HEALTHCARE ADMINISTRATION, LEADERSHIP, AND MANAGEMENT (HALM) THE ESSENTIALS

FIRST EDITION

EDITED BY
DANIEL A. HANDEL, MD, MBA, MPH, CPE

FOREWORD BY
PETER ANGOOD, MD

American Association for
PHYSICIAN
LEADERSHIP

978-1-960762-29-0 Print
978-1-960762-30-6 eBook
Published by **American Association for Physician Leadership, Inc.**
PO Box 96503 | BMB 97493 | Washington, DC 20090-6503

Website: www.physicianleaders.org

13 8 7 6 5 4 3 2 1

Copyedited, typeset, indexed, and printed in the United States of America

PUBLISHER
Nancy Collins

PRODUCTION MANAGER
Jennifer Weiss

DESIGN & LAYOUT
Carter Publishing Studio

COPYEDITOR
Patricia George

Dedication

This book is dedicated to my father, David J. Handel (1946–2024). He was an accomplished healthcare administrator during his career and showed me the importance of the impact we can all have on improving the health of the communities we serve. He took great joy in developing programs and people that will long outlive him, which is something I carry forward to this day. Without his example, I would never have taken the path of physician leadership.

Acknowledgments

AS THIS IS MY FIRST FORAY into being the lead editor on a textbook, I truly appreciate the guidance of Nancy Collins and her team from the American Association for Physician Leadership (AAPL). When I came up with the idea for this textbook, the AAPL was the natural choice to be the publisher, and they have reaffirmed that decision at every step of the way. It was apparent early on that they have the textbook development process down to a science, for which I was grateful. I would also like to thank all of the contributors for their expertise. We were able to recruit phenomenal content experts from a wide range of backgrounds who offer knowledge and perspectives from which you will benefit.

Lastly, I would like to thank you, the reader, in advance, for providing feedback as you read through this book and reflect on it later. The content and knowledge will certainly evolve in this novel board certification process, and we will update this textbook to reflect those changes. However, we will need you to guide us to improve the content and better support future physician leaders, whether they are preparing for the HALM board certification exam, are just starting their HALM fellowship, or are looking for a resource to be better physician leaders.

Table of Contents

SECTION 7: LEADERSHIP IN PATIENT SAFETY AND QUALITY IMPROVEMENT

SECTION 8: ORGANIZATIONAL LEADERSHIP AND COMMUNICATION SKILLS

SECTION 9: PROFESSIONALISM AND ETHICS

About the Editor

Dan Handel is the vice president and chief medical officer for the Central Area of Atrium Health (part of Advocate Health) in Charlotte, North Carolina, and is a clinical professor of emergency medicine at Wake Forest University. In this role, he focuses on quality and patient safety, along with patient logistics, and continues to practice part-time as an emergency physician. He is also the program director for the Healthcare, Administration, Leadership and Management (HALM) ACGME-accredited fellowship at Atrium Carolinas Medical Center, only the third accredited program in the country.

Prior to this, he was the vice president and chief medical officer of Indiana University Health's South Central Region. In this role, he was responsible for overseeing patient logistics, case management, quality and safety, credentialing, and the Southern Indiana Physicians medical group for an 11-county region. Prior roles included being the chief medical officer at the Medical University of South Carolina and vice chair for clinical affairs in the Department of Emergency Medicine at Oregon Health & Sciences University (OHSU) in Portland, Oregon.

Handel was raised in Indianapolis, Indiana. He received his Doctor of Medicine degree from Northwestern University, along with a Master's in Public Health. In June 2014, he completed his Healthcare MBA from OHSU, where he also served on the faculty of the Division of Management, teaching process improvement and value streams.

He has a Lean Six Sigma black belt certification and holds advanced degrees in public health, aeronautics, and business. He lectures nationally on process improvement and improving patient flow. He is a Certified Physician Executive and Fellow of the American College of Emergency Physicians and American College of Healthcare Executives.

Contributor List

Greg Adams, DO, MBA
Assistant Professor
Department of Emergency Medicine
University of Colorado School of Medicine

Smita Agarkar, MD, CPE, FAAPL, FAPA
Service Chief, Quality and Patient Safety Chair
Gracie Square Hospital
Associate Professor of Clinical Psychiatry
Weill Cornell Medicine

Timothy Craig Allen, MD, JD, FCAP, FASCP
Professor and Chair, Department of Pathology,
Corewell Health's Oakland University William Beaumont School of Medicine

Peter Angood, MD, FRCS(C), FACS, MCCM, FAAPL(Hon)
President and CEO
American Association for Physician Leadership

Bryan N. Becker, MD, MMM, CPE, FACP, FAAPL
Professor of Medicine
Anne Burnett School of Medicine, Texas Christian University

Steven Brass, MD, MPH, MBA, FACHE
Executive Vice President and Chief Medical Executive
Harris Health System
Associate Professor of Neurology
Baylor College of Medicine
Associate Professor of Neurology
UT Health Houston

Parveen Chand, MHA, FACHE
Chief Operations Officer
Ascension St. Vincent Indiana

Edgar G. Chedrawy, MD, MSc, FRCSC, FACS, MHA, CPE, FAAPL, MCPDC
Chief Medical Executive
Clemenceau Medical Centre

Roz Cordini, JD, MSN, RN, CHC, CHPC
Senior Vice President, Regulatory Compliance & Audit Services
Coker Group

Reka Danko, MD
Chief Medical Officer
Saint Mary's Regional Medical Center (Reno, NV)
Corporate Medical Director of Utilization Management
Prime Healthcare
Clinical Associate Professor
University of Nevada, Reno School of Medicine

Maggie DiCostanzo, Esq.
Director
Fennemore Business and Finance Group

Karen M. Eastmond, CHC, CHPC, MBA
Vice President
Coker Group

Robbie Freeman, DNP
Chief Digital Transformation Officer
Mount Sinai Health System

Nicholas Gavin, MD, MBA, MS, CPE
Vice President/Chief Clinical Innovation Officer
Mount Sinai Health System
Associate Professor of Emergency Medicine
Icahn School of Medicine at Mount Sinai

Amin Hakim, MD, FIDSA, CPE, FACPE
Vice President, Clinical Operations
United Healthcare New York

Maria Hamilton, MBA, FACHE
Vice President, Chief Operational Excellence Officer
Penn State Health
Co-Director
Health Systems Science Academy, Penn State College of Medicine

Daniel A. Handel, MD, MBA, MPH, CPE
Vice President/Chief Medical Officer
Central Area, Atrium Health
Clinical Professor of Emergency Medicine
Wake Forest University School of Medicine

Robert E. Harbaugh, MD, FAANS, FACS, FAHA
Chief Medical Officer
Milton S. Hershey Medical Center
Senior Vice President
Penn State Health Academic Practices

Amy Harrington, MD, CPE, FAPA
Interim President
UMass Memorial Medical Group

Beth K. Herman, DEd
Associate Designated Institutional Official
Penn State Hershey Medical Center

Amy M. Herold, MD, MBA, MPH, FACOG
Chief Administrative Officer/Chief Medical Officer
Providence Queen of the Valley Medical Center

Rex Hoffman, MD, MBA, FACHE, CPE
Chief Medical Officer
Providence Holy Cross Medical Center
Interim Chief Medical Officer
Providence Cedars Sinai Tarzana Medical Center

Rubayet Hossain, MD, MBA
Clinical Informatics Core Faculty, Emergency Medicine
Mount Sinai Health System
Assistant Professor of Emergency Medicine
Icahn School of Medicine at Mount Sinai

Julie T. Joseph, MD, MBA, MPH, CPE

Mountasser Kadrie, PhD, MHA, FACHE, FACMPE, FHIMSS
Associate Professor of Clinical Research and Leadership
Program Director, Clinical Operations and Healthcare Management Program
Program Director, Biomedical Informatics
Academic Coordinator, Healthcare MBA
The George Washington University School of Medicine and Health Sciences

Andrew S. Karson, MD
Professor of Internal Medicine
UMass Memorial Medical Group

Vijay P. Khatri, MBChB, MBA, FACS, FSSO, FASGO
Professor of Surgery and Oncology
California Northstate University College of Medicine
Medical Consultant
Medical Board of California-Enforcement Department (Executive Office)
Editor-in-Chief
Surgical Oncology (Elsevier Science)

Doug Koekkoek, MD, FACP, SFHM
Independent Consultant and Mentor

George T. "Deuce" Lukemeyer, II
Consulting Principal
PYA, PC

Brian P. McDonough, MD, FAAPL, FAAFP, CPE
Chairman of Graduate Medical Education and DIO
Saint Francis Hospital
Clinical Professor of Family Medicine, Temple
University-Lewis Katz School of Medicine

Mark D. Olszyk, MD, MBA, CPE
ice President/Chief Medical Officer
rroll Hospital
Chair
land Board of Physicians

ael Patrick, Jr., MD, FAAP
Director of Digital Health
de Children's Hospital
Professor of Pediatrics
ate University College of Medicine

adive, MD, MMHC

sen, MA, MBA, CISSP

isors, LLC

dical University of South Carolina,
Science University

Amyn M. Rojiani, MD, PhD, CPE, DFAAPL
Chair, Department of Pathology
Penn State Health
University Chair in Pathology
Penn State College of Medicine
Clinical Service Chief,
Penn State Health Hershey Medical Center

Anne Roberts, Esq., CPMSM, CPCS
System Vice President, Medical Affairs Operations
The Mount Sinai Health System

Adia K. Ross, MD, MHA
Associate Professor of Medicine
Wake Forest School of Medicine
Chief Medical Officer
Atrium Health Wake Forest Baptist- High Point Regional Hospital

Brijen Shah, MD, AGAF
Vice President of Medical Affairs
Mount Sinai Health System
Professor of Medicine/GI, Geriatrics and Medical Education
Icahn School of Medicine at Mount Sinai

Anthony D. Slonim, MD, DrPH, FAAPL
Professor, Internal Medicine, Pediatrics and Health Systems
Virginia Tech-Carilion School of Medicine

Nikhil Sood, MD
Assistant Clinical Professor
University of Arizona College of Medicine – Phoenix
Hospitalist
Banner Health

Dusko J. Stojkov, JD, LLM
Attorney, Principal
Offit Kurman

Jacob Swartzwelder, CPC, CPMA, CRC, CIC, CEMC
AAPC Approved Instructor
AAPC National Advisory Board Officer
Director, Coding Operations
Coker

Jennifer Wiler, MD, MBA, FACEP
Professor, Department of Emergency Medicine
University of Colorado School of Medicine

Jamie Wooldridge, MD, MS-PopH, CPE
Professor of Pediatric Pulmonology
University of Rochester Medical Center

David Zaas, MD, MBA
President
Atrium Health Wake Forest Baptist
Professor
Wake Forest University School of Medicine

Preface

GROWING UP, I DIDN'T UNDERSTAND what my father did for a living as a healthcare administrator. From my teenage lens of the world, he went to work in a hospital wearing a suit every day. I didn't appreciate it at the time how he was able to help patients and the health of a community despite having no clinical background. In my idealistic mind, I decided I was actually "going to help people," and that crystallized my decision to go to medical school.

Fate and karma have a way of showing one the error of their ways. I thought I was going to be a health services researcher coming out of my emergency medicine residency in Cincinnati and moved across the country to do a research fellowship in Oregon. Six months into the fellowship, I was working one of those rare emergency department (ED) shifts that overlapped with my department chair. He mentioned that our hospital was going live with this new electronic health record called "Epic," and given my interest in operations research, he asked if I wanted to be the physician champion for its implementation in the ED.

Thus prematurely ended my research fellowship. I was probably not destined to be a full-time researcher anyways, as the thought of perpetually chasing grant funding was not at all appealing to me. I spent the next year working on the implementation of Epic, and when the ED medical director position opened up, I was asked to take that on as well. During the next six years, we made a lot of strides improving the quality and efficiency of care provided to our patients, and I learned a lot in the process.

Despite what we were able to accomplish within the walls of the ED, there were still constraints and barriers that prevented us from delivering the best care possible. Even though we had eliminated ambulance diversion, we continued to struggle with ED boarding, where patients spend extended periods of time in the ED awaiting an inpatient hospital bed. It was crippling at times and long overdue to be fixed. Realizing the only way for me to remedy this was to go upstream and work at the hospital level, I was fortunate to be selected as a chief medical officer (CMO) for the first time in 2014.

As all conversations tend to come full circle, I had a conversation with my now-teenage son when he was visiting me at work. "Chief...Medical...Officer," he slowly enunciated as he read my business card on my desk. "Dad," he asked, "do you arrest doctors?"

I smirked at the underlying logic of my then 12-year-old. "Son, that's about a good of an explanation as any," I replied. My two boys vaguely understood what it meant to be an emergency physician, but were in the same position I had been 30 years before.

Explaining what it means to be a healthcare leader is hard.

Robert E. Harbaugh, MD, FAANS, FACS, FAHA
Chief Medical Officer
Milton S. Hershey Medical Center
Senior Vice President
Penn State Health Academic Practices

Amy Harrington, MD, CPE, FAPA
Interim President
UMass Memorial Medical Group

Beth K. Herman, DEd
Associate Designated Institutional Official
Penn State Hershey Medical Center

Amy M. Herold, MD, MBA, MPH, FACOG
Chief Administrative Officer/Chief Medical Officer
Providence Queen of the Valley Medical Center

Rex Hoffman, MD, MBA, FACHE, CPE
Chief Medical Officer
Providence Holy Cross Medical Center
Interim Chief Medical Officer
Providence Cedars Sinai Tarzana Medical Center

Rubayet Hossain, MD, MBA
Clinical Informatics Core Faculty, Emergency Medicine
Mount Sinai Health System
Assistant Professor of Emergency Medicine
Icahn School of Medicine at Mount Sinai

Julie T. Joseph, MD, MBA, MPH, CPE

Mountasser Kadrie, PhD, MHA, FACHE, FACMPE, FHIMSS
Associate Professor of Clinical Research and Leadership
Program Director, Clinical Operations and Healthcare Management Program
Program Director, Biomedical Informatics
Academic Coordinator, Healthcare MBA
The George Washington University School of Medicine and Health Sciences

Andrew S. Karson, MD
Professor of Internal Medicine
UMass Memorial Medical Group

REFERENCES

1. Kaiser F, Schmid, Schlüchtermann J. Physician-Leaders and Hospital Performance Revisited. *Social Science & Medicine.* 2020;249, 112831, ISSN 0277-9536, https://doi.org/10.1016/j.socscimed.2020.112831.
2. Tasi MC, Keswani A, Bozic KJ. Does Physician Leadership Affect Hospital Quality, Operational Efficiency, and Financial Performance? *Health Care Manage Rev.* 2019;44(3):256–262. doi: 10.1097/HMR.0000000000000173
3. See H, Shreve L, Hartzell S, et al. Comparison of Quality Measures From US Hospitals with Physician vs. Nonphysician Chief Executive Officers. *JAMA Netw Open.* 2022;5(10):e2236621. https://doi:10.1001/jamanetworkopen.2022.36621.
4. Gupta AK. Physician Versus Non-physician CEOs: The Effect of a Leader's Professional Background on the Quality of Hospital Management and Health Care. *J Hosp Admin.* 2019;8(5):47–51. https://doi.org/10.5430/jha.v8n5p47.
5. ACGME. Health Care Administration, Leadership, and Management. Overview. https://www.acgme.org/programs-and-institutions/institutions/sponsoring-institution-based-fellowships/health-care-administration-leadership-and-management/

Foreword

AT SOME LEVEL, ALL PHYSICIANS can be considered to be leaders — an expectation that society has of the medical profession. The American Association for Physician Leadership (AAPL) delivers on supporting this expectation by maximizing the potential of physician leaders to create personal and organizational transformation in the healthcare industry, which simultaneously benefits patient outcomes, augments workforce wellness, and improves healthcare delivery nationally and internationally.

For 50 years, AAPL has been the world's premier organization for supporting all aspects of physician leadership in every sector of healthcare. AAPL is the only professional organization that focuses solely on providing information resources, leadership and management education, career development services, and thought leadership research designed for the physician workforce, the organizations where physicians are engaged or represented, and the healthcare industry overall.

Since its founding in 1975, beyond the greater than quarter-million physicians already influenced, thousands of physicians and other inter-professional clinicians continue to participate annually with AAPL's leadership development approaches. AAPL has an active individual membership community and an organizational constituency located in upwards of 40 countries.

AAPL was originally initiated by Roger Schenke as the American College of Physician Executives (ACPE). Schenke had identified a crucial gap in the medical profession's education system: the need for physicians to be educated and trained in management and leadership principles. At that time, the association primarily focused on educating mid-career physicians in pursuit of administrative roles within hospitals.

To this day, medical training and business courses in higher education still do not effectively, or adequately, provide medical professionals with an in-depth understanding of these principles. Since its inception, AAPL has remained the premier organization for leadership development among healthcare professionals. As healthcare continues to evolve rapidly, the need for developing improved leadership and management skills remains crucial.

Recognizing the necessity of a broader perspective for those physicians interested in leadership or management roles, in 2012 the association was rebranded as AAPL, and its mission has continually evolved to better meet and anticipate the leadership needs of physicians, organizations, and patients in this complex industry.

While the core mission of enhancing physician leadership skills has remained consistent over time, AAPL has adopted a deeper and more comprehensive approach to leadership development by diversifying its programs, products, and services, as well as by expanding its offerings to include inter-professional healthcare leaders and their respective organizations. The association continues to evolve as a significant thought leader and influencer in the international healthcare industry as well.

The industry-standard physician leadership credential, Certified Physician Executive (CPE), originated with AAPL. The CPE program now has amassed nearly 30 years of competency-based, educational programming and credentialing experience with physician leadership. There are almost 5,000 CPE program alumni, and they come from a wide range of backgrounds, institutions, and countries. These alumni, individually and collectively, have created significant levels of institutional and industry-wide change as a result of their CPE education and related experiences.

Numerous institutions and search companies recognize the significance and impact from these alumni and frequently seek CPE-credentialed physicians when considering physician leaders in their programs. Additionally, a large number of hospitals and health systems train members of their medical staff with the educational course offerings from the AAPL CPE program and encourage their staff to obtain the full CPE credential.

Graduates of all AAPL programs, including the CPE program, have become transformative leaders at various levels of healthcare in both traditional and nontraditional roles. This community of healthcare leaders has successfully shifted their organizations' foci toward true patient-centered, value-based care by integrating innovative practices to enhance organizational performance and improve health outcomes through inter-professional collaboration.

AAPL's core mission remains constant: to improve the overall quality, safety, efficiency, and value of contemporary healthcare by leveraging the widely recognized legacy relationship between patients and physicians — a relationship that continues to be the dominant driver of the healthcare industry (and its various sectors) across all continents.

The CPE Capstone event, among all the AAPL successes over this half-century of AAPL experience, deserves special mention. As currently structured, the CPE Capstone is experienced over a long weekend of focused activities specifically designed to truly transform the physician leader toward a seasoned and mature appreciation for leadership in healthcare.

Participants typically apply to the Capstone event through their AAPL educational programming, but an alternate application process is available for those with an already established master's degree credential. Regardless of the approach, uniformly, all participants rate the experience highly (average Net Promoter Scores of 80-90) and value the impact of their experience for the duration of their careers. The peer-to-peer networking and life-long professional relationships formed are incalculable.

Nonetheless, there has been a gradual recognition within the formal medical education enterprise of related associations that medical training should provide medical trainees with an improved approach to leadership and management principles. The Accreditation Council for Graduate Medical Education (ACGME) and the American Board of Medical Specialties (ABMS) have each launched new initiatives focused on "healthcare administration leadership and management," or HALM.

The ACGME has set criteria for accreditation of institutional fellowship training programs in HALM (https://www.acgme.org/programs-and-institutions/institutions/sponsoring-institution-based-fellowships/health-care-administration-leadership-and-management/), and a number of education programs have begun to implement these fellowship training programs. Similarly, within the ABMS, the American Board of Emergency Medicine (ABEM) is now recognized as the administrative board inside the umbrella of ABMS for setting a new board certification program for qualified applicants in HALM (https://www.abem.org/subspecialty-get-certified/health-care-administration-leadership-and-management-halm/).

At the time of this writing, three other ABMS Boards had also decided to work with ABEM in this regard: 1) the American Board of Anesthesia (ABA), 2) the American Board of Family Medicine (ABFM), and 3) the American Board of Preventive Medicine (ABPM). It is expected that other ABMS Boards will gradually embrace this board certification opportunity as well.

With the widely recognized and extensive long-term legacy of AAPL in this educational arena, both ACGME and ABMS solicited and embraced AAPL in their development of these HALM initiatives from the beginning. And while it may initially appear counter-intuitive, the leadership of AAPL is very supportive of these HALM initiatives, has embraced the opportunity of this transition in medical education, and has readily initiated its own set of programs, products, and services oriented toward the support of HALM activities and its eventual community. Additionally, AAPL remains in close contact with ACGME and ABMS/ABEM, plus the other ABMS constituent Boards, on the future evolution of HALM activities.

In this regard, AAPL launched a new journal in 2023 fully focused on HALM: the *Healthcare Administration Leadership & Management Journal* (*HALM Journal*) (https://www.physicianleaders.org/publications/halmj). The association also launched a HALM online community for those interested in peer-to-peer networking and already has numerous competency-based educational offerings in support of HALM.

In addition to the existing deep well of AAPL information resources for HALM, the AAPL educational offerings also provide valuable content for fellowship training programs, board certification preparation, and continuing medical education (CME), as well as for the eventual maintenance of certification (MOC). AAPL remains as a resource for individuals seeking advanced experience with HALM as well as for institutions offering or considering offering HALM fellowship programs.

The well-established AAPL CPE credential, the CPE Capstone event, and the developing HALM initiatives will become complementary to each over time. This type of complementarity already exists with the AAPL CPE credential and the variety of university-based master's degree programs.

The growing community hosted by AAPL for all types of physician leaders supports everyone, regardless of credentials and/or number of credentials. AAPL is clearly the community of choice for physician leadership and intends to remain as the premiere leadership association for many years to come.

All of which brings us to the topic of a HALM textbook. AAPL recognized, given AAPL's expertise and history of successful publications, that a textbook for the rapidly evolving HALM environment was needed, almost immediately, by those institutions and individuals with an interest in pursuing a variety of activities with HALM. Fortunately for AAPL, an exceptional lead editor became readily evident: Dan Handel.

Dan Handel, MD, MBA, MPH, CPE, FACHE, FACEP, is vice president, chief medical officer, Central Area, for Atrium Health ,and clinical professor in the Department of Emergency Medicine at Wake Forest University. His areas of research includes access to care, health policy, and emergency department crowding. He is the author of 52 peer-reviewed publications, 16 articles, 3 textbooks, 17 book chapters, and 22 abstracts.

Handel, together with his 44 expert contributors from across the nation and representing various specialties, have put together an exceptional resource that is certain to become recognized as the leading authority in HALM education. This new AAPL *Healthcare Administration, Leadership, and Management* textbook covers all of the relevant topic areas for anyone pursuing HALM education and board certification. It is also an invaluable resource for those who are responsible for developing a training program in HALM that will be able to withstand the rigor of an ACGME accreditation review, and a program where graduates will be able to pass HALM board certification comfortably.

AAPL remains recognized internationally as the predominant physician leadership professional association, given that its breadth and depth of resources are second to none. AAPL is exceedingly proud to be able to bring this HALM textbook forward to the healthcare industry. Moreso, AAPL is extremely grateful to the editor and contributors for their energy, expertise, and efforts in making this textbook such an exceptional offering.

This resource promises to be an essential element toward facilitating the birth and growth of a new, rich community of HALM alumni and committed physician leaders. The eventual benefits to the healthcare industry on a global basis are already incalculable.

On a personal level, it has been humbling to observe and learn from the individuals committed to not only developing the various HALM initiatives across the United States, but also to those developing this new HALM textbook and the host of other HALM resources gradually coming to the surface. The constellation of these resources is invaluable because they will eventually create significant change and the betterment of our industry. Thanks to each and every one who have become connected as a result of embracing the concept of HALM.

For those not yet fully appreciative of what HALM represents, start with this book; it is exceptional and will provide all you need to upgrade your awareness and understanding.

Peter Angood, MD
American Association for Physician Leadership
www.physicianleaders.org
April 2025

SECTION 1

Business of Healthcare

CHAPTER 1

Market, Competition, and Community Needs Analysis

Parveen Chand, MHA, FACHE

HALM COURSE CONTENT:

- 1.2 Business plan development (e.g., framework, adding new services, return on investment)
- 1.9 Interpretation of market data (e.g., market analysis, market research, sales, advertising)
- 1.10 Methods of determining community gaps/needs for health services (community need)
- 1.11 Methods for determining the fair market value for services provided (clinical, academic affiliations, teaching, or research)
- 1.19 Mergers and acquisitions
- 1.20 Vendors and payer relations
- 1.22 Business community relations
- 1.23 Advertising and marketing
- 1.25 Collaborating with competitors

CASE SCENARIO:

A not-for-profit network with several critical-access hospitals, community hospitals, as well as a large tertiary, quaternary academic medical center is contemplating establishing a second community cancer center in a major metropolitan service area. The service area covers 2.5 million residents with an aging demographic in a very competitive market void of any for profit entities. Also being contemplated is the potential to merge or acquire a private oncology practice or recruit and directly employ more providers.

How will the services be defined? Who will receive services? Who will provide and staff these services? Where will the services be offered? How will the services be reimbursed? Who will be first to serve that portion of the market? How will the services be organized and how will compliance and regulatory standards be met? Will a certificate of need be needed, and what are the risks? How will the services be marketed and promoted?

These, along with other questions, will need to be answered when developing a strategic plan as well as a business plan for the service. A physician leader, partnering with others to define need, must interpret complex data and determine whether their mission aligns and supports building a program, or partnering with a competitor.

Business Plan Development

By 2031, the United States is projected to spend $7.1 trillion on healthcare-related services,[1] and organizations are weighing options to gain a competitive advantage, increase market share and profit, or in some cases, to remain viable or pivot. Consequently, strategic as well as business planning models must continue to evolve.

The overarching framework of the National Institute of Standards and Technology's Baldrige Performance Excellence Program, encompasses the necessary criteria into an overall process to yield higher and long-term sustainable progress (see Figure 1).[2] This model has been used successfully across multiple industries and is a benchmark of high-performing organizations. The model considers all stakeholders, the leadership structure(s), how information flows throughout an organization, how decisions are made, the infrastructure that is used, key attributes of the workforce, the operational rigor, and how results inform the overall cycle.

The iterative process can help strengthen the strategic planning process, and using this framework repeatedly may help organizations or even a service line or a division improve results, increase buy-in, and ultimately lead to higher profits, increased market share, and improved results across multiple key performance indicators.

Similarly, *Healthcare Strategic Planning*[3] by Alan Zuckerman, offers a practical guide and insights to address internal and external pressures, adapting quickly and achieving longer term goals. His follow-up work, *Advancing the State of the Art in Healthcare Strategic Planning,*[4] builds on how healthcare organizations can learn from other industries and incorporate real-time data, encouraging innovation and creativity; move to a more "bottom up" rather than "top down" approach; evolve to continuous improvement processes (the last two attributes are similar to the Baldrige framework); and move from static to dynamic planning (incorporating planning at all levels of the organization, not just the top).

Further, the often-referenced book titled *Blue Ocean Strategy*[5] by W. Chan Kim and Renée Mauborgne, focuses on a multi-step strategy-visualization process to help

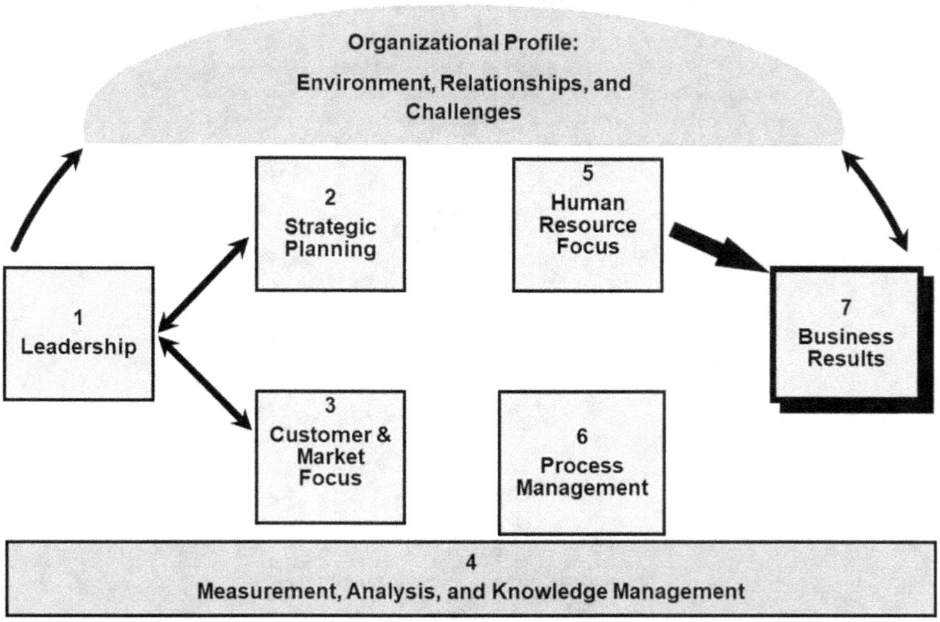

FIGURE 1. Baldrige Framework Model

corporations reach beyond a current and existing demand, often in untapped new market spaces which are often ripe for growth, even creating new revenue streams.

Using the value innovation tool may help an organization uncover true value between its costs for a good or service and what increasing buyer value can be achieved by raising and creating factors the industry has not offered before.

The Value Agenda framework[6] by Porter and Lee argues that creating value across the healthcare enterprise or ecosystem eventually may be the only driving path to future relevance as we move away from fee-for service, meet consumer demand, fight for scarce resources, and operate in a complex legislative environment. In an increasingly digital age, information technology in many cases will be the enabling infrastructure to create that value (Figure 2).

This framework builds on Porter's book *The Five Forces That Shape Industry Competition*[7] published in 2008. The five forces are competition, the threat of new entrants to the industry, supplier bargaining power, customer bargaining power, and the ability of customers to find substitutes for the services or products.

Today, while the five-forces model must be adapted to rapid technological change and the importance of collaboration across many industries, it's a reliable way to guide companies needing to navigate industry-specific challenges. Barriers to entry — specifically the role of an advantage gained by an incumbent and more recently the role of government policy — are more relevant now than ever.

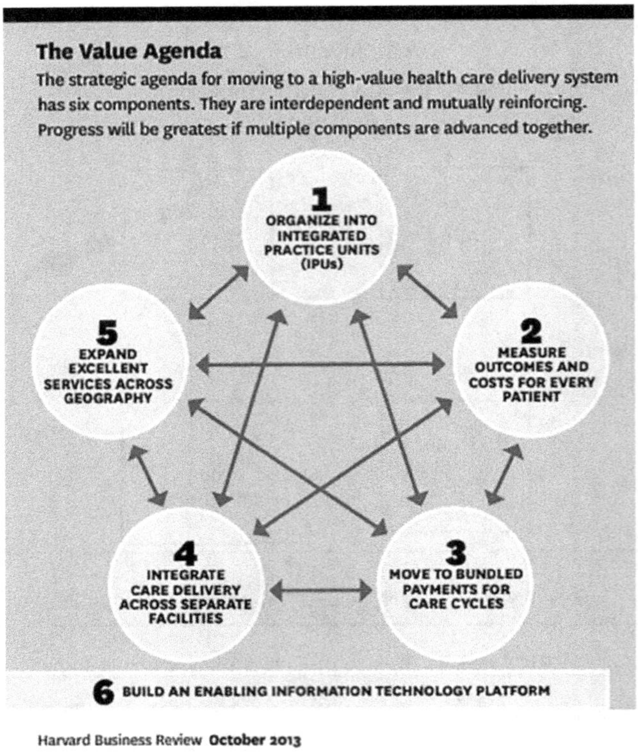

FIGURE 2. The Value Agenda

Developing a specific business plan is a critical process for ensuring that the business idea is viable, sustainable, and aligned with regulatory requirements. Development encompasses identifying market opportunities, assessing healthcare needs, and setting long-term goals. The planning process typically includes financial forecasting, resource allocation, regulatory compliance, and risk management, while also considering technological advancements and patient outcomes.

The fundamental elements of the plan include:

1. *Executive Summary:* In the summary, describe the business, including the type of service or product intended to be offered. In the case scenario above, it could simply be "expansion of cancer care services in primary service area" or "establishing a new cancer center in an underserved part of the market." The overview should encapsulate the "why" behind the proposal and the intended target market and specify how the proposal will meet the need, along with its financial feasibility.
2. *Project Description:* Relationship to Mission and Vision: What is the core mission and long-term vision of the healthcare business? This section should describe the aspirations for growth and impact and illustrate a direct tie back to the vision.
3. *Strategic Importance, Alignment and Supporting Objectives:* Short-term and long-term goals should be readily identified. Leveraging a template like the one featured

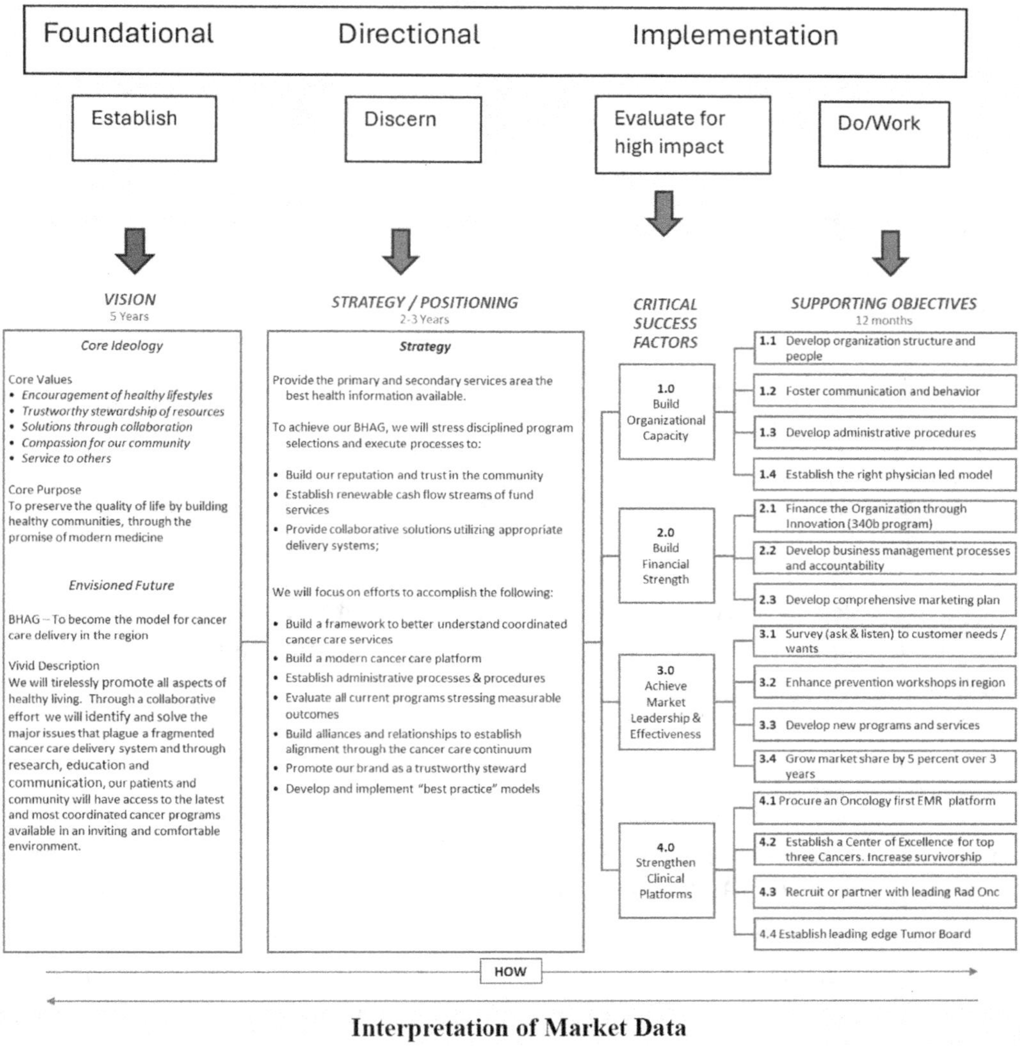

FIGURE 3. Example of Template to Identify Key Steps That Align With Strategy to Achieve a Desired Outcome

in Figure 3 will outline key steps that align with strategy to achieve a desired outcome by highlighting elements important to your plan and elements that show up in your business plan.

The next element of a business plan is current market position, projections, assumptions, assessment, and competitive factors. Analyze the current healthcare industry, focusing on trends, market growth, regulatory landscape, and economic conditions. Tools from state hospital associations or the 2024 Environmental Scan from the American Hospital Association[8] can offer insights into the market. For example, Figure 4 illustrates that nationally there is an opportunity to expand outpatient services overall, by 2033.

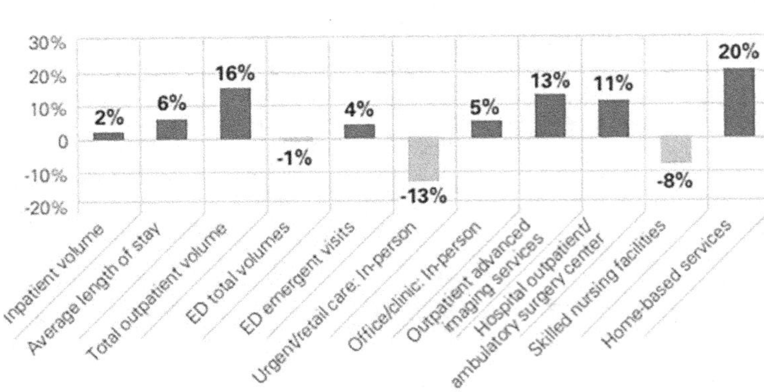

- 28% of evaluation and management visits will occur virtually by 2033.
- As the population continues to age and chronic disease incidence rises, there will be increased demand across many sites of care.
- Patient acuity will continue to rise.
- Care redesign will be critical to prevent the acute exacerbation of medical conditions.

Data from "2023 Impact of Change® Forecast Highlights," Sg2, a Vizient company, accessed Aug. 8, 2023. Used with permission of Vizient, Inc. All rights reserved. Impact of Change®, 2023; HCUP National Inpatient Sample (NIS). Healthcare Cost and Utilization Project (HCUP) 2019. Agency for Healthcare Research and Quality, Rockville, MD; Proprietary Sg2 All-Payer Claims Data Set, 2021; The following 2021 CMS Limited Data Sets (LDS): Carrier, Denominator, Home Health Agency, Hospice, Outpatient, Skilled Nursing Facility; Claritas Pop-Facts®, 2023; Sg2 Analysis, 2023

FIGURE 4. Projected Increase in Care in Alternative Settings by 2033.

Disease-specific tools like the National Cancer Institute Surveillance Epidemiology and End Result Program database offer relevant information to inform the market analysis.

OPERATIONAL ISSUES

Once the needed services are identified, the location, hours of operation, designated space, clinical equipment needs, information technology standards and platform, staffing, and quality standards must be determined. The estimated volume projections are translated into objective values that include throughput metrics, the number of exam rooms and procedure suites for example, total square footage, and capital equipment needed. The analysis is based on plans to develop clinical services, offer innovative technologies, and account for anticipated demographic changes.

The assessment should project both near-term (e.g., three years) and long-term (e.g., 7–10 years) facility requirements and should be stress-tested against other benchmarks to give an overall confidence level of success.

As a part of this process, the organization should take a close look at current operational performance compared to industry benchmarks and not lose an opportunity to improve workflows, leverage technology, and look for ways to better serve the patient or community need. There will be a fine balance between meeting current and forecasted need, what is affordable, and what allows for the most flexibility in the future.

Understanding key regulatory and compliance issues that the healthcare business must navigate, such as HIPAA, FDA regulations, or healthcare licensing requirements, can also influence the operating model and impact the budget. If building a new structure, the 2022 *Guidelines for Design and Construction*[10] provided by Facility Guidelines Institute is an invaluable resource.

If a project is approved, this operational framework will be the basis of designing and physically building a new program and will form the basis of how you will operate the new or expanded service.

MARKETING PLAN, SALES, AND PRICING STRATEGY

This section of the plan could include traditional marketing (print ads, radio), digital marketing (search engine optimization, social media), and community outreach (health fairs, partnerships with local businesses, churches or social service agencies). The section explains how to attract and retain patients or clients.

If selling a product, describe the sales channels (direct sales, online, third-party distributors). For a healthcare service organization, outline the approach for patient acquisition and retention, such as referrals, partnerships with other healthcare providers, or advertising. Recently, healthcare organizations have taken a play from the pharmaceutical industry book and have hired physician liaisons to help market, coordinate care, and promote services.

Research the pricing model, including whether insurance will be accepted, sliding scale fees will be offered, or whether the organization will charge out-of-pocket. Ensure that pricing is competitive while still allowing for profitability. The pricing strategy needs to account for the payer mix (mix of insured, government pay, or self-pay) and should be reflected in the financial model.

Highlight strategies for maintaining patient loyalty, such as follow-up care, personalized services, or loyalty programs, and include how to use current methods to measure, track, and influence consumer experience by understanding consumer expectations.[11]

Return on Investment

Next, a financial pro forma for the program is developed based on as much historical financial information as is available with respect to the projected new volumes (Figure 5). To develop a holistic perspective, the analysis should factor in the contemplated financial investments, including facility construction and equipment. The result of this analysis typically is expressed on a net present value (NPV) basis, where multiple years of future returns are compared to near-term financial investments. Any project with a positive NPV is considered financially viable.

Leaders must make many calculated decisions, and a well-thought-out business plan positions projects on their own merits. These plans can offer clarity, leverage potential partnerships, demonstrate feasibility, and in many organizations is a next step to allocate funding at a board level. Specificity minimizes future risk and models a more accurate financial picture.

Elements of the financial pro forma include:

MEDICAL CENTER A
SUMMARY
FINANCIAL PROJECTION

	2024	2025	2026	Year 1	Year 2	Year 3	Year 4	Year 5
TOTAL								
Medical Office Building - Financial Projections								
Revenue	$648,000	$661,760	$667,840	$887,840	$1,107,840	$1,107,840	$1,107,840	$1,107,840
Total Expenses	$523,879	$617,094	$651,418	$1,048,748	$1,163,448	$1,168,248	$1,173,368	$1,178,488
Operating Margin	$124,121	$44,666	$16,422	($160,908)	($55,608)	($60,408)	($65,528)	($70,648)
Total Depreciation	$150,119	$256,774	$299,738	$582,688	$582,688	$582,688	$582,688	$582,688
Capital Expenditures	$0	$0	$0	($5,659,000)	$0	$0	$0	$0
Direct Net Income (Cancer Ctr, Radiology, CT, MRI)	$1,190,433	$1,401,325	$549,077	$882,236	$1,005,848	$1,177,159	$1,213,741	$1,251,102
(Adding) Medical Group Practice	$0	$0	$0	$846,451	$871,875	$897,977	$924,926	$952,723
Net Cash Flow	**$1,464,673**	**$1,702,765**	**$865,237**	**($3,508,533)**	**$2,404,803**	**$2,597,416**	**$2,655,827**	**$2,715,865**
					7 YR NPV:	**$6,453,614**		
					7 YR IRR:	**38.85%**		
					12 YR NPV:	**$11,506,921**		
					12 YR IRR:	**42.76%**		
					20 YR NPV:	**$15,800,553**		
					20 YR IRR:	**43.36%**		
BASE								
Medical Office Building - Financial Projections								
Revenue	$648,000	$661,760	$667,840	$667,840	$667,840	$667,840	$667,840	$667,840
Total Expenses	$523,879	$617,094	$651,418	$655,898	$660,698	$665,498	$670,618	$675,738
Operating Margin	$124,121	$44,666	$16,422	$11,942	$7,142	$2,342	($2,778)	($7,898)
Total Depreciation	$150,119	$256,774	$299,738	$299,738	$299,738	$299,738	$299,738	$299,738
Capital Expenditures	$0	$0	$0	$0	$0	$0	$0	$0
Direct Net Income (Cancer Ctr, Radiology, CT, MRI)	$1,190,433	$1,401,325	$549,077	$560,903	$572,370	$583,607	$594,520	$605,072
Net Cash Flow	**$1,464,673**	**$1,702,765**	**$865,237**	**$872,583**	**$879,250**	**$885,687**	**$891,480**	**$896,912**
				20 YR NPV:	**$7,333,956**			
INCREMENTAL								
Medical Office Building - Financial Projections								
Revenue				$220,000	$440,000	$440,000	$440,000	$440,000
Total Expenses				$392,850	$502,750	$502,750	$502,750	$502,750
Operating Margin				($172,850)	($62,750)	($62,750)	($62,750)	($62,750)
Total Depreciation				$282,950	$282,950	$282,950	$282,950	$282,950
Capital Expenditures				($5,659,000)	$0	$0	$0	$0
Net Cash Flow				($5,548,900)	**$220,200**	**$220,200**	**$220,200**	**$220,200**
Direct Net Income (Cancer Center, Radiology, CT, MRI)				**$321,333**	**$433,478**	**$593,552**	**$619,221**	**$646,030**
					7 YR NPV:	**-$2,134,797**		
					7 YR IRR:	**-1.34%**		
					12 YR NPV:	**-$523,036**		
					12 YR IRR:	**8.70%**		
					20 YR NPV:	**$846,426**		
					20 YR IRR:	**12.52%**		
Medical Group Contribution Margin				**$846,451**	**$871,875**	**$897,977**	**$924,926**	**$952,723**
					7 YR NPV:	**$2,206,476**		
					7 YR IRR:	**20.93%**		
					12 YR NPV:	**$5,590,933**		
					12 YR IRR:	**27.07%**		
					20 YR NPV:	**$8,466,597**		
					20 YR IRR:	**28.56%**		

FIGURE 5. Example Pro Forma

- *Revenue:* Define how the business will generate revenue. Will insurance providers offer reimbursement? Will there be a charge per consultation or will the business offer subscription-based services? How certain are payer contracts into the future?
- *Start-up Costs:* Detail initial capital requirements, including costs for equipment, licensing, facility setup, marketing, salaries, and legal fees.
- *Financial Projections:* Include detailed financial projections for at least 3-5 years. This should include:
  - *Profit and Loss Statement:* Revenue, cost of goods sold, operating expenses, and net profit.
  - *Cash Flow Statement:* Inflows and outflows of cash, helping to ensure the business maintains liquidity.
  - *Balance Sheet:* Overview of assets, liabilities, and equity.

- *Break-even Analysis:* When the healthcare business is expected to become profitable.
- *Funding Requirements:* If seeking external funding (e.g., investors, loans, grants), how much capital is needed and how it will be used.

Net present value and the internal rate of return are two calculations that help organizations determine if a project is worth taking a risk on. Organizations often vet projects using internal metrics to benchmark against. It is not uncommon to have several business plans competing for the same scarce resources during annual capital cycles.

PROJECT RISK AND ALTERNATIVES

Regulatory Compliance and Risk: Ensuring adherence to laws (such as Certificate of Need requirements), policies, and accreditation standards within the healthcare sector. Highlight the challenges and risks of navigating healthcare regulations and compliance. Three key risk categories include:

- Market Risks: Identify market-related risks such as changes in healthcare regulations, competition, or economic downturns. For example, if an institution intends to use bond financing to fund a project, it may be important to understand the bond issuance process.[12]
- Operational Risks: These could include the failure of medical equipment, staff turnover, or disruptions in supply chains. For example, determine if employees are represented by a union, and if so, what will be the impact if there is a work strike?
- Financial Risks: Discuss potential risks such as unexpected costs, cash flow problems, or dependence on insurance reimbursement.

PROJECT TIMELINE

A proposed timeline with milestones is essential to a business plan. Each work stream with appropriate action steps should be shown with anticipated completion dates (Figure 6).

EXIT STRATEGY/CONTINGENCY PLANS

To help leaders think through possible future scenarios, the business plan in its entirety, either through a rigorous financial stress test or multiple scenario planning models, should account for either an exit strategy (discontinue or reduce service footprint) or a contingency plan (calculated risk and loss levels, ability to shift payer mix, ability to joint venture in the future, ability to partner with a private equity firm, etc.). This section should illustrate the overall discernment process, including an exit strategy if needed.

Stakeholder Groups	10/21	10/28	11/4	11/11	11/18	11/25	12/2	12/9	12/16	12/23	12/30	1/6
Core Group	•	•	•	•	•	•	•	•	•	•		•
Joint Group Meeting		•			•			•	•			•
Workstream 1: Medical Oncology Alignment												
Develop vision for broader regional collaboration												
Collect and analyze practice data to supplement current state assessment												
Define transactional models available to both groups												
Document evolving terms and requirements for partnership clinical / business architecture												
Create pro forma to demonstrate impact of partnership												
Workstream 2A: Campus A Planning												
Conduct space utilization study using data reports and walk-throughs												
Identify opportunities for optimization of campus												
Profile the investment requirements for . clinic												
Create pro forma to demonstrate impact of space optimization												
Workstream 2B: Campus B Planning												
Forecast future cancer volumes split between Campus A and Campus B												
Identify core services on the campus												
Create a preliminary program plan for the campus												
Define partnership structures with aligned physician groups for Campus B												
Profile the investment requirements for the campus												
Create pro forma to demonstrate impact of a Campus B												

FIGURE 6. Example Project Timeline

Determining Community Gaps/ Needs for Health Services

Working with key community partners, local and state health departments, and social service organizations is often useful not only to identify gaps in care and better understand financing and reimbursement mechanisms, but also to evaluate partnership opportunities and foster community engagement. At the conclusion of a community needs assessment survey, the data collection and analysis generate actionable steps and often highlight areas for collaboration.

Key steps to assessing community needs include:

- *Clearly define the community.* Be as specific as possible. For example, the community may be a portion of the region that is underserved with limited access for transportation to receive timely infusion treatment.
- *Build in community engagement* by engaging with public and private organizations to identify and solve for gaps. This step often can elicit multiple viewpoints for the same problem. An example may be an unmet need for language interpretation services, causing delays in care.
- *Collect data.* Data from surveys, interviews, and other forms of community outreach can provide qualitative and quantitative data. Interviews, for example, can highlight perceptions within the community that may not be accurate.
- *Commission, create, and complete a community needs assessment report.* The report should highlight all parties involved, funding source(s), data summary, methodology, and key findings from the analysis. Each partner then can determine how to prioritize the information and incorporate it into both strategic and financial plans.
- *Develop an action-oriented improvement plan.* A needs assessment builds toward a plan to remedy the problems faced by the community over a specific period.

Most provider organizations are required to complete a community assessment every three years.[13]

Methods for Determining the Fair Market Value for Services Provided

Key regulatory considerations must be addressed in the valuation process, as the healthcare industry is highly regulated. Key regulatory issues that generally apply to transactions between physicians and hospitals or other medical facilities include the anti-kickback statutes (AKS),[14] the Ethics in Patient Referrals Act (Stark Law), and the IRS's intermediate sanctions regulations and prohibitions against private inurement.

Generally, provider compensation fair market value (FMV) methodologies include:

- *Administrative*: Qualitative analysis of the role and services using benchmarks for proposed administrative time.
- *Call Coverage*: Consider the type of work and the degree to which normal income-generating activities are disrupted. Use specific market data, percentage of clinical benchmarks, and a burden approach.
- *Clinical Time*: Blend of full-time equivalent, productivity based, and collections based.
- *Physician Executive*: Possible to consider role, status, and service line (revenue).
- *Research and Teaching*: Evaluated using a blend of academic and clinical benchmarks as well as impact to billable activity.
- *Clinical Support*: Evaluated using a time-based approach (e.g., physician extenders).[15]

The American Institute of Certified Public Accountants has published several valuation processes that can be used to evaluate FMV of a business entity or asset.[16] The three approaches are:

- *Market Approach*: This method compares the asset (practice, contract, business, etc.) to similar businesses, business ownership interests, or securities that have been transacted upon. This method is limited because quality public data may be lacking or unavailable.
- *Cost Approach*: This methodology is used as a general way of determining value of an asset by quantifying the amount of money required to replace the future service capability of the service being valued. This is also referred to as the asset-based approach.
- *Income Approach*: This is a general way of determining a value using one or more methods that convert the economic benefit into a single value or amount.

The relevance of FMV equates to any exchange of value between healthcare providers receiving payments under federally funded programs and can apply to several types of transactions, including joint ventures, business acquisitions, income guarantees, leasing arrangements, payments to physicians for clinical or administrative roles, call coverage, equipment leases, space rental agreements, other leasing arrangements, or even providing anything of value at no cost.

Mergers and Acquisitions

While many healthcare organizations, especially hospitals, are faring better than they did a few years ago, mergers and acquisitions (M&A) continue to be a strategy used to leverage scale and size and reduce operating expenses, improve quality, and improve access to care. The American Hospital Association (AHA) describes mergers and acquisitions as one of the most important tools that some hospitals use to manage financial pressures and increase patient access to care.[17] While mergers and acquisitions have declined year over year, 2024 saw almost 1,400 deals across the healthcare sector compared to 828 in 2019 — a 70% increase.[18]

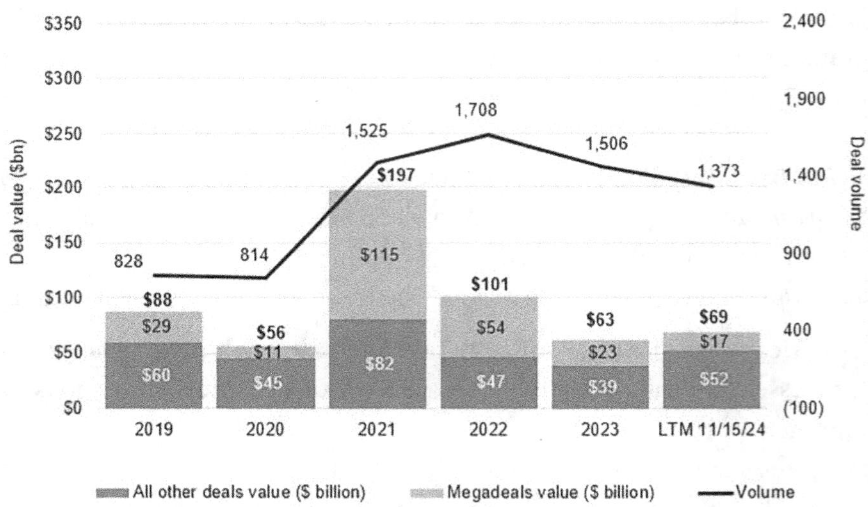

Source: LevinPro HC, Levin Associates, 2024, November, levinassociates.com
LTM 11/15/24 refers to the period from November 16, 2023, through November 15, 2024. Megadeals are those valued at $5 billion or greater. Totals may appear not to sum due to rounding.

FIGURE 7. 2019-2024 Health Services Deal Value

M&A models include:

- *Horizontal consolidation.* Two or more health systems or hospitals offering similar services combine to reduce expenses, share services and resources including staff.
- *Vertical consolidation.* One organization purchases another healthcare services organization to access new patients or sources of revenue. Acquisition of a physician practice is an example of a vertical merger.

- *Private equity (PE) activity.* Over the past decade, PE firms have invested over $750 billion to create value across vertical and horizontal sectors in research, life sciences, and specialty physician practices.[19]

While PE activity is projected to increase, there is a growing scrutiny and concern of private equity-backed deals, and the Department of Justice and the Federal Trade Commission have indicated a renewed focus on antitrust enforcement. The FTC's own study[20] found that several recent hospital mergers have resulted in price hikes and reduced quality care and outcomes.

Vendors and Payer Relations

Apart from the care delivery side of a healthcare organization, it is necessary to understand two other dynamics that ultimately impact the profitability and sustainability of a healthcare enterprise. First, understanding the complexity of the healthcare supply chain, from manufacturers to distributors, to logistics and ultimately to providers and patients is paramount to realizing an opportunity to increase value. Finding supplies, buying and managing stock, and understanding patient needs and delivering medical products in a timely fashion are some of the pressures supply chain operators face.

In a recent McKinsey and Company survey,[21] the importance of clinical engagement was identified as a critical element to a high-performing supply chain. Organizations should consider executive clinical sponsorship on key initiatives formalizing specialty-focused committees with key users, like orthopedics or oncology, and staff with dedicated resources and subject matter expertise at every level.

Beyond these fundamentals, organizations should consider building a data analytics infrastructure with easily accessible tools and dashboards embedded into daily operations. Many suppliers and group-purchasing organizations offer contract incentives that can be realized only if the right structures and tools are in place. Evidence indicates that providers realize cost savings of 10–18% by using group purchasing organizations (GPOs), relative to the costs providers would have incurred if they negotiated prices on their own.[22]

Similarly, payer relationship management is crucial and requires subject-matter expertise, as providers can likely deal with multiple "payers," including insurance companies, government programs, employers, and even individuals, as all are considered payers. A report by the Healthcare Financial Management Association titled "Bridging the Provider Divide"[23] shows a deteriorating relationship between providers and payers:

- Nearly 60% of health system CFOs surveyed said their relationships with health plans has changed for the worse over the past three years.

- 80% cited an "intentional or systematic effort" by payers to increase denials.
- 75% of respondents stated the need to add financial services staff in the past three years to manage a substantial increase in the denials.

Physician leaders can improve payer relationships through several key strategies:

- Become comfortable with being transparent.
- Understand the payer mix, contract terms, and length of contract.
- Design processes and systems to gather data, compare trends, and monitor collections and denials by payer type.
- Formulate strong network relationships with payers, not just during contract negotiations.
- Build a team of subject-matter experts.

Business Community Relations

A community health needs assessment survey is better-informed when many partner organizations are involved. Business community relationships can be formed to build on existing board relationships, civic endeavors, and coalition building and philanthropic ventures to improve access, equity, and health outcomes. Benefits of partnerships include:

- Trust-building.
- Sharing of costs and reduction of expenses, as well funding and investments to allow for scale and improve access.
- Enhanced technology and innovation collaboration.
- Workforce development.
- Policy and legislative change.
- Enhanced health and public safety education and awareness.

Increasingly, changes to Medicaid policies[24] are placing more responsibility on the shoulders of healthcare organizations, which are then turning to the local business community for support. Understanding the role of the local institution, often the economic engine in a community, and how it partners with local and area businesses can lead to collaboration to build a workforce, enhance access, finance projects and capital, and impact social determinants of health. Further, the U.S. Chamber of Commerce has advocated that the business community at large help prioritize "Access and Affordability, Wellness, Innovation and Value."[25]

Advertising and Marketing

Once decisions to fund, build, or expand and open new services have been made, it's time to inform the public, referring physicians, and providers as well as employers. As the healthcare industry evolves, consumer expectations are shifting toward greater convenience, personalization, and digital engagement. Health systems must develop plans to stay ahead of the latest marketing trends to meet these demands.

To build a marketing or promotional plan, organizations need to consider their online presence, use of traditional media, relationship management with referring providers, internal communications (internal stakeholders), and direct-to-employer marketing, and develop a unique or difficult to imitate brand presence that helps differentiate services.

Focusing on quality as a major component of the marketing strategy is increasing. According to Healthgrades research, 57% of consumers are more concerned with quality than they were before the pandemic, and 35% are researching hospital quality more than they had before the start of COVID-19.[26]

Determining where to place limited resources for a marketing or advertising campaign using traditional media is part of the process, and in an advancing digital age, online marketing and promotional tools can reduce barriers to engagement and foster loyalty. As consumers become more selective in their search for healthcare, moving from a traditional physician-focused marketing to a more personalized patient-centric approach is warranted.

Another Healthgrades study[27] found that patient reviews topped physicians' list of factors that matter most to them when making referrals, followed by office location, board eligibility or certifications, and medical school and residency training. Brand recognition, reputation, and even affiliation are powerful revenue multipliers and, like most industries, healthcare consumers want the best possible overall experience when seeking services and institutions that prioritize customer satisfaction and engagement are more likely to report successful customer outcomes.

Collaborating with Competitors

As markets further consolidate and evolve, legislative pressures increase, and margins decline, healthcare organizations will likely need to look to each other to solve for complex issues and to continue to serve the community. For example, it is not uncommon for two entities to share the burden of trauma coverage in a market on an annual rotating basis or, in rare cases, a rotating weekly basis, or sharing physician resources across multiple hospitals due to an inability to recruit in some geographies.

In some markets, competitors have formulated relationships to partner on joint ownership of hospitals or conduct the due diligence on lab services from a simple reference lab agreement to joint venture to acquisition.

Healthcare organizations should consider the value proposition of each model to determine the best solution for each organization, as a partnership may help reduce costs, increase access, and improve outcomes and quality.

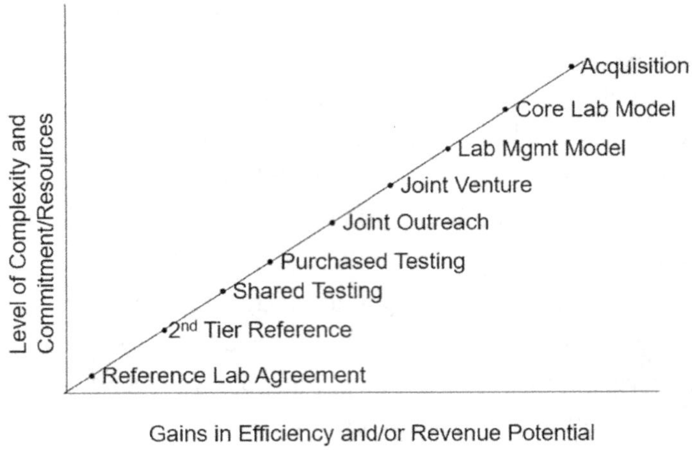

FIGURE 8. Models to Consider

Chapter Summary

Alignment between leadership, between its board, and between its mission and actions is likely the single biggest factor of success in any organization. Leveraging the organization's strategic planning process, developing a business plan supported by a comprehensive market and needs assessment, and performing a financial feasibility assessment paves the path forward. Then, work begins on licensing, hiring the right staff, negotiating with vendors and suppliers, credentialing and enrolling providers, negotiating contracts, marketing, and promoting services as well as engaging the community.

REFERENCES

1. Keehan SP, Fiore JA, Poisal JA, et al. National Health Expenditure Projections, 2022–31: Growth to Stabilize Once the COVID-19 Public Health Emergency Ends. *Health Affairs,* 2023;42(7):886–898. https://doi.org/10.1377/hlthaff.2023.00403
2. Baldrige Excellence Framework. NIST. August 10, 2016. Accessed January 19, 2025. https://www.nist.gov/baldrige/publications/baldrige-excellence-framework
3. Zuckerman AM. *Healthcare Strategic Planning, 3rd Ed.* Chicago, IL: Health Administration Press; 2016.
4. Zuckerman AM. Advancing the State of the Art in Healthcare Strategic Planning. *Frontiers of Health Services Management* 2006;23(2):3–16. https://essentialhospitals.org/wp-content/uploads/2022/07/Advancing_the_State_of_the_Art_in_Healthcare.2-1-1.pdf
5. Kim WC, Mauborgne R. *Blue Ocean Strategy.* Boston, MA: Harvard Business Review Press; 2015.
6. Porter MD, Lee TH. The Strategy that Will Fix Healthcare. *Harvard Business Review.* 2013. Accessed December 1, 2024. https://hbr.org/2013/10/the-strategy-that-will-fix-health-care
7. Porter MD. The Five Forces That Shape Strategy. *Harvard Business Review.* 2008. Accessed November 5, 2024. https://hbr.org/2008/01/the-five-competitive-forces-that-shape-strategy
8. 2024 Environmental Scan. American Hospital Association. December 20, 2024. Accessed January 19, 2025. https://www.aha.org/environmentalscan/2024

9. Surveillance, Epidemiology, and End Results Program. National Cancer Institute. 2018. Accessed January 19, 2025. https://seer.cancer.gov/
10. 2022 *Guidelines for Design and Construction.* Facility Guidelines Institute. Accessed January 19, 2025. https://www.fgiguidelines.org/
11. Anderson J. Why Bond Insurance Is Making a Comeback in Healthcare. *HFMA*. June 25, 2021. Accessed January 19, 2025. https://www.hfma.org/finance-and-business-strategy/capital-finance/why-bond-insurance-is-making-a-comeback-in-healthcare/
12. Pennel CL, McLeroy KR, Burdine JN. Matarrita-Cascante D. Nonprofit Hospitals' Approach to Community Health Needs Assessment. *Am J Public Health*. 2015;105(3):e103–e113. doi: 10.2105/AJPH.2014.302286
13. 42 U.S.C. section 1320a-7b(b)
14. 2023 MGMA DataDive Provider Compensation. Accessed January 19, 2025. https://www.mgma.com/datadive/provider-compensation
15. Valuation Services: Statement of Standards for Valuation Services No.1, Appendix B. AICPA & CIMA. 2023. Accessed January 19, 2025. https://www.aicpa-cima.com/topic/valuation-services.
16. AHA Statement to Ways and Means Subcommittee on Consolidated Markets. May 17, 2023. Accessed January 19, 2025. https://www.aha.org/testimony/2023-05-17-aha-statement-ways-and-means-subcommittee-consolidated-markets
17. PricewaterhouseCoopers. Health Services: US Deals 2025 Outlook. *PwC.* Accessed January 19, 2025. https://www.pwc.com/us/en/industries/health-industries/library/health-services-deals-outlook.html
18. The Growing Role of Private Equity in Healthcare. GrantThorton. September 26, 2023. Accessed January 19, 2025. https://www.grantthornton.com/insights/articles/health-care/2023/the-growing-role-of-private-equity-in-healthcare
19. U.S. Federal Trade Commission. FTC Policy Paper Warns About Pitfalls of COPA Agreements for Patient Care and Healthcare Workers. August 15, 2022. Accessed January 19, 2025. https://www.ftc.gov/news-events/news/press-releases/2022/08/ftc-policy-paper-warns-about-pitfalls-copa-agreements-patient-care-healthcare-workers
20. Bowen B, Galceran BC. Optimizing Health System Supply Chain Performance. McKinsey & Company. August 23, 2022. Accessed January 19, 2025. https://www.mckinsey.com/industries/healthcare/our-insights/optimizing-health-system-supply-chain-performance
21. Leibowitz J, O'Brien D. Five Things To Know About the Role of GPOs in the Healthcare Supply Chain. *Managed Healthcare Executive*. September 14, 2017. Accessed January 19, 2025. https://www.managedhealthcareexecutive.com/view/five-things-know-about-role-gpos-healthcare-supply-chain
22. Williams J. Bridging the Payer-Provider Divide. HFMA. October 24, 2024. Accessed January 19, 2025. https://www.hfma.org/revenue-cycle/bridging-the-payer-provider-divide/
23. Hinton E, Diana A. Medicaid Authorities and Options to Address Social Determinants of Health. KFF. January 29, 2024. Accessed January 19, 2025. https://www.kff.org/medicaid/issue-brief/medicaid-authorities-and-options-to-address-social-determinants-of-health-sdoh/
24. Buchongo P. The Importance of Cross-Sector Partnerships in Enabling Better Health Outcomes. *Chief Healthcare Executive*. November 3, 2024. Accessed January 19, 2025. https://www.chiefhealthcareexecutive.com/view/the-importance-of-cross-sector-partnerships-in-enabling-better-health-outcomes-viewpoint
25. Healthgrades. Special Report: Three Years Later, COVID-19 Continues to Impact Patient Behavior. Healthgrades. Accessed January 19, 2025. https://b2b.healthgrades.com/insights/special-reports/three-years-later-covid-19-continues-to-impact-patient-behavior/
26. Viscomi L. What Physicians Value Most When Making Referrals. Healthgrades. July 7, 2023. Accessed January 19, 2025. https://b2b.healthgrades.com/insights/blog/what-physicians-value-most-when-making-referrals/

CHAPTER 2

Contracts and Negotiations

Maggie DiCostanzo, Esq., and Dusko Stojkov, Esq.

HALM CORE CONTENT:

- 1.4 Contracts legal and financial implications
- 1.12 Negotiation strategies and techniques
- 1.18 Stark, antitrust, and kickback laws related to physician services
- 1.21 Contract and vendor sourcing
- 1.24 Taxation law

CASE SCENARIO:

A hospital purchases two additional hospitals located in other counties, creating a new regional health system. Each hospital has its own vendor contracts with varying terms and conditions. The health system aims to integrate and standardize contracts across all facilities, developing template agreements for future use. Questions to consider include:

- What are the legal issues associated with contracting?
- What negotiating issues will arise, and how can they be addressed?
- What are some key contract provisions to address?
- What compliance laws can affect contract terms?
- What are the financial implications of contracting?
- Can vendor sourcing be beneficial?
- Are there tax implications of contracting?

THE DAILY OPERATION of a healthcare entity involves numerous contracts, each with its own unique risks and each addressing specific needs. These needs can range from product purchase agreements to service contracts, pricing agreements, rebate agreements, evaluation agreements, licensing agreements, evaluation agreements, and subscription agreements, to name just a few.

Not only are there myriad agreement types, the topics addressed in the agreements are numerous as well, including medical device purchases, consumable purchases, laboratory testing services, medical waste disposal services, physical facility services, equipment loaners, and coding and billing services.

Contracting in healthcare is unique due to healthcare-specific regulatory requirements such as state and federal Stark (self-referral), anti-trust, and anti-kickback (fee splitting) laws. Negotiating terms can be difficult, especially when a large, national, or international corporate vendor entity has more leverage than a regional hospital. Standardizing contracts and their terms can reduce variance and risk over the long term.

Contracts: Legal Issues

Black's Law Dictionary defines a contract as "[a]n agreement between two or more persons which creates an obligation to do or not to do a particular thing."[1] Applicable law to any contract is determined by individual state statutory and/or common law and may be interpreted by the courts when disputes arise.

Common law contracts are governed by the Restatement (Second) of Contracts. That Restatement defines a contract as "[a] promise or a set of promises for the breach of which the law gives a remedy, or the performance of which the law in some way recognizes a duty."[2] In some instances, the Uniform Commercial Code is applicable to a contract, particularly in cases of secured transactions.

While contracts may be verbal or in writing, if a state follows the statute of fraud, in order to be enforceable, the contract must be in writing. Of course, the healthcare system will want its contracts to be in writing, as doing so would help to provide clear expectations of the parties and, if needed, enforceability and damages for any breach by the entity with whom the system contracts.

A legally enforceable contract is evidenced by an (1) offer, (2) acceptance of that offer, and (3) adequate consideration. Consideration is when one party gives something of value and the other party receives that value. Perhaps the clearest example is that one party pays the other party money in exchange for the other party providing a service.

If a contract is breached, the law provides remedies to the non-breaching party that may include general damages, consequential damages, and specific performance. If a contract is breached, one must determine whether the breach was "material" or "immaterial." Only a material breach terminates an agreement.

Generally, whether a contract was breached is a determination of fact involving an analysis using a five-prong test.[3] A hospital can, however, agree on specific circumstances that will constitute a breach in an agreement at the outset. Note that wrongly claiming a material breach occurred can itself be a breach.

If a party to a contract believes that a material breach has occurred, that party should follow the requirements on breach notification outlined in the contract. Regardless, a best practice is to provide written notification of a claimed breach, specifically identifying the reasons for the breach.

Working with an attorney can minimize risk and enhance a successful termination or at least enhance supportive evidence for termination should the matter lead to litigation. Note that oftentimes, a contract will include an opportunity for the breaching party to cure a breach after receiving notice of an alleged breach from the non-breaching party.

Contracts: Negotiating Strategies/Issues

Negotiating a contract requires understanding the hospital's goals and priorities with the contract and its subject. Some contract terms may be more important in one contract than in another, depending on the circumstances. Essential terms can include termination, *force majeure*, warranty, return policies, remedies, confidentiality, dispute resolution, limitation of liability, and indemnification provisions. In addition, standardizing contracts can reduce variance and risk over the long term.

When drafting and negotiating contracts, think about what could go wrong after the contract is signed and negotiate the contract so as to minimize the impact on the hospital should that wrong occur. For example:

- Is there a risk that the vendor will not meet certain required quality metrics?
- Is there a risk that the vendor's product might fail?
- Is there a risk of unauthorized access to protected health information (PHI)?

To address the first risk, incorporating those metric requirements into the contract is not enough; also incorporate the implications to the vendor of not meeting those requirements and provide the hospital with a remedy if the vendor fails to meet those requirements.

With regard to the second risk, a warranty provision and a return policy become particularly important: What is warranted? For how long? And what is the remedy?

For the final issue, terms should spell out the obligations of the vendor should unauthorized access to PHI occur. Who determines whether unauthorized access occurred? How soon must the vendor notify the hospital of the unauthorized access? Who will bear the cost of patient notification of the unauthorized access?

These are just a few examples that show that the analysis is fact-specific, dependent on the goals of the hospital, the risk, the things that could go wrong, and the sophistication of the parties, to name just a few.

Even if a healthcare system implements template agreements, negotiating with vendors may still be necessary. A vendor might reject using the system's template and instead require use of its own standard contract. For this reason, it is important to have standard negotiating terms in place and also to have identified those contract provisions about which the system will not negotiate or revise.

The system also might encounter "contracts of adhesion." These are boiler plate contracts where a party has no input in the terms of the contract. These contracts are more apt to arise with technology terms and conditions. For example, there may be a link referenced in a contract that, when accessed, leads to a standardized set of terms and conditions that are not editable. While these types of contracts can be beneficial to one party, they can be disadvantageous to the other, and in this situation, that is the hospital. More negotiating may be involved, or the system would need to conduct a risk–benefit analysis before moving ahead with such a contract.

Compliance: Stark, Anti-Trust, and Anti-Kickback Laws Related to Physician Services

Stark Law. Generally, the Stark law prohibits a physician from making a referral to an entity for any provision of "designated health services" if the physician has a financial relationship with that entity, unless the situation falls within a Stark Law exception.[4] Oftentimes, in efforts to provide supportive evidence of the intent of the parties, a contract includes a provision that states that the fees paid by the hospital to the vendor are not based on referrals.

Anti-Kickback Statute (AKS). The federal AKS makes it unlawful to knowingly and willfully solicit or receive any remuneration in return for purchasing, leasing, ordering, or arranging for or recommending the same of any product, facility, service, or item for which payment may be made under a federal healthcare reimbursement program.[5] Certain exceptions, or safe harbors, exist and are set forth in the AKS law. One example is the "discount safe harbor," which provides that certain rebates and discounts are not subject to the AKS.

Note that many states have enacted their own self-referral prohibitions and anti-kickback laws that in some instances are broader in scope than the federal laws. For example, the state compliance laws may not be limited to the involvement of federal healthcare programs but may also apply to non-government payers.

Excluded Providers. The system's hospitals should not contract with an entity or individual that a hospital knows or should have known has been excluded from a federal healthcare program.[6] A hospital that contracts with an excluded provider does so at risk of civil monetary penalties and, worse, becoming an excluded provider from federal healthcare programs itself. To reduce such risk, a clause in the contract should state that the vendor is not excluded from a federal healthcare program. This clause can be in the form of a statement or a warranty.

HIPAA. A hospital is a "covered entity" as defined by HIPAA and accordingly is required to comply with HIPAA laws and regulations. If PHI is received, used, or maintained by the vendor, then the vendor is a "business associate" who must comply with HIPAA, and the parties must enter into a business associate agreement that addresses permitted uses and disclosures of the PHI by the vendor. The business associate agreement is another type of contract that can be standardized by the healthcare system. It can be a stand-alone agreement or part of a vendor-hospital agreement.

Anti-discrimination Laws. Hospitals that qualify as federal contractors must notify a contracted vendor that by providing services to the hospital as a "covered federal subcontractor," the vendor may be subject to certain anti-discrimination laws. Such anti-discrimination laws may include non-discrimination laws, affirmative action laws, and Executive Orders.

Contracts: Financial Implications

The financial management goals of contracts include cost-savings, compliance, risk reduction, and enhanced vendor relationships. Centralizing and unifying financial management in the healthcare system can further achieve these goals. Using a centralized electronic contract management program can help with timing and other efficiencies. Further, the creation of standardized contract templates for oft-used types of contracts can enhance timing and predictability, reduce negotiations and errors, and reduce compliance risk.

Operational inefficiencies in contract management can affect finances in many ways, including:

- Finance charges for late or missed payments.
- Lost money due to missed opportunities.
- Breach of warranty damages.
- Contract errors resulting in negative financial consequences.
- Civil monetary penalties for non-compliance.
- Legal fees.

As an example, price reductions and rebates raise compliance concerns, particularly with the AKS. The key is for a price reduction or rebate to satisfy the AKS discount safe harbor. A "discount" is defined as "a reduction in the amount a buyer…is charged for an item or service based on an arms-length transaction."[7]

The law also requires that a hospital report the discount to the federal healthcare program. Oftentimes, parties include a provision in the contract that addresses discounted pricing and party obligations related to discounted pricing. One important aspect of this safe harbor is the need for the vendor to cooperate with the hospital by providing the hospital with pricing and discount information.

Contract and Vendor Sourcing

Vendor sourcing is an important aspect of contracting. Vendor sourcing is a strategic practice that can mitigate risk, lower costs, improve compliance, and enhance vendor relationships. Usually, vendor sourcing is done internally by a hospital's procurement team, which can also be centralized for the system.

The process may follow like this:

1. *Define the Hospital's Needs.* Identify the scope of work, quality requirements, and pricing expectations.
2. *Evaluate the Market.* Who are possible vendors? What are their capabilities? Do they align with the hospital's defined needs?
3. *Prepare a Request for Proposal (RFP).* Draft an RFP about the hospital's needs and requirements and use it to solicit bids from the identified vendors.
4. *Evaluate the Proposals.* Evaluate and compare the vendor proposals based on hospital needs and requirements, including price, timing, and capabilities.
5. *Select a Vendor and Negotiate Final Terms.* Finalize contract terms and a contract for signing.
6. *Sign the Contract.*

After signing, the healthcare system should monitor and evaluate vendor performance. This may include regular meetings and communication with the vendor, analysis of benchmarks, and performance review. The vendor sourcing could be unified within the system to further enhance efficiencies.

Taxation Law

Standardization of contracts requires the involvement of many different systems and hospital team members, including risk management, supply chain, legal, IT, and the chief financial officer (CFO). With the CFO, who is tasked with addressing the legal and tax implications of the consolidation, the process might proceed as follows:

Sales and Use Tax. The CFO's tax manager points out potential sales and use tax issues: "Each state has different rules regarding sales tax on medical supplies and equipment. We need to review our purchasing processes to ensure we are not overpaying sales tax on exempt items or underpaying on taxable items."

She provides an example: "In New Jersey, prescription drugs and prosthetic devices are exempt from sales tax, while in Illinois, prescription drugs are taxed at a reduced rate of 1%. We need to ensure our accounting systems accurately track these distinctions. We need to carefully review our sales of medical services, durable medical equipment, and mobility-enhancing equipment. Many states have specific exemptions or reduced rates for these items when sold to patients or healthcare providers." Specifically:

- New Jersey provides exemptions for prescription drugs for human use, prosthetic devices, and durable medical equipment for home use.[8]
- Illinois imposes a reduced tax rate of 1% on prescription and nonprescription medicines for human use.[9]
- Massachusetts exempts certain medical equipment if prescribed by a physician, including kidney dialysis machines, enteral and parenteral feeding devices, oxygen concentrators, and hospital beds for home use.[10]

- California provides that sales of mobility aids such as wheelchairs, crutches, canes, and walkers to healthcare facilities for patient use are generally taxable but may be exempt if ordered for a specific patient as directed by a physician.[11]
- New York exempts from tax drugs and medicines for human use and medical equipment and supplies required to correct or alleviate physical incapacity.[12]
- Ohio exempts drugs dispensed with a prescription[13] and taxes prosthetic devices sold without a prescription.[14]

Income Tax Considerations. The CFO's controller raises concerns about the income tax implications of the consolidation: "The consolidation may affect our nexus in different states. We need to review our operations in each location to determine if we would be creating new income tax filing obligations. With the rise of telehealth services, we need to consider the income tax implications of providing services across state lines. Some states have adopted market-based sourcing rules for services, which could impact our tax liability.

"Also, we need to consider tax implications of software and technology purchases. Many states have complex rules around the taxability of software as a service (SaaS) and other digital products. For instance, if we license technology and pass the cost to the patient, many states use the "true object" test to determine whether the primary purpose is the provision of medical services (likely non-taxable) or the sale/license of technology (potentially taxable)." A number of states have implemented market-based sourcing rules for services.[15]

Tax-Exempt Status Considerations. The CFO's tax advisor cautions: "As a nonprofit entity, we need to be careful that our new contractual arrangements don't jeopardize the system's tax-exempt status. Any agreements with for-profit entities should be at arm's length and serve a charitable purpose. We need to be particularly careful with our sales activities. While many of our healthcare services are exempt, sales of non-medical services could be taxable. We should review our sales tax collection policies."[16]

A tax law action item list for contracting includes:

1. Engage a tax professional to review sales and use tax compliance and income tax nexus issues.
2. Review telehealth services for potential multi-state tax implications.
3. Analyze technology purchases and contracts for potential sales tax obligations.
4. Evaluate revenue streams for potential taxable sales activities.

Chapter Summary

Healthcare contracting is a multidiscipline area, requiring the involvement of physician leaders, healthcare executives, and advisors who understand and can operationalize financial, compliance/regulatory, legal, tax, and risk matters. When considering standardizing vendor contracts across a system, develop an action plan that includes:

1. Review all existing contracts for legal enforceability and compliance issues.
2. Develop standardized contract templates that address key legal and compliance requirements.
3. Implement a centralized contract management system to track all agreements across the organization.
4. Conduct training for staff on new contracting procedures, key contract provisions, and compliance requirements.
5. Establish a regular contract review process to ensure ongoing compliance and optimization.

REFERENCES

1. Contract. *Black's Law Dictionary*. 6th ed., 1990.
2. Restatement (Second) of Contracts §1.
3. Restatement (Second) of Contracts §241.
4. 42 U.S.C. §1395nn.
5. 42 U.S.C. §1320a-7b(b)(1)(B).
6. See 42 U.S.C. §1320a-7.
7. 42 C.F.R. §1001.952(h)(5).
8. N.J.S. § 54:32B-8.1.
9. Illinois Admin. Code tit. 86, §130.311(a).
10. Massachusetts G.L. c. 64H, §6(l); Technical Information Release TIR 85-7.
11. Cal. Code Regs. tit. 18, §1591.2(c).
12. N.Y. Tax Law §1115(a)(3); 20 N.Y.C.R.R. §528.4(a)(1).
13. Ohio R.C. §5739.02(B)(18).
14. Ohio R.C. §5739.01(B)(1).
15. *See, e.g.*: Cal. Rev. & Tax. Code § 25136-2; Mass. Gen. Laws ch. 63, §38(f); N.Y. Tax Law §210-A(10); 35 ILCS 5/304(a)(3)(C-5)(iv); 72 P.S. §7401(3)2.(a)(16.1)(C); Ohio Rev. Code Ann. §5733.05(B)(2)(c)(ii); Mich. Comp. Laws §206.665(1)(e).
16. See, Internal Revenue Code Section 501(c)(3); Treasury Regulations Section 1.501(c)(3)-1(d)(1)(ii); IRS Rev. Rul. 69-545, 1969-2 C.B. 117 (the IRS providing examples illustrating whether a nonprofit hospital claiming exemption under Code section 501(c)(3) is operated to serve a public rather than a private interest); IRS Publication 4221-PC, "Compliance Guide for 501(c)(3) Public Charities."

CHAPTER 3

Optimizing Revenue and Margins

George "Deuce" Lukemeyer, II

HALM CORE CONTENT:

- 1.6 Fundamental productivity measures
- 1.7 Funding sources
- 1.8 GME reimbursement models and associated regulatory / compliance law
- 1.15 Reimbursement methodologies
- 1.16 Centers for Medicare and Medicaid payer-based models
- 1.17 Revenue generation

CASE SCENARIO:

Physician leaders of an independent, recently established multispecialty physician group face significant challenges balancing practice revenue growth, personal income, work/life balance, and overall financial and clinical quality success. Within the group, the desires of individual physicians to understand the factors influencing and contributing to financial success vary.

What core concepts affecting revenue generation are important for the group's physician leaders to understand? What inventory of sources are available for alternative revenue streams? What forms do reimbursement models take? What is the role of governmental programs and payers? What strategies exist for increasing revenue?

Fundamental Productivity Measures

Contributing to the overall work output, or productivity, of the medical group underpins the ability to generate revenue for physicians of all specialties. Productivity can be measured in myriad ways, but at a minimum, the total work effort should contribute to improving financial results without compromising clinical quality.

Traditional, long-established physician-productivity measurements include:[1]

- *Patient volume* – Count of patient encounters.
  Maintaining overall patient volume is critical to financial sustainability. In its most basic form and with all patient encounters of equal intensity and duration, a physician who sees 20 patients per day is more productive at generating revenue than a physician who sees 10.
- *Efficiency* – Count of patient encounters per unit of time.
  Adding an efficiency metric correlates productivity across time. A physician who sees 15 patients in an eight-hour day has lower productivity efficiency than a physician who sees 10 patients in a half-day of four hours. Revenue generation relies heavily on efficiency.
- *Collections* – Patient and insurance reimbursement
  Using collections as a measure of productivity is popular due to the direct link with money coming into the practice. One commonly cited flaw of collections as a productivity measure is that it includes contractual adjustments from payers. Meaning that physicians who see indigent patients or patients covered by less-desirable payers receive a lower attributable value for the same work effort.
- *Relative value units*
  Consistently increasing in use, the relative value unit (RVU) is a national standard set by the Centers for Medicare and Medicaid Services (CMS) in 1992 to determine the monetary value paid to providers for professional services based on the skills and resources used. Agnostic to the payer, RVUs are a barometer of practice efficiency and patient complexity and are used to normalize work performance across providers.[2]

A Current Procedural Terminology (CPT) code specifies a procedure or treatment performed in patient care and each carries an RVU value. RVUs are broken into three components:

1. Work RVU (wRVU) represents the provider's time, effort, and skill required and accounts for just over 50% of the total RVU.
2. Practice expense RVU (peRVU) represents the costs incurred by the practice for overhead such as staff salaries, occupancy costs, equipment, and supplies. The peRVU accounts for approximately 44% of the total RVU.
3. Malpractice RVU (mpRVU) represents the costs associated with professional liability insurance. The mpRVU accounts for approximately 6% of the total RVU.

The Geographic Practice Cost Index (GPCI) standardizes Medicare payments by adjusting for geographic cost differences. The GPCIs are applied in the calculation of a Medicare payment schedule amount by multiplying the RVU value for each component by the GPCI for that component of each CPT code. Medicare then reimburses professional services using a monetizing value called a conversion factor (CF) assigned per RVU. Medicare reimburses for professional services through a formula defined as {(wRVU * GPCI) + (peRVU * GPCI) + (mpRVU * GPCI)} * CF.[3]

Metrics such as hours per patient day, cost per patient day, and units of service per labor hour represent important concepts for physician leaders to understand as they measure productivity, resource consumption, and efficiency.

- *Hours per patient day*

  The formula for hours per patient day (HPPD) is the total number of productive hours worked by all staff divided by the total number of patient days. The significance of HPPD lies in its ability to track how efficiently resources, including drilling down to discrete job types and role, are used.[4]
- *Cost per patient day*

  The formula for cost per patient day is the total patient-related expenses divided by the number of patient days in a given period. Similar to HPPD, cost per patient day measures the ability to deliver care efficiently.
- *Units of service per labor hour*

  Frequently referred to as work hours per unit of service (WHPUOS), this metric allows physician leaders to ensure staff are productive. The formula divides the total number of hours worked by the volume of service units in that time.

  The challenge with WHPUOS is determining "unit of service." For example, an emergency department leader may define the unit of service as admissions. If five nurses are working a 12-hour shift each, the total work hours is 60. In this example, the 60 hours would be divided by admissions in that time period as a measure of staff productivity.[5]

Monitoring and growing individual and group productivity is critical for physician leaders to understand as it is the base driver for generating revenue, achieving financial soundness, and delivering individual and group success.

Funding Sources

Physician leaders must understand all the options for securing funds necessary to establish, maintain, and expand healthcare operations. These options include bonds, philanthropy, grants, and foundations.

- *Issuing Bonds*

  Companies use bonds with the intent of borrowing money from investors. Bond issuers are obligated to pay regular fixed interest payments to these investors, known as bondholders. Additionally, the bond issuer is obligated to repay the bondholder's original invested amount at an agreed-upon time known as the bond maturation date.

- *Philanthropy*
  Leveraging philanthropic sources is an increasingly common strategy for securing medical practice funding. In an era of pressure to decrease the overall cost of care combined with shrinking, or even nonexistent, positive margins, philanthropy has become a strategic imperative and source of new revenue. Grateful patient fundraising has evolved over the past decade. The goal is for healthcare organizations to build relationships with and raise funds from patients and their families who have had positive experiences.
- *Grant writing*
  Government, private, and corporate grants represent another source of funding for healthcare. The art of grant writing involves crafting a compelling proposal that aligns with the prospective funding source's priorities. The key components to a successful grant request include an executive summary, a needs assessment, a description of how the funds will be used, and a proposed budget.[6]
- *Foundations*
  In the same continuum as seeking philanthropic funding and grant writing, foundations, both public and private, represent another potential source of funding. Because foundations differ by design, instead of the specificity inherent to grant writing during a snapshot in time, the approach to foundations centers on relationships that endure for long periods.

GME Reimbursement Models and Associated Regulatory Compliance

Hospitals that host graduate medical education (GME) programs are saddled with additional costs, and academic physicians are burdened with potentially decreased efficiency due to the presence of residency training programs and residents.

The costs associated with residents and residency training programs are bucketed into two components: direct costs and indirect costs. Direct costs, or direct medical education DME) costs, relate to items such as resident stipends, supervisory physician salaries, and associated program administrative costs.[7] Medicare payments for DME are calculated based on the number of full-time equivalent residents in the teaching hospital's training program(s). The methodology is based on a hospital-specific base period of time per resident, calculated as the hospital's allowable costs of GME divided by its number of residents.[8]

Indirect costs, or indirect medical education (IME) costs, reimburse for the higher patient care expenses and increased complexity of cases that teaching hospitals often encounter. Medicare payments for IME are calculated based on a formula established by CMS to account for several factors, including the hospital's ratio of residents to beds, Medicare patient population, and Medicare disproportionate share (DSH) adjustment.

The ratio of residents to beds reflects the teaching hospital's capacity to train residents and interns. Teaching hospitals with a higher ratio of residents to beds are likely to receive higher IME payments due to their greater educational impact. The hospitals' Medicare population is used to increase payments made to those hospitals training healthcare professionals who care for Medicare beneficiaries. The DSH adjustment increases payments due to the teaching hospitals' significantly higher proportion of low-income and uninsured patients to adjust for the hospital's higher level of uncompensated care.[9]

Compliance issues in GME center on ensuring resident physicians receive adequate training, adhere to work hours restrictions, receive proper supervision, document patient encounters accurately, and bill appropriately.

Oversight of GME programs occurs primarily through the Accreditation Council for Graduate Medical Education (ACGME). The ACGME is an independent, 501(c)(3), not-for-profit organization that sets and monitors professional educational standards essential in preparing physicians to deliver safe, high-quality medical care to all Americans.[10]

Balancing a positive and supportive resident learning environment with patient safety, quality of care, and resident well-being is the core responsibility of ACGME oversight. Starting in 2003, the ACGME enacted duty hours restrictions to include an 80-hour work week maximum, a mandatory eight-hour break between shifts, one day off per week on average during the course of a month, and a 24-hour maximum shift duration.[11]

In addition, ACGME established "Milestones" to represent a framework of competencies for effective supervision of residents. The goal is for all graduating learners to achieve basic abilities in key areas to care for patients when in practice through competency-based medical education. The ACGME and the American Board of Medical Specialties developed six core competencies necessary for a practicing physician.[12]

1. Patient Care and Procedural Skills
2. Medical Knowledge
3. Practice-based Learning and Improvement
4. Interpersonal and Communication Skills
5. Professionalism
6. Systems-based Practice

The billing process in teaching settings occurs in two ways.

1. The Medicare physician fee schedule guides reimbursement when services are performed by a resident with a teaching physician present during the critical or key portions of the encounter or when provided by a resident under a primary care

exception within an approved GME program. Teaching physicians who involve residents in the care of patients must include the GC modifier indicating the service has been performed in part by a resident under the direction of a teaching physician.[13]

2. Patient care services performed by an intern or resident within the scope of his or her training program are reimbursed as provider services through GME and IME.

Reimbursement Methodologies

Physician reimbursement for work output takes multiple forms. Common methodologies include fee-for-service models, value- and risk-based models, as well as academic institution-specific models and government payers.

- *Fee for Service*
  Fee for service is a reimbursement model whereby physicians are paid a set fee for each service they render. The fee paid accounts for the complexity, duration, and intensity of the service. From the physician practice perspective, the primary advantage of the fee-for-service model is the opportunity for increased revenue due to reimbursement, at an agreed-upon fee schedule set by the provider and the payer, for each service provided. Critics of this model argue it incentivizes providers to perform more procedures rather than focusing on the patient's overall health.[14]
- *Managed Care*
  Managed care plans represent the major form of reimbursement for physician practices today. Conceptually, the goal of managed care is to effectively control costs while simultaneously improving quality by regulating the use of medical services. Managed care takes many forms, but all are designed to expand the patient population and associated revenue streams available to physician practices. Plans include:
  1. Health maintenance organizations (HMOs) typically reimburse physicians under a model referred to as capitation. Capitated plans reimburse physicians using a predictable, upfront, set amount of money necessary to cover the predicted cost of all or some of the services provided to specific patients over a certain period of time.[15] Conceptually, the typical HMO is designed to improve outcomes by requiring a primary care physician be assigned to the patient to ensure preventative care.
  2. Preferred provider organizations (PPOs) are networks of physicians and facilities that offer lower out-of-pocket costs for members using in-network physicians and facilities. The PPO model is intended to offer participating physicians a way to expand their patient base, streamline operations, and ensure prompt and fair reimbursement.[16]
  3. Point of service (POS) plans are less common than HMOs and PPOs and are designed to combine features of both. Patients covered by a POS plan are typically required to have a primary care provider but are also able to self-refer within the POS network.[17]

The terms *value-based plans* and *risk-based plans* are frequently used interchangeably; both incentivize providers for positive patient outcomes and lower cost. Value-based care reimbursement focuses on the quality of care rather than the quantity of care.[18] Risk-based reimbursement is tied to the physicians' ability to keep actual healthcare expenses below a budgeted allowance and share in the savings compared to budget.[19] The subtle, yet important, distinction is value-based plans focus reimbursement more on positive outcomes while risk-based plans incentivize more for cost reduction.

Enhanced payment is a form of reimbursement that is available to physicians and academic medical centers. Typically, academic medical centers provide healthcare to large numbers of Medicaid patients. Upper payment limit (UPL) is a form of enhanced payment that applies specifically to Medicaid enrollees. UPL payments are constructed to allow individual states to improve reimbursement on Medicaid patients to match:[20]

- The Medicare rate.
- The average commercial rate.
- The Medicare equivalent of the average commercial rate.

Centers for Medicare and Medicaid Services Payer-Based Models

The Centers for Medicare and Medicaid Services (CMS) reimburses physicians for professional services performed for enrollees in government-run payer programs, Medicare and Medicaid. Each program generally follows the same payment *methodology* options (fee for service, HMO, capitation, value-based, risk-based, etc.) described above.

Medicare is federal health insurance for people 65 and older. The two most common models are:

- Original Medicare, also known as Part A – Hospital Coverage and Part B – Medical Coverage, represents the traditional fee-for-service model where Medicare reimburses a set amount based on services rendered. Medicare typically pays the physician practice 80% of the annually published Medicare Physician Fee Schedule with the beneficiary responsible for 20% as deductibles, copayments, and coinsurance.
- Medicare Advantage, or MA plans, also known as Part C, is coverage through a Medicare-approved private health insurance company. MA plans cover Part A and Part B, and frequently offer extra coverage such as vision, hearing, and dental. Most MA plans also include prescription drug coverage, known as Part D. From a reimbursement perspective, physicians active in MA plans can choose to participate with the plan in significant shared-savings payment opportunities.

Medicaid payer-based models follow the same payment methodologies discussed above, fee-for-service and variations of managed care, including coverage delivery through private insurance companies, but with one import distinction: Medicare is a federal program administered by CMS, which is a division of the Department of Health and Human Services, while Medicaid is a joint federal and state program. Medicaid programs are intended to help cover medical expenses for people with limited income and less-than-adequate resources. The federal government has general rules that all state Medicaid programs must follow, but each state runs its own program. This means the eligibility requirements and benefits provided can vary from state to state.[21]

Revenue Generation

The most typical and elemental form of generating revenue within a physician practice is by filing a claim for reimbursement from a third party. Today's electronic medical record (EMR) systems integrate medical history with revenue-capture functions such as claim management and payment processing. Billing effectively for physician services can be distilled to eight steps:[22]

1. Registering.
2. Establishing financial responsibility.
3. Checking the patient in/out.
4. Coding the encounter.
5. Preparing/transmitting claims.
6. Monitoring payer adjudication.
7. Generating statements for patients/accounting for patient and payer payments.
8. Properly documenting the services.

Physicians affect this process the most directly in step four, coding the encounter. Coding accurately is critical to all parties involved with a patient visit. Inaccurate coding delays reimbursement to the physician practice and severely restricts practice cash flow. Physician, patient, and insurer benefit from the reduced administrative costs associated with accurate coding.

Identifying new ways of generating revenue within the practice, such as adding ancillary services and physician extenders, can be effective revenue-capture tactics.

Adding ancillary services requires understanding services that are currently referred out. Examples of ancillary services that most medical practices could implement include lab and imaging. The determination to add ancillary services should focus on patient convenience and include an analysis of potential volume for generating new revenue with additional staffing and equipment costs.

Adding physician extenders to serve appropriate patient encounters that do not pay well is another effective tactic for generating revenue. Utilizing lower cost providers adds efficiency to the practice by freeing up the physician to perform the higher billable encounters. Patient convenience is often the driver through improved patient access and shorter wait times associated with extenders.

Innovative pricing strategies can enhance payer contracting efforts. Price transparency allows consumers of healthcare services to compare prices across entities. It is also a prerequisite for effective pricing strategies. Insurers and employers could significantly bend the cost curve merely by steering away from providers that are outliers on price or quality. The two critical questions each physician practice should ask itself are:

1. How do my in-network rates compare to my competitors at the service line level and by market?
2. Are my rates an outlier within the market?

Answers to those two questions allow development of practice-specific pricing strategy. The strategy results from identifying the services inside the practice with:

- Above-average quality at a rate below the market median.
- Below-average quality at a rate above the market median.
- High volumes and comparatively low rates.
- Low volumes and comparatively high rates.[23]

Physician leaders who determine their practice reimbursement rates do not reflect their value and quality will be able to engage payers equipped with identifiable data substantiating that current rates are not competitive and should be aligned with the organization's true value.[24] Strategies such as cost-plus pricing, where a markup is added to the actual cost associated with providing the service, and bundled pricing, where multiple services that complement each other are offered together for a single price, surface as a result of this process.[25]

Chapter Summary

Effective physician leaders understand how generating revenue intersects with productivity measures, funding sources, graduate medical education, government programs, and private payer reimbursement methodologies. This knowledge base drives the strategic and tactical approach necessary to secure financial, clinical quality and work/life success at a group and individual level.

REFERENCES

1. Moore KJ. A Productivity Primer. *Fam Pract Manag.* 2022:9(5):72–73. https://www.aafp.org/pubs/fpm/issues/2002/0500/p72.html.
2. SCP Health. Using RVUs to Measure Provider Productivity. SCP Health blog.. November 2024. https://www.scphealth.com/blog/using-rvus-to-measure-provider-productivity/.
3. Seidenwurm DJ, Burleson JH. The Medicare Conversion Factor. *Am J Neuroradiol.* 2014;35(2):242–243.
4. ShiftMed. How to Optimize Your HPPD Goal for Healthcare Excellence. Shiftmed Insights. October 10, 2023. https://www.shiftmed.com/insights/knowledge-center/how-to-effectively-manage-your-hppd-goal/.
5. Shiftwizard. WHPUOS Analysis: Reducing Healthcare Labor Costs. Shiftwizard.com. https://www.shiftwizard.com/reduce-healthcare-costs-whpuos/#:~:text=It's%20the%20job%20of%20health-

care,is%20worthwhile%20for%20the%20hospital.

6. Livingston T. Master Grant Writing: Tips and Tools for Securing Essential Funding. BlueNotary. October 4, 2024. https://bluenotary.us/grant-writing/#:~:text=What%20is%20the%20key%20to,proposal%20to%20meet%20their%20objectives.
7. Institute of Medicine. Committee on Implementning a National Graduate Medical Education Trust Fund. Washington, DC: National Academies Press; 1997. Overview of Graduate Medical Education and the Distribution of a Trust Fund. https://www.ncbi.nlm.nih.gov/books/NBK233558/.
8. CMS. Direct Graduate Medical Education (DGME). CMS.gov. September 9, 2024. https://www.cms.gov/medicare/payment/prospective-payment-systems/acute-inpatient-pps/direct-graduate-medical-education-dgme.
9. MD Clarity. Indiret Medical Education (IME). RCM Glossary. MD Clarity. https://www.mdclarity.com/glossary/indirect-medical-education-ime#:~:text=future%20healthcare%20professionals.-,Difference%20between%20Indirect%20Medical%20Education%20(IME)%20and%20Direct%20Medical%20Education,of%20medical%20residents%20and%20interns.
10. ACGME. About the ACGME. Accreditation Council for Graduate Medical Education. https://www.acgme.org/about/overview/.
11. Grabski DF, Goudreau BJ, Gillen JR, et al. Compliance with the Accreditation Council for Graduate Medical Education Duty Hours in a Residency Program: Challenges and Solutions in a Teaching Hospital. *Surgery.* 2020;167(2):302–307.
12. Eno C, Correa R, Stewart NH, Lim J, et al.. Milestones *ACGME Guidebook for Residents and Fellows. Accreditation Council of Graduate Medical Education; 2020.* . https://www.acgme.org/globalassets/pdfs/milestones/milestonesguidebookforresidentsfellows.pdf.
13. CMS. Guidelines for Teaching Physicians, Interns and Residents. CMS Medical Learning Network. March 2017. https://med.jax.ufl.edu/compliance/documents/medicare-mln.pdf.
14. Streamline Health. Fee-for-Service vs Value-Based Care: The Differences You Should Know. Streamline Health. August 31, 2023. https://streamlinehealth.net/fee-for-service-vs-value-based-care/.
15. CMS. Capitation and Pre-payment. CMS.gov. https://www.cms.gov/priorities/innovation/key-concepts/capitation-and-pre-payment#:~:text=Capitation%3A%20A%20way%20of%20paying,to%20cover%20the%20predicted%20cost.
16. Prime Health Services. Expanding Horizons: The Upsides of PPO Network Participation for Medical Providers. Prime Health Services. https://www.primehealthservices.com/upsides-of-ppo-network-participation-for-medical-providers/.
17. PayrHealth. Payor Contracting: How Managed Care Contracts Impact Reimbursement. PayrHealth blog. https://payrhealth.com/blog/how-managed-care-contracts-impact-reimbursement#health-maintenance-organizations-hmo.
18. foresee Medical. What Is Value-Based Care. foresee Medical. https://www.foreseemed.com/value-based-care#:~:text=Value%2Dbased%20healthcare%20delivery%20is,health%20outcomes%20and%20reduce%20costs.
19. Robeznieks A. Moving to New Payment Models: What You Need to Know. American Medical Association. https://www.ama-assn.org/practice-management/payment-delivery-models/moving-new-payment-models-what-you-need-know#:~:text=Under%20risk%20or%20budget%2Dbased,population%20with%20a%20particular%20condition.
20. Medicaid.gov. Medicaid Downloads UPL Instructions. Medicaid.gov.. https://www.medicaid.gov/medicaid/downloads/upl-instructions-qualified-practitioner-services-replacement-new.pdf.
21. U.S. Department of Health and Human Services. Answers about Medicare and Medicaid. hhs.gov. https://www.hhs.gov/answers/medicare-and-medicaid/what-is-the-difference-between-medicare-medicaid/index.html.
22. MedicalBillingandCoding.org. Medical Billing and Coding, 3.03: The Medical Billing Process. MedicalBillingandCoding.org. https://www.medicalbillingandcoding.org/billing-process/.

23. Trilliant Health. Field Guide to Survive Healthcare's Negative-Sum Game. Chapter 4: Developing Effective Pricing Strategies. March 20, 2024. Trilliant Health. https://fieldguide.trillianthealth.com/pricing-strategies/#:~:text=%E2%80%9CThe%20worship%20of%20premium%20pricing,that%20produces%20optimum%20market%20standing.%E2%80%9D.
24. McKinsey & Company. How Price Transparency Could Affect US Healthcare Markets. McKinsey & Company Healthcare. April 2, 2024. https://www.mckinsey.com/industries/healthcare/our-insights/how-price-transparency-could-affect-us-healthcare-markets.
25. Supra. Pricing: Industries, Case Studies, Campanie. Supra. https://supra.tools/healthcare-pricing-strategies.

CHAPTER 4

Financial Principles and Procedures

Mountasser Kadrie, PhD, MHA, FACHE, FACMPE, FHIMSS

HALM CORE CONTENT:

- 1.1 Accounting principles, financial controls, P&L, and financial statements
- 1.3 Capital budgeting and asset management (e.g., funding sources, long-term implications of capital planning, such as depreciation)
- 1.5 Financial decisions' impact on operations, health care, human resources, and quality of care
- 1.13 Operating budget principles (e.g., fixed vs. flexible, zero-based, variance analysis, contribution margin)
- 1.14 Prioritization of capital resources and associated conflict resolution

CASE SCENARIO:

As the new CFO of a large multispecialty group practice, you are tasked with developing a new comprehensive financial plan. Similar to past years, the proposed financial expenditures far exceed the projected revenues, and it is up to you to balance all of the requests with the overall priorities and objectives of the organization.

Effective management of financial affairs is an essential management and leadership task that helps healthcare leaders assess and support their organizations' financial survival and sustainability. These leaders develop, deploy, and implement financial plans to keep sight of their entities' mission, vision, and competitive position. They determine, achieve, and assess goals and objectives, addressing various promising opportunities and demanding challenges.

A HEALTHCARE ORGANIZATION should manage its financial affairs effectively and efficiently to ensure long-term viability. Healthcare leaders must focus on generating accurate financial information, managing the revenue cycle, understanding complex methods of reimbursement from payers, analyzing the approaches to recording expense information and controlling costs, integrating financial reporting systems for efficient decision-making and management oversight, developing realistic budgets, and leveraging strategic planning to ensure a long-term competitive advantage position.

Accounting Principles, Financial Controls, and Financial Statements

The International Financial Reporting Standards, or IFRS, set the most commonly used accounting principles on a global scale.[1] Like other industries in the United States, the healthcare industry follows the widely used Generally Accepted Accounting Principles (GAAP), developed by the Governmental Accounting Standards Board.[2] The six basic GAAP principles are consistency, regularity, sincerity, permanence of methods, non-compensation, and full disclosure. Other GAPP principles include accrual, historical cost, materiality, conservatism, periodicity, and prudence.

In the United States, all publicly traded companies are required to follow GAAP principles; private firms and nonprofits may elect to follow GAAP principles, or they may be required to follow those regulations at the request of investors, lenders, or other partners.

Firms that do not follow GAAP principles tend to report their financial information using other comprehensive basis of accounting (OCBOA) principles.

FINANCIAL CONTROLS

Financial controls are the processes and policies that help organizations monitor and manage their financial resources. These controls are a core part of an organization's operational efficiency and resource management, helping organizations prevent or detect accounting errors, keep accounting records accurate and reliable, deter fraudulent activity, promote accountability, ensure financial and accounting information integrity, and achieve operations, reporting, and compliance objectives.

Critical components of financial controls include:

- Monitoring cash flow projections.
- Analyzing balance sheets and income statements.
- Reconciling accounts payable and receivable records.
- Ensuring compliance with regulatory requirements.
- Regularly conducting risk-based analysis to obtain information on the company's current status.

- Reporting and substantiating balance sheets, budgets, cash flow statements, asset statements, and financial projections before release.

A strong handle on the environment is critical for the success of an internal control system. This involves establishing clear policies and procedures and emphasizing ethical and legal behavior and integrity.

FINANCIAL STATEMENTS

There are four essential types of financial statements: income statement, balance sheet, statement of cash flows, and statement of owner's equity. The primary financial statements used in a healthcare organization are the balance sheet, income statement, and statement of cash flows.[3]

The income statement (profit and loss), the most important financial statement, lists revenue, expenses, operating and total margins, and cash flow profit margin. Income statements are created several times during the year and show financial trends and comparisons over time.

The balance sheet offers a financial assessment of the organization at a given time. It comprises three components: assets, liabilities, and net position. Balance sheets are typically prepared monthly or quarterly to ensure the Assets = Liabilities + Equity equation is always balanced.

The statement of cash flow provides a detailed description of an organization's cash flow during a specific time. It shows how much cash flows into and out of the organization, giving the manager an understanding of performance and signaling the need to adjust strategies if needed.

Income statements can be examined using vertical and horizontal analysis. One method is not better than the other; both are necessary to provide insight into an organization.[4] Horizontal analysis of financial statements evaluates the statements over different periods and vertical analysis analyzes how the numbers in a single period affect each other.[5] Both analyses are important for a financial manager to understand because they can tell different things about an organization's performance and make different decisions.

Horizontal and vertical analyses both play a significant role in long-term financial viability by identifying patterns and relationships in financial data, which is essential for making evidence-based decisions about future investments, cost management, and strategic adjustments and alignments.[6] They also enable healthcare organizations to benchmark their performance against industry standards or historical data, which is crucial for evaluating competitive position, organizational performance, and operational effectiveness.

By understanding financial trends and structures, healthcare leaders can make more informed decisions regarding strategic initiatives, operational improvements, and financial management, thus supporting sustained financial stability and growth.

Capital Budgeting and Asset Management

Strategic planning and capital budgeting are critical to an organization's strategic vision because they allocate resources toward initiatives that shape the organization's future. They help healthcare organizations respond to changes and dynamics in the external environment, such as evolving patient needs, technological advancements, or regulatory shifts.

By funding capital projects, organizations can expand their services, improve infrastructure, and enhance technology, all of which contribute to long-term growth and competitiveness. A well-planned capital budget ensures that investments are made in areas that align with the organization's strategic goals, such as improving patient care, expanding market reach, or adopting new technologies.[7]

Moreover, capital budgets provide a framework for prioritizing projects based on their ability to deliver value. This framework ensures that resources are used effectively and that the organization can achieve and sustain its objectives financially.

Healthcare managers must thoroughly understand the complexities of capital investment opportunities.[3] Otherwise, they may take a risk that might hurt the organization's long-term viability.

Balancing fiscal needs with available funds includes:

- Establishing a capital allocation management plan to identify key activities that need funding.
- Developing an evidence-based decision framework to determine the capital project's needs.
- Establishing criteria to identify what project will be approved.
- Developing a multi-year plan for future investment.
- Deploying a performance monitoring system.

Understanding and assessing the problematic decision-making factors when evaluating capital project proposals and setting realistic budgets and strategic implications involves identifying financial constraints and balancing financial, operational, and strategic considerations, all while ensuring that the organization's long-term goals support the project. Managers must assess the project's financial viability through cost-benefit analysis, return on investment, and availability of funds. Regulatory and compliance matters add another layer of complexity, as healthcare is a highly regulated industry.

Capital budgets are integral to an organization's strategic vision for several reasons. They facilitate investments in projects that support long-term strategic objectives, such as expanding service offerings, enhancing patient care, and improving operational efficiency.[7] Aligning capital expenditures with strategic priorities ensures that investments contribute to the organization's mission and vision. Investments in infrastructure and technology are crucial as they help maintain high standards of care and operational excellence.[8]

The complexity of factors influencing the decision-making process and the subsequent approval or denial of these proposals are fundamental to effective management and strategic planning. Managers must carefully evaluate the financial implications of capital projects, including the initial costs, potential long-term benefits, and overall return on investment. This financial scrutiny involves a detailed capital budget and analysis of projected revenues, cost savings, and efficiencies the project is expected to bring. Additionally, identifying and securing appropriate funding sources is important; these sources can include internal reserves, loans, grants, or bonds, each with financial implications and requirements.

Every proposed investment must be assessed for its immediate financial viability and how well it fits the organization's long-term strategic plan.[9] Consequently, it's important to understand market trends and patient needs. For example, investing in digital health technology might be strategically advantageous if there is a growing demand for telehealth services and to keep pace with technological advancements and evolving patient expectations.

Additionally, capital budgeting helps manage long-term financial commitments by ensuring that significant expenditures are planned and financed to align with the organization's financial health and sustainability.[7] Strategic capital investments can enhance operational efficiency by using depreciation planning for equipment and facility modernization or process improvements, leading to cost savings, better resource utilization, and improved patient outcomes.[8] These long-term investments also offer a competitive advantage by enhancing the organization's capabilities and service offerings, attracting more patients, and strengthening its market position.

Healthcare leaders can use capital budgets as evidence-based tools for performance measurements, resource allocation, flexibility, and accountability. Performance measurements provide structured performance analysis and return on investment (ROI). Resources are put in place to arrange and allocate the organization's final resources and the most demanding projects.

Finally, flexibility allows an organization to adjust a budget according to the wavering market conditions. The organization's priorities will change, with the market conditions being as ever-changing as they are. By combining these attributes, capital budgets can guide organizations to make informed decisions and expedite efficiency, growth, and competitive leverage.

Financial Decisions' Impact On Operations, Healthcare, Human Resources, and Quality of Care

Financial management is essential for planning, decision-making, allocating resources, and achieving goals. In healthcare, data can be demonstrated in financial statements such as a balance sheet, income statement, and cash flow statement. Understanding and leveraging this data is beneficial for an administrator to make solid financial, operational, and strategic decisions.

Healthcare executives (clinicians and business leaders) are responsible for ensuring strong financial performance. They do this through managing the workforce, using intelligent spending practices, influencing third-party payer contracts, managing capital and contracts, addressing and improving the quality of patient care, and controlling operational risks.[10]

These executives also play a key role in creating viable financial policies and realistic and meaningful budgeting targets. These decisions can improve the profit margin and the quality of care for the patient and targeted population.

Even in nonprofit organizations, a healthy profit margin is essential to provide salary and compensation increases, purchase new equipment, remodel facilities, and start new service lines that the community needs. While healthcare focuses on providing exemplary patient care, care can occur only by ensuring viable and sustainable finances. Healthcare executives should prioritize financial health outcomes so the healthcare team can focus on the patient's health.

While financial stability is necessary for a healthcare organization to grow, financial excellence can also lead to a competitive market advantage. Increased financial performance provides funds to reinvest in the organization or offer new services. Studies show a positive correlation between financial performance and the quality of the care supplied.[11] This may be due to the ability to pay competitive wages and attract a higher caliber quality of staff. To be competitive, healthcare organizations must employ high-quality staff, provide various services, provide the latest technology and equipment, and be innovative in care delivery. That requires significant financial funds earned through patient care revenue, investments, or private or public funding. Smart financial management is the foundation.

In addition to making active decisions to increase revenue and distribute spending, financial data can allow an administrator to plan and forecast for the future; once they understand where current expenses and incomes are occurring, they can make small changes that can significantly improve future income.[12]

To make informed and due diligence decisions, healthcare leaders use forecasting and valuation methods. These methods are crucial in helping healthcare leaders and professionals achieve sustainable and viable financial outcomes for their organizations. By utilizing forecasting techniques, healthcare administrators can predict future financial conditions based on historical data, trends, and various external factors, such as regulation changes.

This forward-looking approach enables healthcare leaders to anticipate potential financial challenges and opportunities, allowing for proactive adjustments to budgets and resource allocations. On the other hand, valuation methods assist in assessing the worth of healthcare assets, including facilities, equipment, and services.[13] Accurate valuation helps leaders make informed decisions regarding investments, mergers, acquisitions, and other strategic initiatives.

Together, these methods provide a comprehensive understanding of current financial health and prospects, enabling healthcare leaders to create, integrate, and optimize data-driven decisions that enhance operational efficiency, optimize resource utilization, and ensure long-term financial strategic stability. By integrating robust forecasting and valuation practices into their financial strategies, healthcare professionals can better navigate the industry's complexities, ultimately contributing to their organization's overall success and sustainability.

Operating Budget Principles

Budgeting is essential to an organization's strategic, financial, and operational success because the budget drives most of the operational decision-making for the budget period. Budgeting ensures the revenues are higher than costs for some time and can help managers control a company's operations when done right.

Budgeting is one of the leading performance indicators for almost all organizations and will be the main benchmark for the following year, so it is important to get it right. Budgeting allocates resources to produce the best output according to the revenue levels involved.[7] A budget is an evidence-based estimate of revenue and expenses over a given timeframe. When developed properly, a budget can help managers oversee the organization by providing objective data to report if revenue is higher or lower than anticipated and expenses are higher or lower than anticipated. It provides objective data on a timely basis so that identified budget variances can be modified and the organization can remain financially successful.

Employees and managers must have the opportunity to participate in the budget development process, as their participation allows employees to be heard and educated on the process, which can ensure that all levels understand the consequences of the budget. Healthcare leaders can prioritize plans that foster growth and sustainability by supporting the budget with the organization's strategic plan.

Financial budgeting also promotes stability by helping organizations manage cash flow, control costs, and prepare for unexpected expenses, which reduces the risk of financial crises. The organization's budget should consider the strategic plan, planned capital expenditures, and expected revenue and expenses while considering any anticipated market changes for the budget period.[9] If the budget is unrealistic or not in line with the organization's strategic plan, leaders continually will have to explain the variance in actual performance from the budget. For instance, it is hard for healthcare leaders to make their case for additional staff or capital and operational spending areas if they are not meeting some of their budget targets, whether reasonable or not.

Healthcare leaders can choose from a variety of budget types, including a fixed budget versus flexible, zero-based budget (ZBB). The choice is related to the organization's budgeting and financial issues.

In fixed budgeting, healthcare leaders have a specific amount of funds to allocate to cover all activities and expenses; in flexible budgeting, leaders move the funding among areas, depending on how productive that area is.

ZBB is one of the most commonly used budgeting methods in the healthcare space. Leaders have a fixed amount, but it is based on a forward-looking projection of how much costs and expenses will be. All identified expenses must be justified for each new period. This budgeting model is very tight and aims to avoid all expenditures that are not considered essential to the organization's successful (profitable) operation. This kind of bottom-up budgeting can be an effective way to "shake things up," especially in tight profit margins, as is the case for most healthcare organizations.

Many healthcare organizations with extensive integrated health systems use financial variance analysis to optimize financial and operational performance outcomes. Variance analysis is a technique that compares actual performance to a planned outcome to identify and understand differences. Financial variance analysis (FVA) in healthcare refers to the process of comparing a healthcare organization's actual financial performance (like costs and revenue) against its pre-established budget or projected figures, allowing them to identify areas where spending deviates from expectations and take corrective actions to improve financial efficiency and control costs.

In healthcare, FVA can be used to:

- *Improve efficiency*: Identify areas for improvement and set priorities.
- *Control costs*: Compare actual results to a standard of performance to identify and investigate differences.
- *Enhance quality of care:* Provide insights into the quality, effectiveness, and efficiency of care delivery.
- *Manage risk*: Identify the sources of deviations from standards and suggest corrective actions.
- *Explain costs*: Explain costs and charges to interested groups.

Variance analysis can be applied in many areas of healthcare, including:

- *Personnel costs:* Compare costs across similar sites to identify opportunities to reduce costs.
- *Budgeting:* Compare budgeted amounts to actual amounts spent to identify fiscal variances.
- *Clinical Outcomes:* Compare actual performance to planned outcomes to identify sources of deviations.
- *Patient Satisfaction:* Compare actual performance to planned outcomes to identify sources of deviations.

Contribution margin is another financial concept that healthcare leaders must focus on to ensure long-term organizational financial viability. The contribution margin is a crucial organizational performance measure because it provides a clear picture of how much revenue from a specific service or procedure is available to cover fixed costs, allowing healthcare providers to identify which services are most profitable, make informed decisions about resource allocation, and ultimately ensure financial stability by maximizing the revenue that contributes to covering overhead expenses like facility costs and staff salaries.

Prioritization of Capital Resources and Associated Conflict Resolution

Many healthcare organizations (HCOs) face financial challenges due to increasing government regulation, new payment models, and increased financial obligations from merging HCOs into large health conglomerates. Working capital is the money organizations use to run day-to-day operations. HCOs are placing greater emphasis on their working capital and cash management. Efficient working capital management allows HCOs to reduce their holdings of current assets, such as medical supplies and accounts receivable, which earn no interest income and require financing with short-term debt.[14]

In addition to paying off short-term obligations, working capital can be used for additional investment into new technology and partnerships, which ultimately increase revenue while improving the efficiency of clinical operations and overall patient care. Efficient working capital management can be achieved by implementing just-in-time inventory practices, streamlining supply chain processes, improving billing and collection processes, negotiating favorable payment terms with suppliers and insurance companies, and utilizing cash forecasting techniques.[14]

Overall, a medical facility must have the money it needs to provide services to patients while the facility waits to get paid for the services they have provided. This highlights the importance of assessing working capital, including cash balance and accounts receivable. Working capital is the difference between current assets and liabilities. One of the ways to improve an HCO's working capital is to focus on the revenue cycle, optimize payment, minimize the collection period, and maximize the payment period.[15]

To be efficient, healthcare organizations need to implement strategies to optimize payments and minimize the collection period on accounts receivable. The first strategy is clinical documentation integrity (CDI). CDI focuses on accurate physician documentation, and it is a process that frustrates and annoys many physicians, mainly because they often need help understanding its importance. The ultimate financial goal is ensuring prompt, adequate payment for services, but the services must be appropriately documented to be accurately billed.[16] The claim will be paid if a patient's chart is coded and the bill is submitted accurately and in line with the services provided.

Suppose a claim is denied, threatening payment. In that case, a hospital starts down the path to denials management, which is time-consuming and expensive. Denial claims have increased substantially over the last few years.[17] This money may never make it to the hospital as accounts receivable if the denials management process is not optimized.

Chapter Summary

Healthcare organizations with strong financial positions have been shown to offer quality healthcare services and have a greater chance of long-term viability. Agile financial management in healthcare organizations helps organizations align financial accountability with the organization's overall strategic goals and support strong competitive positions and healthy financial outcomes.

REFERENCES

1. Palmer B. What Are the International Financial Reporting Standards (IFRS)? Investopedia. June 10, 2024. Accessed December 15, 2024. https://www.investopedia.com/terms/i/ifrs.asp
2. Fernando J. Generally Accepted Accounting Principles (GAAP): Definition and Rules. Investopedia. June 27, 2024. Accessed December 15, 2024. https://www.investopedia.com/terms/g/gaap.asp
3. Pink GH, Song PH. *Gapenski's Understanding Healthcare Financial Management, 8th ed.* Health Administration Press; 2019.
4. Stobierski T. How to Read and Understand a Cash Flow Statement. Harvard Business School blog. April 30, 2020. Accessed December 15, 2024. https://online.hbs.edu/blog/post/how-to-read-a-cash-flow-statement
5. Tuovila A. Horizontal Analysis: What It Is vs. Vertical Analysis. Investopedia. March 3, 2024. Accessed December 15, 2024. https://www.investopedia.com/terms/h/horizontalanalysis.asp
6. Kelkar G. Vertical and Horizontal Analysis tor Finances: How To Choose Between the Two? Emeritus blog. February 26, 2024. Accessed December 15, 2024. https://emeritus.org/blog/finance-vertical-and-horizontal-analysis/
7. Homauni A, Markazi-Moghaddam N, Mosadeghkhah A, et al. Budgeting in Healthcare Systems and Organizations: A Systematic Review. *Iranian J Public Health*. 2023;52(9):1889–1901. https://doi.org/10.18502/ijph.v52i9.13571
8. Huebner C, Flessa S. Strategic Management in Healthcare: A Call for Long-Term and Systems-Thinking in an Uncertain System. *Int J Environ Res Public Health*. 2022;19(14):8617. doi: 10.3390/ijerph19148617
9. Zhang R, Bohlen J. Healthcare Business Budgeting. In: *StatPearls [Internet].* Treasure Island, FL: StatPearls Publishing; January 7, 2023. https://www.ncbi.nlm.nih.gov/books/NBK589707/
10. Eisenstein L. Objectives of Financial Management in Healthcare. BoardEffect.com blog. July 8, 2020. Accessed December 15, 2024. https://www.boardeffect.com/blog/objectives-financial-management-healthcare/
11. Bhati D, Deogade MS, Kanyal D. Improving Patient Outcomes Through Effective Hospital Administration: A Comprehensive Review. *Cureus.* 2023:15(10):e47731. https://doi.org/10.7759/

cureus.47731

12. Park YJ, Shon J, Lu J. Predicting Organizational Mortality: How Financial Management Matters. *Administration & Society*. 2021;54(5):828–856. https://doi.org/10.1177/00953997211045068
13. Hutto, J. How Much Is Your Medical Practice Worth? A Comprehensive Guide to Valuation Methods. JamesMoore. November 13, 2024. Accessed December 15, 2024. https://www.jmco.com/articles/healthcare/medical-practice-valuation-methods/
14. Rauscher S, Wheeler J. The Importance of Working Capital Management for Hospital Profitability: Evidence from Bond-Issuing, Not-for-Profit U.S. Hospitals. *Healthcare Manage Rev.* 2012;*37*(4):339–346. https://doi.org/10.1097/hmr.0b013e3182224189
15. Cleverley WO, Cleverley JO, Parks AV. *Essentials of Health Care Finance: 9th ed.* Jones & Bartlett Learning, LLC; 2024.
16. Limjoco CM. Clinical Documentation Integrity: Fostering Collaboration and Embracing a Long-Term Vision. *J AHIMA*. March 21, 2024. Accessed December 15, 2024. https://journal.ahima.org/page/clinical-documentation-integrity-fostering-collaboration-and-embracing-a-long-term-vision
17. Healthcare Financial Management Association. Navigating Payer Practices to Reduce Denials and Enhance Outcomes. *HFMA*. March 3, 2023. Accessed December 15, 2024. https://www.hfma.org/revenue-cycle/navigating-payer-practices-reduce-denials/

SECTION 2

Care Innovation, Health Equity, and Population Health

CHAPTER 5

Care Innovation

Bryan N. Becker, MD, MMM, FACP, CPE

HALM CORE CONTENT:

- 2.3 Healthcare trends and barriers across the continuum of care (e.g., extended care, acute hospital care, ambulatory care, home care)
- 2.4 Non-traditional settings and methods to improve access
  - 2.4.1 Hospital at Home
- 2.5 Patient-centered care
- 2.8 Telehealth impact and other emerging technologies
- 2.9 Value-based care models
  - 2.9.1 ACOs
  - 2.9.2 Bundled payment models
  - 2.9.3 Clinically integrated networks
  - 2.9.4 Co-management agreements
  - 2.9.5 MIPS/MACRA
  - 2.9.6 The transition from volume to value-based care implementation

CASE SCENARIO:

A 72-year-old man with a history of obesity, chronic kidney disease stage 3b, heart failure, osteoarthritis with significant degenerative changes in both of his knees, hypertension, and hyperlipidemia wants to change his primary care physicians. He chooses a primary care physician who is part of an accountable care organization. His new physician assesses his medical conditions and starts a regimen for treatment of his knee pain with different medications, physical therapy, and a weight-loss program.

After six months, the patient's knee pain persists, and the physician refers the patient for an orthopedic evaluation. The decision is made to have a knee replacement. The patient undergoes total knee arthroplasty and is sent home from the hospital after two days with his regular medications as well as home physical therapy, home health to monitor his cardiac status, a course of anticoagulation administered regularly by the patient and his caregiver, and a device to monitor his vital signs and post-operative recovery including increasing ambulation and flexibility exercises in his home.

WITH MOUNTING PRESSURES FROM RISING COSTS, uneven health outcomes, and increasing consumer demands for higher-quality care, the traditional fee-for-service (FFS) model in the United States is challenged. In response, the U.S. healthcare ecosystem has been shifting in fits and starts with care innovation across care environments. Payment innovation has accompanied operational innovation, with value-based care (VBC), better aligning reimbursement with high-quality, cost-effective care.

Access and the Contemporary U.S. Healthcare Landscape

Although many individuals in the United States have health insurance, there are still barriers to access; the complexity in using healthcare coverage is one obstacle.[1] Long wait times for appointments, difficulty finding in-network physicians, and transportation all may lead to care delays.[2]

While hospitals retain a prominent position in U.S. healthcare, only 8% of the U.S. population had an overnight hospital stay in 2018.[3] This is counterbalanced by a vast amount of outpatient activity with more than 1 billion office visits annually in the United States.[4] Notably, there are also shifts in post-acute and long-term care. More than 68,000 post-acute and long-term care providers cared for 7.3 million individuals, according to the 2020 National Post-acute and Long-term Care Study.[5] Care innovation is necessary in each of these domains to improve outcomes, quality, and effectiveness.

Hospital at Home

The concept of hospital at home (HaH) allows patients to receive hospital-level care in their homes. This includes daily physician or nurse visits, monitoring of vital signs, laboratory testing, intravenous (IV) fluid and medication administration, and hospital transfer if needed. This care is supported by advanced medical technologies and multidisciplinary teams. The model has gained interest due to its ability to improve outcomes and patient satisfaction while reducing healthcare costs.

HaH's origins can be traced to early 20th-century healthcare delivery when house calls and care in the home were standards of practice. Even with the expansion of hospitals after the Hill-Burton Act, at-home care continued for less intensive needs.

Burton and Leff tested a HaH model in the 1990s.[6] They demonstrated that acute care at home for older adults resulted in better patient outcomes and lower costs compared to traditional hospitalization. The COVID-19 pandemic created a watershed moment for HaH care. Hospitals with overwhelming capacity constraints adopted HaH to manage non-COVID and low-acuity COVID-19 cases. CMS also launched the Acute Hospital Care at Home program in 2020, allowing hospitals to bill Medicare for HaH services. This, combined with greater trust in home-based care, has driven more acceptance of HaH.

HaH COMPONENTS

HaH programs comprehensively screen patients with clear inclusion and exclusion criteria that include clinical stability, home safety, and caregiver availability.[7] Patients who may benefit from HaH include those with pneumonia, chronic obstructive pulmonary disease (COPD) exacerbations, heart failure, cellulitis, or infections that require IV antibiotics.

A standard HaH care team includes physicians who oversee patient care via telehealth and in-home visits, advanced practice professionals (APPs) such as nurse practitioners or physician assistants, and nurses who provide in-person care, administer medications, monitor clinical conditions, and identify necessary social support services. HaH teams also may include pharmacists, physical therapists, occupational therapists, social workers, or dietitians.

Improvements in technology have fortified HaH, with remote patient monitoring (RPM) and telehealth making it easier to monitor patients, perform HaH virtual consultation, and communicate with patients and caregivers. In addition to intensive care coordination and individualized care plans, HaH requires that teams bring testing equipment into the home for laboratory and imaging studies. HaH models also facilitate home delivery of medications, durable medical equipment, and supplies.

HaH programs have protocols to escalate care and transfer the patient to a hospital if needed. They partner with social services to support patient needs such as transportation, food security, or home safety. HaH programs also educate patients and caregivers about clinical conditions, treatment, and emergency protocols.

The CMS Acute Hospital Care at Home program has a list of requirements for HaH programs, including compliance with the Condition of Participation standards for hospitals, daily assessment by the physician in-person or via telehealth, twice-daily evaluation by a registered nurse or paramedic, immediate connectivity to a nurse if needed, a 30-minute response time for a decompensating patient, and data submission to CMS. Regulations also may vary by state in APP scope of practice, coverage for certain services, and whether home health licensing is necessary.

HaH TODAY AND TOMORROW

The benefits of HaH make a compelling case for its expansion. HaH has reduced the cost of care by 38% with fewer laboratory and imaging tests and consultations compared to inpatient hospitalization according to one study.[8] HaH patients also had increased levels of activity and decreased readmissions.

Based on early experience with the Acute Hospital at Home waiver, complex patients receiving HaH had 0.5% mortality during HaH and lower mortality compared to similar patients who were hospitalized with a lower readmission rate as well.[9,10] Such data continue to support expansion of HaH and evolution in the capabilities of the teams that deliver it.

Patient-Centered Care

Demographic shifts in the U.S. population are reflected in greater diversity in opinions, languages, and culture in the population. As such, clinicians must individualize their care more than ever to make it equitable and patient-centered. Patient- or person-centered care (PCC) integrates the values, beliefs, and preferences of the patient in shared decision-making as an acknowledgment of patient autonomy.[11] This leads to a plan of care that is appropriate and acceptable for the patient. PCC enhances patient satisfaction and is associated with decreasing admissions, readmissions, and length of stay in various studies.

One often-seen tension is the pull between evidence-based practice and PCC. One multicenter analysis noted that organizations with strong improvement-oriented cultures, accountability, and regular, meaningful staff engagement were more likely to provide evidence-based clinical care and effectively incorporate patient and family preferences in developing and implementing the plan of care, reducing that tension.[12]

IMPLEMENTING PCC

PCC requires a commitment to transformation. While there is no definitive PCC playbook, insights from a qualitative study suggest seven domains are critical for PCC in any organization: leadership, patient and family engagement, staff engagement, a focus on innovation, alignment of staff roles and priorities, synchronization of organizational structure and process, and a caring environment.[13]

As value-based care has matured, PCC is now recognized as an important, although not yet dominant, quality measure. The alignment of PCC and VBC is complicated by the paucity of applicable patient experience and preference measures, and cost calculations that are payer- instead of patient-focused.

Strategies have been proposed to align PCC and VBC, including using patient-reported outcome measures (PROMs) in clinical trials, general practice, and in value calculations, and purposeful integration of patient preference in clinical decisions and guidelines. As care innovation advances, organizations will likely need to incorporate PCC and PROMs more extensively to inform feedback related to clinical care and operational decisions.

Telehealth and Emerging Technologies

Although telehealth emerged from the COVID-19 pandemic, its history is actually decades old. NASA and the Nebraska Psychology Institute piloted closed-circuit television for remote monitoring and consultation in the 1960s.[14] Programs such as Project ECHO in New Mexico developed simultaneous specialty care and educational uses for telehealth platforms.[15]

Today, telehealth is an essential element of care delivery. Digital cameras and wearables assist telehealth with real-time imaging and biometric measurement. Telehealth can also support remote robotic surgery, intensive care unit capabilities, behavioral healthcare, and diagnostics in teleradiology and telepathology.

Post-COVID-19, telehealth continues to be a means of healthcare access, although its use has declined for some; 48% of all Medicare beneficiaries were telehealth users in 2020, and 24% were telehealth users in 2023 based on Part B claims.[16] It is interesting to note demographic differences in telehealth adoption among patients. Telehealth use has been lower among individuals who lack insurance coverage, among young adults, and among residents in the Midwest compared to other parts of the United States.[17] CMS recognized the importance of telehealth by adding a number of Current Procedural Terminology (CPT) and Healthcare Common Procedure Coding System (HCPCS) codes for telehealth services that have been updated annually.

Remote patient monitoring has been adopted as a component of telehealth in various clinical settings, be it inpatient, outpatient, or at home. RPM interventions based on measured data have been integrated into COPD and heart failure management, post-operative care for patients' status-post arthroplasty, neonatal care, home and remote cancer care, diabetes management, home dialysis, and most recently, COVID-19.

Combining RPM with patient education has a positive effect on patient outcomes. CMS and commercial payers have acknowledged the increasing relevance of RPM with reimbursement for a set of RPM CPT codes. The 10-fold increase in RPM use for Medicare beneficiaries since COVID-19[18] suggests there is expanding interest in using RPM to enhance patient care.

Accountable Care Organizations

The term "Accountable Care Organization" was introduced by Elliott Fisher and colleagues at Dartmouth in 2006. They envisioned ACOs as groups of providers, including

TABLE 1. Select Advanced APMs from CMS that Function as ACOs[20]

Model Name	Track	Effective Start	Effective End
States Advancing All-Payer Health Equity Approaches and Development (AHEAD) Model	Hospital Global Budget and Primary Care Tracks	07/01/2024	12/31/2034
Enhancing Oncology Model Risk Arrangement 2		07/01/2023	06/30/2028
Kidney Care Choices	Option Level 2 and Professional	01/01/2022	12/31/2026
Making Care Primary	Track 2 and Track 3	07/01/2024	12/31/2034
ACO Realizing Equity Access and Community Health (REACH)		04/01/2021	12/31/2026

hospitals, physicians, and other caregivers, who would take collective responsibility for a defined population's care with shared clinical and financial accountability and quality measurement. Section 3022 of the Patient Protection and Affordable Care Act (ACA) of 2010 created the Medicare Shared Savings Program (MSSP). This program encouraged healthcare organizations and physicians to form ACOs to manage and be accountable for the care of Medicare beneficiaries.

ACOs have continued to evolve since their inception, with payers adopting ACO principles in VBC contracts and CMS bringing new models forward, such as the Pioneer ACO Model, which tested more advanced ACOs, and the Next Generation ACO Model that allowed for greater financial risk and reward. ACOs now include physician-led, hospital-based, and integrated delivery system ACOs. In 2022, more than 11 million Americans were receiving healthcare through 1,000-plus ACOs in the United States.

ACOs have met with headwinds even as they have grown in number.[19] Some organizations have struggled to meet savings targets or manage downside risk in advanced models. Hospital ACOs can experience misalignment with incentives. Coordinating care across diverse providers can be logistically challenging. Critics also argue that ACOs may not sufficiently address social determinants of health. CMS has recognized many of these factors in new ACO models.

CMS continues to adjust the ACO model as one of several advanced alternative payment models (APMs) (see Table 1). There are newer specialty-care ACO constructs, such as the Enhancing Oncology Model and Kidney Care Choices models, and, recognizing potential shortcomings of primary care-focused ACOs, CMS created the States Advancing All-Payer Health Equity Approaches and Development Model (AHEAD Model) and the ACO Primary Care Flex Model.

The AHEAD model collaborates with states to decrease healthcare costs, improve population health, and advance health equity. The ACO Primary Care Flex Model is designed to increase program participation for low-revenue ACOs and rural providers. It features a prospective payment option and a one-time payment to cover administrative costs.

TABLE 2. Design Elements for Bundled Payment[25]

Design Element	Examples
Covered Services	Surgical Care: Pre-op, Surgery, Inpatient Post-op, Follow-up Oncology Care: Assessment, Diagnosis, Staging (imaging, biopsy, pathology), Treatment (surgery, chemotherapy, radiation), Follow-up Chronic Care, such as diabetes care in primary care, annual or more frequent diabetic check-ups such as nutrition, eye exams, foot exams, education, other screening tests, such as CKD
Payment Methodology	Prospective, Retrospective, or Combination
Accountable Entity	Provider-led entity — hospital or physician practice
Episode of Care Definition	Defined length of time, such as one year, totality of services encompassed
Risk Sharing	Shared savings between insuring entity and providers, or providers bear 100% of risk, or progressive increase in provider risk over time
Risk Adjustment	Severity-adjusted budget per episode; risk stratification by comorbidities and diagnosis
Distribution of Payments Among Participating Providers	Incentive payments indexed by resources managed, patient experience, and clinical performance
Payment and Quality Outcomes	Must meet quality standards to participate in shared savings

ACOs have delivered more than $21 billion in total savings since they started, including $4.3 billion in Medicare savings in 2022 with 69% of ACOs achieving shared savings in the last performance year.[21] Research indicates that ACOs have resulted in modest improvements in quality, although they have leveraged care plans, home visits, clinician-specific data, and care coordination for medically complex patients far more frequently than non-ACO organizations.[22]

Bundled Payments

Another form of APM is bundled payment. These payment models incentivize providers to deliver coordinated, high-quality care by offering a fixed payment for an entire episode of care, covering all services provided during that period (see Table 2). Bundled payments gained attention initially in the 1980s and 1990s. The Medicare Participating Heart Bypass Demonstration (1984–1989) provided bundled payments for coronary artery bypass graft (CABG) surgeries, covering hospital and physician services. It demonstrated cost savings and maintained quality.

Bundled payment models expanded at the start of the century with large employers, such as Walmart and Lowe's, and employer coalitions partnering with health systems to negotiate bundled payment contracts for high-cost procedures, such as joint replacements and certain cardiac procedures. The ACA formalized bundled payments as part of payment reform, and CMS launched the three-year Acute Care Episode (ACE) Demonstration. This demonstration covered all Part A and B services for 28 cardiac and nine orthopedic inpatient surgical procedures and services.[23]

This heralded a series of additional initiatives that included the Bundled Payments for Care Improvement (BPCI) from CMS. This encompassed four payment models covering 48 clinical episodes.[24] The Comprehensive Care for Joint Replacement was released as a mandatory model in 2016, along with BPCI Advanced as a voluntary model. Certain design elements are integral for bundled payments.

It is essential to define an episode of care, which includes all related care services, such as diagnostics, treatments, hospital stays, rehabilitation, and follow-ups, within a specified time frame, usually 30 or 90 days. Episodes can be related to procedural (e.g., joint replacements, cardiac surgery), acute (e.g., pneumonia, myocardial infarction), or chronic conditions (e.g., diabetes management).

Payment is a single negotiated amount paid to cover all services within the episode. The models that determine payment can be prospective — payment is made up front and distributed among the providers involved in the bundle — or retrospective — providers are reimbursed fee for service initially and total costs are reconciled against the bundled payment after the episode. Providers may share in savings if costs are less than the bundle price or absorb losses if costs exceed them.

To be effective, bundles require significant collaboration across the episode care continuum (e.g., hospitals, physicians, post-acute care facilities). Care pathways or standardized protocols for the episode ensure consistent, evidence-based care. A review of 20 studies confirmed that bundled payment maintains or improves quality of care while lowering costs for total joint replacement.[26] However, for other conditions or procedures, data showing improvements was less consistent.

CMS has added a new model to better assess the effectiveness of bundled payment: the Transforming Episode Accountability Model (TEAM). TEAM bundles payments for lower-extremity joint replacement, hip and femur fractures, CABG, spinal fusion, and certain abdominal surgical procedures.[27] TEAM as a mandatory model is also designed to address health equity and incorporate regional pricing. Hopefully, TEAM will yield data that can establish the true effectiveness of this care innovation.

Clinically Integrated Networks

Clinically integrated networks (CINs) grew out of a trend of vertical integration in healthcare in the early part of the 21st century. The Federal Trade Commission (FTC) defines a clinically integrated structure as a joint contracting program that includes:

- Independent contracting, especially if payers and the network cannot agree on terms.
- Price setting only for services that are part of the clinically integrated program.
- Sharing of substantial financial risk in the arrangement by all physician participants.

- No unnecessary exchange of pricing information.
- No assistance in the refusal of or restriction of physicians in contracting with payers.[28]

There are three main types of CINs: a joint venture physician-hospital organization, a subsidiary or subsidiaries of a health system, or independent practice associations (IPAs).[29] In general, CINs can withstand FTC scrutiny if they demonstrate:

- Active participation by physicians in developing and operating the CIN.
- Shared goals of quality, efficiency, decreased utilization, and lower costs.
- Processes for reviewing clinician performance and removing inefficient clinicians.
- Development and implementation of evidence-based clinical guidelines.
- Use of interoperable health information technology to ensure care integration.
- A nonexclusive network.
- Restricted access to provider pricing data.

Healthcare systems view CINs as a lever to increase their breadth of clinicians and services across multiple settings, thereby improving population health and negotiating leverage with payers.

Organizations that have successfully created large CINs have developed common clinical protocols, expanded quality measurement, and increased meaningful performance feedback to clinicians.[30] They also have realized efficiencies by co-locating practices and driving health information exchange across electronic health record (EHR) platforms.

Still, there is limited information regarding the actual performance of CINs. CINs do appear to have met or exceeded many of their goals of care related to reducing utilization, managing clinical conditions, and improving patient experience. The inherent challenge with such reporting is that comparisons are often against internal data or generalized CMS data. Nonetheless, CINs appear to have staying power as aggregators of physicians and clinical services.

Co-Management Agreements

The most traditional example of co-management is a hospital contracting with a physician group to co-manage a service line. Another example is an arrangement between providers to co-manage different aspects of patient care. A specialist may provide surgical care and then refer the patient back to their primary care provider for post-surgical monitoring.

When co-management aligns a hospital and physicians, those physicians can focus on improving quality and efficiency in that service line in exchange for compensation payable by the hospital. These arrangements can cover one hospital or an entire health system and can be applied to any service line such as orthopedic surgery, cardiology, or maternal care. By increasing efficiency, reducing waste, and increasing profitability, co-management agreements have "legitimate business and medical purposes."[31]

There are two types of co-management arrangements. The first is direct contract co-management in which the physicians are individually engaged or engaged as a group. The other model is the limited liability company (LLC) model. In the LLC model, the hospital contracts with a management company, the LLC, formed to co-manage the service line. This LLC can be wholly owned by the physicians or jointly by the physicians and the hospital.

In both constructs, fees are paid as hourly- and performance-based services. Hourly-based services are administrative, such as clinical workflow improvements, scheduling, oversight of other clinicians in the service line, credentialing, patient case management, materials management across the service line, program development, and medical staff committee service and leadership.

Performance-based services are clinical in nature and focus on achieving pre-determined quality outcomes for the designated service line. Performance-based compensation is variable in that, based on service line performance, physicians may receive any compensation amount from $0 up to a maximum incentive amount consistent with fair market value (FMV) by a third-party valuation firm.

There are important guardrails to consider when establishing or reviewing a co-management agreement.

- Does the arrangement satisfy a legitimate business need of the parties?
- Is the referring party the best or only party to deliver the services for the need?
- Are the services (and fees) tailored and limited so that there is no question about their purpose and intent?
- Would the arrangements be reasonable if no referrals were received?

Successful co-management agreements improve clinical outcomes, patient satisfaction, service line efficiency, and effectiveness. These agreements help physicians retain autonomy over their practice and provide an avenue for them to share in financial rewards of strategically aligned programs. Hospitals benefit from the focus on quality and cost and have a legal protection through such constructs in providing performance-based incentives. There is little published data evaluating co-management agreements, likely due to their distribution and application across different environments.

MIPS and MACRA

The merit-based incentive payment system (MIPS) and the Medicare Access and CHIP Reauthorization Act of 2015 (MACRA) are milestones in transforming Medicare payment models. Prior to MACRA, Medicare physician reimbursement was largely determined by the sustainable growth rate (SGR) formula. The SGR, however, required annual congressional interventions to avert reductions in payment.

MACRA repealed the SGR formula in 2015, with an intent to end the annual cycle of fiscal adjustments to physician payment. It also established a framework for transitioning from volume- to value-based reimbursement through the MIPS and alternate payment models (APMs). The legislation simplified existing quality programs, rolling them into MIPS, and provided incentives for participation in APMs, which involved more risk-sharing but offered greater potential rewards.

MIPS consolidated the physician quality reporting system (PQRS), value-based payment modifier (VBM), and CMS EHR Incentive Program, known as "Meaningful Use," into a single performance-based payment system with four categories:

1. Quality (45% of the MIPS score): Performance across quality measures, including patient outcomes, practice improvement, and guideline adherence.
2. Cost (15% of the MIPS score): Cost-efficiency of care, including total cost of care during the year or a specific episode of care.
3. Improvement Activities (15% of the MIPS score): Efforts to improve practice, such as care coordination, patient engagement, and health equity.
4. Promoting Interoperability (25% of the MIPS score): The use of certified EHR technology.

Providers with high MIPS scores earn positive payment adjustments funded by penalties for lower-scoring providers, creating a budget-neutral system.

APMs offer a separate pathway to accept financial risk and accountability for patient outcomes. Providers participating in qualifying APMs are exempt from MIPS and receive a higher Medicare conversion factor update, +0.75% versus +0.25%, beginning in 2026 while also being eligible for model-specific performance payments. APMs also include a separate lump sum incentive payment that expires at the end of the 2024 performance year and the requirement that participants meet a threshold percentage of payments or patients through qualifying APMs.

These thresholds scale up in the 2025 performance year, making it more difficult to be a qualifying provider. APMs include ACOs (see Table 1) as well as other payment structures, such as BPCI-Advanced, the Maryland Total Cost of Care (TCOC) Model—Care Redesign Program, and the concluding Vermont Medicare ACO Initiative.

CMS is not the only entity supporting and evaluating APMs. Several states and payers have APMs as well, including episode-based payment, Medicaid APMs, and second-generation patient-centered medical home tracks.

Data regarding the impact of these programs are mixed. For instance, MIPS scores do not necessarily correlate with performance, as seen in a study of more than 80,000 primary care physicians.[32] Physicians with low MIPS scores had worse performance on diabetic eye examinations, hemoglobin A1c screening, and mammography screening compared to physicians with high MIPS scores. However, physicians with low MIPS scores had better performance with regard to influenza vaccination and tobacco screening. Interestingly, physicians with low MIPS scores and better patient outcomes cared for more multimorbid and vulnerable patients.

The Ongoing Shift from Volume to Value

The transition from volume to VBC in U.S. healthcare requires a fundamental shift in how medical services are delivered and reimbursed. Changes in reimbursement have been essential with VBC to overcome FFS inertia. The ability of these care innovations and payment models to effect change is predicated upon:

- Improvements in data quality and delivery.
- Analytics and population health management tools that make it easier to identify, communicate with, and treat at-risk patient groups.
- Workflow changes combined with technology that makes it easier to engage in evidence-based practice.
- Physician leadership for the culture shift necessary for team-based PCC.

By prioritizing value, the U.S. healthcare system aims to achieve the "Triple Aim": better patient experience, improved population health, and reduced per capita costs. With the right tools and more financial alignment, it may even improve clinician engagement and access to resources for all patients, supporting the parameters that now define the Quadruple and Quintuple Aims as well.

Chapter Summary

Multiple areas of care innovation are occurring simultaneously with shifts in reimbursement in the United States. As healthcare organizations adjust to incorporate the innovations that will work best for their patients, they also continue to examine and create structures that can allow them to deliver care more broadly with greater alignment across services and physicians.

REFERENCES

1. Levitt L, Altman D. Complexity in the US Health Care System Is the Enemy of Access and Affordability. *JAMA Health Forum.* 2023;4(10):e234430. doi:10.1001/jamahealthforum.2023.4430
2. Telesford I, Winger A, Rae M. Beyond Cost, What Barriers to Health Care Do Consumers Face? Peterson-KFF Health System Tracker. August 22, 2024. Accessed November 20, 2024. https://www.healthsystemtracker.org/chart-collection/beyond-cost-what-barriers-to-health-care-do-consumers-face/#Percent%20of%20adults%20who%20delay%20or%20did%20not%20get%20health%20care,%20by%20type%20of%20care,%202022.
3. Centers for Disease Control and Prevention. National Ambulatory Medical Care Survey: 2019 Summary Tables. CDC National Center for Health Statistics. Accessed November 11, 2024. https://www.cdc.gov/nchs/data/ahcd/namcs_summary/2019-namcs-web-tables-508.pdf.
4. Centers for Disease Control and Prevention. Table P-10a. National Ambulatory Medical Care Survey: 2019 Summary Tables. CDC National Center for Health Statistics. Accessed November 11, 2024.

https://ftp.cdc.gov/pub/Health_Statistics/NCHS/NHIS/SHS/2018_SHS_Table_P-10.pdf, retrieved November 11, 2024.

5. Lendon JP, Caffrey C, Melekin A, et al. Overview of Post-acute and Long-term Care Providers and Services Users in the United States, 2020. In: National Health Statistics Report 208. Hyattsville, MD: National Center for Health Statistics; August 27, 2024. Accessed November 15, 2024. https://www.cdc.gov/nchs/data/nhsr/nhsr208.pdf.
6. Leff B, Burton L, Mader SL, et al. Hospital at Home: Feasibility and Outcomes of a Program to Provide Hospital-Level Care At Home for Acutely Ill Older Patients. *Ann Intern Med.* 2005;143(11):798–808. doi: 10.7326/0003-4819-143-11-200512060-00008. PMID: 16330791.
7. Kanagala SG, Gupta V, Kumawat S, et al. Hospital at Home: Emergence of a High-Value Model of Care Delivery. *Egypt J Intern Med.* 2023;35:21. https://doi.org/10.1186/s43162-023-00206-3.
8. Levine DM, Ouchi K, Blanchfield B, et al. Hospital Level Care at Home for Acutely Ill Adults: A Randomized Controlled Trial. *Ann Intern Med.* 2019;172(2):77–85. https://doi.org/10.7326/M19-0600.
9. Levine DM, Souza J, Schnipper JL, et al. Acute Hospital Care at Home in the United States: The Early National Experience. *Ann Intern Med.* 2024;177(1). https://doi.org/10.7326/M23-2264.
10. CMS. Fact Sheet: Report on the Study of the Acute Hospital Care at Home Initiative. Centers for Medicare and Medicaid Services News Release. September 30, 2024. Accessed December 4, 2024. https://www.cms.gov/newsroom/fact-sheets/fact-sheet-report-study-acute-hospital-care-home-initiative.
11. Institute of Medicine. *Toward Health Equity and Patient-Centeredness: Integrating Health Literacy, Disparities Reduction, and Quality Improvement: Workshop Summary.* Washington, DC: The National Academies Press; 2009.
12. Engle RL, Mohr DC, Holmes SK, et al. Evidence-based Practice and Patient-Centered Care: Doing Both Well. *Health Care Manage Rev.* 2021;46(3):174184. https://doi:10.1097/HMR.0000000000000254. Epub 2019 Jun 24.
13. Bokhour BG, Fix GM, Mueller NM, et al. How Can Healthcare Organizations Implement Patient-Centered Care? Examining a Large-Scale Cultural Transformation. *BMC Health Serv Res.* 2018;18:168. https://doi.org/10.1186/s12913-018-2949-5.
14. Anawade PA, Sharma D, Gahane S. A Comprehensive Review on Exploring the Impact of Telemedicine on Healthcare Accessibility. *Cureus.* 2024;16(3):e55996. https://doi:10.7759/cureus.55996.
15. Arora S, Thornton K, Murata G, et al. Outcomes of Treatment for Hepatitis C Virus Infection by Primary Care Providers *NEJM.* 2011;364:2199–2207. doi:10.1056/NEJMoa1009370.
16. CMS. Medicare Telehealth Trends Report. Centers for Medicaid and Medicare Services. July 15, 2024. Accessed December 2, 2024. https://data.cms.gov/sites/default/files/2024-09/c213a5e9-9e70-4b46-b5f1-2fb941ea0f6c/Medicare%20Telehealth%20Trends%20Snapshot%2020240827_508.pdf,
17. Lee EC, Grigorescu V, Enogieru I, et al. Updated National Survey Trends in Telehealth Utilization and Modality (2021-2022). ASPE Office of Health Policy Issue Brief. April 19, 2023. Accessed November 14, 2024. https://aspe.hhs.gov/sites/default/files/documents/7d6b4989431f4c70144f209622975116/household-pulse-survey-telehealth-covid-ib.pdf
18. Parikh H, Tarosky A, Maglione A. OIG Report Recommends Increased Oversight of Medicare's Reimbursement for Remote Patient Monitoring (RPM). Nixon Peabody Insights. October 8, 2024. Accessed December 2, 2024. https://www.nixonpeabody.com/insights/alerts/2024/10/08/oig-report-recommends-increased-oversight-of-medicares-reimbursement-for-remote-patient-monitoring,
19. Khullar D, Schpero WL, Casalino LP, et al. Accountable Care Organization Leader Perspectives on the Medicare Shared Savings Program: a Qualitative Study. *JAMA Health Forum.* 2024;5(3):e240126. doi:10.1001/jamahealthforum.2024.0126.
20. Quality Payment Program. 2023 and 2024 Comprehensive List of APMs. QPP. December 26, 2023. Accessed November 12, 2024. https://qpp.cms.gov/resources/document/3ad0ec11-dc16-4af0-8a98-ddd8b8ae660f.
21. CMS. Performance Year Financial and Quality Results. Centers for Medicare and Medicaid Services.

2023. Accessed November 22, 2024. Accessed November 22, 2024. https://data.cms.gov/medicare-shared-savings-program/performance-year-financial-and-quality-results.

22. Bao C, Bardhan IR. Measuring Value in Health Care: Lessons from Accountable Care Organizations. *Health Affairs Scholar.* 2024;2(3):1–8. https://doi.org/10.1093/hasschl/qxae028
23. CMS. Medicare Acute Care Episode (ACE) Demonstration. Centers for Medicare and Medicaid Services. Accessed December 4, 2024. https://www.cms.gov/priorities/innovation/innovation-models/ace
24. CMS. Bundled Payments for Care Improvement (BPCI) Initiative General Information. Centers for Medicare and Medicaid Services. Accessed December 4, 2024. https://www.cms.gov/priorities/innovation/innovation-models/Bundled-Payments
25. Struijs J, de Vries EF, Baan CA, et al. Bundled Payment Models Around Work: How They Work, and What Their Impact Has Been. The Commonwealth Fund. April 6, 2020. Accessed October 22, 2024. https://www.commonwealthfund.org/publications/2020/apr/bundled-payment-models-around-world-how-they-work-their-impact.
26. Agarwal R, Liao JM, Gupta A, Navathe AS. The Impact of Bundled Payment on Health Care Spending, Utilization, and Quality: A Systematic Review. *Health Aff.* 2020;39(1):50–57. https://doi.org/10.1377/hlthaff.201900784.
27. Shashikumar SA, Ryan AM, Maddox KEJ. Medicare's New Mandatory Bundled-Payment Program—Are We Ready for TEAM? *NEJM*. 2024;391(22):2065–2067. doi.10.1056/NEJMp2410850.
28. Schaff MF, Anderson GD. The Nuts and Bolts of Establishing a Clinically Integrated Network, Las Vegas, NV. November 2015:American Health Lawyers Association, Physicians and Hospitals Law Institute, Accessed February 17, 2025, http://cdn2.hubspot.net/hub/345447/file-2402958872-pdf/HORNE_The_Nuts__Bolts_012315.pdf?t=1422568193753.
29. Hart J. Clinically Integrated Networks. The Business of Primary Care. Accessed February 17, 2025, https://www.thebusinessofprimarycare.com/articles/clinically-integrated-networks.
30. Ridgely MS, Timbie JW, Duffy E, Wold LJ, Buttorff C. Consolidation by Any Other Name? The Emergence of Clinically Integrated Networks. *Health Serv Res.* 2020;55(Suppl 1):114. Accessed November 1, 2024. https://doi.org/10.1111/1475-6773.13493
31. U.S. Department of Health & Human Services, Office of Inspector General. Re: OIG Advisory Opinion No. 12-22. U.S. Department of Health and Human Services. January 7, 2013. Accessed December 4, 2024. https://oig.hhs.gov/documents/advisory-opinions/658/AO-12-22.pdf.
32. Bond AM, Schpero WL, Casalino LP, Zhang M, Khullar D. Association Between Individual Primary Care Physician Merit-based Incentive Payment System Score and Measures of Process and Patient Outcomes. *JAMA*. 2022;328(21):2136–2146. doi:10.1001/jama.2022.20619.

CHAPTER 6

Health Equity

Jamie Wooldridge, MD, MS-PopH, CPE

HALM CORE CONTENT:

- 2.1 Health disparities
- 2.6 Social determinants of health

CASE SCENARIO:

D'Wayne is a 10-year-old black male with moderate persistent asthma living in inner-city Rochester, New York. Over the last year, he has experienced five visits to the children's hospital emergency room resulting in three hospitalizations, including one admission to the intensive care unit, where he required non-invasive positive pressure.

He missed 20 days of school last year due to his asthma symptoms. He lives with his mother and two other siblings in an apartment building with neighbors who smoke. His mother has a high school diploma and works in a hair salon. He is often responsible for taking his own medications. Pharmacy records indicate that his daily controller inhaler is refilled about 50% of the expected times.

What are the factors contributing to D'Wayne's poorly controlled asthma? How can his healthcare team improve his asthma control to keep him out of the hospital and in school?

UNDERSTANDING HEALTH EQUITY is a key component of understanding population health. An appreciation of what good health is and how it affects an individual's life is foundational to understanding health equity.

Good health is defined as a complete physical, mental, and social well-being of an individual.[1] Good health is more than the absence of disease. The ability to maintain and enjoy good health is the right of every human being without distinction of race, religion, political belief, economic or social condition.[1] Good health includes child development, both physical and mental. Governments are responsible for the health of their people through adequate medical care and social measures.

Ensuring good health is economically beneficial to countries and governments. Improving the health of a population through actions such as vaccines, appropriate antibiotic usage, good sanitation, and adequate nutrition expands the labor force and increases productivity. McKinsey Global Institute estimates that in the United States, every $1.00 invested into improving the health of the population will result in $3.90 of economic benefit.[2] This benefit translates to a 10% ($2.94 billion) increase in Gross Domestic Product (GDP) by 2040. It also improves individual lives with a 33% reduction in the poor health of individuals and 22 additional healthy days per person per year.[2] One has to wonder what worthy actions could happen for individuals, families, and employers with 7 billion annual additional healthy days in the United States (a number based on a total population of 314 million).

Every country around the world would experience similar economic benefits by ensuring good health for its population. The categories of interventions to achieve good health are: (1) therapeutic (direct medical interventions); (2) environmental, social, or behavioral; and (3) prevention and health promotion, with variations across the groups for optimal impact for each country.

Specific interventions within these three categories include but are not limited to, vaccines, medications, safe childbirth, alcohol and drug abuse prevention, insect spray and nets, access to specialty surgery, behavior change, and dietary interventions. Within the United States, the top five interventions by highest impact are (1) medicines for heart disease, stroke prevention, and diabetes; (2) psychological counseling and talking therapies; (3) smoking cessation; (4) supported behavior change; and (5) vaccines.[2]

Every country experiences significant barriers to good health, ranging from the individual to the systemic level. This chapter explores these barriers and possible solutions that can be piloted by individual providers and health teams across partnerships between healthcare institutions and the community. This work forms the basis of population health.

A few key terms are important to understand with regard to the barriers to good health in communities.

Health equity is the attainment of the highest level of health for all people.[3] Achieving health equity requires valuing everyone equally with focused and ongoing societal efforts to address avoidable inequalities, historical and contemporary injustices, and social determinants of all health.[3]

Equality and equity are often mistakenly understood as the same (Figure 6). Health equality means everyone is given the same tools and assistance to overcome their individual barriers to good health.

Health disparities are preventable differences in the burden of disease, injury, violence, or opportunities to achieve optimal health experienced by a socially disadvantaged population.[4] Equity customizes tools to identify and address the disparities.

Social determinants of health (SDoH) are the conditions in the places where people live, learn, work, play, and worship that affect a wide range of health risks and outcomes. SDoH are shaped by the distribution of money, power, and resources at global, national, and regional levels.[5] Ideally, SDoH are addressed at the institutional and societal levels to offer equal opportunities for good health (Figure 1).

FIGURE 1. Addressing Social Determinants of Health

Health Disparities in the United States

Health outcomes and healthcare spending in the United States are appalling, with significant disparities compared to other high-income countries. Utilizing data from the Organization of Economic Co-operation and Development (OCED), The Commonwealth Fund compared 38 high-income countries, including the United States, Australia, Canada, France, Germany, Japan, the Netherlands, New Zealand, Norway, South Korea, Switzerland, and the United Kingdom.[6]

Comparatively, the U.S. has the lowest life expectancy at 77 years compared to the overall average of 80.4 years and Canada at 81.7 years.[6] The U.S. has the highest rate of avoidable deaths per 100,000 people at 336 compared to the OCED average of 225 and some countries with a rate of half of that.[6] The U.S. also has the highest rate of infant and maternal deaths with the maternal death rate being almost 2.5 times higher than the OCED average. Adults in the United States are most likely to have multiple chronic conditions compared to all other high-income countries with obesity rates almost double the OCED average.

The U.S. is a significant outlier in deaths from physical assault, including gun violence, with a rate seven times higher than all other high-income countries.[6] The United States is also an outlier in healthcare spending, with 17.8% of GDP going to healthcare compared to the OCED average of 9.6% over the last 40 years. Lastly, the United States is the only high-income country that does not guarantee healthcare coverage.[6]

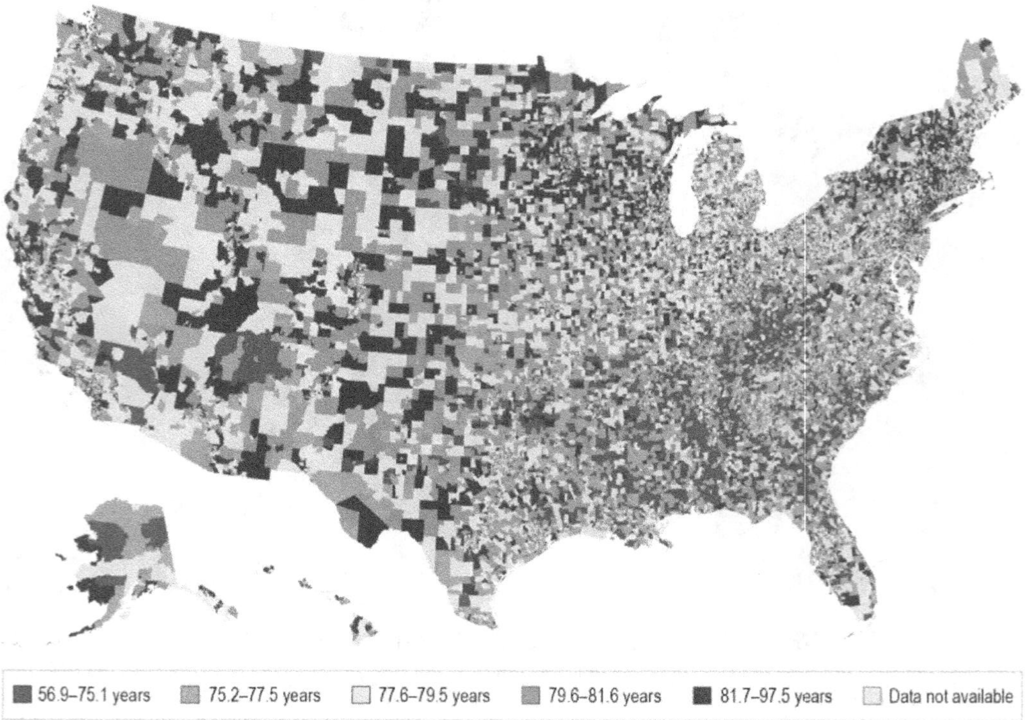

FIGURE 2. CDC Data Visualization of Life Expectancy at Birth by Census Tract

These poor outcomes are not equally distributed across the United States. Instead, there is a wide variation in outcomes, which are monitored by census tracks, small subdivisions of a county averaging about 4,000 inhabitants. Within the United States, the life expectancy at birth ranges from 56.9 to 97.5 years across census tracts. This is a difference of 20-30 years in life expectancy, often with the same cities, counties, and/or states (Figure 2).[7] The Centers for Disease Control and Prevention, National Center for Health Statistics has published a data visualization gallery that includes an interactive map allowing a person to look up life expectancy at birth by census tract throughout the country.[8]

Analysis of demographics across counties reveal possible causes for the large variation in life expectancy. In Monroe County, New York, which includes the city of Rochester, inner city census tract #23 has an average life expectancy at birth of 69.5 years compared to a census tract #128 at 87.6 years. Demographic data from these two census tracts demonstrate significant disparities nearly identical to those found across the U.S. (Table 1).[9]

Individuals living in inner-city Rochester are more likely to be single, black females with only a high school education living in poor housing and living on an income below the poverty level. Compare this to someone living in suburban Rochester who is more likely to be a married, white female with a college education in good housing and with an income well above the poverty level. It is easy to see how the poor health and significantly lower life expectancy of inner-city Rochester are connected to the significant other demographic disparities.

TABLE 1. U.S. Census Bureau Demographic Disparities[9]

Demographic	Downtown Rochester (#23)	Rochester Suburb (#128)
Median Age (yrs)	31.9	33.5
Sex (female)	54%	56%
Race & Ethnicity		
White	22%	76%
Black	43%	5%
Hispanic	22%	9%
Median Household Income	$19,740	$72,413
Persons Below Poverty Line	44.2%	9.6%
Number of Households	1919	2235
Marital Status	24%	48%
Women Ages 15-50 Who Gave Birth in the Past Year	8.7%	1.9%
Number of Housing Units	2231	2400
Single Unit Structure	44%	51%
Occupied	86%	93%
Education Level		
High School Grad	75.2%	99.8%
Bachelor's Degree or Higher	13%	74.6%

Regarding mortality, although the rates of heart disease in the U.S. are similar across racial and ethnic groups, black, non-Hispanic adults are dying from heart disease at higher rates of 50-100 more deaths per 100,000.[10] When extrapolating these rates across the total population of black and white individuals in 2019 with heart disease, there may have been >25,000 preventable deaths of black individuals. Additionally, black, non-Hispanic individuals with cancer have a similar significantly higher mortality compared to other racial and ethnic groups.[10]

Black people are disproportionately impacted by human immunodeficiency virus (HIV) compared to other racial or ethnic groups. From 2015 to 2019, new diagnosis of HIV rates in black, non-Hispanic individuals was four times higher compared to all individuals in the United States. The death rates from HIV are more than four times higher in black, non-Hispanic, individuals compared to all other racial and ethnic groups.[10] Barriers to healthcare, racism, stigma, homophobia, and poverty are known contributors to these disparities.[11]

CAUSES OF HEALTH DISPARITIES

Health disparities result from systemic differences in the opportunities groups have to achieve optimal health, leading to unfair and avoidable differences in health outcomes.[12] The elements of social identity and geographic location that create disparity in opportunities for good health include race and ethnicity, gender, employment, socioeconomic status, disability, immigration status, geography, and more.[13]

These systemic differences generate large, preventable differences in health outcomes such as life expectancy, implying that one's zip code is more important to health than one's genetic code.[14] Policies that foster inequities at all levels (from organization to community to county, state, and nation) are critical drivers of inequities.[13]

Throughout the history of the United States, people have been "sorted" into resource-rich or resource-poor neighborhoods and schools based on race and socioeconomic status.[15] An example of this sorting is the practice of redlining, which was the systematic denial of mortgages, insurance loans, and other financial services to residents within the "redlined" zip codes of a city based on race or ethnicity.

This practice was created in the 1930s using color-coded maps ranking loan "worthiness" of neighborhoods with the red neighborhoods considered too risky for lending programs and homeownership.[16] Most of the red areas were neighborhoods with a majority of black residents.

The overlapping maps of redlined neighborhoods in cities from the 1930s almost exactly match the neighborhoods with low life expectancy today. See Figure 3 for a redlining map for Rochester, New York from 1938 and a map of life expectancy by census tracts for 2010–2015.

One example of the causal relationship between the practice of redlining and healthcare disparities is evidenced by rates of tobacco use. Underperforming schools are often located in previously redlined neighborhoods and have lower rates of high school graduation.[17] Adults with no high school diploma or high school equivalency

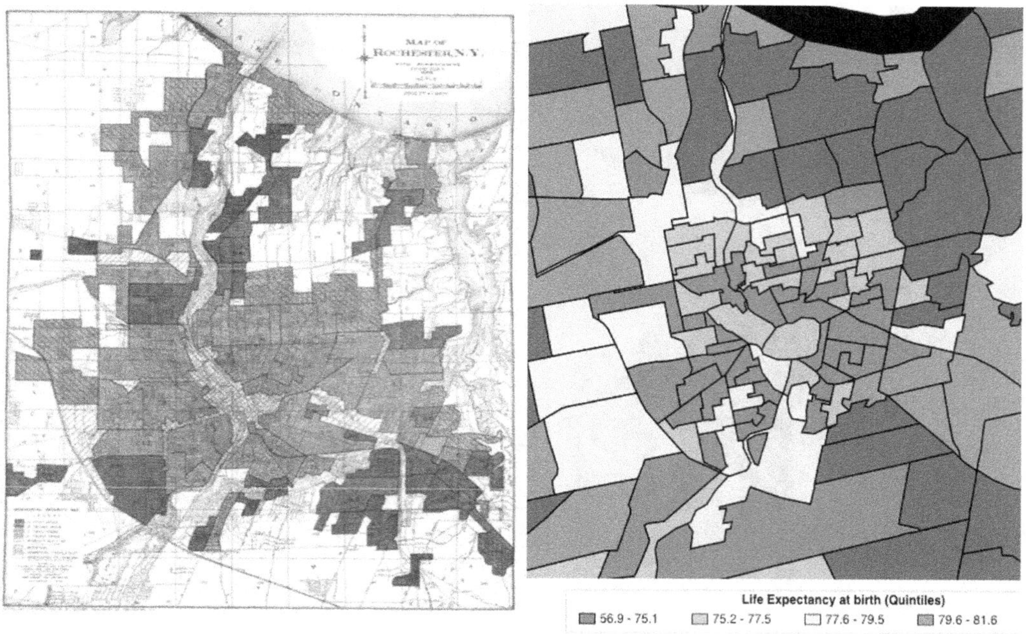

FIGURE 3. Home Owners' Loan Corporation "redlining" map of Rochester, NY from 1930s compared to Life Expectancy at Birth for U.S. States and Census Tracts, 2010–2015

diploma (GED) were over four times as likely to smoke cigarettes as those with a bachelor's degree or higher in 2019.[10]

Social Determinants of Health

Social determinants of health (SDoH) are the conditions of the places where people live, learn, work, play, and worship that affect a wide range of health risks and outcomes.[5] Many factors determine the health, good or poor, of an individual, with healthcare accounting for only about 20% (Figure 4).

Instead, socioeconomic factors and health behaviors contribute 70% to an individual's health. Therefore, to improve patients' health, healthcare providers must extend beyond diagnostic and therapeutic interventions prescribed in hospitals and clinics. Without consideration of SDoH, the gains from provided care can be lost when the patients return home.

SDoH is divided into five categories: (1) economic stability, (2) education access and quality, (3) healthcare access and quality (4) neighborhood and built environment, and (5) social community and context (Figure 5). Healthy People 2030 is a program from the Office of Disease Prevention and Health Promotion through the U.S. Department of Health and Human Services to improve health and well-being over the next decade.[3] Healthy People goals in addressing SDoH are:

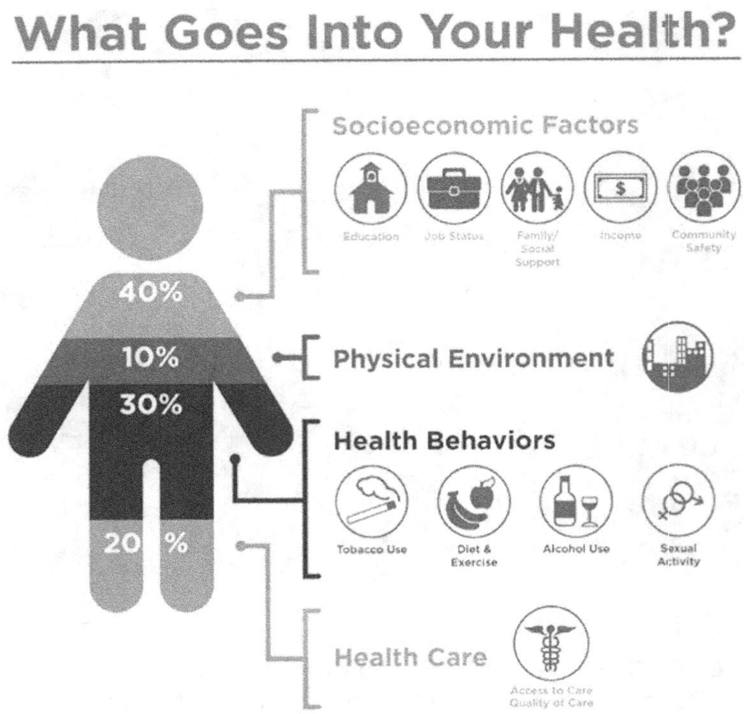

FIGURE 4. Factors That Contribute To Our Health

Source: Institute for Clinical Systems Improvement, Going Beyond Clinical Walls: Solving Complex Problems, 2014.

FIGURE 5. SDoH as outlined in Healthy People 2030

Source: Institute for Clinical Systems Improvement, Going Beyond Clinical Walls; Solving Complex Problems, 2014.

- Economic stability: Help people earn steady incomes that allow them to meet their health needs.
- Education Access and Quality: Increase educational opportunities and help children and adolescents do well in school.
- Healthcare Access and Quality: Increase access to comprehensive, high-quality healthcare services. (See Chapter 7)
- Neighborhood and Built Environment: Create neighborhoods and environments that promote health and safety.
- Social Community and Context: Increase social and community support.[3]

ECONOMIC STABILITY

Individuals who are unemployed or living in poverty have less access to nutritious food and adequate housing. Additionally, the stress of economic instability contributes to health conditions. In the U.S., one in 10 individuals lives below the poverty level.[18] To compound the health impact of economic stability, individuals with disabilities and/or chronic medical conditions often experience limitations in their ability to work. Many other people may have steady employment yet do not earn enough to afford healthy food and safe housing.

Programs and studies have proven the possibility of improving economic instability for individuals. One study enrolled 345 employed, single mothers earning an income of no more than 200% of the 2017 federal poverty level. The mothers were randomized to receive a financial education and coaching program or no intervention program. They were followed over 12 months. Results showed those receiving the program experienced a significant reduction in financial stress, were more likely to stop smoking, and reduced their need to seek medical care.[19]

A second program, the Enhanced Transitional Job Demonstration (ETJD) program funded by the Employment and Training Administration of the U.S. Department of Labor, included multiple interventions targeting people recently released from prison or low-income parents who had fallen behind in child support payments. These interventions improved employment and increased child support payments for the participants.[20]

EDUCATION ACCESS AND QUALITY

Children from low-income families, those with disabilities, and those who routinely experience forms of bullying are more likely to struggle with math and reading. These children have decreased rates of high school graduation, are less likely to find safe, high-paying jobs, and are more likely to have health problems like heart disease, diabetes, and depression.[3]

The stress of living in poverty also affects children's brain development, creating challenges that poorly funded schools may not be able to support. The most startling evidence of the impact of education on health is a study using U.S. vital statistics comparing the number of deaths avoided through medical care to the number of avoided deaths if more adults were college-educated. The study found that improved education decreased deaths by a ratio of 8:1 compared to medical care.[15]

Community programs offering vocational training, alternative schooling, social-emotional skills training, college-oriented programming, mentoring and counseling, attendance monitoring and contingencies, and case management demonstrated an 8.5% median increase in the rate of high school graduation compared with students not receiving these programs.[21]

Programs focused on early education for low-income children had a pronounced long-term effect, with decreased crime rates, decreased rates of teen pregnancy, improved self-regulation and emotional development, and improved health outcomes. Every dollar invested in early-education programs resulted in a $3.39 increase in earnings gains.[22]

NEIGHBORHOOD AND BUILT ENVIRONMENT

Racial and ethnic minorities and people with low incomes are more likely to live in neighborhoods with high rates of violence, unsafe air and/or water, and other health risks.[23] Children living in lower-opportunity neighborhoods are less likely to attend preschool and graduate from high school, have fewer green spaces in which to play, experience more days of extreme heat, are more likely to lack health insurance, and live in homes with incomes below the federal poverty level.[3]

There are multiple programs to improve neighborhoods and thus improve the health and well-being of their residents. For example, community development financial institutions (CDFIs) provide access to affordable capital and financial services to low-income communities. CFDIs utilize federal resources from the U.S. Department of Treasury CDFI Fund to attract private investment to build affordable housing, small businesses, and community facilities. CFDIs have headquarters in all 50 states and U.S. territories.[24]

Another example is the Gem City Market in Dayton, Ohio, which is a worker- and member-owned grocery store in the downtown area that provides healthy food options and employment opportunities. The market was established in partnership with a community action group, the Dayton city government, and a local bank.[7]

SOCIAL AND COMMUNITY CONTEXT

Research shows individuals who lack social support are at increased risk for physical and mental health problems. Unsafe neighborhoods, discrimination, and poverty have a negative effect on the health of individuals, but often are out of their control.[3] The negative effects can be reduced through positive relationships at home, work, and within the community, as well as through social support in the form of community organizations and religious community organizations offering emotional support, practical assistance, stress management, and guidance in accessing needed resources. Interestingly, data have shown that perceived support, the belief that help is available if needed, rather than actual support, has a strong link to improving health outcomes.[25]

Chapter Summary

Every human being has the right to good health. Ensuring good health is economically beneficial at all levels from individuals to countries and governments. However, disparities exist, preventing individuals from achieving good health. By identifying and addressing social determinants of health, these disparities can be reduced. Physician leaders must reach outside their clinical domain to partner with individuals and communities to tackle social determinants of health and help their patients achieve good health.

REFERENCES

1. Constitution of World Health Organization. World Health Organization. Accessed July 15, 2022. https://www.who.int/about/governance/constitution
2. Remes J, Linzer K, Singhal S, Dewhurst M, et al. Prioritizing Health: A Prescription for Prosperity. McKinsey Global Institute. July 6, 2020. Accessed December 10, 2024. https://public.tableau.com/views/PrioritizingHealthAprescriptionforprosperity/PrioritizinghealthAprescriptionforprosperity?showVizHome=no&%3AshowVizHome=no#2
3. Office of Disease Prevention and Health Promotion. *Healthy People 2030*. Washington, DC: US Department of Health and Human Services:. Accessed December 15, 2024. https://odphp.health.gov/healthypeople/about/promoting-healthy-people-2030
4. Centers for Disease Control and Prevention. Office of Minority Health. Health Disparities. July 2024. Centers for Disease Control and Prevention. Accessed December 10, 2024. https://www.cdc.gov/minority-health/about/#cdc_health_equity_health_disparities-health-disparities
5. World Health Organization. Social Determinants of Health. WHO. Accessed December 15, 2024. https://www.who.int/health-topics/social-determinants-of-health#tab=tab_1
6. Gunja MZ, Gumas ED, Williams RD. U.S. Health Care from a Global Perspective, 2022: Accelerating Spending, Worsening Outcomes. Issue Brief. The Commonwealth Fund. January 31, 2023. https://doi.org/10.26099/8ejy-yc74
7. Community Health and Economic Prosperity: Engaging Businesses as Stewards and Stakeholders—A Report of the Surgeon General [Internet] (US Department of Health and Human Services) 2021. https://odphp.health.gov/healthypeople/tools-action/browse-evidence-based-resources/community-health-and-economic-prosperity-engaging-businesses-stewards-and-stakeholders-report-surgeon-general
8. Life Expectancy at Birth for U.S. States and Census Tracts, 2010-2015. Center for Disease Control and Prevention Accessed January 7, 2025. https://www.cdc.gov/nchs/data-visualization/life-expectancy/index.html
9. Census Reporter. American Community Survey (ACS), US Census Bureau Accessed December 10,

2024. https://censusreporter.org

10. Health, United States, 2020–2021: Annual Perspective (National Center for Health Statistics) 2023. https://www.cdc.gov/nchs/data/hus/hus20-21.pdf
11. HIV national strategic plan for the United States: A roadmap to end the HIV epidemic 2021–2025 (U.S. Department of Health and Human Services) 2020. https://files.hiv.gov/s3fs-public/HIV-National-Strategic-Plan-2021-2025.pdf
12. Braveman P. Health disparities and health equity: concepts and measurement. *Annu Rev Public Health*. 2006;27:167-94. doi:10.1146/annurev.publhealth.27.021405.102103
13. In: Baciu A, Negussie Y, Geller A, Weinstein JN, eds. *Communities in Action: Pathways to Health Equity*. National Academies of Sciences, Engineering, and Medicine; Health and Medicine Division; Board on Population Health and Public Health Practice; Committee on Community-Based Solutions to Promote Health Equity in the United States; 2017:chap The Root Causes of Health Inequity.
14. *Beyond Health Care: New Directions to a Healthier America*. 2009. https://www.rwjf.org/en/insights/our-research/2009/04/beyond-health-care.html
15. Woolf SH, Johnson RE, Phillips RL, Philipsen M. Giving everyone the health of the educated: an examination of whether social change would save more lives than medical advances. *Am J Public Health*. 2007;97(4):679-83. doi:10.2105/AJPH.2005.084848
16. Jackson C. What is Redlining? *The New York Times*. August 22, 2021:9. https://www.nytimes.com/2021/08/17/realestate/what-is-redlining.html
17. Lindsey Burke JS. *Housing Redlining and Its Lingering Effects on Education Opportunity*. 2021. March 11, 2021. https://www.heritage.org/education/report/housing-redlining-and-its-lingering-effects-education-opportunity
18. Semega J, Kollar M, Creamer J, Mohanty A. *Income and Poverty in the United States*. Bureau USC; 2020. *Current Population Reports, P60-266(RV)*. https://www.census.gov/content/dam/Census/library/publications/2019/demo/p60-266.pdf
19. White N, Packard K, Kalkowski J, et al. Improving Health through Action on Economic Stability: Results of the Finances First Randomized Controlled Trial of Financial Education and Coaching in Single Mothers of Low-Income. *Am J Lifestyle Med*. May-Jun 2023;17(3):424-436. doi:10.1177/15598276211069537
20. Barden B, Juras R, Redcross C, Farrell M, Bloom D. *New Perspective on Creating Jobs – Final Impacts of the Next Generation of Subsidized Employment Programs*. Office of Planning R, and Evaluation, Administration for Children and Families, U.S. Department of Health and Human Services; 2018. https://clear.dol.gov/Study/New-perspectives-creating-jobs-Final-impacts-next-generation-subsidized-employment-programs
21. *Social Determinants of Health: High School Completion Programs*. Services UDoHaH; 2013. *Guide to Community Preventive Services*. https://www.thecommunityguide.org/findings/social-determinants-health-high-school-completion-programs.html
22. Kay N, Pennuci A. *Early Childhood Education for Low-Income Students: A Review of the Evidence and Benefit-Cost Analysis*. 2014.
23. Social Determinants of Health: Know What Affects Health. Centers for Disease Control and Prevention. Accessed December 5, 2024. https://www.cdc.gov/socialdeterminants/index.htm
24. *Community Health and Economic Prosperity: Engaging Businesses as Stewards and Stakeholders—A Report of the Surgeon General*. 2021. https://www.hhs.gov/sites/default/files/chep-sgr-full-report.pdf
25. Uchino BN. Understanding the Links Between Social Support and Physical Health: A Life-Span Perspective With Emphasis on the Separability of Perceived and Received Support. *Perspect Psychol Sci*. May 2009;4(3):236-55. doi:10.1111/j.1745-6924.2009.01122.x

CHAPTER 7

Population Health

Amin Hakim, MD, FIDSA, CPE, FACPE

HALM CORE CONTENT:

- 2.2 Healthcare access, quality, cost, resource allocation, accountability, and the community
- 2.7 Community social services relations

CASE SCENARIO:

A provider organization has a value-based contract (VBC) with a payer. The contract calls for improving care and satisfaction scores and reducing costs among the payer's members. Both organizations are challenged by several issues, including data and patient and provider engagement. While the contract lists performance indicators, the organizations' perspectives differ regarding their responsibilities and implementation. How should they manage the care of their shared patients/enrollees? Both have data that help them track and trend performance against the VBC goals.

PROVIDERS' CLOSER RELATIONSHIP with the patients affords them faster access to some data and better opportunities to influence outcomes. The payers may have better access to certain data and resources that can support providers and patients.

What does each party bring to the table, and what is each one accountable for? How would they collaborate toward achieving VBC goals? What challenges do they face and would they overcome them?

Whether they work in the provider or payer setting, physician leaders play a key role in achieving VBC goals, and their input has risen in importance, given the growth of VBC arrangements among government and private payers. Their insights guide the planning, implementation, and evaluation of resource allocation to improve access to care, improve quality cost and coordination of care, and manage internal and external collaborations.

TABLE 1. Percentage of Population Aged 16 Years and Older Who Opted To Forgo Care

Country	Consultation		Test, Treatment, F/U		Prescribed Meds.	
	2016	2020	2016	2020	2016	2020
Australia	8.9	10.2	7.7	13.9	6.5	8.5
Canada	6.4	5.2	5.8	5.7	10.5	9.3
France	N/A	3.3	N/A	6.2	N/A	5.1
Germany	2.8	3.5	4.7	4.2	3.2	6.2
Netherlands	6.0	4.2	7.0	3.5	7.0	3.4
New Zealand	14.3	12.9	9.7	8.4	5.8	6.7
Sweden	3.5	6.3	3.3	5.2	6.3	6.6
Switzerland	19.6	18.3	12.5	14.3	11.3	9.1
United Kingdom	3.8	4.6	2.8	3.5	2.2	5.6
Non-U.S. Average	**8.3**	**8.3**	**6.7**	**6.5**	**5.9**	**6.3**
United States	**21.8**	**26.8**	**19.5**	**26.4**	**18.1**	**23.1**

N/A: Not available, F/U: Follow-up
Source: OECD Health Data, July 2024. U.S. peer countries were selected based on those typically used in comparisons published by the Commonwealth Fund. Most data were unavailable for years other than 2016 and 2020.

Healthcare Access

Access to care is a complex issue with multifaceted challenges that require a combination of policy changes, system reforms, and community-based initiatives in order to improve access and ultimately improve healthcare quality, optimize cost, and reduce disparities in experience and outcomes. The challenges that Americans face are many and include:

- *Affordability*: A fragmented insurance system and high out-of-pocket costs, including those receiving coverage through their employers, create significant barriers.[1] Many patients forego medical care at three- to four-fold higher rates than those living in other industrialized countries because of high deductibles and cost-sharing requirements (Table 1). Lack of affordability disproportionately affects low-income patients who, even with sliding-scale fees, are more likely to report difficulties accessing care, delaying care due to cost, and forgoing care altogether.[2–5]
- *Availability*: Shortages of primary care providers and limited options for after-hours care have resulted in limited availability of healthcare services, particularly in rural areas.[6–7] The net loss of primary care clinicians compounds the U.S. ranking among its peer nations as having the least physicians per capita in this specialty.[8] Unfavorable reimbursement in the face of higher work intensity has also discouraged prospective candidates from entering the field.

- *Social determinants of health (SDoH):* Factors such as poverty, lack of transportation, and unsafe environments impede access to care because they influence an individual's ability to prioritize and utilize healthcare services, even with insurance coverage.[3–5] Additionally, unfavorable employment compensation, benefits, and/or rules lead to the inability to afford time off from work for medical appointments, which also hinders access to care.
- *Structural barriers:* Separate and unequal system-based practices based on state of residence, insurance type, socioeconomic status, and other factors limit access and contribute to unequal outcomes.[7] For instance, hospital systems may offer different speeds of appointments based on insurance coverage — fastest for commercial insurance and slowest for Medicaid enrollees.
- *Implicit and explicit bias*: Implicit and explicit biases among clinicians can limit access to care, thus creating or reinforcing health inequalities.[7] For example, some providers choose not to accept some or all forms of government insurance or may render services only in certain settings, which may impede access to care.

Addressing these barriers would necessitate a serious commitment to value regardless of political affiliation, personal or other gains, lobbying, or other persuasions. A multipronged multistakeholder approach would include:

- *Expanding insurance coverage*: The number of uninsured individuals has dropped by about 50% since the Affordable Care Act went into effect in 2010, but millions still lack coverage.[8] Subsidized private insurance and other forms of coverage have improved affordability, but more action is needed to achieve better health outcomes.
- *Strengthening primary care*: Various administrations have employed a variety of initiatives to increase the availability of primary care, particularly in underserved areas.[1,7] Those efforts have included loan forgiveness, higher reimbursement and novel payment models, and investment in training programs, but will take a long time to bear fruit.
- *Addressing SDoH and inequity*: Policy initiatives to remove barriers and improve equity have driven and sometimes mandated efforts by providers and payers to tackle individual patient SDoH needs. Increasing workforce diversity, promoting cultural competence among healthcare workers, and investing in community outreach and collaborative activities hold promise for reducing inequity.[5]
- *Improving patient engagement and health literacy*: Targeted efforts to enhance patient communication, health literacy, and shared decision-making empower patients and improve their understanding of healthcare options.[3,7] These efforts should address language barriers and employ culturally sensitive approaches.
- *Promoting integrated care*: Accountable care organizations and value-based care models incentivize and encourage collaboration among providers, as well as integration of behavioral health and other services in primary care.[7,9] Such models may also foster partnerships with community-based organizations (CBOs) to address SDoH.

- *Engaging CBOs*: Providers and payers may implement community-based interventions, which can play a crucial role in mitigating local barriers to access related to SDoH. Examples include programs that provide specialized meal delivery to food-insecure patients with diabetes or facilitate early inhaler refills for patients with asthma ahead of wildfire smoke events.[10]
- *Investing in technology*: Utilizing technology like telehealth, streamlined electronic medical records, dashboards, and patient portals may improve access to care, particularly in areas with limited clinical resources.[3]

Healthcare Trends

The healthcare landscape is evolving rapidly, and several trends have shaped medical management programs and will continue to do so. Among them are:

- *Growth of VBC:* The focus is on value rather than volume of services. Value is commonly described as quality (clinical +/- consumer experience) divided by cost.[2] While the specifics may differ, healthcare purchasers, employers, and governments want better value.
- *Evolving quality measures*: Metrics for the quality of acute and preventive care, chronic disease control, and patient experience may be rotated and weighed differently every year, thus requiring vigilance by measurement and operational teams. Governmental and private payers have increasingly emphasized outcome over process measures in VBC models.
- *SDoH and equity*: Addressing SDoH needs and reducing disparities are increasingly incorporated into both clinical initiatives and VBC models.[11,12] CMS has been implementing programs since 2023 to measure and improve inequity disparities.[13]
- *Strained revenue*: Unfavorable Medicare reimbursement, a common benchmark for private payers, and rising costs have significant effects on revenues and margins. Pay-for-performance models often entail deferred payment by several years for government-program payers. For example, services provided in 2025 will yield a Medicare Advantage plan's star rating in 2027 with payment of quality bonus to eligible plans in 2028. Revenue volatility may reduce payers' SDoH-oriented benefits and may affect provider and payer programs.
- *Emerging technologies*: New medical devices and drugs are usually more expensive than comparable existing ones, and novel approaches such as cell, gene, and immune therapies may have exorbitant prices. Clinical leaders may steer the choice of technology to lower cost, such as type of non-invasive colorectal cancer screening. Intervention programs may utilize telehealth, wearables, remote patient monitoring, and health apps.
- *Shrinking experienced workforce*: All healthcare organizations are struggling to recruit and retain experienced clinicians. They will face further shortages in primary care providers in the future, which may affect preventive care.[14]

- *Rise of private equity (PE) ownership*: PE firms are increasingly investing in provider, payer, and other healthcare organizations. The impact of investor ownership on costs and quality varies depending on market and regulatory conditions, but the experience is generally negative, with worse quality and higher cost than comparators.[15] Such ownership is often associated with operational and staffing cuts, and liquidating assets rapidly for maximum return.
- *Polarization of politics*: Shifts in political winds can lead to significant swings in federal and state funding programs. A transactional approach to healthcare, underfunding of public health, and the lack of coherent long-term planning that is safeguarded from the whims of political parties undermine efforts to improve the well-being of all citizens.
- *Privatized government insurance*: More than 50% of seniors had joined private Medicare Advantage payers by 2024, and most Medicaid-eligible persons are enrolled in like health plans. Higher private enrollment rates are expected in future years. Private insurance may be associated with better quality than traditional coverage, but higher administrative burdens and other issues pose challenges for providers and patients. High copays, deductibles, and coinsurance may discourage individuals from seeking care.
- *Unforeseen events*: The COVID-19 pandemic, economic downturns such as the Great Recession, and natural disasters have repeatedly stressed the healthcare system. While temporary regulatory and contractual allowances apply during such events, utilization and cost may rise significantly while the health status and preventive care decline. Long-term post-COVID-19 pandemic clinical and actuarial consequences are expected to persist for years to come.[16] Individuals forgo medical care due to financial constraints during such periods, potentially leading to delayed diagnoses, disease progression, and ultimately higher costs.

Trends in Quality of Care

Despite gains in various leading and lagging quality indicators over the past two decades,[17] the United States has lagged significantly behind its international peers, ranking last among them on multiple measures such as avoidable mortality and hospitalizations (Figures 1 and 2). Improvements are necessary and actionable by addressing the factors noted above and other challenges.

Trends in Cost of Care

Rising healthcare costs are driven by preventable events, complex care needs of an aging population, pricier medical technology, administrative complexity, mergers and acquisitions, inflation, fraud, and other factors. Attempts to curtail cost include

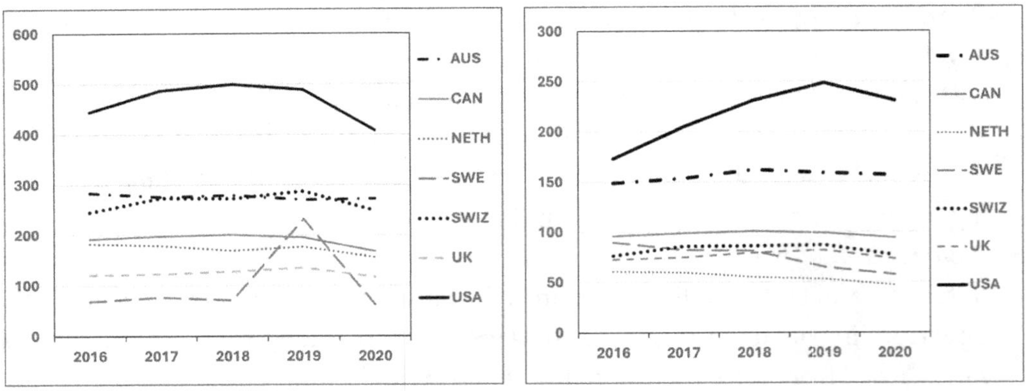

Congestive Heart Failure & Hypertension

Diabetes

FIGURE 1. Total avoidable mortality, deaths per 100,000 inhabitants, standardlzed rate. Healthcare Quality and Outcomes. OECD Health Data, July 2024. U.S.-peer countries were selected based on data availability every year in the data set (2005 was not included because Australia's data were missing; data were incomplete for 2021 and 2022); countries were selected based on those frequently used in global comparisons published by the Commonwealth Fund.

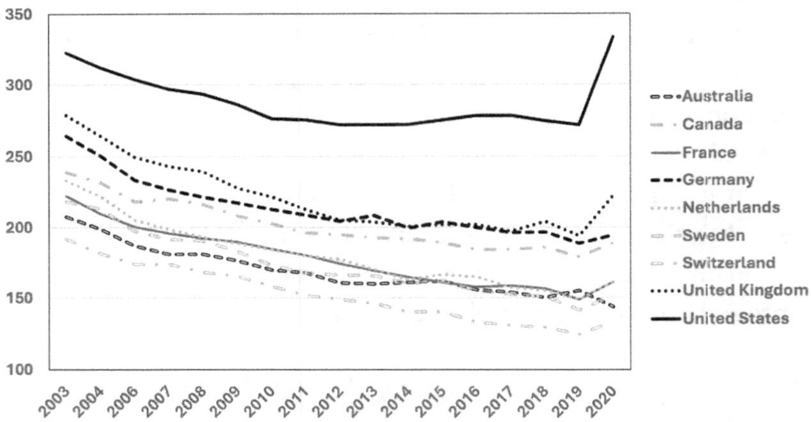

FIGURE 2. Illustrative condition-specific avoidable hospitalizations per 100,000 inhabitants. COVID-19 hospitalizations reduced avoidable admissions in 2020. Healthcare Quality and Outcomes. OECD Health Data, July 2024. U.S.-peer countries were selected based on data availability every year in the data set; countries were selected based on those typically used in comparisons published by the Commonwealth Fund.

risk-sharing and capitation arrangements, attention to behavioral health and SDoH, care coordination and integration, and innovative service models, to name a few.

Healthcare spending in the United States far exceeds that of its peers (Figure 3) and healthcare costs are projected to continue rising in the coming years.[18] Care abandonment in the U.S. is significantly higher than in similar countries (Table 1), which

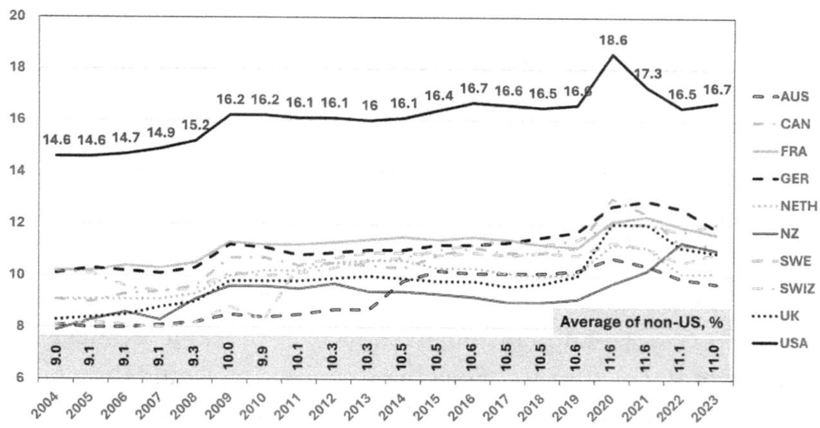

FIGURE 3. Health expenditure, percentage(%) of gross domestic product (GDP). OECD Health Data, July 2024. U.S.-peer countries were selected based on those typically used in comparisons published by the Commonwealth Fund.

would undermine provider and payer efforts, and needs solutions at the societal level. Investing in public health activities can reduce healthcare spending, particularly in low-resource communities.[19]

Resource Allocation

Evaluation of the impact of clinical programs and the return on investment (ROI) from value-based care agreements guide resource allocation to yield optimal benefits. Intensive interventions are reserved for more complex, higher-risk patients. Clinical leaders should estimate the costs associated with each intervention, including staff, software, etc., which may be attributed to a particular program wholly or partially when resources are shared with other departments. Likewise, benefits are forecasted according to the methodology selected by the financial team; the latter may allow either direct or indirect gains.

Value estimation relies on both evidence-based knowledge and informed experience and may include customer experience and retention, reduction in healthcare disparities, and other nontraditional indicators. Challenges in determining the value of interventions include annual variations, the amount of time some outcomes may take to materialize, and the difficulty in attributing outcomes to specific interventions due to the complex interplay of factors and concurrent initiatives.

Assessment methods vary among organizations and may be conducted by healthcare economics or actuarial teams that might use a particular approach, and methodology may change over time depending on the preferences of the financial leadership. This exercise is conducted annually and periodically during the year; the analysis informs budgeting, resource allocation, program realignment, and negotiations. Program budgeting and marginal analysis (PBMA), cost-benefit analysis, and other methods are used in public health planning and are applicable to clinical programs.[20]

Organizations may use formal and rapid estimation methods and may aim for a standard ROI (e.g., 2:1 or higher) or context-specific ones. When program leaders have to use zero-based budgeting, they should consider the benefits of different tactics; for example, deploying a few nonclinical staff instead of adding a nurse may grow the program's capacity while improving clinicians' efficiency.

Stakeholders should be mindful of short-term gains in pre/post comparisons or first-year evaluations because of diminishing returns over time. Physician leaders should understand and provide input into how the organization would distribute financial gains, such as how the latter would be allocated to providers, teams, or resources. Budgeting and resource allocation are subject to competing priorities, management changes, reduced budgets, etc. Clinical leaders should be adaptable while advocating for optimal resources and should share challenges with their teams for transparency and ideation.

Accountability

Accountability stems from agreement among stakeholders on the goals and objectives that drive their activities. Expectations should be based on establishing and documenting SMART (Specific, Measurable, Attainable, Relevant, Time-bound) goals[21] and sharing them with stakeholders for implementation.

The aims and key outcomes should be informed by data and quality improvement tools; accountability will rely on tracking and trending results with regular updates to the participants. The latter includes leadership, liaisons, care team members, and providers. The format of the information shared with them will vary depending on the role of the recipient; aggregate data for all audiences — particularly leaders — and provide detailed patient-level data for the care team and providers.

A plan or program description would outline what, who, and when; would be updated at least annually; and would meet regulatory and/or accreditation requirements. Detailed process descriptions, such as swim lane workflows delineate the responsibilities and accountability of each party. Program operations entail frequent meetings with stakeholders to jointly share, discuss, update, plan, and facilitate activities. Periodic trend review by providers and payers is important and may be held in one or more forums, such as joint (clinical) operational meetings and care management rounds.

When aggregate results deviate from the desired targets, program leaders and contributors should conduct drill downs into the data and use quality improvement tools such as a root cause analysis to identify opportunities for improvement. Armed with that analysis, they may seek additional data, reinforce knowledge, address process gaps, and/or redesign the intervention.

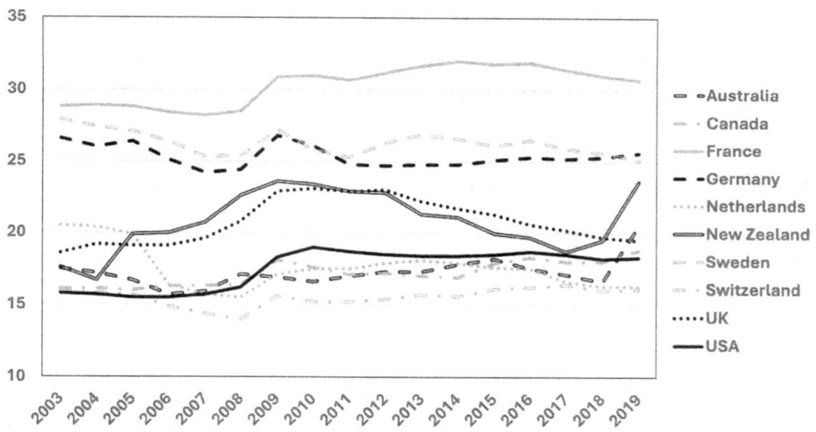

FIGURE 4. Public social expenditure, percentage (%) of gross domestic product (GDP). Health Expenditure and Financing. OECD Health Data, July 2024. U.S.-peer countries were selected based on data availability every year in the data set; countries were selected based on those typically used in comparisons published by the Commonwealth Fund.

Physician leaders play a crucial role in the successful design and implementation of VBC and related programs, and their contributions can serve organizations best through formal team management rather than in a consultative capacity. They provide informed guidance and support for team members and providers in addition to trusted accountability within and outside the organization. Their expertise and leadership are essential for achieving desired goals thanks to their ability to drive improvement in the face of a constantly changing environment and rising rates of clinician burnout.

Community and Social Services

The United States has historically spent less money on social programs than or about the same as its international peers (Figure 4). Those services include paid sick leave, rehabilitation services, residential care, and pensions. While public social spending has increased since 2009, it remains below that of several other countries. The U.S. lags behind all or most of its peers in spending on family programs, unemployment, incapacity, and housing, among other areas. The relatively recent focus on addressing SDoH needs through the healthcare system is laudable but upstream solutions akin to those of other countries may yield health and well-being outcomes similar to theirs.

Routine screening for determining unmet social needs and providing referrals to community resources and social services addresses socioeconomic factors that hinder access to care. This focus can involve connecting patients with services related to housing, food assistance, transportation, and other essential needs.[10,22,23] Programs like the Accountable Health Communities incentivize healthcare organizations to address unmet needs.[22] Both provider and payer organizations engage community-based organizations and social services to provide support in navigating SDoH resources through live and digital solutions. The key strategies for successful support programs include:[12,22,24,25]

- Multidisciplinary care, which casts a wide net both within and outside the organization.
- Assessment of community health needs and assets, typically conducted by provider organizations.
- Patient screening and referral programs, performed by providers and payers.
- Partnerships with CBOs through formal contracts; payers use subcontractor arrangements that facilitate payment for CBO services that are otherwise not reimbursable.
- Integration of social workers into the assessment, guidance, and coordination of access for individuals who qualify for various community and social services.
- Deployment of community health workers, particularly those recruited from the same community to complement other support programs.

Social workers, community health workers, and other support staff address patients' SDoH needs by facilitating access to CBOs and social services that may yield significant savings. Social and CBO services include assistance with housing, food, employment, financial assistance, disability issues, protective services, legal advice, and representation.

CBOs also provide resource navigation advice, support for self-management of chronic conditions, and linkage to other services. Clinical-community and other partnerships were demonstrated to yield substantial reductions in mortality and cost.[26] Despite limitations, a growing body of literature shows that the use of social services and other SDoH interventions optimizes healthcare utilization, cost, and quality.

A two-year analysis of a call center-based process for referral to social services showed a 10% greater cost reduction among Medicare beneficiaries who benefited from this initiative than a comparable group whose needs were not met.[27] Greater reductions were achieved among high-risk patients and those managed by risk-bearing entities.

Chapter Summary

Physician leaders can drive significant improvements in quality, health status, satisfaction, and cost. Successful program implementation requires broad collaboration, thoughtful planning, effective communication, ongoing monitoring, information sharing, and engagement of nontraditional partners including community-based organizations. The healthcare sector will continue to evolve leading to both headwinds and opportunities to achieve program goals.

REFERENCES

1. Blumenthal D, Gumas ED, Shah A, et al. Mirror, Mirror 2024: A Portrait of the Failing U.S. Health System — Comparing Performance in 10 Nations. *The Commonwealth Fund*. September 2024. Accessed October 11, 2024. https://doi.org/10.26099/ta0g-zp66.
2. Singh GK, Daus GP, Allender M, et al. Social Determinants of Health in the United States: Addressing Major Health Inequality Trends for the Nation, 1935-2016. *Int J MCH AIDS*. 2017;6(2):139–164. doi: 10.21106/ijma.236.
3. Okunrintemi V, Khera R, Spatz ES, et al. Association of Income Disparities with Patient-Reported Healthcare Experience. *J Gen Intern Med*. 2019 Jun;34(6):884–892. doi: 10.1007/s11606-019-04848-4.
4. Haggerty J, Levesque JF, Harris M, et al. Does Healthcare Inequity Reflect Variations in Peoples' Abilities To Access Healthcare? Results From a Multi-Jurisdictional Interventional Study in Two High-Income Countries. *Int J Equity Health*. 2020 Sep 25;19(1):167. doi: 10.1186/s12939-020-01281-6.
5. Travers JL, Cohen CC, Dick AW, Stone PW. The Great American Recession and Forgone Healthcare: Do Widened Disparities Between African-Americans and Whites Remain? *PLoS ONE*. 2017;12(12): e0189676. https://doi.org/10.1371/journal.pone.0189676.
6. Clarke JL, Bourn S, Skoufalos A, et al. An Innovative Approach to Health Care Delivery for Patients with Chronic Conditions. *Popul Health Manag*. 2017 Feb;20(1):23–30. doi: 10.1089/pop.2016.0076.
7. Fiscella K, Sanders MR. Racial and Ethnic Disparities in the Quality of Health Care. *Annu Rev Public Health*. 2016;37:375–394. doi: 10.1146/annurev-publhealth-032315-021439.
8. The Peterson Center on Healthcare and KFF. Total Share of U.S. Population Uninsured, 2010–First Quarter of 2023. *Health System Tracker*. https://www.healthsystemtracker.org/indicator/access-affordability/percent-uninsured/#Total%20share%20of%20U.S.%20population%20uninsured,%20 2010%20-%20first%20quarter%20of%202023. Accessed December 21, 2024.
9. Caldararo KL, Nash DB. Population Health Research: Early Description of the Organizational Shift Toward Population Health Management and Defining a Vision for Leadership. *College of Population Health Faculty Papers*. 2017; Paper 79. Accessed September 16, 2024.https://jdc.jefferson.edu/healthpolicyfaculty/79.
10. Baum A, Batniji R, Ratcliffe H, et al. Supporting Rising-Risk Medicaid Patients Through Early Intervention. *NEJM Catalyst*. 2024;5(11):1–21. doi.org/10.1056/cat.24.0060.
11. Wammes JJG, van der Wees PJ, Tanke MAC, et al. Systematic Review of High-Cost Patients' Characteristics and Healthcare Utilisation. *BMJ Open*. 2018;8:e023113. doi: 10.1136/bmjopen-2018-023113.
12. Ravaghi H, Guisset AL, Elfeky S, et al. A Scoping Review of Community Health Needs and Assets Assessment: Concepts, Rationale, Tools and Uses. *BMC Health Serv Res*. 2023 Jan 17;23(1):44. doi: 10.1186/s12913-022-08983-3.
13. Centers for Medicare & Medicaid Services. CMS Focus on Health Equity. Measures Management System. Accessed September 16, 2024. https://mmshub.cms.gov/about-quality/quality-at-CMS/quality/cms-focus-on-health-equity.
14. National Center for Health Workforce Analysis. Health Resources & Services Administration. State of the Primary Care Workforce, 2024. Accessed December 12, 2024. https://bhw.hrsa.gov/sites/default/files/bureau-health-workforce/state-of-the-primary-care-workforce-report-2024.pdf.
15. Borsa A, Bejarano G, Ellen M, Bruch JD. Evaluating Trends in Private Equity Ownership and Impacts on Health Outcomes, Costs, and Quality: Systematic Review. *BMJ* 2023; 382:e075244. doi:10.1136/bmj-2023-075244.
16. Centers for Medicare & Medicaid Services. Announcement of Calendar Year (CY) 2023 Medicare Advantage (MA) Capitation Rates and Part C and Part D Payment Policies. Accessed September 16, 2024. https://www.cms.gov/files/document/2023-announcement.pdf.
17. The Peterson Center on Healthcare and KFF. *Health System Tracker*. Accessed September 16, 2024. https://www.healthsystemtracker.org/dashboard/.

18. Mays GP, Mamaril CB. Public Health Spending and Medicare Resource Use: A Longitudinal Analysis of U.S. Communities. *Health Serv Res.* 2017;52:2357–2377. https://doi.org/10.1111/1475-6773.12785.
19. Howard SW, Bradford N, Belue R, et al. Building Alternative Payment Models in Health Care. *Front. Health Serv.* 2024;4:1235913. doi: 10.3389/frhs.2024.1235913.
20. Mitton C, Dionne F, Donaldson C. Managing Healthcare Budgets in Times of Austerity: The Role of Program Budgeting and Marginal Analysis. *Appl Health Econ Health Policy.* 2014 Apr;12(2):95–102. doi: 10.1007/s40258-013-0074-5.
21. Ogbeiwi O. Why Written Objectives Need To Be Really SMART. *Bri J Healthcare Management.* 2017;23(7):324–336.
22. Ruiz Escobar E, Pathak S, Blanchard CM. Screening and Referral Care Delivery Services and Unmet Health-Related Social Needs: A Systematic Review. *Prev Chronic Dis.* 2021 Aug;12;18:E78. doi: 10.5888/pcd18.200569.
23. National Academies of Sciences, Engineering, and Medicine. *Metrics That Matter for Population Health Action: Workshop Summary.* Washington, DC: The National Academies Press, 2016. DOI: 10.17226/21899.
24. Fiore JA, Madison AJ, Poisal JA, et al. National Health Expenditure Projections, 2023-32: Payer Trends Diverge as Pandemic-Related Policies Fade. *Health Aff* (Millwood). 2024 Jul;43(7):910–921. doi: 10.1377/hlthaff.2024.00469.
25. Edwards ST, Saha S, Prentice JC, Pizer SD. Preventing Hospitalization with Veterans Affairs Home-Based Primary Care: Which Individuals Benefit Most? *J Am Geriatr Soc.* 2017 Aug;65(8):1676–1683. doi: 10.1111/jgs.14843.
26. Honeycutt AA, Khavjou OA, Tayebali Z, et al. Cost-Effectiveness of Social Determinants of Health Interventions: Evaluating Multisector Community Partnerships' Efforts. *Am J Prev Med.* 2024 Dec;67(6):916–923. doi: 10.1016/j.amepre.2024.07.016.
27. Pruitt Z, Emechebe N, Quast T, et al. Expenditure Reductions Associated with a Social Service Referral Program. *Popul Health Manag.* 2018 Dec;21(6):469–476. doi: 10.1089/pop.2017.0199.

SECTION 3

Governance

CHAPTER 8

Health Systems Governance

Adia Ross, MD, MHA, and David Zaas, MD, MBA

HALM CORE CONTENT:

- 3.1 Health system governance structure (e.g., bylaws, articles of incorporation) and operations (e.g., board member selection, education, orientation, monitoring, and assessment)
  - 3.1.1 Board member conflicts of interest, dualities of interest
  - 3.1.2 Administrative staff conflicts of interest, dualities of interest
- 3.2 Health system governing board models, roles, and responsibilities, e.g.:
  - 3.2.1 Financial oversight (nonprofit vs. for-profit settings)
  - 3.2.2 Patient safety and assurance of the quality of care
  - 3.2.3 Preservation of assets, reputation, and risk management
  - 3.2.4 Statutory and regulatory compliance
  - 3.2.5 Strategic planning
- 3.8 Organizational-level committee structure and participation
- 3.9 Management of single-entity versus federation of entities
- 3.10 Matrix management (e.g., medical group, health plan)
- 3.11 Coalition building
- 3.12 Managing competition (internal and external)
- 3.13 Interface to medical transport systems
- 3.14 Foundational model and health system direction

CASE SCENARIO:

A multi-state hospital system is considering acquiring another hospital. The hospital is geographically located outside of its primary service area. What governance structures and governing bodies should they consider creating or modifying to ensure that the new hospital is aligned with the mission and vision of the parent organization? When evaluating the new hospital's local governance structure, what factors should they review?

Health System Governance Structure

THE GOVERNANCE OF HOSPITALS and the effectiveness of the governance models is an important topic for physician leaders to understand. It is important to understand how hospitals are governed and held accountable to their community and larger organizations for the long-term stewardship of healthcare services in their community.

This chapter will define hospital and health system governance and review the distinct types of internal and external governance structures. A key focus will be on how governance structures support and ensure high-quality care is provided to the entity's community.

DEFINING HOSPITAL GOVERNANCE

Hospital governance can be defined as a "set of structures and processes that define the strategic direction for the hospital and the means by which resources are assembled and allocated to achieve them.[1] Hospitals and health systems are responsible and accountable for providing excellent, reliable, safe care in a sustainable way. The World Health Organization defines five key areas of organizational accountability:[1]

1. Compliance, ethics, and risk management: Adhering to legal and ethical standards for how resources are allocated and care is delivered; assessment and mitigation of organizational risk.
2. Clinical governance and reputation management: Ensuring healthcare is delivered in a safe manner and rooted in acceptable standards of care.
3. Financial stewardship and preservation of assets: Tracking how funds are allocated and ensuring financially sustainable business practices and robust financial controls.
4. Political and governmental accountability: Enabled through government regulations.
5. Patient accountability and transparency: Promoting patient engagement and public engagement at all levels of organizations.

Internal and external governance models hold health systems accountable for their mission to their community. Table 1 describes the most common mechanisms.

Impact of Hospital Ownership Structure on Governing Board Configurations

In the United States, there are three main types of hospital corporate ownership structures: not-for-profit charitable hospitals, for-profit (publicly or privately owned) hospitals, and government entities. Federal, state, and local laws dictate how governing bodies must be structured. Each hospital type has different governing board require-

TABLE 1. Examples of External and Internal Governance Structures

	Types	Sample List of Tactics
External Governance	Governmental agencies	Impose government regulations about corporate responsibility, mandated quality, and fiscal standards.
	Accreditation bodies	Establish standard of care guidelines for certification. Compliance may lead to increase market share and more favorable payer contracts.
	Reputational programs	Define excellence performance, which may drive consumer behavior.
Internal Governance	Hospital and health system boards	Align the organization's strategic goals and priorities.
	Internal alignment structures	Establish national or regional service line structures. Integrate key support functions (e.g., supply chain, pharmacy, IT, HR). Establish hospital committees. Use matrix management to promote clinical integration across care settings.

ments and composition.[2,3] The most frequent type of hospital ownership structure is not for profit or government owned.[3]

EXTERNAL GOVERNANCE STRUCTURES

All hospitals that receive governmental funding must adhere to the standards of the Centers for Medicare and Medicaid Services (CMS). CMS dictates the specific roles and responsibilities that hospital governing bodies must fulfill. This is achieved through the CMS Conditions of Participation (COPs). According to CMS, all hospitals must have a governance structure that "is legally responsible for the conduct of the hospital."[4] Based on the various hospital configurations (Table 2), there may be other regulatory or legal requirements that the hospital boards are required to meet.

Lastly, most hospitals and health systems use organizations called deeming bodies. Deeming bodies are organizations that CMS delegates authority to validate that a given hospital meets the regulatory requirements for the COPs. Organizations such as The Joint Commission[5] and DNV[6] may have additional requirements for certification.

INTERNAL GOVERNANCE STRUCTURES

Many hospitals are affiliated with or owned by larger health systems. Health systems can have one centralized governing body that manages all facilities as a single entity or decentralized governing bodies with a federation of governing bodies. Many of the options for structure are dictated by state law.

TABLE 2. Board Composition Types[2,3]

Types of Boards		
Board Type	**Board Composition and Selection**	**Other Key Facts**
For-profit hospital	May be privately owned or publicly traded. If privately owned, board is usually composed of owners or individuals selected by the owners. If publicly owned, the board members are elected shareholders of the company; board members must be publicly disclosed. The hospital is subject to corporate laws as well as federal and state laws.	Board must act to the benefit of shareholders and to increase shareholder value. Represents approximately 36% of the types of hospitals in the U.S.
Not-for-profit hospital, tax-exempt	Hospital must focus on the charitable mission of the hospital or system. Board selects its own members and removes them (with cause).	These organizations are considered charitable organizations and therefore subjected to IRS rules around board independence. Represents approximately 49% of U.S. hospitals.
Government owned, public entity hospital	Boards are either elected or appointed by elected officials or a governmental agency. Board members cannot be selected by board or removed by the board.	Board meetings are open to the public and press with only limited ability to go into confidential closed sessions. Represents approximately 14.7% of U.S. hospitals.

Organizations with decentralized governing bodies can have multiple governing bodies within a governing body hierarchy.[7] The hierarchical structure may include national, regional, multi-state, or single-state governing bodies. The responsibilities of the multiple governing bodies may vary as outlined in the hospital bylaws and articles of incorporation. This structure allows facilities to leverage centralization to maintain market share, seize on capital investment opportunities, eliminate care variation through standardizing practices, and gain efficiencies in supply chain and resource allocation.[8]

A given hospital board may report out to other boards within the health system and to a "parent" or system board. As a result, each governing board may have specific responsibilities and functions delegated to it, but the parent or system board may have ultimate authority.[7]

At an entity level, most hospitals have a structure in which both the organized medical staff and the executive leadership team report to a local governing body. The organized medical staff, through its medical executive committee, is responsible for the quality of care provided to patients, and the CEO or facility executive is responsible for managing the hospital. The typical local hospital structure is shown in Figure 1.

Key considerations when determining governance structure are:[8]

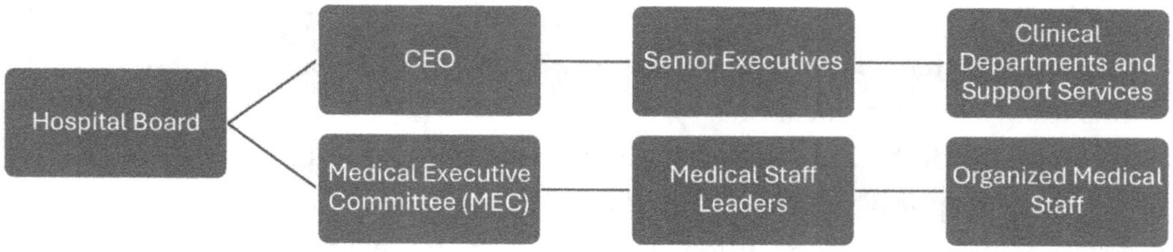

FIGURE 1. Typical Local Hospital Governance Structure

- Size of the system.
- Geographic locations of entity facilities.
- Diversity of the patient populations served.
- Cultures and subcultures across the organization.

KEY HOSPITAL GOVERNING BODY ROLES AND RESPONSIBILITIES: FIDUCIARY DUTIES AND MANAGING CONFLICTS OF INTEREST

Individual board members are considered stewards and fiduciaries of the organization they oversee and are responsible for the care that the hospital provides. There are several key areas that a hospital governing body is legally responsible for overseeing to remain compliant with the CMS COPs.[4] This list applies to all hospitals that receive Medicare funding.

- Approve the hospital's written scope of services.
- Appoint the CEO who is responsible for managing the hospital.
- Ensure performance improvement activities occur and that the scope of performance improvement reflects the complexity of the facility.
- Approve the structure of the medical staff.
- Along with the leaders of the medical executive committee and the hospital leadership team, define conflicts of interest that could affect patient care or hospital operations.
- Ensure a regular evaluation of the culture of safety and quality using validated instruments.
- Ensure care of patients occurs under the appropriately licensed professionals and that those professionals are available on-call and throughout a patient's hospitalization.
- Ensure that the facility has an institutional plan that includes an operating budget and capital expenditures. This plan must be reviewed and updated annually. The plan must be under the direction of the governing body and prepared by a committee that is representative of the board, administrative staff, and medical staff.
- Review and ensure the adequacy of contractors for services in both scope and nature of services to ensure safe, effective care.

- Ensure that emergency services meet all regulatory and statutory requirements and have written policies and procedures around the provision of emergency care, including all off-site locations.
- Approve the organized medical staffs credentialing process.
- Review and approve all medical staff bylaws.
- Establish a complaint resolution process and ensure that patients and families are aware; this responsibility can be delegated to the complaint resolution committee.
- Appoint qualified infection preventionist(s) to administer the hospital's infection prevention and control program.
- Appoint a qualified individual (or individuals) to oversee the antibiotic stewardship program.

Depending on the type of hospital corporate structure, the entity may be subject to other legal or regulatory statutes.

Each hospital must have written hospital bylaws that codify the governing body's responsibilities and detail what responsibilities are delegated to the medical executive committee or CEO.

The key themes of board responsibilities fall into three main fiduciary categories: duty of care, duty of loyalty, and duty of obedience.[9]

Duty of care requires that board members act in good faith, including making informed decisions, being engaged in discussions to determine the completeness of the information presented to them, and exercising business judgment in the best interest of the organization without self-interest.

Duty of loyalty (also known as duality of interest) requires board members to avoid conflicts of interest, such as serving on multiple boards with competing interests, which could make it difficult for them to consider strategic priorities, investments, and initiatives for the organization with its best interests solely in mind.

Duty of obedience requires board members to comply with all laws, rules, and regulations as well as bylaws and corporate articles. By adhering to the duties of care, loyalty, obedience board members can be protected from individual lawsuits through board immunity.[9]

In addition, the board is responsible for creating its own structures to ensure that it runs effectively, including creating processes for board orientation, comprehensive conflict of interest statements and disclosure policies, ethics training, evaluation, recruitment, board policies, establishing committees, selection of officers, etc.

Lastly, it is the responsibility of the governing bodies to ensure that administrative, clinical staff, and organized medical staff act in ways that are in the best interest of the hospital and the patients it serves. As a result, hospitals should ensure that their conflict-of-interest statements and disclosure policies also include their hospital providers and administrative professionals.

Role of Board Committees

Federal regulations do not require that a hospital board establish committees. However, depending on the state in which the board is incorporated, state corporate law may dictate that some committees be established. If there is no legal requirement to establish committees, the hospital bylaws can dictate whether board committees are required based on the entity and community needs. The hospital bylaws can also stipulate which committees are required to be standing committees versus ad hoc.

A board's committee structure can serve as an effective way for the board to fulfill its duties. Governing boards can empower their subcommittees to make decisions that are binding. The most common board committees are:[9]

- Governance
- Nominating
- Credentialing and Medical Safety
- Patient Safety and Clinical Quality
- Finance
- Compensation
- Strategic Planning
- Executive
- Community Benefit

Board-Specific Responsibilities Related to Quality and Safety

Hospitals are required to have structured effective, ongoing, hospital-wide, data-driven quality assessment and performance improvement (QAPI) plans.[4] It is the responsibility of the board, in collaboration with the CEO and medical executive committee, to ensure that certain elements are fulfilled with the program and are available to be presented to CMS upon request:[4]

- Reflects the complexity of the services provided.
- Is inclusive of all hospital departments and services including contracted services.
- Ensures that the program focuses on indicators related to "improved health outcomes and the prevention and reduction of medical errors."
- Ensures that the focus of the QAPI includes priority areas for improvement and that these improvement efforts are evaluated.

One area of focus has been whether a board is actively involved in assessing the effectiveness of the QAPI plan at their hospital. CMS now stipulates that the hospital board must be engaged and periodically review the hospital's QAPI program.

Hospitals that are high performers in quality-of-care measures review their quality dashboards at least quarterly, appoint board members with healthcare quality expertise, and tie the compensation of their CEOs in part to quality metrics.[10,11]

Internal Governance Structures: Role of Hospital and Health System Executive Leadership in the Organization Foundation Model and Setting Health System Direction

The board delegates the responsibility of corporate and clinical management to the CEO and medical staff, respectively.[9] The CEO is responsible for managing the daily operations of the hospital, while the medical executive committee is responsible for overseeing the performance of the members of the organized medical staff.

The board should be focused on long-ranging strategic planning and the ongoing assessment of the hospital's ability to fulfill its mission. Execution and tactic deployment is the responsibility of the executive team. As corporate board expert David Nadler stated, "[boards] should be seats of challenge and inquiry that add value without meddling and [should] make CEOs more effective but not all-powerful."[12]

Due to the complexity of care and the need for economies of scale, many hospitals choose to affiliate or be owned by larger entities. In addition, because the healthcare landscape continues to shift from "volume to value," unique competitive forces have led health systems to integrate with other entities across the care continuum.

To receive the maximal benefit of integration, additional internal governance mechanisms must be implemented to manage the connection between entities to ensure coordination of care occurs across the care continuum and to continually meet stakeholder and patient needs.

As they begin to integrate with each other, organizations can use three main types of alignment or internal governance tactics: structural, functional, and process.[13] Table 3 describes each type of integration.

Structural Integration as a Governance Tool to Manage Competition

Entity-specific competitive pressures and unsustainable costs influence health system strategies around the type of structural integration that they pursue. There are two types of structural integration: vertical and horizontal. Figure 2 provides an example of vertical versus horizontal integration.[14]

Vertical integration occurs when an organization purchases another organization along the care continuum. Vertical integration usually combines "buyers" and "sellers"

TABLE 3. Types of Hospital Integration[13]

Type of Integration	Description	Examples
Structural integration	Usually involves operational, financial, and legal structures that bind the entities together.	Integration of hospital operations across entities, creating a single EHR.
Functional integration	Formal process and protocols are designed to coordinate activities and support shared accountability among entities through centralized decision-making.	Centralizing HR, IT, supply chain, pharmacy, planning and budgeting.
Process (or clinical integration)	The integration of patient care across people, functions, and entities.	Standardizing service lines, utilizing the EHR to create standardized protocols, implementing team-based care models.

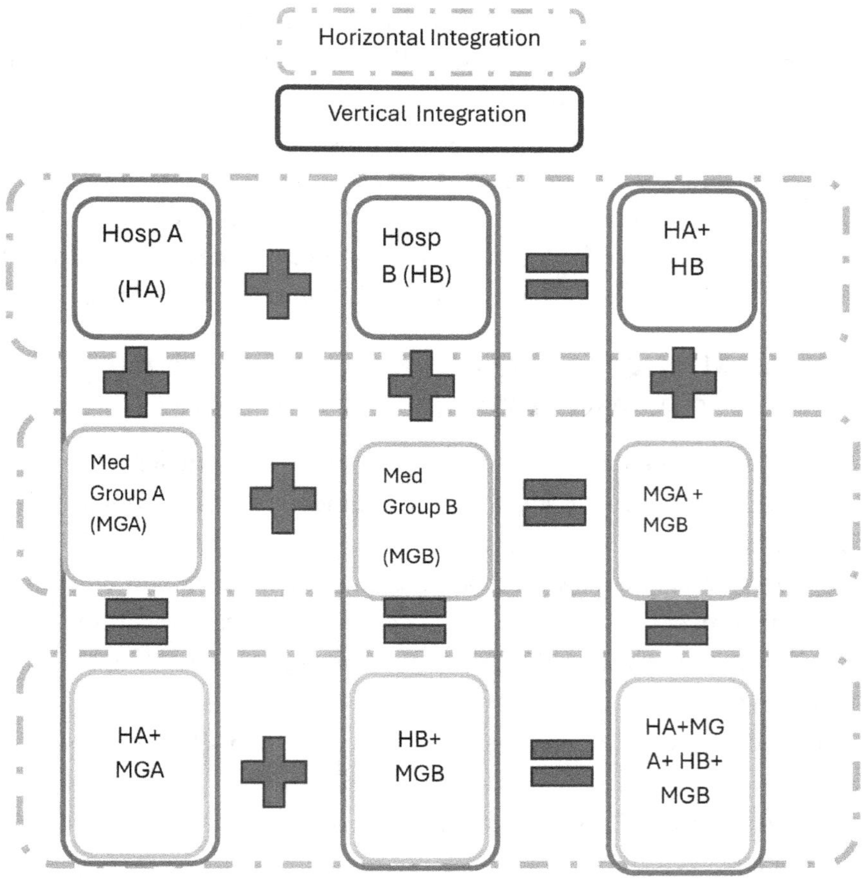

FIGURE 2. Vertical versus Horizontal Integration

to decrease the transaction costs associated with non-integrated services across the care continuum, as well as increase network size.[15]

Horizontal integration occurs when an organization expands by purchasing an entity similar to its existing entity. This acquisition can increase total market share. It also can allow health systems to develop "hub" and "spoke" models that facilitate more complex care to be provided at the" hub" and less complex at the "spokes." In summary, horizontal integration helps with economies of scale, and vertical integration benefits economies of scope.[15,16]

Leveraging Service Line Management for Health System Clinical Integration and Through the Implementation of Matrix Management

Healthcare organizations must be organizationally resilient. To retain high performance in the face of rapidly changing regulatory requirements, workforce challenges, and evolving technology and market and clinical complexity, health systems must constantly evolve their complement of services and organizational structure.

Care at the patient's bedside is inherently multidisciplinary; it requires various disciplines to effectively "govern" the patient's care. However, historically, health systems have not been as clinically integrated with regard to administration. This traditional structure can make it more difficult to make strategic or financial decisions across the care continuum, eliminate care variation, or meet stakeholder demands for transparency.[10]

TRADITIONAL VERSUS MULTIDIVISIONAL ORGANIZATIONAL STRUCTURES

Traditional organizational structures align staff and providers in departments and care settings; they rely on top-down, single-command hierarchies. Functional departments are well-defined with single-line authority, usually to a CEO or facility executive. However, this structure alone without additional mechanisms to promote multidisciplinary administrative thinking and process development, leads to discipline-centered thinking, misaligned incentives and rarely serves patient care needs in their entirety.[17]

An alternative to the traditional organizational structure is a multidivisional structure that includes service (or product) lines designed to meet specific patient population needs. There has been some evidence to support that such structures lead to lower re-admissions, less ED utilization, improved patient satisfaction and improved clinical outcomes.[17]

A matrix administrative governance system is often established to promote the use of this new structure. This structure seeks to align functional (subject matter expertise or service line) expertise with a project or whole business unit (i.e., hospital operational and patient flow expertise of a hospital entity structure).

TABLE 4. Examples of Typical Roles within the Matrix Administrative Governance System[17,18,19]

Role	Responsibility
Entity Facility Executive (ex. Hospital CEO)	• Responsible for coordinating all activities within the entity inclusive of service lines. • Has ultimate P+L accountability for the entire organizational unit.
Entity Senior Executive (ex. Hospital CMO)	• Entity senior executive who may have delegated P+L accountability for service line performance at the individual entity. • Responsible with service line executive to ensure local goals align with service line priorities.
Service Line Executive	• Responsible for cascading the strategic vision and tactics specific to their individual service line. • Assists the entity service line leader in day-to-day operations. • Works closely with entity leadership to enact local plan deployment. • Usually has dual reporting relationship to a health system service line executive and an entity facility executive.
Assigned Entity Matrix Service Line Manager	• Assigned to a specific facility or entity. • Charged within enacting the service lines strategies locally. • Has dual reporting to a local entity senior leader and service line leader.
Front-line staff within the matrix	• Responsible for day-to-day patient care or support services for the service line. • Usually only has one supervisor (the entity service line manager)

The most effective matrix models align high-level strategic goals with the need for local, coordinated execution within a given hospital and require strategic collaboration or coalition building. These coalitions are important to ensuring strategies align with various stakeholders' needs and that buy-in exists for key initiatives.

Coalition building is important from idea generation to execution.[20] There are five main roles in a matrix administrative system. Table 4 outlines each role and its function.

Hospital Governance Structures and Interface with Medical Transportation

Interaction with medical transportation teams, both internal and external to health systems, helps to ensure patients have access to care. Many health systems collaborate with county emergency medical services and transportation companies to develop shared protocols policies and governance structures to ensure that care delivered pre-hospitalization meets acceptable standards.

Chapter Summary

The governance of health systems is complex and includes both internal and external governance mechanisms to ensure that high-value, reliable, and safe care is provided to patients. There are different governing bodies and mechanisms that exist with specific roles and responsibilities to ensure this occurs.

Governance and management are related but are not the same. Administrative structures can be deployed within a health system to ensure both occur. It is important for physician leaders to understand this topic to be effective patient advocates within a complex system.

REFERENCES

1. Jalilvand MA, Raeisi AR, Shaarbafchizadeh N. Hospital Governance Accountability Structure: A Scoping Review. *BMC Health Serv Res.* 2024;24:47. https://doi.org/10.1186/s12913-023-10135-0
2. Orlikoff J. *Effective Governance Systems.* Trustee Insights. American Hospital Association. April 2022. Accessed December 1, 2024. https://trustees.aha.org/system/files/media/file/2022/04/TI_0422_orlikoff.pdf
3. Welch WP, Xu L, De Lew N, Sommers BD. *Hospital Ownership Data Brief.* US Department of Health and Human Services Office of the Assistant Secretary of Planning and Evaluation Services. August 2023. Accessed November 29, 2024. https://aspe.hhs.gov/sites/default/files/documents/582de65f285646af741e14f82b6df1f6/hospital-ownership-data-brief.pdf
4. Conditions of Participation for Hospitals. 42 § 428 (2024) eCFR :: 42 CFR Part 482 -- Conditions of Participation for Hospitals.
5. The Joint Commission's Requirements on Boards. Accessed November 1, 2024. https://www.jcrinc.com/-/media/jcr/jcr-documents/our-priorities/board-education/joint-commission-requirements-for-the-board-071123-final-version.pdf
6. DNV. National Integrated Accreditation For Healthcare Organizations (NIAHO®) Accreditation Requirements, Interpretive Guidelines & Surveyor Guidance for Hospitals. Accessed on December 1, 2024. https://www.dnv.us/services/acute-care-hospital-accreditation-219000/
7. Wagner S. *A Taxonomy of Healthcare Boards.* Trustee Insights. American Hospital Association. September 2023. Accessed November 1, 2024. https://trustees.aha.org/system/files/media/file/2023/09/TI_0923_orlikoff_interview_3.pdf
8. Murphy S, Peisert KC, Murphy CJ. Board Organization and Structure: An Intentional Governance Guide: Trends, Tips and Tools. The Governance Institute. Fall 2015 Accessed November 23, 2024. https://nrchealth.com/wp-content/uploads/2017/05/Board-Organization-Structure_An-Intentional-Governance-Guide_Patrick-M....pdf
9. Anning D, Entin F, Totten M. The Guide to Good Governance for Hospital Boards. Center for Healthcare Governance. December 2009. https://trustees.aha.org/sites/default/files/trustees/09-guide-to-good-governance.pdf
10. Jha A, Epstein A. Hospital Governance and the Quality of Care. *Health Aff* (Millwood). 2010 Jan-Feb;29(1):182–187. https://www.healthaffairs.org/doi/10.1377/hlthaff.2009.0297. Epub 2009 Nov 6.
11. Tsai TC, Jha A, Gawande A, Huckman RS, Bloom N, Sadun R. Hospital Board and Management Practices Are Strongly Related to Hospital Performance on Clinical Quality Metrics. *Health Aff (Millwood).* 2015;34(8):1304–1311. Accessed November 29, 2024 https://www.healthaffairs.org/doi/pdf/10.1377/hlthaff.2014.1282
12. Nadler D. Building Better Boards. *Harvard Business Review,* May 2004. Accessed November 1, 2024. https://hbr.org/2004/05/building-better-boards .
13. Ridgely MS, Buttorff C, Wolf LJ, et al. The Importance of Understanding and Measuring Health System Structural, Functional, and Clinical Integration. *Health Serv Res.* 2020;55(Suppl. 3):1049–1061. https://doi.org/10.1111/1475-6773.13582
14. Heeringa J, Mutti A, Furukawa MF, Lechner A, Maurer KA, Rich E. Horizontal and Vertical Integration

of Health Care Providers: A Framework for Understanding Various Provider Organizational Structures. *Int J Integr Care*. 2020;20(1):2. https://doi.org/10.5334/ijic.4635.

15. Thaldorf C, Liberman A. Integration of Health Care Organizations: Using the Power Strategies of Horizontal and Vertical Integration in Public and Private Health Systems. *Health Care Manag (Frederick)*. 2007 Apr-Jun;26(2):116–127. doi: 10.1097/01.HCM.0000268614.41115.fc. PMID: 17464224.
16. Khuntia J, Ning X, Stacey R. Competition and Integration of US Health Systems in the Post-COVID-19 New Normal: Cross-sectional Survey *JMIR Form Res.* 2022;6(3):e32477 doi: 10.2196/32477
17. Westphal JA. Resilient Organizations: Matrix Model and Service Line Management. *J Nurs Adm.* 2005 Sep;35(9):414-419. doi: 10.1097/00005110-200509000-00012. PMID: 16200010.
18. Finerty SZ. *Master the Matrix: 7 Essentials for Things Done in Complex Organizations.* Columbus, SC: Two Harbors Press; 2022.
19. Hall K. *Making the Matrix Work: How Matrix Managers Engage People and Cut Through Complexity.* Finland: Nicholas Brealey Publishing; 2014.
20. DeLuca JR. *Political Savvy: Systematic Approaches to Leadership Behind-the-Scenes*. Berwyn, PA: Evergreen Business Group; 1999.

CHAPTER 9

Medical Staff Governance & Leadership

Doug Koekkoek, MD, FACP, SFHM

HALM CORE CONTENT:

- 3.3 Health system physician leadership roles
- 3.4 Medical staff structure and its relationship to governing bodies (e.g., board oversight of credentialing, privileging, employed vs. voluntary models, and disciplinary process)
- 3.5 Medical staff call obligations and compensation

CASE SCENARIO:

Dr. JS is a seasoned vascular surgeon hoping to move his practice to the hospital. Although he has been in practice for many years across town at a competing hospital system, he has had two partners retire recently, so he is closing that practice and joining an existing practice at the hospital.

He applies for privileges through an online application that performs criminal and malpractice background checks; verifies his medical school, residency, and fellowship credentials; and ensures his specialty board certification is current.

His application is approved by the Credentials Committee, Medical Executive Committee, and community board. After a provisionary review of a specified number of procedures through a focused professional practice evaluation (FPPE), he is granted full privileges and begins his clinical work at the facility.

Dr. JS enjoys several years of active practice and becomes a respected member of the medical staff. This year, several complaints surfaced through the variance reporting system that his clinical skills are "slipping," as evidenced by long operating room times and several cases with complications. Simultaneously, a review of his ongoing professional practice evaluation (OPPE) metrics by the department chair shows a slightly higher operative mortality rate and higher than predicted "return to the operating room in 24 hours" than his peer vascular surgeons. How does the hospital evaluate and manage this situation to ensure quality care is provided to its patients and it prevents any risk of harm to patients?

THE PRACTICE OF MEDICINE in the United States is a privilege earned by years of education and training. For physicians, that unique and privileged status as a profession means the profession must self-regulate its quality and professional behaviors.[1] The AMA's code of ethics describes it as,

> *Peer review by medical societies, hospital credentials and utilization committees, or other bodies, has long been established by organized medicine to scrutinize professional conduct. The peer review process is intended to balance physicians' right to exercise medical judgment freely with the obligation to do so wisely and temperately. Medicine has a long tradition of self-regulation, based on physicians' enduring commitment to safeguard the welfare of patients and the trust of the public. The obligation to report incompetent or unethical conduct that may put patients at risk is recognized in both the ethical standards of the profession and in law and physicians should be able to report such conduct without fear or loss of favor.*[1]

This obligation to self-govern and manage the quality of its peers is formalized in medical staff structures through bylaws, policies, and the committees described in those documents.

Bylaws, Credentials, Privileges

Medical staff bylaws are the highest order of regulatory documents for the professional medical staff. They are voted on by the entire medical staff, approved by the community board or governing body, and therefore designed to be permanent. Bylaws outline the various categories of medical staff — active, affiliate, and courtesy — and typically describe the various elected offices of the medical staff, including chief of staff (or president of the medical staff), credentials committee chair, departments and their associated chairs, and the membership of the Medical Executive Committee (MEC).

Also included in the bylaws are the qualifications for these roles, the nomination and election process, and the terms of these various offices and committees.[2] The credentialing, peer review, and professionalism policies are often referenced in the bylaws, but are typically a second order of documents and fall under the purview of the Medical Executive Committee and so can be changed and revised more easily because they do not require a vote of the entire medical staff.

Often, these other important policies are assembled into the Medical Staff Rules and Regulations or may be described as the Medical Staff Polices. These documents and policies describe in detail the process and checks and balances that ensure a thorough and fair process in granting privileges and providing oversight to clinical quality.

The Credentials Policy becomes an important policy for each medical staff leader as well as the hospital administrator to understand. The Credentials Policy outlines the process and standards for appointment and reappointment to the hospital's medical staff and the process by which privileges to do various tasks and procedures in the hospital is granted. Privilege criteria are developed by specialty. Those criteria include the required formal education, training, and prior volumes to demonstrate competence.

Under the Credentials Policy, most specialties will have a set of "core" privileges that all specialists who have completed the specified residency or fellowship training will have mastered, and a set of "special" privileges for more unique or less commonly performed procedures that must be individually granted. At the time of reappointment (typically a two-year interval), a physician must reapply for privileges.

At the time of reappointment, the department chair is tasked with reviewing a physician's medical staff file to ensure the training and experience are in place, adequate volumes have continued to be performed, and no quality or professionalism concerns exist. If recommended by the department chair, endorsed by the Credentials Committee, and approved by the MEC and Community Board, the entire two-year cycle begins again.

A point of clarification. *Membership* on the medical staff and *privileges* in the hospital are related but technically different things. A physician has membership based on meeting the medical staff criteria — licensure, board certification, malpractice coverage, references, etc.

Medical staff membership is typically separated into active, affiliate, or courtesy staff categories based on how much volume of work is done in that hospital. Each membership category has specific rights and responsibilities with respect to committee participation, voting on medical staff business, access to continuing education, and other medical staff services.

Privileges, on the other hand, codify what type of clinical work or procedural activity can be done in the hospital where a physician has membership. Privileges are requested at each reappointment cycle and are specific to the physician's specialty. Specific privileges are available if a physician demonstrates appropriate training and recent volume at any facility to ensure adequate competency to perform the specific procedure or clinical activity.

So, membership is about what administrative and committee functions a physician can participate in as a member, while privileges describe what clinical activity the member can perform in the hospital.

Focused Professional Practice Evaluation and Ongoing Professional Practice Evaluation

CMS requires hospital accrediting surveys, which typically are delegated to one of several accrediting organizations, including Det Norske Veritas (DNV) or The Joint Commission. CMS requires that the medical staff performs a preliminary review of physician proficiency at the time of granting privileges.[3] These accrediting surveys all have a Medical Staff portion where the reviewing entity ensures this oversight of competency and privileges is occurring. The Joint Commission refers to the initial evaluation as a focused professional practice evaluation (FPPE).[4]

CMS also requires regular, ongoing review of physician competency, which The Joint Commission refers to as ongoing professional practice evaluation (OPPE). Each hospital has some latitude in selecting what goes into those evaluations. These practice evaluations can take the form of chart reviews, procedure observation, or specific performance metrics (mortality rates, unexpected return to the operating room, readmission rates, etc.) If metrics are selected, they must be relevant to the specific specialty of the provider and measurable at the individual provider level.[5]

A focused professional practice evaluation can also be conducted on a periodic basis for a specific provider and involve a specified privileged activity when quality concerns arise. The "for cause" FPPEs must be confidential and conducted according to the hospital's peer review policy.

Variance Reporting and Protecting Quality of Care

Hospitals invariably employ some type of confidential quality and safety reporting, referred to by terms such as incident reporting systems, variance reporting systems, unusual occurrence reporting systems, and patient safety reporting systems. To succeed, these systems need a supportive environment that protects the privacy of staff who report occurrences.

Ideally, the systems should be used by a broad range of personnel, not just physicians. The events must be cataloged, tracked, and the information disseminated in a timely fashion. And finally, a reliable process must be in place for reviewing reports and developing action plans.[6]

The professional medical staff have accountability for professionalism concerns and clinical competency concerns that are brought forward in the variance reporting system. Professionalism issues may include rude behavior, inappropriate language, privacy or HIPPA infractions, and other concerns. Clinical competency may stem from cognitive or physical impairments that influence the ability to safely deliver care. Gaps in knowledge or technical proficiency also fall under clinical competency concerns.

A process should be in place whereby concerns identified in the variance reporting system, whether professionalism or clinical competency, can be referred to the medical staff structure.[7] Typically, this referral process is codified in the bylaws, professionalism policy, and the peer review policy of the medical staff. The ideal process maintains a high degree of confidentiality, includes an opportunity for the practitioner to convey their recollection of the clinical event or circumstances, and philosophically should be oriented to encourage continuous improvement rather than punitive or disciplinary in nature.

Adverse events and clinical errors must be thought of as important learning opportunities for an entire department. That way, the process can mitigate future safety concerns for the broader medical staff rather than just an individual physician.

There are, of course, "never events" that may result in the loss of privileges or result in a practitioner losing their membership on the medical staff, but those tend to be the exception and result from intentional or egregious actions that take the practitioners far outside the standard of care or represent permanent changes in the physical health of the provider.

Examples of these "never events" exist in both the clinical competency and professionalism domains. Clinical competency concerns that lead to the removal of privileges include physical dexterity and cognitive changes in the physician. Examples are a physician who suffers a stroke that impairs their manual dexterity, uncorrectable loss of visual acuity, and early onset dementia.

Professionalism concerns that could lead to the loss of membership on the medical staff may include ignoring relationship and sexual boundaries with a patient, illegal use or diversion of controlled substances, or intentionally causing physical harm to a patient or caregiver. When privileges are restricted or when membership is unilaterally terminated by leadership, those circumstances are reportable to the State Board of Medicine and the National Practitioner Data Bank (NPDB).[8]

Some evaluations of clinical competency and professionalism take time, and because the decisions have a profound effect on future patient care and the career of a physician, they should not be made in haste. For these reasons, it is often necessary to ask a physician to voluntarily refrain from practice for a finite time frame to allow time for the investigation or evaluation.

When a physician voluntarily refrains from exercising a privilege, it is not considered a reportable event to the NPDB or State Medical Board. If, however, the practitioner does not willingly choose to refrain from practice, the MEC can temporarily suspend a physician's privileges. Because this is an adverse action by the MEC, it becomes a reportable event.

In situations where there may be immediate risk to patient safety, the chief of staff, working in concert with the hospital administrator, can temporarily suspend a physician's privileges pending a more formal decision by the MEC.

Peer Review and Performance Improvement Plans

Many concerns identified by variance reporting and other direct complaints to the medical staff office will, with further investigation, be found to have no merit. Other concerns may simply require brief education on hospital policy or a reminder of expected professional behavior. An even smaller subset will require a performance improvement plan to be put in place.

Most hospitals use a combination of hospital personnel and department chairs to do the initial data gathering and clinical circumstances review. The evaluation should include input from the physician involved. Many times, a peer specialty reviewer is needed to provide specific input when the department chair may not have direct clinical experience in a highly specialized clinical area.

Medical staff policy dictates at what time this evaluation is brought to the peer review committee to make decisions on what action is needed, if any. Confidentiality and impartiality are key fundamentals for a peer review committee to successfully carry out its work without injuring the reputation of its physician workforce. Peer review committee members may have concerns about legal action against them if they put in place a corrective action or restriction of privilege against a colleague, but all 50 states have peer review protection statutes that confer immunity.[9] If a medical staff member in a leadership role on the peer review or MEC is following their medical staff policies and maintaining confidentiality, the medical staff leader has little to worry about in this regard.

Professionalism concerns of a minor nature are best dealt with in a graduated or progressive fashion. A simple conversation between department chair and physician to alert them to the complaint, remind them of the medical staff professionalism policy, and the expectations around behavior, may be all that is necessary.

If ongoing professionalism concerns occur, the medical staff leadership has other interventions at their disposal to encourage a change in behavior. Those interventions may include requiring the physician to explain themselves to the MEC, complete an appropriate educational seminar or curriculum to address the behavior, have privileges temporarily restricted, or participate in an organized coaching or mentoring program.

In instances where the physician involved has no insight or if no improvement is noted, the medical staff can move to terminate membership. All conversations and interventions should be documented in the physician's medical staff office file.

Clinical concerns tend to be addressed with education and retraining if possible. A follow-up focused professional practice evaluation (FPPE) is often used to ensure the intervention has resulted in satisfactory, sustained improvement. And like professionalism concerns, documentation of clinical concerns and the recommended performance improvement plan is of paramount importance to gauge improvement and to ensure future leadership is aware of prior concerns or deficits.

The "Fair" Hearing

Most medical staff bylaws have provisions to ensure due process is provided to physicians on the medical staff with respect to decisions about membership, privileges, or a performance improvement plan.

Typically, these provisions outline a process where a physician member who disagrees with a decision of the MEC that terminates their membership or impacts their ability to exercise their privileges is offered the opportunity to have a group of previously uninvolved medical staff members review the evaluation and decision-making process to assess whether the decision was made in compliance with the medical staff bylaws and policies.

While technically not a legal proceeding and usually conducted without legal representation from either side, these reviews are referred to as a hearing or a "fair hearing." The evaluation is meant to focus on whether the peer review committee and MEC followed its process rather than to revise the recommended action against the physician.

If the hearing finds the process was aligned with all medical staff bylaws and policies, the action will stand. A physician may still sue the hospital or medical staff at this point, but as stated previously, there is broad protection and immunity here for medical staff leaders acting in good faith and according to the governing documents.

Physician Leadership Roles in the Hospital

Most hospitals have an elected leader of the medical staff designated either the chief of staff or president of the medical staff. Typically, a candidate for this position is nominated by either the medical staff or MEC and endorsed by the hospital administration before being put to a vote of the entire medical staff. Many hospitals have a process such that there are progressive roles that must be held before being eligible for the chief of staff such as department chair, secretary or treasurer of the medical staff, and even a probationary period of vice chief of staff or president-elect before they are moved to the lead role.

The chief of staff or president of the medical staff position is typically of limited tenure — often two years. This finite duration of term presents some problems in continuity with physician issues of professionalism or clinical competency that play out over many years, but it ensures mitigation against any cronyism or personal bias, and builds redundancy and depth in the hospital's clinical leadership.

In contrast to the limited term and elected nature of the chief of staff/president of the medical staff role, most hospitals now employ a vice president of medical affairs (VPMA) or a chief medical officer (CMO).[10] Historically, the VPMA title predates the

CMO title, but both are employed leadership roles that are not elected by the medical staff and that report directly to hospital administration.

The VPMA role was developed to provide corporate expertise, consistency, and longevity to the ranks of the hospital physician leadership and was often viewed as a disciplinary role that worked closely with hospital operations to ensure physician compliance with hospital policy, state and local laws, as well as regulatory and accreditation standards. The VPMA would refer physician non-compliance to medical staff committees and ensure that policy was upheld.

The limited scope of VPMA has now been largely replaced with the broader role of the CMO.[11] The CMO still has responsibility for the medical staff office and ensuring physician compliance with policy and regulatory statutes but has been given more accountability for overall hospital quality and safety performance and a host of new obligations around strategy, growth, and innovation of clinical services in the hospital.

Especially with movement toward value-based care revenue, the management of appropriate utilization and cost-effectiveness of the care model are now very important and represent areas the VPMA typically did not address.

Similar to the distinction between the elected medical staff roles of chief of staff/president and the CMO, there are elected departmental physician leadership roles that exist alongside employed medical director roles. What looks somewhat redundant on the surface actually has important distinctions when dissected more fully.

In most non-academic settings, the department chair leadership role is an elected medical staff leader for each specialty area, such as surgery, medicine, anesthesia, obstetrics, and emergency medicine. These chair positions are time-limited, elected by their peers, and for the most part concern themselves with the medical staff affairs of credentials, privileges, peer review, and professionalism issues. The chair may be engaged with quality and patient safety but primarily from the standpoint of the physician's practice and behavior.

Contrast this with an employed medical director or service line physician leader who has responsibility for business development and administrative management of a group of employed physicians, including compensation and scheduling, cost-containment initiatives, and equipment purchasing decisions.

The Changing Nature of Hospital Call Requirements

Requirements for physicians to participate in emergency department subspecialty "call" are included in the Medical Staff Bylaws, Medical Staff Rules and Regulations, or Policies of the Medical Staff. These requirements are aligned with the hospital's Emergency Medical Treatment and Labor Act (EMTALA) obligations and ensure the hospital can reliably provide a full complement of specialty services.

Because these policies are a requirement of a physician's medical staff membership and privileges, there is a strong incentive to participate and take part in the specialty call coverage; otherwise, the physician risks losing the ability to admit and manage patients in the hospital. The medical staff obligation to take emergency call historically has not included any financial incentive.

With the development and spread of ambulatory surgery centers and the expanded ability to provide care in non-hospital settings, however, many medical subspecialists no longer depend on the inpatient setting for a viable practice. Consequently, specialists who do not need inpatient privileges may request a call coverage stipend from the hospital to compensate them for providing this call coverage for the hospital, or they may decide to drop their hospital privileges.

There is also recognition that, depending on the volume of specialty call requests, this commitment can be disruptive for a physician's practice, and especially in essential specialties like general surgery, orthopedics, neurosurgery, and urology, the hospital may want to provide a per-day stipend to secure predictable coverage of specialty call and consultation.

Third-party "fair market value" assessments by specialty are available regarding what a hospital can pay for these call services and not run the risk of overpayment and an anti-kickback statue violation. As a result, most hospitals now have a complicated list of arrangements for emergency call coverage. Some of that coverage is non-reimbursed medical staff obligations and some includes a daily stipend that is negotiated each year and varies in amount across specialties.

Chapter Summary

The functional processes and committees of the professional medical staff remain an important component in hospitals across the United States to ensure quality and clinical competency in the physician workforce is maintained. Even with the advent of physician-owned hospitals, integrated hospital systems associated with insurers, or hospitals with fully employed physician models, the framework of the professional medical staff is often used to organize the routine review and monitoring of competency and professionalism. A firm understanding of these basic governance structures is necessary background for all hospital administrators.

REFERENCES

1. American Medical Association. Chapter 9: Professional Self-Regulation. AMA Code of Medical Ethics. American Medical Association. Accessed November 1, 2024. https://code-medical-ethics.ama-assn.org/chapters/professional-self-regulation.
2. Credentialing Resource Center. What Should Be Covered by Medical Staff Bylaws? Credentialing Resource Center Digest. January 29, 2024. Accessed November 1, 2024. https://credentialingresourcecenter.com/articles/what-should-be-covered-medical-staff-bylaws.

3. Federal Register. Title 42, Chapter IV, Subchapter 6, Part 482.12 Conditions of Participation: Governing Body. Accessed November 1, 2024. https://www.ecfr.gov/current/title-42/chapter-IV/subchapter-G/part-482.
4. The Joint Commission. Focused Professional Practice Evaluation (FPPE)—Understanding the Requirements. What Are the Key Elements Organizations Need To Understand Regarding the Focused Professional Practice Evaluation Requirements? The Joint Commission. Accessed November 1, 2024. https://www.jointcommission.org/standards/standard-faqs/critical-access-hospital/medical-staff-ms/000001485/.
5. Makary MA, Wick E, Freischlag JA. PPE, OPPE, and FPPE: Complying with the New Alphabet Soup of Credentialing. *Arch Surg.* 2011;146(6):642–644.
6. Reporting Patient Safety Events. PSNet. Rockville, MD: Agency for Healthcare Research and Quality, 2019. Accessed November 1, 2024. https://psnet.ahrq.gov/primer/reporting-patient-safety-events#:~:-text=Institution%20must%20have%20a%20supportive%20environment%20for%20event,place%20for%20reviewing%20reports%20and%20developing%20action%20plans.
7. Macrae C. The Problem with Incident Reporting. *BMJ Quality & Safety* 2016;25:71–75.
8. National Practitioner Data Bank. What You Must Report to the NPDB. US Department of Health & Human Services. Accessed November 1, 2024. https://www.npdb.hrsa.gov/hcorg/whatYou-MustReportToTheDataBank.jsp#:~:text=The%20NPDB%20collects%20information%20and%20maintains%20reports%20on,by%20private%20accreditation%20organizations%20and%20peer%20review%20organizations.Protect Peer Review Privileges, or Risk Serious Consequences. Healthcare Risk Management. February 1, 2022. Accessed November 1, 2024. https://www.reliasmedia.com/articles/149011-protect-peer-review-privileges-or-risk-serious-consequences#:~:text=To%20pro-tect%20patient%20safety.
9. Olszyk MD. *The Chief Medical Officer's Essential Guidebook.* Washington, DC: American Association for Physician Leadership; 2023.
10. Hoffman R. *I Want to be a Chief Medical Officer, Now What?* Washington, DC: American Association for Physician Leadership; 2024.

SECTION 4

Healthcare Policy, Law, and Advocacy

CHAPTER 10

Hospital/Medical Center Accreditation

Maria Hamilton, MBA, FACHE, and
Amyn M. Rojiani, MD, PhD, CPE, DFAAPL

HALM CORE CONTENT:

- 4.5 Continual readiness for accrediting/regulatory organization inspection and compliance (e.g., JC, ACGME, OSHA, FDA, NRC, CDC, state, federal/tribal accreditation/certification/licensure)

CASE SCENARIO:

The following announcement was sent to the medical staff:

"A patient safety alert is being issued for a wrong-site surgery that took place in our hospital last week. This is our fifth wrong site procedure when considering all procedural sites during the last 12 months. When we account for near misses, this event is the 40th event involving actual or potential wrong-site surgery.

"Without exception, all areas of the hospital must adhere to the time-out procedure as outlined in the hospital's Universal Protocol policy. The key components of this policy include pre-procedural verification, the site marking, and the time out. This policy serves our patients by preventing mistakes in surgery as described in The Joint Commission National Patient Safety Goals."

THE STANDARDIZED APPROACH to transparently communicating patient safety events to physicians, administrators, and hospital staff is embedded in highly reliable organizations that seek to ensure that patient safety is at the forefront of healthcare delivery.[1–3] Patient safety is a core learning concept taught in undergraduate medical education and demonstrated through the systems-based practice competency for graduate medical education, which sets an expectation that residents understand the complex systems of healthcare and craft potential systems solutions.

Accreditation History

The history of evaluating hospitals through accreditation standards can be traced back to 1910 when Ernest Codman, MD, proposed his "end result idea."[4,5] The core principle of this idea was that hospitals would ensure that patients were followed long enough after their illness to see if the treatment they received had in fact worked. In the spirit of continuous improvement, if the treatment did not yield a positive result, what could be planned and studied in the future so that adjustments could be made for better performance with the next patient?

The American College of Surgeons (ACS) used this "idea" to begin promoting evidence-based medicine as a way to improve health outcomes. In 1917, the ACS began using these evidence-based standards to inspect hospitals and ensure patients were receiving the best care.[6,7] The establishment of both a structure, which included patient safety performance standards, and a process, which included hospital inspections, gave birth to The Joint Commission as an independent organization that evaluated healthcare organization outcomes in providing safe, effective, and patient-centered care. Founded in 1951, The Joint Commission was formed as an independent, not-for-profit organization and is the most widely known accreditation agency for U.S. hospitals.

The mission of The Joint Commission is to ensure patients receive quality care that is patient-centered, safe, and of the highest value. The Joint Commission's stated mission is: "To continually improve healthcare for the public, in collaboration with other stakeholders, by evaluating healthcare organizations and inspiring them to excel in providing safe and effective care of the highest quality and value."[8]

The Joint Commission accomplishes this by creating quality standards that hospitals must meet to achieve and sustain hospital accreditation. One set of standards is known as the National Patient Safety Goals (NPSGs).[9] These goals were established in 2002 to help hospitals prioritize and eliminate potential patient safety events at a national level and are set forth by The Joint Commission to address specific areas of concern and improve patient outcomes.

As shown in Figure 1, several topic areas are addressed in the NPSGs, including preventing mistakes in surgery, using medications safely, and improving communication between healthcare team members.

The Centers for Medicare and Medicaid Services (CMS) has mandated external reviews of healthcare organizations through accreditation processes since 1965. CMS has specific written requirements for hospitals. Known as Conditions of Participation (CoPs), organizations must achieve these standards in order to receive payments from CMS. In lieu of directly surveying hospitals, CMS allows several other organizations to grant accreditation via a process known as "deemed status." Hospitals that are surveyed by agencies such as The Joint Commission and who achieve full accreditation after

The Joint Commission

2025 Hospital National Patient Safety Goals

(Easy-To-Read)

Identify patients correctly	
NPSG.01.01.01	Use at least two ways to identify patients. For example, use the patient's name *and* date of birth. This is done to make sure that each patient gets the correct medicine and treatment.
Improve staff communication	
NPSG.02.03.01	Get important test results to the right staff person on time.
Use medicines safely	
NPSG.03.04.01	Before a procedure, label medicines that are not labeled. For example, medicines in syringes, cups and basins. Do this in the area where medicines and supplies are set up.
NPSG.03.05.01	Take extra care with patients who take medicines to thin their blood.
NPSG.03.06.01	Record and pass along correct information about a patient's medicines. Find out what medicines the patient is taking. Compare those medicines to new medicines given to the patient. Give the patient written information about the medicines they need to take. Tell the patient it is important to bring their up-to-date list of medicines every time they visit a doctor.
Use alarms safely	
NPSG.06.01.01	Make improvements to ensure that alarms on medical equipment are heard and responded to on time.
Prevent infection	
NPSG.07.01.01	Use the hand cleaning guidelines from the Centers for Disease Control and Prevention or the World Health Organization. Set goals for improving hand cleaning.
Identify patient safety risks	
NPSG.15.01.01	Reduce the risk for suicide.
Improve health care equity	
NPSG.16.01.01	Improving health care equity is a quality and patient safety priority. For example, health care disparities in the patient population are identified and a written plan describes ways to improve health care equity.
Prevent mistakes in surgery	
UP.01.01.01	Make sure that the correct surgery is done on the correct patient and at the correct place on the patient's body.
UP.01.02.01	Mark the correct place on the patient's body where the surgery is to be done.
UP.01.03.01	Pause before the surgery to make sure that a mistake is not being made.

FIGURE 1. National Patient Safety Goals[9]

their respective survey are determined to meet or exceed CMS requirements and, as a result, the hospital can receive payments by CMS programs.[10]

In September 2008, CMS granted deeming status to DNV (Det Norske Veritas) which is a competitor of The Joint Commission. This accreditation organization combines a traditional accreditation process, using National Integrated Accreditation for

Healthcare Organization (NIAHO) standards, with ISO9001 quality standards and is conducted annually as opposed to every three years.[11] Approximately 300 hospitals across the country have chosen to transition from JC accreditation to the DNV accreditation process over the past 15 years.

Hospital Accreditation Process

The overall process of evaluating hospitals is to review the standards that have been developed and ensure that the hospital meets those expectations for delivering safe patient care. Many of the JC standards overlap with CMS Conditions of Participation standards.[10] The objective of the survey process is to provide guidance to the organization, identify areas of opportunity, and recommend areas of focus to achieve accreditation status and ensure key patient safety processes are embedded in the fabric of the organization.

The standards are divided into chapters and include areas such as leadership, provision of care, infection prevention, medication management, and environment of care. In total, there are 18 chapters with more than 240 associated standards.

For Joint Commission accreditation, the organization must participate in a full survey every 18–36 months in order to demonstrate their commitment to continuous improvement and patient safety as well as maintain their payment status with CMS. The survey process includes an unannounced visit to the healthcare facility where surveyors will use the tracer methodology to evaluate the hospital's performance against the standards and the elements of performance embedded in each standard.

It is an expectation that healthcare organizations are always prepared for the unannounced survey from The Joint Commission and that the hospital has a culture and mindset of continuous survey readiness. This is accomplished by establishing standard work that allows for multidisciplinary collaboration among the healthcare team to look for performance gaps and to work together to design systems to enhance patient care.

The key process The Joint Commission uses is the tracer methodology, in which surveyors follow a number of patients in their journey through the entire healthcare delivery system.[12] The Joint Commission surveyors speak with doctors, nurses, quality and patient safety staff, and ancillary staff to review the organization's current care processes and recommend areas for improvement. The Joint Commission uses a tool to score the organization in each of the standards. There are associated elements of performance (EP) that determine if the organization has met the standard.

Once the surveyors have completed their unannounced visit, the hospital receives a comprehensive score in the form of the SAFER™ (Survey Analysis for Evaluating Risk) matrix.[13] This matrix (see Figure 2) was first implemented by The Joint Commission in 2017 and is a valuable tool to communicate to the organization the levels of risk and associated deficiencies to the standards that were identified when the surveyors were onsite.

Each area that requires improvement will be placed in the SAFER matrix according to the likelihood of patient/staff/visitor harm and the scope of the observations recorded during the survey. The standards listed on the matrix need to have associated action plans in order to demonstrate evidence of standards compliance.

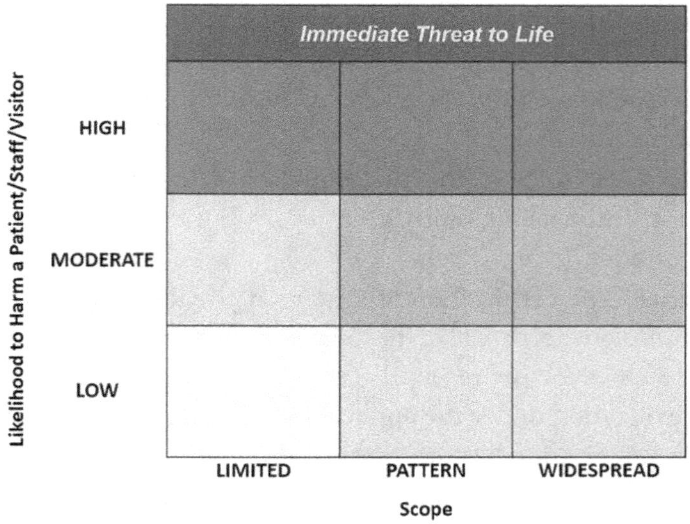

FIGURE 2. The Joint Commission SAFER™ Matrix

It is important to remember that there may still be an element of subjectivity in where a surveyor places requirements for improvement (RFI) and elements of performance (EP) relative to the likelihood of harm and scope of the non-compliance. For example, an element may have a low likelihood of harm but may be widespread in scope, or it may have a high likelihood of harm but be very limited in its scope of occurrence. It's important to be familiar with the following accreditation definitions:

Standard: An overarching regulatory requirement with which healthcare organizations are expected to comply. It is composed of individual elements of performance.

(TJC) The Joint Commission: A nonprofit organization that accredits more than 21,000 healthcare organizations and programs in the United States. (JCAHO is the old acronym.)

Element of Performance (EP): The procedural steps you must use to become compliant with a standard.

Tracer Methodology: Uses information from an organization to follow the experience of care, treatment, or services for a number of patients through the organization's entire healthcare delivery process. Tracers allow surveyors to identify performance issues in one or more steps of the process or interfaces between processes.

Requirements for Improvement (RFI): Areas of non-compliance within the organization found during the survey.

Survey Analysis for Evaluating Risk (SAFER)™: Prioritizes resources and focuses corrective action plans in areas that are in most need of compliance activities and interventions.

CMS Conditions of Participation (CoPs): Requirements developed by CMS that healthcare organizations must meet to participate in federally funded healthcare. In total, there are 24 CMS CoPs.

ESC: Evidence of Standards Compliance: A report that shows how a healthcare organization has addressed the requirements for improvement (RFIs) identified by The Joint Commission surveyors.

Condition Level Findings: High risk, frequently widespread findings that require immediate interventions and another survey by The Joint Commission to ensure compliance.

Deemed Status: CMS certification process for a provider or supplier for Medicare participation, based on meeting all of the following criteria: (1) The provider or supplier has voluntarily applied for and received accreditation from a CMS-approved national accrediting organization under the applicable Medicare accreditation program; (2) the accrediting organization has recommended the provider or supplier to CMS for Medicare participation; (3) CMS has accepted the accrediting organization's recommendation; and (5) CMS finds that all other participation requirements have been met. Thus, it is important to regularly monitor and conduct mock surveys, either using internal resources or external consultants, or applying various tools that may facilitate accreditation.[14,15]

In addition to accreditation standards, there are additional regulatory requirements that are both mandatory and voluntary at local, state, and federal levels. This section will describe those various agencies and the oversight each provides to ensure patients who receive care in a hospital setting are receiving the highest quality healthcare in a highly reliable healthcare delivery system.

Department of Health

The department of health (DOH) is responsible for the licensure and oversight at the state level for individual hospitals that meet certain criteria. Although the requirements may be somewhat different from one state to another, the broad principles as seen at the DOH of the Commonwealth of Pennsylvania apply to regulations defined by most states.

In addition to granting hospital licenses, the DOH also conducts surveys on behalf of CMS, investigates patient complaints, and reviews patient safety events that have been reported to the state through the mandatory state reporting processes.[16] If a complaint is submitted or an event is reported, DOH surveyors conduct surveyor-led investigations at the facility. During this process, the DOH surveyors review relevant medical records, interview staff, and conduct a preliminary investigation to determine if the hospital adhered to established policies and procedures.

If there is a finding of non-compliance, the hospital must create a written plan of correction and submit that plan to the DOH in a timely manner. A revisit to the hospital will ensure compliance and implementation of the action plan.

If a hospital determines that it would like to offer a new service, the hospital must notify the department of health so that the DOH surveyors are able to conduct an onsite review and determine if the hospital meets the requirements as set forth by the DOH. This is known as a "certificate of need" (CON) requirement.[17] This is a requirement in 35 states and DC, which mandate justification of major expenses to contain the cost of healthcare delivery by evaluating the need for the new service or equipment. The department of health reserves the right to approve or deny requests based on the information they receive and the rationale for the request. Failure to meet any hospital standards at the state level could result in penalties to the hospital, up to and including revocation of the hospital license.

Occupational Safety and Health Administration (OSHA)

The Occupational Safety and Health Administration (OSHA) is a part of the United States Department of Labor and was established in 1970. OSHA's mission is "to assure America's workers have safe and healthful working conditions free from unlawful retaliation." OSHA conducts its mission by setting and enforcing standards; enforcing anti-retaliation provisions of the OSHA act and other federal whistleblower laws; providing and supporting training, outreach, education, and assistance; and working collaboratively with state OSHA programs as well as ensuring that they are at least as effective as federal OSHA, furthering a national system of worker safety and health protections.

OSHA's regulations for hospitals ensure patients and staff remain safe from harm. Standards have been created to address relevant areas of focus to include bloodborne pathogens, personal protective equipment, and respiratory protection.[18] The hospital must create policies and procedures to address these topics as well as provide training and evaluation of program effectiveness. "Failure of hospitals to meet OSHA requirements results in financial penalties to the institution."[18]

OSHA violations in healthcare are relatively limited, particularly given the behemoth size of U.S. healthcare institutions. The most frequently issued citations were for violations of the following OSHA standards: bloodborne pathogen, hazard communication, respiratory protection, control of hazardous energy, formaldehyde, asbestos, wiring methods, components, and equipment and exit route (maintenance, safeguards, and features) standard.[19] Each of these elements therefore requires particular attention by leadership and staff in preparation for an accreditation survey.

Food and Drug Administration

The Food and Drug Administration (FDA) is a federal agency that is part of the Department of Health and Human Services and was established to regulate food, drugs, medical devices, radiation-emitting products, vaccines, blood, biologics, animal and veterinary, cosmetics, and tobacco products.

As described in part in their mission statement, "the Food and Drug Administration is responsible for protecting the public health by ensuring the safety, efficacy, and security of human and veterinary drugs, biological products, and medical devices; and by ensuring the safety of our nation's food supply, cosmetics, and products that emit radiation."[20]

The FDA regulates medical device safety in hospitals and ensures that any devices purchased are safe and effective for use on patients. The hospital's supply chain management structure should develop a robust process for purchasing, using, and maintaining medical devices in accordance with FDA regulations.

Nuclear Regulatory Commission (NRC)

Congress created the Nuclear Regulatory Commission (NRC) in 1974 as an independent agency. According to its stated mission, "the NRC licenses and regulates the nation's civilian use of radioactive materials to provide reasonable assurance of adequate protection of public health and safety and to promote the common defense and security, and to protect the environment."

Its regulatory mission covers three areas of focus: reactors, materials, and waste.[21] Accordingly, hospital administration and physician leaders should understand diagnostic and therapeutic use of nuclear materials and their mandatory requirements at the local, state, and federal government levels.

Centers for Disease Control and Prevention (CDC)

The Centers for Disease Control and Prevention (CDC) is a national public health organization that protects safety through the control and prevention of disease, injury, and disability. It focuses its attention on infectious disease, environmental health concerns, health and equity promotion, occupational safety, and food-borne pathogens. CDC provides many resources to support both individuals and communities from health threats and to design resilient systems to prevent disease.[22]

Laboratory Accreditation

Recognizing that the vast majority of significant clinical decisions are based on test results from pathology laboratories, it is essential that providers and patients have full confidence in the quality, precision, consistency, and timeliness of results. In that context, lab accreditation goes a long way in ensuring that the laboratory has met well-defined, stringent criteria for equipment calibration, test protocols, personnel qualifications, and ongoing safety standards.

A second, and perhaps equally important, practical reason for ensuring accreditation is that it allows for reimbursement from insurance providers. While being essential for reimbursement by federal and state healthcare agencies, accreditation is a requirement for private insurers as well. This accreditation standard is thus mandated to ensure that patients get diagnostic results from a lab that is committed to meeting appropriate quality standards.

The primary entity in the United States that governs clinical laboratory accreditation is CLIA (Clinical Laboratory Improvement Amendments). It is overseen by the Centers for Medicare & Medicaid Services.[23] CLIA amendments provide a baseline regulatory framework with minimum standards for quality and patient safety that are applicable to all laboratories, as mandated by federal law. Compliance with CLIA regulations is essential for laboratories to conduct testing on human specimens and obtain necessary certifications for reimbursement from insurance providers.

CLIA generally requires all facilities that perform even one applicable test, including waived tests, on "materials derived from the human body for the purpose of providing information for the diagnosis, prevention, or treatment of any disease or impairment of, or the assessment of the health of, human beings" to meet certain federal requirements.

If a facility performs tests for these purposes, it is considered a laboratory under CLIA and generally must apply and obtain a certificate from the CLIA program that corresponds to the complexity of tests performed. However, a CLIA certificate may not be needed if the laboratory is located in the states of New York or Washington, as those states operate their own laboratory regulatory programs. As of the date of this publication's release, there are seven CMS-approved accreditation organizations:

- Association for the Advancement of Blood and Biotherapies (AABB)
- American Association for Laboratory Accreditation (A2LA)
- Accreditation Association for Hospitals and Health Systems/ Healthcare Facilities Accreditation Program (AAHHS/HFAP)
- American Society for Histocompatibility and Immunogenetics (ASHI)
- Commission on Laboratory Accreditation (COLA)
- College of American Pathologists (CAP)
- The Joint Commission

While some of the above agencies are specific to certain subspecialty areas, such as blood bank or histocompatibility, the two entities most frequently used to meet CLIA requirements are The Joint Commission and CAP. Accreditation of clinical laboratories by both of these agencies requires substantial commitment of time and resources.

The College of American Pathologists (CAP), the leading organization of board-certified pathologists, serves patients, pathologists, and the public by fostering and advocating excellence in the practice of pathology and laboratory medicine worldwide. CAP meets the full accreditation standards put forth by CLIA, and goes much further to include its own rigorous standards, including areas such as quality management, personnel qualifications, facilities and safety, and analytical performance.[24]

CAP accreditation is voluntary but far exceeds CLIA requirements. CAP certification represents a strong commitment to enhanced proficiency and quality.[25] Monitored by a biennial external inspection process and an alternate year documented self-inspection, most institutions maintain tight regulatory control over items that are on CAP's accreditation checklist, thus ensuring high-quality standards and continuous quality improvement.

Unlike The Joint Commission, CAP capitalizes on the power of peer inspections, with inspection teams consisting of highly skilled and trained laboratory professionals who themselves understand the logistical and quality challenges that institutions face.

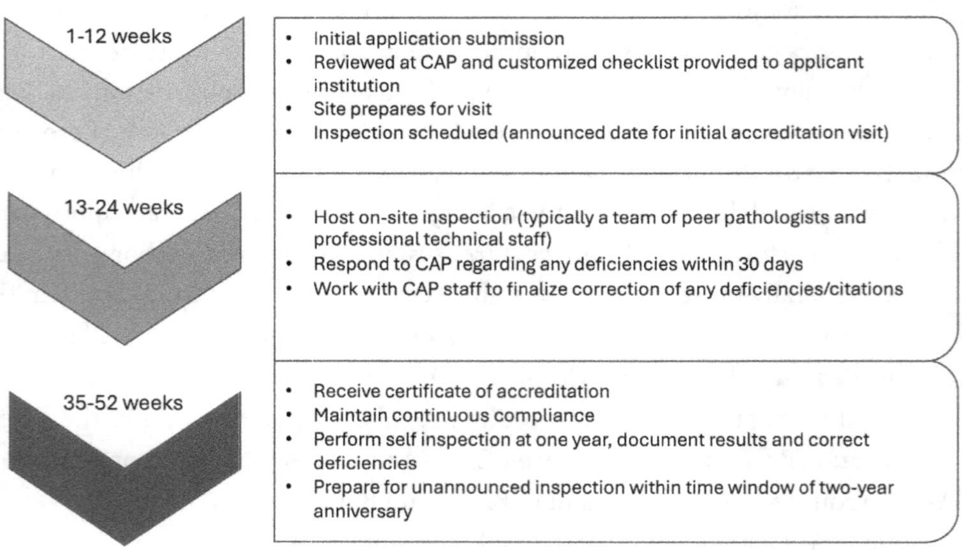

FIGURE 3. CAP Accreditation Process and Timeline

Adapted from https://www.cap.org/laboratory-improvement/accreditation/accreditation-process

Healthcare institutions may apply for initial accreditation according to the timeline in Figure 3. Once accredited, the institution will be inspected every two years by a peer team, typically as an unannounced visit, within a three-month window. Institutions are thus encouraged to maintain professionalism, accountability, continuous quality improvement, high proficiency standards, and a constant state of accreditation readiness.

Chapter Summary

Creating a culture of patient safety is the responsibility of all members of the healthcare team. Accreditation structures and processes can be leveraged internally to continuously improve patient safety throughout the healthcare organization. On a broader scale, government organizations exist to provide all workers and citizens public health and safety measures and standards to ensure the highest quality and safety at the local, state and national levels through the creation of regulations.

As the move to value-based care increases and the interface of quality and cost become more intertwined it will be important for physician leaders to understand and encourage an environment of continuous improvement through continuous survey readiness processes and ensure a broad understanding of the public health structures which exist at the various microsystem and macrosystem levels.

Healthcare leaders must be knowledgeable about regulatory requirements and accreditation standards and implement the appropriate policies and procedures to support the requirements. Additionally, hospital leadership should design ongoing education and training programs to support the organization as new standards are designed, developed, and implemented.

REFERENCES

1. Rotteau L, Goldman J, Shojania KG, et al. Striving for High Reliability in Healthcare: A Qualitative Study of the Implementation of a Hospital Safety Programme. *BMJ Qual Saf.* 2022;31(12):867–877. doi:10.1136/bmjqs-2021-013938
2. Wachter RM, Gupta K. *Understanding Patient Safety.* 3rd ed. The McGraw-Hill/Medical; 2018.
3. Harvard Health Publishing. Medical Errors: Honesty Is the Best Policy. Harvard Health Blog. October 3, 2016. Accessed January 4, 2025. https://www.health.harvard.edu/blog/medical-errors-honesty-is-the-best-policy-2016100310405
4. Kaska SC, Weinstein JN. Historical Perspective. Ernest Amory Codman, 1869-1940. A Pioneer of Evidence-Based Medicine: The End Result Idea. *Spine (Phila Pa 1976).* 1998;23(5):629–633. doi:10.1097/00007632-199803010-00019
5. Nakayama DK. Ernest Amory Codman and the End Result Idea in Surgical Quality. *Am Surg.* 2023;89(11):4237–4240. doi:10.1177/00031348221148344
6. Hoyt DB, Ko CY, Opelka FG. A Century of Surgical Quality: Origins, Evolution, and Future Directions. *Am J Med Qual.* 2024;39(6):285–289. doi:10.1097/JMQ.0000000000000205
7. Hines K, Mouchtouris N, Knightly JJ, Harrop J. A Brief History of Quality Improvement in Health Care and Spinal Surgery. *Global Spine J.* 2020;10(1 Suppl):5S–9S. doi:10.1177/2192568219853529
8. The Joint Commission. Who We Are. https://www.jointcommission.org/who-we-are/. Accessed January 4, 2025. https://www.jointcommission.org/who-we-are/
9. The Joint Commission. 2025 Hospital National Patient Safety Goals. Accessed January 4, 2025. https://

www.jointcommission.org/-/media/tjc/documents/standards/national-patient-safety-goals/2025/hap-npsg-simplified-2025-accessible.pdf

10. Federal Register. Providers or Suppliers That Participate in the Medicaid Program Under a CMS-approved Accreditation Program. Title 42 Chapter IV Subchapter G Part 488 Subpart A : § 488.6 Accessed January 15, 2025. https://www.ecfr.gov/current/title-42/chapter-IV/subchapter-G/part-488/subpart-A
11. Gamache C. Choosing the Right Agency for Hospital Accreditation: The Joint Commission vs. DNV. The ISO 9001 Group. June 29, 2023. Accessed January 4, 2025. https://iso9001group.com/hospital-accreditation-the-joint-commission-vs-dnv/
12. Siewert B. The Joint Commission Ever-Readiness: Understanding Tracer Methodology. *Curr Probl Diagn Radiol.* 2018;47(3):131–135. doi:10.1067/j.cpradiol.2017.05.002
13. The Joint Commission. Survey Analysis for Evaluating Risk® (SAFER™). Accessed January 9, 2025. https://www.jointcommissioninternational.org/-/media/jci/jci-documents/accreditation/why-jci/jci-safer-matrix-brochure_insights.pdf
14. Dewan S, Sibal A, Uberoi RS, et al. The Apollo Accreditation Program: A Web-based Joint Commission International Standards Compliance Management Tool. *World Hosp Health Serv.* 2014;50(4):31–34.
15. Van KA, Nogueira L, Gustafson D, et al. The Culture of Patient Safety Practice: Systematic Review. *Urol Pract.* 2017;4(4):296–301. doi:10.1016/j.urpr.2016.08.003
16. Commonwealth of Pennsylvania. Hospital Regulations. Accessed January 9, 2025. https://www.pa.gov/agencies/health/facilities/in-patient-healthcare-facilities/hospitals/hospital-regulations.html
17. National Council of State Legislatures. Certificate of Need State Laws. Updated February 26, 2024. Accessed January 9, 2025. https://www.ncsl.org/health/certificate-of-need-state-laws
18. U.S. Department of Labor Occupational Safety and Health Administration. OSHA Standards. Accessed January 9, 2025. https://www.osha.gov/healthcare/standards
19. Alder S. OSHA Violation Cases in Healthcare. *The HIPAA Journal.* November 7, 2023. Accessed January 9, 2025. https://www.hipaajournal.com/osha-violation-cases-in-healthcare/
20. Food and Drug Administration. What We Do. Accessed January 9, 2025. https://www.fda.gov/about-fda/what-we-do#mission
21. United States Nuclear Regulatory Commission. NRC Mission. January 9, 2025. https://www.nrc.gov/about-nrc.html
22. Centers for Disease Control and Prevention. About CDC. Accessed January 9, 2025. https://www.cdc.gov/about/cdc/index.html
23. Centers for Medicaid and Medicare Services. CLIA Accreditation and Testing. Accessed January 9, 2025. https://www.cms.gov/medicare/quality/clinical-laboratory-improvement-amendments/accreditation-exemptions
24. College of American Pathologists. Laboratory Accreditation Program. Accessed January 9, 2025. https://www.cap.org/laboratory-improvement/accreditation/laboratory-accreditation-program
25. Zneimer SM, Hongo D. Preparing for Clinical Laboratory Improvement Amendments (CLIA) and College of American Pathologists (CAP) Inspections. *Curr Protoc.* 2021;1(12):e324. doi:10.1002/cpz1.324

CHAPTER 11

Graduate Medical Education (GME) Accreditation

Robert E. Harbaugh, MD, FAANS, FACS, FAHA; Beth K. Herman, DEd; and Amyn M. Rojiani, MD, PhD, CPE, DFAAPL

HALM CORE CONTENT:

- 4.6 GME policies and accreditation requirements

CASE SCENARIO:

Dr. James Endrado is the internal medicine residency program director at Elsewhere Hospital, the main teaching hospital of Elsewhere State University. The program has 18 residents over a three-year program and five ACGME-accredited fellowships.

Dr. Endrado is a highly skilled internist who primarily provides coverage on the renal service, although often helps out with other services if needed. He is very well-liked by his peers and even more so by residents and medical students.

He was very surprised when he was told at a meeting with the designated institutional official (DIO) that the program was being cited by the Accreditation Council for Graduate Medical Education (ACGME) for his inadequate time commitment to the program. There had been no complaints, and as far as he was aware, all paperwork had been completed and submitted on time.

On further inquiry it was determined that ACGME had concluded, based on a review of documented call schedules, service assignments, etc., that Dr. Endrado was committing no more than 0.3 FTE to the residency program administration.

Although, in all respects, the residency program was successful in its training goals and boasted significant accomplishments, it did not meet accreditation requirements ACGME II.A.2.[1] The program director and, as applicable, the program's leadership team, must be provided with support adequate for administration of the program based upon its size and configuration.

Number of Approved Resident Positions	Minimum Support Required (FTE)
<7	0.20
7-10	0.4
>10	0.5

According to requirement II.A.2.b), programs with more than 15 residents must appoint an associate program director(s). The associate program directors(s) must be provided with support equal to a dedicated minimum time for the administration of the program as illustrated below.

Number of Approved Resident Positions	Minimum Support Required (FTE)
<15	0.0
16-20	0.1
21-25	0.2

The Accreditation Council for Graduate Medical Education (ACGME) and institutional policies, procedures, and infrastructure created to meet the ACGME requirements play crucial roles in maintaining high standards for graduate medical education (GME) in the United States. The primary function of the ACGME is to ensure that residency and fellowship programs provide high-quality training that meets the needs of the public, the healthcare system, and the residents and fellows.

To ensure success in these goals, the ACGME defines common program requirements that are applicable to all residency and fellowship programs. "The ACGME Common Program Requirements are a basic set of standards (requirements) in training and preparing resident and fellow physicians.[2] These requirements set the context within clinical learning environments for development of the skills, knowledge, and attitudes necessary to take personal responsibility for the individual care of patients. In addition, these requirements facilitate an environment where residents and fellows can interact with patients under the guidance and supervision of qualified faculty members who give value, context, and meaning to those interactions."[2] Categories of these requirements effective July 1, 2025, are oversight, personnel, resident appointments, educational program, evaluation, and the learning and working environment.[2]

These common program requirements are applicable across the spectrum of specialties and define the key areas for any training program. Further requirements, including the length of the training program specific to each specialty, are defined by each respective review committee. The ACGME helps to maintain these standards in the following ways:

- Setting accreditation standards for more than 13,000 residency and fellowship programs in 146 specialties and subspecialties.
- Curriculum development that ensures residents are exposed to a comprehensive, evidence-based knowledge base that prepares them for independent practice.
- Faculty qualifications that ensure mentors are properly trained, qualified, and engaged in the educational process.
- Fostering learners' well-being by requiring institutional policies and infrastructure needed to maintain the mental, emotional, and physical well-being of learners.
- Program evaluations that ensure programs have mechanisms in place to assess residents' progress and the effectiveness of the education.
- Yearly surveys of learners and mentors to assess the health of the program.

MILESTONES AND COMPETENCY-BASED ASSESSMENT

The ACGME implements the Milestones framework, which outlines specific developmental stages (Milestones) that residents should achieve during their training.[3,4] These Milestones are divided into the six competencies developed by the ACGME and the American Board of Medical Specialties. These competencies provide a framework that describes the domains required for physicians to enter autonomous practice. These competencies are:

- Patient Care and Procedural Skills – Residents must provide care that is patient-centered, compassionate, equitable, appropriate, and effective.
- Medical Knowledge – Residents must demonstrate knowledge of established and evolving biomedical, clinical, epidemiological, and social-behavioral sciences.
- Practice-based Learning and Improvement – Residents must demonstrate the ability to investigate and evaluate their care of patients, to appraise and assimilate scientific evidence, and improve patient care.
- Interpersonal and Communication Skills – Residents must demonstrate interpersonal and communication skills that result in the effective exchange of information.
- Professionalism – Residents must demonstrate a commitment to professionalism and adherence to ethical principles.
- Systems-based Practice – Residents must demonstrate an awareness of and responsiveness to the larger context and system of health care, including the structural and social determinants of health.

Programs must assess residents' progress toward these Milestones and provide feedback to help guide their development. This approach moves away from solely time-based training toward competency-based training. The Milestones serve as a template for continued growth and level of proficiency attained by each individual trainee using the Dreyfus model of adult skill acquisition.[5] Residents progressively develop from Level 1 to Level 5.

Level 1 describes what would be expected of a novice in the specialty (a starting resident or fellow). Level 2 designates an advanced beginner; Level 3 focuses on competence; Level 4, or proficiency in the Dreyfus schema, is a graduation target, but not a requirement of the ACGME, as each program or institution sets the requirements for graduation. Level 5 describes expertise or aspirational performance for a resident or fellow who is acting as a role model or coach for others. The Milestones are not included in determining the accreditation status by the review committees.

The Accreditation Process – Residencies and Fellowships

Each ACGME-accredited residency and fellowship is reviewed by a review committee (RC).[6,7] The 28 specialty-specific RCs are composed of physicians who have demonstrated expertise in and commitment to graduate medical education, a resident member representing the interests of the learners, and a member of the public representing the interests of the patients.

Five accreditation statuses are offered:[8]

1. Initial Accreditation – New Program Accreditation (8.4% of programs)
2. Continued Accreditation (89.9% of programs)
3. Continued Accreditation with Warning (1.1% of programs)
4. Probationary Accreditation (0.2% of programs)
5. Withdrawal of Accreditation (0.4% of programs)

New Program Accreditation

Before a residency or fellowship program can begin training, it must apply for accreditation to the specialty-specific RC, meet ACGME standards for training in that specialty, and be awarded initial accreditation status by the RC. If initial accreditation is not awarded, the decision may be appealed to the ACGME, and a hearing will be held.

During the 2023–2024 academic year, 175 ACGME programs received initial accreditation and were newly accredited. The establishment of a new residency or fellowship program often requires several years from concept to accreditation.

One of the most significant hurdles to the establishment of a residency program is funding. GME program funding may be obtained from public or private sources. Public sources[9,10] include the Centers for Medicare & Medicaid Services, which is by far the largest source of federal funding. The Health Resources and Services Administration (HRSA), including the Children's Hospital GME Program, supports specific programs.

The Department of Veterans Affairs and Department of Defense are also important but have limited resources.

Securing the appropriate financial backing must be completed prior to the preparation and submission of an application to the ACGME. A detailed budget that includes salaries, benefits, administrative faculty time, recruitment, and operating costs should be prepared. Once this funding is secured, the application process for accreditation can be pursued.

SPONSORING INSTITUTIONS

The ACGME requires the residency and fellowship programs to have one sponsoring institution (SI) that has the ultimate financial and academic responsibility for one or more accredited graduate medical education programs, and that has the primary purpose of providing educational programs and/or healthcare services. General teaching hospitals make up 44% of all SIs. Academic medical centers total 15% of SIs.

The SI is required to complete an institutional self-study every 10 years prior to an institutional site visit. Residents rotate at unique, participating sites, including ambulatory care clinics, other teaching hospitals, federally qualified health centers, and other clinical experiences.

PROGRAM DIRECTOR

There must be one faculty member appointed as program director with authority and accountability for the overall program, including compliance with all applicable program requirements. The program director must have responsibility, authority, and accountability for: administration and operations; teaching and scholarly activity; resident recruitment and selection, evaluation, and promotion of residents, and disciplinary action; supervision of residents; and resident education in the context of patient care.

DIO AND INSTITUTIONAL BUY-IN

The initial step in starting a new residency program is to meet with the sponsoring institution's designated institutional official (DIO) — the individual who provides institutional oversight of all residency and fellowships within the purview of that institution. The sponsoring institution has oversight of all training programs. Established academic partners have expertise in developing new residency programs in community hospitals and in the academic medical center.

SITE SELECTION

The primary training site must be clearly defined. Factors such as patient volume, diversity of patients, teaching faculty, and facilities are important considerations when identifying the primary teaching site. A program director and program coordinator must be appointed and placed at the primary teaching site.

CURRICULUM DEVELOPMENT

An educational curriculum and vision should be developed and detailed and the patient population, facilities, clinical programs, and faculty opportunities should be defined. The clinical rotations and block schedule will be built utilizing the curriculum. An application to the ACGME will require a minimum of one year for preparation, submission, and completion of a site visit. A carefully thought-out timeline is critical to mapping the implementation of a new training program.

SITE VISITS

ACGME sends trained surveyors to perform on-site visits to programs to evaluate how well programs are adhering to accreditation standards. Site visits can be routine or requested by the specialty-specific RCs because of concerns they may have.

Continued Accreditation

Accredited programs undergo regular reviews and evaluations by the ACGME specialty-specific RCs. In general, all the elements to be addressed in the initial accreditation process must be followed. Additionally, these assessments consider factors such as the program's curriculum, clinical training opportunities, resident performance and well-being, and institutional support. The ongoing accreditation assessment recognizes there is a historical perspective as well as access to data from the ACGME annual residents survey.[11-13]

CITATIONS OR AREAS FOR IMPROVEMENT

The ACGME RC will issue a citation when an area is not in substantial compliance with the ACGME program requirements or institutional requirements. The accredited program is required to respond to the citation. Areas for improvement (AFI) are not as significant as a citation, and the RC assumes the concerns will be reviewed and addressed. If not addressed, the AFI may result in a citation.

Categories for common citations are:

- Program Director Responsibilities
- Faculty Responsibilities
- Evaluations – Program, Faculty, Resident
- Educational Program
  - Procedural Experience
  - Service to Education Imbalance
  - Supervision
  - Duty Hours
  - Scholarly Activity Requirement

ADDRESSING COMMON CITATION CATEGORIES

Corrective actions and preventative steps may be taken to address common citations.[14-18] These include:

Program Director Responsibilities. One of the most frequent citations is in the area of "protected" time for the program director (see case scenario above). It is imperative that the program director be allocated the required time to effectively carry out their duties. This means that they should be free of clinical, research, or other administrative duties for the specified time.

Each RC determines the required protected time based on the size of the program. Program directors must provide a learning and working environment in which residents have the opportunity to raise concerns and provide feedback in a confidential manner. The program director must provide clear communication forums for residents, ensure residents understand the policy and resources available, and solicit feedback from residents.

Faculty Responsibilities. Faculty members must demonstrate a strong interest in the education of residents. Sufficient time must be devoted to the educational program to fulfill their supervisory and teaching responsibilities. Faculty members must administer and maintain an educational environment conducive to educating residents. Through faculty evaluations and feedback from residents, faculty members will identify trends in teaching assessments.

Evaluations. Evaluations of the program, faculty, and residents must be conducted regularly and completed according to a defined schedule. They must be completed in a timely manner that ensures anonymity, without any fear of reprisals and as objectively as possible.

Resident evaluations must include a definition of expectations at the start of the rotation, a mid-rotation assessment, followed by a formal end-of-rotation evaluation.

Duty Hours. Residents must accurately log their duty hours. The duty hour logging tool must capture the duty hour violations. Considerations include whether a particular service is creating duty hour violations and whether residents are able to appropriately and safely hand off the care of a patient when they are fatigued.

Documentation. Program leadership should document all issues as they arise. Documentation is essential to identifying trends, addressing concerns, and identifying concerning residents in the program.

Work Hours and Resident Well-Being

Resident well-being is a multidimensional concept that encompasses a variety of factors, including physical, emotional, intellectual, social, and spiritual health. Resident well-being is a continuous process of self-awareness and making healthy choices that can lead to a number of benefits, including increased empathy, a stronger sense of engagement, better clinical performance, a positive attitude, and resilience.

In 2003, the ACGME rolled out significant changes in the work hours for physicians in training. The nationally mandated change now requires that trainees work no more than 80 hours per week. These strict guidelines were implemented following significant concerns regarding medical errors and to protect residents' well-being.

In addition to the maximum 80-hour work week, it also mandated reduced shift length to 30 hours.[19] These shift lengths were modified in 2011 to no more than 16 hours for PGY1s and 28 hours for subsequent year trainees.[20] This helps prevent burnout, fatigue, and errors, ensuring that residents maintain their mental and physical health during training.

Many factors have been identified as contributing to resident well-being, including "a sense of control and autonomy, pursuit and achievement of goals, opportunities for learning, increased confidence and sense of increasing mastery, positive feedback, and positive colleague relationships were all associated with greater well-being, as was sleep and time away from work."[21]

Common areas of concern identified by the annual ACGME surveys include the imbalance of service over education and burnout among trainees.

Disciplinary Actions

Every sponsoring institution must have a policy regarding recruitment, remediation, probation, non-renewal, non-promotion, and dismissal for cause. Attention must be paid to performance characteristics from the initial phase of application review and selection throughout the training period. Early red flags for applicants include:

- Medical students who don't receive any letters of recommendation in their desired specialty.
- Letters of recommendation that are not laudatory or skip details.
- Unexplained gaps of time on their application/curriculum vitae.
- Misdemeanor or felony record.
- Failed boards or shelf exams.
- Transfers from other programs for "weak" reasons. Conversation with the previous program director is essential.

Residents and other trainees must be aware of and stay vigilant for the "Ds" that may affect performance:

- <u>D</u>eprivation (sleep)
- <u>D</u>istraction (finances, distance, divorce/marital difficulties, disease or illness)
- <u>D</u>isability (neuropsychiatric, physical)
- <u>D</u>ependency (alcohol, illicit drugs)

- Disordered personality
- Depression

Early detection of issues associated with the above Ds will avoid future conflict and facilitate adequate support and hopefully successful completion of the training program. It is important to address issues as early and as completely as possible. Meet with the resident, along with someone else present (coordinator), determine facts and challenges, and offer help. Outline a plan for remediation. Remember, remediation is an essential first step prior to any disciplinary action. As always, document the issue, the conversation, the remediation plan, and the criteria for success or failure of the intervention.

REMEDIATION

When remediation is warranted, the program must list the concerns leading to the remediation in detail, utilizing the core competencies and/or milestone(s) as a basis. The clearly defined plan of remediation must include:

- Issues or concerns:
  - The educational prescription that is recommended must be explained and the resident must be involved in determining the personal remediation/improvement plan that will be utilized for each of the specific concerns listed. Resources, if there are any that will be necessary, should be identified and access should be ensured. A faculty mentor for the resident should be identified for the remediation process.
  - Define any other issues from the items listed above as well as issues of professionalism. The latter is a particularly challenging issue and requires significant attention to detail.[22]
- Tools of assessment
  - The specific tools and measures that will be utilized to assess the results of the resident's efforts at remediation should be identified.
- Expected outcome of the remediation
  - Determine what "success" or "progress" will look like and the next steps (continue training, continue training with ongoing assessment, etc.).
  - Define what "lack of success" or "failure" in the process will look like and the next steps (some progress, continued remediation, progression to probation, termination, non-renewal, etc.).
- Timeline for remediation
  - The length of the remediation process should be determined, including specific start and stop dates.
  - The timing of the decision by the program director after review is completed by the clinical competency committee should be specified.

- If remediation is unsuccessful, the program may choose to counsel the resident to consider another program, another specialty, or even another profession. In the case of an appeal, the institutional grievance and due process policy should be followed. Appeals process Institutional Grievance and Due Process Policy should always be followed.

PROBATION

A resident may be placed on probation for:
- Performance.
- Lack of professionalism.
- Behavioral issues/other reported misconduct.
- Failure to progress in the program as outlined in previous action of the clinical competency committee.

NON-RENEWALS/NON-PROMOTION

Regarding the policy on contract renewals, there is no absolute time of renewal (e.g., 120 days). The program should provide a written notice of intent when the resident/fellow agreement will not be renewed, when the resident/fellow will not be promoted to the next level of training, or when the trainee will be dismissed. The resident should be informed upfront and clearly that a delayed promotion or non-promotion may impact future licensure, as this information may be shared with future licensure boards.

Additional Considerations

Quality Assurance. The ACGME promotes continuous quality improvement by requiring residency programs to regularly self-assess and engage in quality improvement processes. The goal is to ensure that programs are not only meeting accreditation standards but also striving to improve in areas like educational content, clinical training, and faculty development.

Public Transparency. The ACGME maintains a database of accredited programs, which allows the public (including potential residents, medical schools, and hospitals) to verify the status of programs. This transparency helps ensure accountability and trust in the GME system.

Collaboration with Other Organizations. The ACGME works in close collaboration with the American Board of Medical Specialties (ABMS), individual ABMS specialty boards, professional societies, medical schools, and healthcare institutions to ensure that GME programs reflect the evolving needs of the healthcare system and the public. The ACGME also works to align training with the changing landscape of medicine, including advances in medical technology and evolving patient care models.

Chapter Summary

GME programs are a vital component of the human resources required to ensure safe and high-quality medical care in this country. These training programs ensure a continuous stream of appropriately trained and experienced healthcare providers necessary to maintain the appropriate staffing and healthcare delivery.

The training process is both long (3-7 years) and complex as it entails not just learning, but learning while actually caring for patients, and it must be closely monitored, with very specific requirements and standards. This oversight is provided through a well-structured, specialty-specific program administered by the ACGME. By overseeing the accreditation process and promoting best practices, the ACGME ensures that GME programs mitigate problems inherent in training programs and provide high-quality education that prepares learners to deliver safe, effective, and ethical patient care.

REFERENCES

1. ACGME. Specialty-Specific Program Requirements: Program Leadership Dedicated Time. 2023. https://www.acgme.org/globalassets/pdfs/specialty-specific-requirement-topics/dio-dedicated_time_program_leadership_102023.pdf.
2. ACGME. Common Program Requirements (Residency). 2025. https://www.acgme.org/globalassets/pfassets/programrequirements/2025-prs/cprresidency_2025.pdf.
3. Kavic MS. Competency and the Six Core Competencies. *JSLS* 2002;6(2):95-97.
4. ACGME. Milestones Guidebook for Residents and Fellows. Secondary Milestones Guidebook for Residents and Fellows 2025. https://www.acgme.org/globalassets/pdfs/milestones/milestonesguidebookforresidentsfellows.pdf
5. Dreyfus SE. The Five-Stage Model of Adult Skill Acquisition. *Bulletin of Science, Technology & Society.* 2004;24(3):177-181 doi: 10.1177/0270467604264992.
6. Zagoria R. The ACGME and the residency review committee: external program review. Accreditation Council for Graduate Medical Education. *Acad Radiol.* 2003;10 Suppl 1:S10-5 doi: 10.1016/s1076-6332(03)80143-5.
7. ACGME. ACGME Specialties. Secondary ACGME Specialties 2025. https://www.acgme.org/specialties/.
8. Data Resource Book: Academic Year 2023-2024. Accreditation Council for Graduate Medical Education. Accessed February 10, 2025. dataresourcebook2023-2024.pdf
9. Heisler E, Mendez B, Mitchell A, et al. Federal Support for Graduate Medical Education: An Overview (CRS Report No. R44376) congress.gov, 2018.
10. He K, Whang E, Kristo G. Graduate Medical Education Funding Mechanisms, Challenges, and Solutions: A Narrative Review. *Am J Surg.* 2021;221(1):65–71 doi: 10.1016/j.amjsurg.2020.06.007 [published Online First: 20200623].
11. ACGME. Resident/Fellow and Faculty Surveys. Secondary Resident/Fellow and Faculty Surveys 2025. https://www.acgme.org/data-systems-technical-support/resident-fellow-and-faculty-surveys/.
12. Clements DS, Miser WF. Understanding and Using the ACGME Resident Surveys to Improve Your Residency Program. *Ann Fam Med.* 2021;19(3):280–281 doi: 10.1370/afm.2704 [published Online First: 20210510].
13. Mitchell KB, Miller T. Getting the Most From the ACGME Annual Resident and Faculty Survey. *Ann Fam Med.* 2017;15(6):591 doi: https://doi.org/10.1370/afm.2163.

14. Elkhaled W, Dulaimy O, Hamad S, et al. Addressing Citations in an ACGME-I Psychiatry Residency Program: From Probationary to Continued Accreditation Within 13 Months. *J Grad Med Educ.* 2024;16(1):11-14 doi: 10.4300/JGME-D-23-00641.1 [published Online First: 20240217].
15. Stansfield RB, Markova T, Baker R. Integration of Continuous Quality Improvement Methods Into Annual Program and Institutional Evaluation. *J Grad Med Educ.* 2019;11(5):585–591 doi: 10.4300/JGME-D-19-00145.1.
16. Levine RB, Hebert RS, Wright SM. Factors Associated with Citation of Internal Medicine Residency Programs for Lackof Scholarly Activity. *Teach Learn Med.* 2005;17(4):328–331 doi: 10.1207/s15328015tlm1704_3.
17. Alweis R, Wenderoth S, Donato A. Effectiveness of Iterative Interventions To Increase Research Productivity in One Residency Program. *J Community Hosp Intern Med Perspect.* 2015;5(6):29203 doi: 10.3402/jchimp.v5.29203 [published Online First: 20151211].
18. Chaloupek M, Graham T, Meyer L. Common ACGME Citations and How to Avoid Them. August 13, 2020. https://gme.med.ufl.edu/wordpress/files/2020/08/2020-8-13-ACGME-Citations-and-how-to-avoid-them-FINAL.pdf.
19. Philibert I, Friedmann P, Williams WT, ACGME Work Group on Resident Duty Hours. New Requirements for Resident Duty Hours. *JAMA.* 2002;288(9):1112-1114 doi: 10.1001/jama.288.9.1112.
20. Nasca TJ, Day SH, Amis ES Jr, ACGME Duty Hour Task Force. The New Recommendations on Duty Hours from the ACGME Task Force. *N Engl J Med.* 2010;363(2):e3 doi: 10.1056/NEJMsb1005800 [published Online First: 20100623].
21. Raj KS. Well-Being in Residency: A Systematic Review. *J Grad Med Educ.* 2016;8(5):674–684 doi: 10.4300/JGME-D-15-00764.1.
22. Domen ER. *Professionalism in Pathology and Laboratory Medicine.* Northfield, Illinois: College of American Pathologists; 2020.

CHAPTER 12

Compliance and Regulatory

Roz Cordini, JD, MSN, RN, CHC, CHPC;
Karen M Eastmond, CHC, CHPC, MBA; and
Jacob Swartzwelder, CPC, CRC, CPMA, CIC, CEMC

HALM CORE CONTENT:

- 4.1 Auditing
- 4.2 Clinician roles and qualifying criteria (e.g., administrative versus clinical)
- 4.3 CMS Conditions of Participation
- 4.4 Compliance and regulatory (e.g., antitrust, conflict of interest, EMTALA, Stark, billing, and coding)
- 4.9 Medicare and Medicaid regulations
- 4.10 Other third-party payment regulations (e.g., PPO, HMO)
- 4.11 Patients' rights laws and regulations (e.g., informed consent, advance directives, involuntary commitments)
- 4.12 Regulatory reporting requirements
- 4.13 Research office leadership compliance and regulation (HIC, IRB, grants management)

CASE SCENARIO:

A physician leader receives reports from a cardiologist that a peer cardiologist is performing stent procedures on patients who do not meet clinical criteria. The physician leader understands the seriousness of the allegations.

What are the regulatory and compliance implications around how this issue is handled?

Hospital leadership involves its compliance officer and legal counsel, who directs a medical necessity review under attorney-client privilege by an external peer. The findings confirm the allegations.

In addition to addressing the physician through the medical staff processes, the hospital understands it has a repayment obligation under the CMS Overpayment Rule possibly going as far back as six years. The Compliance Officer ensures the hospital's legal requirements are met.

What auditing controls should be in place to monitor similar scenarios in the future?

UNDERSTANDING THE CRITICAL ROLE compliance programs play in the medical profession is one of the key requirements for operating a successful practice. For physicians, the intertwining of ethical obligations and regulatory requirements is not merely a bureaucratic necessity; it represents a commitment to integrity, patient welfare, and community trust. As the healthcare landscape evolves with increasing regulatory scrutiny and complex ethical dilemmas, robust compliance programs emerge as essential tools.

Compliance and Regulatory

The foundation of compliance programs lies in the Federal Sentencing Guidelines and the articulation of the framework, which is characterized by the Office of Inspector General's (OIG's) seven key elements that a compliance program must include:[1]

1. Written policies and procedures.
2. Compliance leadership and oversight.
3. Training and education.
4. Communication.
5. Enforcement.
6. Risk assessment.
7. Response.

These elements are a baseline to help healthcare providers develop, at a minimum, key processes, policies, and artifacts to meet their obligation as participants in government programs and to avoid fines, disbarment, and exclusion from participating in federal programs. The OIG requires that providers have "effective" compliance programs that identify issues, correct them, and prevent recurrence.

Centers for Medicare & Medicaid Services Conditions of Participation

An example of a compliance system is the Conditions of Participation (CoPs) and Conditions of Coverage (CfCs) established by CMS that articulate CMS requirements that healthcare organizations need to fulfil in order to initiate and maintain their involvement in Medicare and Medicaid programs. These health and safety criteria form the basis for enhancing quality and safeguarding the well-being of beneficiaries. Additionally, CMS verifies that the standards set by accrediting organizations recognized through a "deeming" process, align with or surpass the Medicare requirements outlined in the CoPs and CfCs.[2]

ACCREDITATION

Accrediting organizations such as The Joint Commission[3] conduct comprehensive evaluations of healthcare providers to verify compliance with Centers for Medicare & Medicaid Services (CMS) guidelines. These organizations assess providers' policies, procedures, and clinical practices, designating "deemed providers" that meet CMS standards. Through rigorous auditing, these organizations help healthcare entities measure, assess, and improve performance to ensure safe, high-quality patient care.

EMERGENCY CARE PROTECTIONS

The Emergency Medical Treatment and Labor Act (EMTALA), enacted in 1986, is a critical federal mandate requiring Medicare-participating hospitals to provide emergency medical treatment to all patients, irrespective of their financial status or insurance coverage.[4] Designed to eliminate the unethical practice of "patient dumping," the law establishes comprehensive on-call requirements for medical staff and provides clear definitions to ensure patient protection and equitable healthcare access.

FRAUD AND ABUSE LAWS

Fraud and abuse prevention is another critical area of healthcare regulation. The Physician Self-Referral law, also known as the Stark Law, prohibits physicians from referring Medicare or Medicaid patients to organizations with which the physician or his or her immediate family member has a financial relationship, unless one of its exceptions applies.[5] The exceptions are strict, and the failure to meet an exception creates a violation regardless of intent. Where a relationship is deemed tainted, no claims may be submitted to governmental payers. Failure to ensure this element is adhered to can result in those billed claims turning into False Claims (see below).

Similar to the Stark Law is the federal Anti-Kickback Statute (AKS), which prohibits the offering, paying, soliciting, or receiving of anything of value by anyone, to induce or reward referrals for items or services covered by federal healthcare programs.[6] The AKS is a criminal law, unlike the Stark law, and requires establishment of knowing and willful intent in order to show a violation. Another difference from the Stark Law is that the AKS has safe harbors rather than exceptions. There is a presumption against a violation if all elements of one of the safe harbors is met. The failure to fully meet the elements does not mean a violation has occurred; however, the farther away from the requirements, the more risk is associated with a relationship.

The federal False Claims Act (FCA) is the U.S. government's primary enforcement tool against healthcare fraud.[7] It imposes liability on any person or entity that knowingly submits false claims to the government or causes another to submit a false claim. The FCA imposes significant penalties on any person or organization that violates the statute, including treble damages (three times each false claim submitted).

FCA penalties are adjusted for inflation annually. As of February 12, 2024, penalties range from $13,946 to $27,894 per violation.[8] In addition, civil and/or criminal penalties may also apply. The FCA includes *qui tam* or whistleblower provisions that allow relators, or private individuals, to file lawsuits on behalf of the government and share in any recovery, thus encouraging whistleblowers to come forward with information about fraud. Many of the laws in this section, where violated, can result in a false claim and be subject to the strict penalties associated with the FCA.

The CMS 60-Day Repayment Rule, initiated in the Affordable Care Act, requires healthcare providers and suppliers to report and return overpayments from Medicare and Medicaid within 60 days of identification.[9] Overpayment means the receipt of any reimbursement from a governmental payer to which the provider or organization is not entitled, whether accidentally or not. The term "identified" is defined and the 60-day repayment period does not run until the overpayment is "identified" following up to a six-month period of diligence in order to determine and quantify an overpayment.

Failure to repay an overpayment within the 60-day time period turns those overpaid claims into false claims. Self-auditing as part of an effective compliance program is critical in order to ensure any overpayments are identified and repaid in a timely manner. Where required due to the systemic nature of an issue creating overpayment is identified, healthcare organizations and providers may be obliged to look back six years to quantify the necessary repayment.

The Beneficiary Inducement Statute prohibits providing or offering any remuneration to Medicare or Medicaid beneficiaries that is likely to influence their selection of a particular provider, practitioner, or supplier. This law seeks to prevent healthcare entities from using remuneration such as free or discounted services to encourage patients to seek services from the provider offering such remuneration in order that they may bill such services to a governmental payer.

The Exclusionary Statute gives the OIG authority to exclude individuals and entities from participating in Medicare, Medicaid, and other federal healthcare programs for various reasons, including fraud, patient abuse, and certain felony convictions. The OIG has both mandatory exclusion authority as well as permissive exclusionary authority with regard to violations of the laws discussed in this section.[10]

Providers are prohibited from billing for services ordered by, or contracting with, individuals or entities that have been excluded from participating in any of the federal healthcare programs, such as Medicare and Medicaid. Significant penalties may result, including repayment of amounts improperly received. As part of its compliance program, providers/entities should check the OIG's List of Excluded Individuals and Entities (LEIE) and state Medicaid exclusion databases before hiring, contracting with, or granting privileges to employees, contractors, or practitioners, and periodically thereafter.

Finally, Civil Monetary Penalties (CMPs) are fines imposed by the government for violations of certain laws and regulations.[11] In healthcare, CMPs can be imposed for a wide range of issues, including violating the AKS, Stark Law, submitting false claims, or failing to report and return overpayments as required by the 60-Day Repayment Rule. These penalties can be substantial, often involving fines of thousands of dollars per violation.

Centers for Medicare & Medicaid Services Regulations

Medicare and Medicaid regulations constitute a significant portion of healthcare law. As an example, CMS has established CoPs and Conditions for Coverage (CfCs) that healthcare providers must meet in order to participate in these programs.[12] In addition, CMS issues National Coverage Determinations (NCDs) for certain tests and procedures that set out if and how certain items and services are covered. Any CMS-recognized accrediting body having deemed status must also have standards that meet or exceed the Medicare standards set forth in the CoPs and CfCs.[2]

The Medicare Secondary Payer Act, for instance, requires group health plans to make Medicare the secondary payer for services provided to working-aged and disabled Medicare beneficiaries.[13] Additionally, regulations governing the Medicare Advantage Program[14] (Medicare Part C) and Voluntary Medicare Prescription Drug Benefit[15] (Medicare Part D) set forth requirements for private insurers who offer Medicare plans, ensuring that beneficiaries receive appropriate coverage and care.

CMS has in place an internet-only manual system that houses its policies and procedures and standard operating procedures addressing each of these areas that are formulated based on laws, regulations, and guidelines, and provide a good reference for healthcare providers and organizations.[16]

Other Key Laws Affecting Providers

The Controlled Substances Act regulates the manufacture, possession, use, and distribution of certain drugs and precursors, focusing on preventing abuse and diversion while ensuring patient access to necessary medications.[17] The act is especially relevant for prescribing practices and pain management.

Workplace safety in healthcare is governed by Occupational Safety and Health Administration (OSHA) regulations, which establish standards for safe working conditions, addressing bloodborne pathogens, hazardous materials, and ergonomics.[18]

State laws further regulate healthcare through stricter fraud and abuse laws, physician licensure and discipline, and prescribing practices. State-specific regulations for health maintenance organizations (HMOs) and preferred provider organizations

(PPOs) insurance plans also interact with federal laws, adding legal complexity for providers.

Antitrust laws, critical in an increasingly consolidated healthcare industry, promote competition and prevent monopolies. Key federal laws include the Sherman Act, which prohibits anticompetitive agreements and monopolization; the Clayton Act, which restricts certain anticompetitive practices like mergers; and the Federal Trade Commission Act, which bans unfair competition. States often supplement these federal antitrust laws.[19]

Clearly, the landscape of healthcare laws and regulations is vast and complex. Healthcare providers, physician leaders, and organizations must maintain robust compliance programs to navigate this ever-evolving environment. Staying informed about these laws and their implications is crucial not only for avoiding penalties and legal issues but also for ensuring high-quality, ethical patient care. As the healthcare industry continues to change and adapt to new technologies and delivery models, it is likely that the regulatory framework will continue to evolve as well, requiring ongoing vigilance and adaptation from all stakeholders in the healthcare system.

Patient Rights Laws and Regulations

Patient rights are a cornerstone of ethical healthcare practice and vital to ensuring individuals receive care that is both respectful and equitable. These rights empower patients to make informed decisions about their healthcare, protect their personal autonomy, and ensure they are treated with dignity. For physicians, understanding and upholding patient rights is not only a legal obligation but also a key component of building trust and fostering positive patient-provider relationships. It is important to know the essential rights of patients, the legal frameworks that protect them, and the critical role healthcare professionals play in maintaining compliance with these standards.

THE PATIENT SELF-DETERMINATION ACT

The Patient Self-Determination Act (PSDA) is a federal law that requires healthcare providers to inform patients of their right to make informed medical decisions, including the right to accept or refuse treatment and to create an advance directive.[20] An advance directive is a legal document specifying a patient's preferences for medical care if they become incapacitated, including wishes regarding life-sustaining treatments in terminal or irreversible conditions.

Providers are obligated to honor advance directives, even if the treatment is deemed futile or unwise. Futile treatment refers to interventions unlikely to yield meaningful benefits. In such cases, providers should speak with patients and families to clarify care goals while respecting patient autonomy. Ethics committees can provide valuable support in navigating complex end-of-life situations.

MEDICARE/MEDICAID PATIENT RIGHTS

Patients enrolled in Medicare and Medicaid have specific rights designed to protect their access to healthcare services and dignity. These rights include the right to receive information about their health plans, the right to participate in their treatment planning, and the right to appeal decisions regarding their care. Patients are also entitled to receive services in a safe and respectful environment, to be assured of the confidentiality of their medical records, to be free from restraint and/or seclusion (except to ensure the immediate physical safety of the patient, a staff member, or others), and to have certain visitation rights.[21]

INFORMED CONSENT

Informed consent, a key Medicare patient right and healthcare principle, ensures patients understand the risks, benefits, and alternatives of a proposed treatment or procedure before agreeing to the treatment. Providers must communicate clearly, allow questions, and confirm patient understanding, as signing a consent form alone may not suffice. Patients must have the capacity to consent; otherwise, consent must be obtained from a surrogate.

Providers should document the consent process, including the information shared and the patient's decision, to reduce legal risk. In emergencies, treatment may proceed in the patient's best interest, with prompt notification to the patient or surrogate when possible.[22,23]

INVOLUNTARY COMMITMENT

Involuntary commitment refers to the legal process by which patients may be admitted to a facility against their will without their consent. This process is typically governed by state law and requires that the patient is a danger to themselves or others or is unable to care for themselves due to their mental condition.

Due process protections must be in place, including the right to a hearing, legal representation, and the right to appeal the commitment. Patients have the right to receive humane care and treatment throughout their commitment.[24] An organization's legal office is of great assistance when the decision to hospitalize a patient against their will is less than clear.

CONFLICTS OF INTEREST

Conflicts of interest occur when a healthcare provider's personal or financial interests may influence their professional judgment. Providers must disclose potential conflicts to ensure transparency, such as relationships with facilities, pharmaceutical, or medical device companies that could affect prescribing decisions. Institutions often have policies to identify, manage, and mitigate conflicts, preserving patient care integrity.[25]

The CMS Open Payments Program requires medical device and pharmaceutical companies to report compensation provided to healthcare providers, including meals, in an online database. Providers can review and dispute inaccuracies in these records, which are publicly searchable and used in compliance programs.

Upholding patient rights is crucial for ethical, equitable, and compassionate care. Providers and leaders should understand these principles to protect patient autonomy and minimize risks, including potential legal consequences of non-compliance.

Clinician Roles and Qualifying Criteria

Medical directors serve essential clinical and administrative leadership roles in healthcare facilities, with positions often required by accreditation standards and Medicare Conditions of Participation for certain facilities such as long-term care,[26] hospice,[27] or dialysis.[28]

Medical directors' core responsibilities include:

- Clinical oversight: Developing clinical guidelines, protocols, and policies to promote patient safety and quality care.
- Quality improvement: Monitoring outcomes, analyzing performance metrics, and leading improvement initiatives.
- Administrative liaison: Facilitating communication between medical staff and administration, advocating for resources.
- Policy development: Creating and updating policies to reflect best practices and regulatory compliance.
- Resource management: Contributing to budgeting and resource allocation decisions.
- Education and research: Overseeing staff education programs and quality improvement projects.

The medical director is a multifaceted role requiring strong clinical expertise, leadership skills, and a commitment to improving patient care within the healthcare organization.[29]

Auditing and Monitoring

Audit programs maintain revenue integrity, ensure adherence to legal standards, and identify providers who pose risks. Programs prevent revenue loss by improving code selection and reduce takebacks through education. Programs ensure compliance with federal, state, and payer guidelines while maintaining accurate code reporting.

Compliance with coding and regulatory guidelines helps avoid penalties. Audits also identify quality concerns and documentation issues that affect patient safety and provider communication.

PURPOSE AND TYPES OF AUDITS

Regular enterprise-wide audits of provider documentation support coding accuracy, compliance, and revenue integrity. Organizations typically use a mix of audit types: internal/external audits to identify risks and opportunities, comprehensive retrospective audits to maintain revenue integrity, focused reviews for specific issues like CPT codes or OIG work plan items, and prospective audits for high-risk services before insurance submission.

CORE AUDIT COMPONENTS

Core audit components are scoping, sampling, and documentation review. Scoping defines objectives, scope, sample size, and guidelines. Sample size varies by audit type: voluntary self-disclosures need 100+ encounters, comprehensive audits need 20 encounters per provider, and focused audits vary based on objectives.

Random sampling software (RAT-STATs) ensures objective findings. Certified auditors review documentation and code selection to identify overcoding, undercoding, and documentation issues, assessing compliance with CPT, ICD-10, CMS, and American Medical Association (AMA) 2023 Evaluation and Management guidelines.[30]

Reports include scoring and financial impacts, with findings potentially leading to focused audits or education. Programs should set quality thresholds and re-audit protocols.

BENEFITS OF REGULAR AUDITS

Documentation audits deliver critical enterprise-level benefits by optimizing financial performance, ensuring regulatory compliance, and enhancing quality of patient care. These systematic reviews identify documentation vulnerabilities, reduce insurance claim denials, and provide targeted provider education. By establishing consistent organizational standards, audits support accurate patient records, streamline revenue cycles, and mitigate compliance risks through proactive identification and correction of documentation practices.

Regulatory Reporting

In the aforementioned complex regulatory landscape, CMS also plays a crucial role in overseeing healthcare programs to ensure that services provided to beneficiaries are of the highest quality.

MERIT-BASED INCENTIVE PAYMENT SYSTEM (MIPS)

The Merit-based Incentive Payment System (MIPS) offers physicians incentives based on quality-of-care metrics, patient health record accessibility and interoperability, patient engagement, and cost efficiency. Participation encourages care process improvements while rewarding patient engagement and quality outcomes.[31]

SUNSHINE ACT

The Sunshine Act requires transparency in financial relationships between physicians and pharmaceutical or medical device companies. Physicians must disclose payments received from these entities, fostering accountability and prioritizing patient needs over financial incentives.

Research Office Leadership Compliance and Regulation

Advancing patient care and tackling healthcare challenges requires a focus on research, which drives innovation in treatments, medications, and technologies. In a dynamic medical landscape, evidence-based practice is key to developing clinical guidelines and best practices.

INSTITUTIONAL REVIEW BOARD (IRB)

An Institutional Review Board (IRB) oversees human subjects research to ensure ethical standards. Human Investigation Committees (HIC) evaluate research protocols, assessing risks and benefits to protect participant welfare while maximizing research value.

GRANTS

Research funding requires effective grant-writing and NIH review of proposals. Proper fund management, financial records, and documentation must demonstrate both ethical compliance and research integrity. The NIH provides financial support for high-quality clinical research, requiring ongoing oversight to ensure regulatory compliance and improve patient care outcomes.[32]

Chapter Summary

The landscape of healthcare compliance and regulation is built upon the Federal Sentencing Guidelines and the Office of Inspector General's seven key elements: policies, leadership, training, communication, enforcement, risk assessment, and response. These elements form the foundation for avoiding fines, disbarment, and program exclusion.

Several critical laws and regulations are important for physician leaders to know, including CMS Conditions of Participation for Medicare/Medicaid participation, EMTALA's guarantee of emergency medical treatment regardless of payment ability, the Stark Law's prohibition on physician self-referral, and the Anti-Kickback Statute's prevention of improper referral payments. The False Claims Act's role in penalizing fraudulent submissions and the 60-Day Repayment Rule's requirement for prompt overpayment returns are also important.

Patient rights deserve significant attention, including the Patient Self-Determination Act's protection of informed medical decisions, informed consent requirements, involuntary commitment processes, and specific Medicare/Medicaid patient protections.

The chapter also explores clinical roles, particularly medical directors' vital leadership functions, and the importance of regular auditing through various approaches to maintain revenue integrity and compliance. The Merit-based Incentive Payment System (MIPS) is examined for its role in incentivizing quality care metrics, while research compliance, including Institutional Review Board oversight and grant management, rounds out the discussion. Throughout, the chapter emphasizes that maintaining robust compliance programs is essential for healthcare organizations to successfully navigate regulatory requirements while delivering high-quality patient care.

REFERENCES

1. U.S. Department of Justice Office of Justice Programs. Federal Sentencing Guidelines: A Report on the Operation of the Guidelines System and Short-Term Impacts on Disparity in Sentencing, Use of Incarceration, and Prosecutorial Discretion and Plea Bargaining. 1991. https://www.ojp.gov/ncjrs/virtual-library/abstracts/federal-sentencing-guidelines-report-operation-guidelines-system
2. Centers for Medicare and Medicaid Services. Conditions for Coverage (CfCs) & Conditions of Participation (CoPs). Updated September 10, 2024. Accessed November 14, 2024. https://www.cms.gov/medicare/health-safety-standards/conditions-coverage-participation.
3. The Joint Commission. What Is Accreditation? Accessed November 14, 2024. https://www.jointcommission.org/what-we-offer/accreditation/become-accredited/what-is-accreditation/
4. 42 U.S.C. Sec. 1395dd.
5. 42 U.S.C. Sec. 1395nn.
6. 42 U.S.C. Sec. 1320a-7b.
7. 31 U.S.C. Sec. 3729-3733.
8. 89 FR 9764, February 12, 2024.
9. 42 C.F.R. Sec. 401.305.
10. 42 U.S.C. Sec. 1320a-7.
11. 42 U.S.C. Sec. 1320a-7a.
12. 42 C.F.R. Part 482.
13. 42 U.S.C. Sec. 1395y(b)(2).
14. 42 C.F.R. Part 422.
15. 42 C.F.R. Part 423.
16. Centers for Medicare and Medicaid Services. Internet-Only Manuals. https://www.cms.gov/medicare/regulations-guidance/manuals/internet-only-manuals-ioms
17. Pub. L. 91-513, Title II, Sec. 202 (Oct. 27, 1970), as amended.

18. 29 C.F.R. Sec. 1910.
19. 15 U.S.C. Ch. 1.
20. 42 U.S.C. Sec. 1395 et. seq.
21. 42 C.F.R. Sec. 482.13.
22. American Medical Association. AMA Code of Ethics, Opinion 2.1.1. AMA. Accessed November 14, 2024. https://code-medical-ethics.ama-assn.org/ethics-opinions/informed-consent.
23. 42 C.F.R.482.13(b)(2).
24. For a list of state involuntary commitment laws, see https://www.bicyclehealth.com/blog/state-by-state-involuntary-commitment-laws.
25. Farhud D, Zokaei S. Conflict of Interest in Medicine and Health. *Iran J Public Health*. 2022;51(7):i–ii. doi: 10.18502/ijph.v51i7.10108. https://www.ncbi.nlm.nih.gov/pmc/articles/PMC9529726/
26. 42 C.F.R. 483.75.
27. 42 C.F.R 418.102.
28. 42 C.F.R. 494.150.
29. Kossaify A, Rasputin B, Lahoud JC. The Function of a Medical Director in Healthcare Institutions: A Master or a Servant. *Health Serv Insights*. 2013 Oct 14;6:105–110. doi: 10.4137/HSI.S13000. PMID: 25114566; PMCID: PMC4089725.
30. American Medical Association. CPT Evaluation and Management (E/M) Code and Guideline Changes. Accessed November 14, 2024. https://www.ama-assn.org/system/files/2023-e-m-descriptors-guidelines.pdf
31. Centers for Medicare and Medicaid Services. What is MIPS? Quality Payment Program. Accessed November 14, 2024. https://qpp.cms.gov/mips/mvps/learn-about-mips
32. National Institutes of Health. Grants Process. Updated July 24, 2024. Accessed November 14, 2024. https://grants.nih.gov/grants-process

CHAPTER 13

Policy, Advocacy, and Philanthropy

Jennifer L. Wiler, MD, MBA, and Greg Adams, DO, MBA

HALM CORE CONTENT:

- 3.6 Public policy, legislative, and advocacy processes
- 3.7 Philanthropic and investment processes
- 4.14 Advocacy and engagement
  - 4.14.1 Lobbying entities
  - 4.14.2 Federal agencies (e.g., MedPac)
  - 4.14.3 Organized healthcare (e.g., NQF, AHA, AMA, etc.)

CASE SCENARIO:

The medical director for an emergency department has noted an increase in patient boarding despite working with hospital leadership on implementing a number of hospital flow tactics. However, the problem persists. Due to the negative quality and safety impact that boarding has on patient care, what other organizations are aware of this issue and working on a solution? Are there any resources from organizations that can help improve processes at the hospital? And are there ways to engage with policymakers?

Public Policy, Legislative, and Advocacy Processes

PUBLIC POLICY REFERS TO THE actions a government takes to address societal issues and promote the welfare of its citizens. It encompasses a range of decisions, laws, regulations, and programs aimed at solving problems or achieving goals in areas like healthcare, education, environment, and economic development.

Development of public policy typically involves five steps:

1. Identification of Issues: Recognizing societal problems or needs.
2. Agenda Setting: Prioritizing issues for government attention.
3. Formulation: Developing strategies and proposals to address the issues.

4. Implementation: Putting policies into action through government agencies.
5. Evaluation: Assessing the effectiveness and impact of the policies.

Public policy is then shaped by the political processes, public opinion, and stakeholder interests. Policies can be at the local, regional, national, or international level. For instance, in 2003, the Framework Convention on Tobacco Control (FCTC) was the first global public health treaty negotiated under the auspices of the World Health Organization (WHO). This international treaty, which sought to reduce tobacco consumption worldwide through measures such as advertising bans, warning labels, smoke-free public spaces, and support for tobacco cessation programs, was originally ratified by 40 counties, then ultimately 181 counties by 2018. It is heralded as one of the most successful pioneering international health policy initiatives to date.[1]

Another example of healthcare-related public policy at the state level involves vaccination requirements. Each state requires children to be vaccinated against certain diseases prior to entering public and private schools. While there is no single federal law requiring vaccination, each state has adopted these requirements into their statutes.[2]

The term *legislative* refers to anything related to the process of making, enacting, or interpreting laws. It typically describes the branch of government or the activities associated with the creation and passage of laws. In the United States, the federal branches of government are legislative, executive, and judicial. These branches work together, with checks and balances, to prevent any one branch from gaining too much power.

The legislative branch makes laws and consists of the House of Representatives and the Senate. First, a bill is introduced in either the House or Senate by a member of Congress. Then, the proposed bill is sent to a legislative committee for review, hearings, and possible amendments. If approved, the bill is then debated by the full chamber where further amendments can be made.

Next, the chamber votes, and if the bill passes, it goes to the other legislative chamber to repeat the process. If the bill is approved by both chambers, but there are differences between the two versions, a conference committee reconciles them. The final bill is then sent to the president, who can sign it into law, veto it, or let it become law without a signature. If vetoed by the president, Congress can override with a two-thirds majority in both chambers.

A healthcare-related example is the precursor version of the Affordable Care Act (ACA). This legislation was originally introduced to both Houses and went through this extensive process. After approval by both chambers and reconciliation of significant differences between the two versions during the Conference Committee, the revised bill was signed into law by President Barack Obama on March 23, 2010.[3]

Although the legislative process took nine months, the process of building the consensus, drafting the bill, and negotiating compromises took several years. Today, it remains one of the most significant and contentious legislative undertakings in

U.S. history. This demonstrates the overall complexity and issues that can arise when creating pieces of legislation.

The executive branch enforces laws and is headed by the president, and includes the vice president, the Cabinet, and federal agencies. An executive order is a directive issued by the president of the United States to manage federal operations and allows the president to enact policy without congressional approval.

A notable example of an executive order related to COVID-19 was issued by President Biden on January 21, 2021.[4] This order aimed to enhance the federal response to the pandemic and promote overall public safety. Some specific actions included a mask mandate on federal property and during interstate travel, a requirement that federal agencies had to follow CDC guidelines, and mandated coordination across agencies to improve testing and vaccine distribution.

Executive orders related to healthcare can significantly impact the direction of policy and the implementation of laws. This impact is achieved by directing federal agencies to take certain actions, adjust regulations, or change the way healthcare programs are run. Depending on the action, the enacted orders can either strengthen or weaken aspects of healthcare law.

In 2017, President Trump implemented an executive order that promoted policies that lowered premiums and reduced the regulatory burdens of the ACA by expanding short-term limited-duration insurance plans which were cheaper, but provided less coverage, than ACA-compliant plans and encouraged state flexibility in healthcare regulations.[5] Essentially, this order attempted to undermine key provisions of the ACA, including the individual mandate.

In 2021, President Biden implemented an executive order focused on strengthening Medicaid and reversed several Trump administration policies that had weakened the ACA, including reversing rules that allowed short-term health plans to be sold.[6]

The third branch of the U.S. government is the judicial branch, which is responsible for interpreting laws. The federal court is composed of three main levels: district courts, circuit courts, and the Supreme Court. The Supreme Court is the highest court in the U.S. judicial system and ensures laws comply with the U.S. Constitution. The Supreme Court has played a pivotal role in shaping the ACA since its passage in 2010 and influenced key aspects of the law's implementation, in particular the individual mandate (*National Federation of Independent Business v. Sebelius*, 2012), Medicaid expansion (*King v. Burwell*, 2015), and state-level decisions (*California v. Texas*, 2021).[7-9]

Regulations are another essential piece of the legislative process. They are detailed rules or directives issued by government agencies to implement and enforce laws enacted by legislative bodies. They provide specific guidance on how laws are to be applied and complied with in practice.

Regulations are more adaptable than laws in that they are more easily modified to adapt to changing circumstances. The rulemaking process allows stakeholder feedback, and when implemented, they are often easier to update and can take less time to modify. Regulations play a crucial role in ensuring the delivery of high-quality healthcare across the U.S.

Each branch of government has the ability to influence the development or implementation of various healthcare regulations. Some common federal examples include:

- The Health Insurance Portability and Accountability Act (HIPAA) regulations were stipulated by the U.S. Department of Health and Human Services (HHS) to protect the privacy and security of patient health information.[10] Essentially, this prevents the dissemination of private health information without explicit patient consent.
- The Occupational Safety and Health Administration (OSHA) created regulations to ensure safe working conditions in healthcare facilities, including personal protective equipment (PPE), infection control procedures, and workplace exposure limits to bloodborne pathogens regulations to protect workers from health hazards.[11]
- The Centers for Medicare & Medicaid Services (CMS) specified the Emergency Medical Treatment and Labor Act (EMTALA) regulations which require hospitals to provide emergency medical treatment to individuals regardless of their insurance status or ability to pay.[12] This ensures that hospitals provide a medical screening exam and necessary treatment to stabilize patients in an emergency and effectively prohibits hospitals from refusing care to patients based on their insurance status or inability to pay.
- The Joint Commission (TJC) specifies the National Patient Safety Goals (NPSG), which set national standards for improving patient safety in healthcare organizations. This includes preventing surgical errors (e.g., ensuring correct-site surgery), improving medication safety, reducing falls, reducing healthcare-associated infections, and improving healthcare equity.[13]
- The Office of Inspector General (OIG), which is a part of CMS, defines the Anti-Kickback Statute (AKS) and Stark Law Regulations.[14] These prevent fraudulent activities related to healthcare services, including prohibiting healthcare providers from receiving or offering improper financial incentives in exchange for patient referrals and ensuring that decisions are based on patient care, not financial gain.
- The Drug Enforcement Administration (DEA) controls the distribution of controlled substances, ensuring their proper use in healthcare settings while preventing misuse and diversion.[15]

Federal Agencies

Federal agencies are entities within the United States government that are responsible for carrying out specific duties and enforcing laws for programs that are under federal legislation. Their comprehensive scope of functions includes regulation, enforcement, research, and policy guidance.

Agencies may function under executive direction, such as the Centers for Disease Control and Prevention (CDC), or work independently, such as the Environmental Protection Agency (EPA). Federal agencies also are diverse in the sectors they work with, including healthcare, defense, and finance.

Federal agencies are integral in healthcare regulation and policy setting within the United States. They ensure compliance and oversee various programs to improve the overall public health of the country. For example, by creating regulations and standards, the Federal Drug Administration ensures the safety of food and drug manufacturing in the United States.[16] Another example involves oversight and enforcement via the Office of Inspector General (OIG). This agency has the authority to investigate fraud, abuse, and waste involving Medicare and Medicaid, along with other HHS programs.[14]

Other key healthcare-related federal agencies include:

- *The Medicare Payment Advisory Commission (MedPAC)*
  MedPAC is an independent congressional agency that was established by the Balanced Budget Act of 1997.[17] The commission advises U.S. Congress on issues that affect Medicare. In addition, they advise Congress on payments for private health plans that are engaged with Medicare's fee-for-service program and provide information on access and quality of care.
- *Agency for Health Research and Quality (AHRQ)*
  AHRQ helps produce evidence to improve healthcare and patient safety in the United States.[18] In 1999, the Healthcare Research and Quality Act established the AHRQ as the lead federal agency on healthcare quality and safety research.[16]
- *Indian Health Services (IHS)*
  The IHS is an agency within the Department of Health and Human Services tasked with providing federal healthcare to American Indians and Alaska Natives.[19] This is accomplished through IHS facilities along with other coordinated outreach programs.
- *Health Resources and Services Administration (HRSA)*
  The HRSA provides healthcare to those who are medically or economically vulnerable and reside in areas that lack access to care.[20] The agency supports health infrastructure by ensuring these medical deserts have adequately trained healthcare professionals providing quality care.

Advocacy and Engagement

Public policy, legislative activity, and regulatory actions can be focused at the local, state, national, or international level. Each of these levels offers distinct opportunities for innovation and creative approaches to addressing complex issues. They each offer physician leaders distinct opportunities and challenges to engage in the process and outcome.

Lobbying Entities and Organized Healthcare

A lobbying entity is an organization or individual that seeks to influence public policy, legislation, or regulations to advance the interests of a specific group, industry, or cause. These entities engage with policymakers at various levels of government to shape decisions that align with their objectives and can include corporate lobbyists, trade associations, public interest organizations, professional groups, and nonprofit advocacy groups.

Lobbying activities may involve direct communication with lawmakers, grassroots mobilization, political action committees (PACs), research and policy reports, and/or coalition-building with other organizations. Lobbying entities are typically required to register with government authorities and disclose their lobbying activities, ensuring transparency and accountability.

Numerous advocacy groups within healthcare seek to influence public policy, legislation, and regulation in ways that align with the interests of stakeholders within the healthcare sector. These organizations represent a broad spectrum of healthcare-related entities, including healthcare providers, insurance companies, pharmaceutical firms, patient advocacy groups, and public health organizations. Their primary goal is to shape the policy landscape in favor of their constituents by engaging with policymakers, regulators and decision-makers at the local, state, and federal levels.

This directly relates to the idea of organized medicine, which refers to the collective efforts of professional medical organizations, associations, and societies that represent and advocate for the interests of physicians, healthcare providers, and the medical profession as a whole. These groups work to shape public policy, improve healthcare delivery, promote professional standards, and address issues affecting medical practice, such as reimbursement, regulations, education, and healthcare access. Key types of healthcare lobby organizations include:

- *Professional Associations*: These societies represent healthcare professionals such as physicians, nurses, and allied health practitioners (e.g., chiropractors, technicians, etc.) and can be focused on one specialty, such as radiologists, nursing home medical directors, and critical care providers. They tend to advocate for policies related to healthcare access, care equity and quality, professional standards, reimbursement, and education.

  An example is the American Medical Association (AMA), which lobbies on behalf of physicians to address issues such as healthcare reimbursement rates, medical licensure, and the regulation of healthcare practices.[21] An example of a specialty specific group is the American College of Emergency Physicians (ACEP), whose goal is to support quality emergency medical care and promote the interests of emergency physicians.[22]

- *Industry Trade Associations*: These organizations represent entire sectors of the healthcare industry, including hospitals, ambulatory surgery centers, employers, medical device manufactures, biotechnology firms, pharmaceutical drug makers, and other healthcare-related services.

  These organizations focus on shaping healthcare policy and regulation that affects industry-wide practices. For instance, the American Hospital Association (AHA) advocates for policies that support hospitals, including funding from states, Medicare and Medicaid, as well as advocating for regulatory flexibility and healthcare infrastructure support.

  Pharmaceutical and biotechnology associations such as the Pharmaceutical Research and Manufacturers of America (PhRMA) focus their lobbying efforts on relevant issues and advocates for policies that protect the interests of pharmaceutical companies, such as drug pricing, intellectual property rights, and regulatory policies that affect drug development and approval.
- *Patient Advocacy Groups*: These organizations focus on advocating for patients' rights, access to healthcare, equity, and the promotion of public health. They often concentrate on specific conditions, diseases, or broader health issues affecting vulnerable populations. There are numerous examples, such as the American Cancer Society and American Diabetes Association, that lobby for increased funding for research, education, and public health awareness and support initiatives for their disease or condition.
- *Health Insurance and Managed Care Organizations*: These entities represent health insurers, accountable care organizations, and managed care organizations. They focus on shaping policies related to coverage, insurance regulations, and the affordability of healthcare.

  An example is America's Health Insurance Plans (AHIP), which is a membership organization of large and small commercial insurers that lobbies on issues such as health insurance reform, Medicaid expansion, reimbursement, and cost control in the health insurance market.
- *Public Health and Advocacy Organizations*: These groups advocate for broader public health policies, health equity, disease prevention, and access to healthcare for underserved populations. They often address systemic issues in healthcare delivery and focus on improving public health outcomes.

  One example is the AARP (formerly the American Association of Retired Persons) which is a prominent nonprofit organization. They advocate for the needs and interests of individuals aged 50 and older, advocating for policies related to Medicare, healthcare access, and aging-related health issues.

Physician leaders are involved in nearly all of these organizations at some point. As such, there is opportunity for participation in all aspects of lobbying. These organizations are set up to engage with lobbying efforts on behalf of its members and key demographics. They have an abundance of resources which can help members become engaged in the process and allow them to further their overall healthcare specific goals. Some examples include letter writing, meeting with lawmakers at the local and federal level, and testifying before legislation. In addition, by creating these relationships with lawmakers, members can provide specialized insight into specific areas of interest and bring certain problems to their attention.

Philanthropic and Investment Processes

Philanthropy refers to the voluntary and intentional act of donating money, resources, time, or effort to support causes that promote the well-being of others. This may be in the form of monetary donations/financial contributions, volunteerism, or resource-sharing which includes goods, services, or expertise.

Physician leaders are often asked to participate in philanthropic activities due to their areas of specific expertise and desire to help those around them. Potential philanthropic activities for physician leaders include contribution of personal time, resources, or expertise toward causes that benefit public health, underserved populations, or healthcare-related charitable organizations. These activities often extend beyond clinical practice and involve initiatives aimed at improving community health, advancing medical research, or supporting medical education.

For instance, physician leaders may be asked to participate in the following types of activities:

- *Community Engagement*: Volunteer time (personal, administrative leadership, or program) to provide free or discounted healthcare services, particularly in underserved or low-income communities.
- *Medical Research*: Work with institutional departments to solicit community or benefactor support for research initiatives. In addition, they may work with philanthropic foundations that fund innovative medical research aimed at advancing treatments or curing diseases.
- *Medical Education*: Lead or support educational programs for future healthcare providers, including mentorship, funding scholarships, or creating opportunities for medical students, residents, or faculty (e.g., "endowed chair").
- *Charitable Donations and Fundraising:* Participate in or lead fundraising efforts for medical charities or healthcare foundations, hospitals, program development (e.g., sexual assault nurse examiner), or nonprofit health organizations to support patient care or medical innovations.

By contributing to the various philanthropic endeavors, physician leaders demonstrate a commitment to advancing healthcare in their communities. It allows them to leverage their expertise and give back in a variety of ways, from training the next generation of physicians to addressing areas of critical healthcare needs.

In addition, participating in philanthropy allows them to build public trust to help further their healthcare organization's strategic missions. All of these avenues have the opportunity to benefit future generations of patients and physicians alike.

Chapter Summary

Policy, advocacy, and philanthropy are three ways physician leaders can drive significant advancements in healthcare at the local and national level. Understanding how public policy is developed allows healthcare leaders to gain in-depth insight into these processes and advocate for change.

Lobbying efforts on behalf of the various advocacy groups are essential in shaping policy and ensure relevant healthcare issues are discussed and insight given by experts in the field. Philanthropic actions of healthcare leaders allow enhancement of research, improved healthcare services to those in underserved areas, and help train the next generation of providers. By participating in these efforts, healthcare leaders can drive change beyond their clinical environments into their communities and wider healthcare landscape.

REFERENCES

1. Craig L, Fong GT, Chung-Hall J for the WHO FCTC Impact Assessment Expert Group, et al. Impact of the WHO FCTC on Tobacco Control: Perspectives from Stakeholders in 12 Countries. *Tobacco Control.* 2019;28:s129-s135.
2. Centers for Disease Control and Prevention. Vaccination Laws. https://www.cdc.gov/phlp/php/publications/vaccination-laws.html Accessed December 1, 2024.
3. Patient Protection and Affordable Care Act, Pub. L. No. 111-148, 124 Stat. 119 (2010). https://www.congress.gov/bill/111th-congress/house-bill/3590.
4. Executive Order on Promoting COVID-19 Safety in Domestic and International Travel. Posted January 21, 2021. Accessed November 20, 2024. https://www.whitehouse.gov/briefing-room/presidential-actions/2021/01/21/executive- order-promoting-covid-19-safety-in-domestic-and-international-travel/
5. Office of the Federal Register, National Archives and Records Administration. DCPD- 201700742 - Executive Order 13813-Promoting Healthcare Choice and Competition Across the United States. Office of the Federal Register, National Archives and Records Administration, 11 Oct 2017. https://www.govinfo.gov/app/details/DCPD-201700742
6. Executive Order on Strengthening Medicaid and the Affordable Care Act. Posted January 28, 2021. Accessed November 19, 2024. https://www.whitehouse.gov/briefing- room/statements-releases/2021/01/28/fact-sheet-president-biden-to-sign-executive- orders-strengthening-americans-access-to-quality-affordable-health-care/
7. National Federation of Independent Business v. Sebelius, 567 U.S. 519 (2012). https://supreme.justia.com/cases/federal/us/567/519/
8. King v. Burwell, 576 U.S. 473 (2015). https://supreme.justia.com/cases/federal/us/576/473/
9. California v. Texas, 593 U.S. (2021). https://supreme.justia.com/cases/federal/us/593/19- 840/

10. Office of the Assistant Secretary for Planning and Evaluation. Health Insurance Portability and Accountability Act of 1996. August 20, 1996. Accessed November 25, 2024. https://aspe.hhs.gov/reports/health-insurance-portability-accountability-act-1996
11. Occupational Safety and Health Administration. About OSHA. Accessed November 25, 2024. https://www.osha.gov/aboutosha
12. Centers for Medical and Medicaid Services. Emergency Medical Treatment and Labor Act (EMTALA). Last Updated September 10, 2024. Accessed November 20, 2024. https://www.cms.gov/medicare/regulations-guidance/legislation/emergency-medical- treatment-labor-act
13. National Patient Safety Goals. The Joint Commission. Accessed November 24, 2024. https://www.jointcommission.org/standards/national-patient-safety-goals/
14. U.S. Department of Health and Human Services Office of Inspector General. About OIG. Accessed November 20, 2024. https://oig.hhs.gov/about-oig/
15. United States Drug Enforcement Agency. Drug Information. Accessed November 24, 2024. https://www.dea.gov/drug-information
16. U.S. Food and Drug Administration. FDA at a Glance. Updated October 16, 2024. Accessed November 24, 2024. https://www.fda.gov/about-fda/economics-staff/fda-glance
17. MedPAC. What We Do. Accessed November 15, 2024. https://www.medpac.gov/what- we-do/#
18. Agency for Healthcare Research and Quality. AHRQ at 20. Last updated July 2022. Accessed November 15, 2024. https://www.ahrq.gov/cpi/about/20timeline.html
19. Indian Health Service. About ISH. Accessed November 16, 2024. https://www.ihs.gov/aboutihs/
20. Health Resources and Services Administration. About HRSA. Last updated July 2024. Accessed November 18, 2024. https://www.hrsa.gov/about
21. American Medical Association. About. Accessed November 20, 2024. https://www.ama- assn.org/about
22. American College of Emergency Physicians. ACEP Values. Accessed November 20, 2024. https://www.acep.org/what-we-believe/acepvalues

SECTION 5

Health Information Technology

CHAPTER 14

Health Information Technology Landscape

Brian McDonough, MD, FAAFP, FAAPL

HALM CORE CONTENT

- 5.1 Applications
- 5.14 Technology lifecycles
- 5.15 Technology policies and regulations
- 5.16 Social media trends

CASE SCENARIO:

A healthcare system recognizes the value of implementing an electronic health record (EHR) system to improve patient care across the continuum. There are numerous vendors from which to choose, and several vendors have dramatically increased market share. How does the system select a vendor?

Their consultants and leadership have discussed this in great detail, and they are aware of certain requirements. The EHR needs to be certified, user-friendly, and reasonably priced. There is also a need to standardize care among the acute care, ambulatory care, and long-term care facilities in the healthcare system, as well as to have the ability to interface with other healthcare systems.

What are the applications needed to help provide quality care? What can be done to reduce physician "pajama time" and improve physician satisfaction and engagement? Finally, what are the organization's requirements for manpower (health informaticists, information technologists, clinical leadership), and how will the organization maximize opportunities to improve the quality of care of their patients?

PHYSICIAN LEADERS MUST UNDERSTAND the process of incorporating electronic health records and other technology applications into the day-to-day care of patients. Certainly, chief medical information officers (CMIOs) must have a detailed knowledge of these tools and work hand in hand with their organizations' chief information officers (CIOs).

In addition, chief medical officers (CMOs) and other members of the C-suite should have more than a passing knowledge; they should have an awareness of technology lifecycles and a clear grasp of policies and regulations because these cross over into every area of healthcare from the bedside to the business office.

Applications

Patient care is complex, and physicians have developed workflows over decades to maintain records of treatment plans and care. Consequently, the implementation of the electronic health record in United States healthcare has not been easy. During the early years of transition, the introduction of technology into the day-to-day life of a physician was disruptive, but the potential to introduce a wide variety of applications could not be overlooked. In particular, the EHR was seen as a tool that could be applied in several key areas:

- Standardization and evidence-based care.
- Communication across the healthcare continuum, including between patients and providers.
- Electronic prescribing of medications and tests.
- Control of medical costs.
- Reduction of medical errors.

With these applications in mind, the Centers for Medicare & Medicaid Services (CMS) instituted an EHR incentive program known as Meaningful Use. The program was introduced in 2009 as part of the Health Information Technology for Economic and Clinical Health (HITECH) Act. Initially, physicians were given incentives to "get on the train." Over time, penalties and payments have been linked to the technology use. The program is now called Promoting Interoperability and requires providers to show that they are using certified EHR technology to ensure quality care.

Without a doubt, there have been tremendous advances since 2009, but it is beyond the scope of this chapter to provide a detailed summary of that journey. In light of some of the noted benefits, it is important to discuss two major barriers to success: the cost of the technology and the impact on physician workflow and job satisfaction.

Regarding cost, the leading vendors in the EHR space are quite different, but there is one area where they are consistent. Depending on size and scope, the cost to implement and maintain an EHR can range from several million dollars to hundreds of millions of dollars.

As great as the cost of equipment and implementation might be, the cost can be greater when it comes to physician engagement and job satisfaction. A National

Academy of Medicine report estimated that more than 50% of the typical workday of a doctor or a nurse is devoted to "treating the screen" rather than the patient.[1]

Many studies reveal that EHRs have been cited as a leading cause of physician burnout.[2] Researchers at Mount Sinai Health System studied the impact of so-called "pajama time" (time working on medical records at home), and their findings suggested that more than 90 minutes on an EHR outside of the typical workday was associated with burnout.[3]

There have been improvements over time, however.[4] There is no doubt progress is being made and artificial intelligence may be a key factor in reducing pajama time as well as onerous "scribing" during patient visits.[5]

Technology Lifecycles

Like other technology tools, EHRs have a technology lifecycle. The early challenges of efficient EHR system development and physician adoption have been replaced by maintaining and optimizing them. In 2021, the National Center for Health Statistics reported that 88.2% of office-based physicians were using any EHR system and 77.8% of these systems were certified. The challenge faced today is developing an evaluation framework for EHR-integrated innovations to support evaluation activities at each of the four information technology lifecycle phases: planning, development, implementation, and operation. Informaticists at the University of Utah and UC San Diego have proposed an evaluation framework called ELICIT — evaluation in life cycle of IT.[6] The detailed framework covers the four lifecycle phases with a focus on three measure levels: society, end-user, and IT. The developers of ELICIT present their tool as just one option but stress the fact that as healthcare evolves and technology improves, there will be a need for evaluation of these systems.

As tools are developed to collect data, we risk drowning in a sea of too much information. Providers complain that they receive pages of extraneous data regarding their patients that can hide the information they need to provide optimal treatment. In a similar manner, the evaluation of the lifecycle of IT depends on randomized controlled studies or RCTs.[7] There needs to be a careful review of data as well as consistent evaluation of the tools to collect data. Data are not limited to provider's notes or hospital-based summaries, and there are now a wide variety of tools used to collect information. The advances seen in wearable devices used for real-time health monitoring and their linkage to the patient health record adds to data that can affect clinical decision-making.[8,9]

By definition, a lifecycle is "the series of changes in the life of an organism." In the past, it may have been considered a liberal use of the term "lifecycle" when it was applied to technology. The emergence of generative artificial intelligence is making the term much more applicable.

Artificial intelligence (AI) has the potential to fundamentally transform the practice of medicine and the delivery of healthcare.[10] As generative AI is introduced into physician practices, it is opening the door for doctors to spend more time with their patients. However, there are concerns that someday AI may replace physicians.[11] AI has the potential to transform medicine but serves as an example of the need to monitor the ever-changing lifecycle of information technology.

Technology Policies and Regulations

Today, the EHR is highly regulated, but it was not always that way. In the early 1960s, the Mayo Clinic, Massachusetts General Hospital, and several other academic inpatient and outpatient medical facilities developed primitive EHRs. Billing and scheduling systems such as COSTAR and PROMIS were developed.[12] At the time, there was a need for large mainframe computers with limited storage. Even at this early stage, it was apparent there would ultimately be a need for clinical support.[13]

The early years of the EHR provide a glimpse at the ingenuity of the pioneers in this area. A review of the literature also reveals a recognition that there was a need for standardization as well as some sort of regulation related to the tools being developed.[14-16]

By the 1990s, it was recognized that paper needed to be replaced, but the transition to electronic medical records appeared cost-prohibitive, and there were many who felt the best-case scenario would be to use electronic records to "complement and not replace" the paper record.[17] From the earliest stages, the electronic health record was seen as a complex web of data — data that needed to be extracted in an organized fashion. Furthermore, the exchange of data needed to be efficient, and this required standards to be implemented.

As early as 1992, Health Level Seven (HL7) was being used by both homegrown and larger vendors.[18] As advances continued and the personal computer became an integral part of the workplace (and home), the expectations grew. Information was being shared from labs, medical devices, and the ambulatory setting. As technology improved, there were additional needs such as Picture Archiving and Communication Systems (PACS).[19] By the turn of the century, it became apparent that technology policies and regulations were required.

After years of discussion and debate, funding for the conversion from paper records to the electronic health record was secured as a provision of the 2009 American Recovery and Investment Act (ARRA). Shortly after, CMS adopted what has been called "The Final Rule" on July 28, 2010.

According to the document, there would be incentive payments to eligible professionals (EPs), eligible hospitals and critical access hospitals (CAHs) participating in Medicare and Medicaid programs that adopted and successfully demonstrated meaningful use of certified electronic health record (EHR) technology. This final rule specifies that the initial criteria EPs, eligible hospitals, and CAHs must meet to qualify for an incentive payment; calculation of the incentive payment amounts; payment adjustments under Medicare for covered professional services and inpatient hospital services provided by EPs, eligible hospitals and CAHs failing to demonstrate meaningful use of certified EHR technology; and other program participation requirements.

Also, the Office of the National Coordinator for Health Information Technology (ONC) issued a closely related final rule that specify the Secretary's adoption of an initial set of standards, implementation, specifications, and certification criteria for electronic health records. ONC had also issued a separate final rule on the establishment of certification programs for health information technology.[20,21]

Regarding the use of the EHR, many of the recommendations, guidelines, and rules were authorized by the Health Information Technology for Economic and Clinical Health (HITECH) Act. This federal law promoted the use of health information technology and was originally passed in 2009 as part of the American Recovery and Reinvestment Act.[22]

HITECH established The Office of The National Coordinator for Health Information Technology (ONC). The Congressional Research Service provided a document on March 17, 2023, which detailed focus areas of the ONC.[23] These focus areas include interoperability, trusted exchange, United States core data for interoperability, health IT certification program, information blocking, health information exchange, and a Health Information Technology Advisory Committee. ONC often works in conjunction with CMS to manage these focus areas.

Social Media Trends

There was a time when a patient's medical record was kept in a chart stored in a doctor's office. In the 1950s and 1960s, a general practitioner kept notes on an index card. In the 1970s, internist Lawrence Reed developed the *SOAP* note (subjective/objective/assessment/plan). Today, he is known as the father of the problem-oriented medical record.[24]

Reed also was an early adopter of primitive electronic health records. In addition to a focus on problem-oriented medical care, he was one of a growing number of physicians who advocated not only informing patients about their personal health issues, but also encouraging them to play an active role in their care.[25,26]

Patients had very limited access to their personal records in the paper world. Now, patients view health information in real time through a personal patient portal. The federal Health Insurance Portability and Accountability Act of 1996 (HIPAA) set standards for medical records and personal health information (PHI). Leaders in healthcare need to know these fundamental rules, and most health organizations have guidelines in place, but the world of social media presents a near and present danger for those involved in healthcare.

Healthcare leaders are obligated to maintain the privacy of patient information while ensuring trust in the medical profession and establishing appropriate boundaries.[27] In addition, connectivity need not come at the expense of professionalism.[28]

The American Medical Association does not pull any punches in their Code of Medical Ethics when it comes to the use of social media:[29]

> *"When using the Internet for social networking, physicians should use privacy settings to safeguard personal information and content to the extent possible, but should realize that privacy settings are not absolute and that once on the Internet, content is likely there permanently. Thus, physicians should routinely monitor their own Internet presence to ensure that the personal and professional information on their own sites and, to the extent possible, content posted about them by others, is accurate and appropriate."*

Three crucial points physician leaders and administrative leaders who offer clinical guidance to providers should abide by:

- Do not use social media to give advice to individual patients. This should be provided in the exam room, by telephone, and/or through the patient portal.
- Never share patient information or photos.
- Do not attempt to change online patient reviews or use friends and family to improve results.

The final point is in response to physicians and healthcare organizations who are being reviewed on social media sites. If someone on social media provides a negative review, it should be taken seriously and objectively analyzed. The reviewer should not be challenged, and the content should not be altered in any way.

The top social media platforms in the United States are always in flux; the percentage of users for each can vary from month to month. At the time of this writing, Facebook, YouTube, and Instagram are the top three social media sites. X/Twitter and LinkedIn are still popular but have seen declines.

Social media sites also vary by the age of the consumer. For instance, Facebook is the most popular social media platform for people over 28, but TikTok is Gen Z's favorite.[30] It is important to not focus on specific social media sites when providing leadership. Rather, focus on organizational policies.

Everything posted on the internet is accessible forever and it is discoverable in a legal environment, thus social media content has been used in malpractice cases.[31] The present use of social media has been compared to use of private investigators in years past. There is little debate that the rapid emergence and exploding usage of online social media networking forums are frequented by millions and present clinicians with new ethical and professional challenges.[32]

Some of the advantages of a social media presence are connectivity, image building, information sharing, and keeping up with the competition. The warnings and concerns shared in this chapter are designed to inform leaders about the need to avoid critical errors but should not discourage them from using these tools to build a brand, educate patients and the public, publicize research, and potentially attract patients.

Chapter Summary

The past 25 years in healthcare have witnessed the dramatic rise of the EHR. Computer technology is now used in virtually every area of the healthcare continuum, and its role is only growing. Health administrators and leaders must recognize these tools can be used to increase access to medical information for patients and providers, but the complexity of these electronic tools can also serve as a barrier.

Those leaders who can harness the technology and break down barriers will improve quality of care. Those who embrace the spirit of innovation and change have an opportunity to dramatically improve the health of patients and the communities served.

REFERENCES

1. National Academies of Sciences, Engineering, and Medicine. *Taking Action Against Clinician Burnout: A Systems Approach to Professional Well-Being.* Washington, DC: The National Academies Press; 2019.
2. Adler-Milstein J, Zhao W, Willard-Grace R, Knox M, Grumbach K. Electronic Health Records and Burnout: Time Spent on the Electronic Health Record After Hours and Message Volume Associated with Exhaustion But Not With Cynicism Among Primary Care Clinicians. *J Am Med Inform Assoc.* 2020;27(4):531–538.
3. Peccoralo LA, Kaplan CA, Pietrzak RH, Charney DS, Ripp JA. The Impact of Time Spent on the Electronic Health Record After Work and of Clerical Work on Burnout Among Clinical Faculty. *J Am Med Inform Assoc.* 2021;28(5):938–947.
4. McDonough B. Finding Optimism in the Future of EMRs. *Physician Leadership Journal.* 2020;7(1):57.
5. Garcia P, Ma S, Shah S. Artificial Intelligence-Generated Draft Replies to Patient Inbox Messages. *JAMA Network Open.* 2024;7(3):e243201.
6. Kukhareva PV, Weir C, Del Fiol G, et al. Evaluation in Life Cycle of Information Technology (ELICIT) Framework: Supporting the Innovation Life Cycle From Business Case Assessment to Summative Evaluation. *Journal of Biomedical Informatics.* 2022;127 (3): 104014 https://doi.org/10.1016/j.jbi.2022.104014
7. Christopoulou SC, Kotsilieris T, Anagnostopoulos I. Assessment of Health Information Technology Interventions in Evidence-Based Medicine: A Systematic Review by Adopting a Methodological Evaluation Framework. *Healthcare.* 2018;6(3):109.
8. Mühlen JM, Stang J, Skovgaard EL, et al. Recommendations for Determining the Validity of Consumer Wearable Heart Rate Devices: Expert Statement and Checklist of the INTERLIVE Network. *Br J Sports Med.* 2021;55:767–779.
9. Guk K, Han G, Lim J, et al. Evolution of Wearable Devices with Real-time Disease Monitoring for Personalized Healthcare. Nanomaterials (Basel). 2019;9(6):813.
10. Bajwa J, Munir U, Nori A, Williams B. Artificial Intelligence in Healthcare: Transforming the Practice of Medicine. *Future Healthc J.* 2021;8(2):e188–e194.
11. Ahuja AS. The Impact of Artificial Intelligence in Medicine on the Future Role of the Physician. *PeerJ.*

2019;7:e7702.

12. Evans RS. Electronic Health Records: Then, Now, and in the Future. *Yearb Med Inform*. 2016;Suppl 1(Suppl 1):S48-61.
13. Shortliffe EH. Computer Programs To Support Clinical Decision Making. *JAMA*. 1987;258(1):61–66.
14. Giokas D. Canada Health Infoway — Towards a National Interoperable Electronic Health Record (EHR) Solution. *Stud Health Technol Inform.* 2005;115:108–140.
15. Tavakoli N, Isfahani SS, Piri Z, Amini A. Patient Access to Electronic Health Record: A Comparative Study un Laws, Policies and Procedures in Selected Countries. *Med Arch.* 2013;67(1):63–67.
16. Shabot MM. Standardized Acquisition of Bedside Data: The IEEE P1073 Medical Information Bus. *Int J Clin Monit Comput.* 1989;6(4):197–204.
17. Rodnick JE. Should the Complete Medical Record Be Computerized in Family Practice? An Opposing View. *J Fam Pract*. 1990;30(4):460–464.
18. Hammond WE. Health Level 7: An Application Standard for Electronic Medical Data Exchange. *Top Health Rec Manage.* 1991;11(4):59–66.
19. Lemke HU. Communication Networks for Medical Image Transmission. *Strahlenther Onkol.* 1993;169(9):512–520.
20. Department of Health and Human Services Centers for Medicare & Medicaid Services Medicare and Medicaid Programs; Electronic Health Record Incentive Program. 42 CRF Parts 412, 413, 422, 495.Federal Register. 2010;75(144).
21. US Department of Health & Human Services. Secretary Sebelius Announces Final Rules To Support 'Meaningful Use' of Electronic Health Records. Press Release. July 13, 2010. https://web.archive.org/web/20100715075135/http:/www.hhs.gov/news/press/2010pres/07/20100713a.html
22. Blumenthal D. Launching HITECH. *N Engl J Med*. 2010;362(5):382–385.
23. The Office of the National Coordinator for Health Information Technology (ONC). *Congressional Research Service.* March 17, 2023. Accessed October 1, 2024. https://crsreports.congress.gov.
24. Aronson M. The Purpose of the Medical Record: Why Lawrence Reed Still Matters. *Am J Med.* 2019;132 (11):1256–1257. doi: 10.1016/j.amjmed.2019.03.051.
25. Weed LL. Medical Records That Guide and Teach. *N Engl J Med.* 1968;278:593–600. https://doi.org/10.1056/nejm196803142781105
26. Weed LL. Medical Records, Medical Education and Patient Care: The Problem Oriented Record as a Basic Tool. Cleveland, OH: Case Western Reserve University Press; 1971.
27. Farnan JM, Snyder Sulmasy L, Worster BK, Chaudhry HJ, Rhyne JA, Arora VM. Online Medical Professionalism: Patient and Public Relationships: Policy Statement from the American College of Physicians and the Federation of State Medical Boards. *Ann Intern Med*. 2013;158(8):620–627.
28. Parikh SM, Liu E, White CB. Connectivity Need Not Come at the Expense of Professionalism [Letter]. *Acad Med*. 2010;85:930.
29. American Medical Association. 2.3.2 Professionalism in the Use of Social Media. Code of Medical Ethics. https://code-medical-ethics.ama-assn.org/sites/default/files/2022-08/2.3.2%20Professionalism%20in%20the%20use%20of%20social%20media%20--%20background%20reports.pdf.
30. HubSpot 2024 Social Medial Marketing Report: Data from 1400+ Global Marketers. HubSpot blog. Accessed November 3, 2024. https://blog.hubspot.com/marketing/hubspot-blog-social-media-marketing-report.
31. Lambert K. Risk Management and Legal Issues with Use of Social Media in the Healthcare Setting. *J Healthc Risk Manag.* 2012;31(4):41–47. https://doi.org/10.1002/jhrm.20103
32. Guseh JS, 2nd, Brendel RW, Brendel DH. Medical Professionalism in the Age of Online Social Networking. *J Med Ethics.* 2009;35(9):584–586.

CHAPTER 15

Information Technology Usability and Interoperability

Smita Agarkar, MD, CPE, FAAPL

HALM CORE CONTENT:

- 5.2 Clinical documentation auditing and improvement strategies (role of physician advisors)
- 5.4 Data and equipment interoperability
- 5.6 Decision support and alert fatigue
- 5.13 Physician and end-user engagement in IT strategies
- 5.17 Workforce engagement and compliance with institutional systems

CASE SCENARIO:

The emergency department (ED) at a local hospital that handles more than 100,000 patients annually is faced with patient flow and clinical efficiency issues due to delays and poor throughput. What role does a physician leader play in managing the ED workflow? Can electronic health record (EHR) functionality help with real-time patient tracking and data-driven clinical decision-making? Effective use of EHR with interoperability between systems helped clear critical cases, alleviating overcrowding during peak hours and reducing length of stay.

THE ROLE OF PHYSICIAN LEADERS in allocating resources while making effective use of EHRs for improving team collaboration strengthens the role of technology integration for patient-centered care.

Data and Equipment Interoperability

Since the federal health information technology (HIT) effort was launched, four overriding national priorities have been articulated: (1) connecting the health system with health data, as with the EHR; (2) supporting patients with information to help them manage their care; (3) advancing health research and innovation; (4) and promoting health and wellness.

An EHR is an electronic version of a patient's medical history that is maintained by the provider and may include all of the key administrative clinical data relevant to that person's care under a particular provider, including demographics, progress notes, problems, medications, vital signs, past medical history, immunizations, laboratory data, and radiology reports. The EHR automates access to this information and has the potential to streamline the clinician's workflow.

EHRs have revolutionized medical practice. The data and the timeliness and availability of those data enable providers to make better decisions and provide quality care. The core benefits of the EHR include:

1. *Cost Reductions:* Lowering transcription costs and re-filing expenses.
2. *Improved Documentation:* Ensuring more accurate records by automated coding.
3. *Error Reduction:* Enhancing patient data access that ensures continuity and preventive alert systems that reduce medical errors.
4. *Better Patient Care:* Facilitating clinical decision-making in disease management, improving patient outcomes.

Although EHR systems are credited with streamlining practice operations, key questions remain regarding the need for standardization in data and equipment interoperability. Lack of standardization has led to delays and disruptions in care and reduced effectiveness and productivity, affecting patient safety as well as revenue.

The first national goal for HIT has been largely realized. Nearly all hospitals and a growing number of physician practices and ancillary care facilities use EHRs to manage patient care (Figure 1).[2]

In 2023, 70% of non-federal acute care hospitals were engaged in all domains of interoperable exchange of summary of care records (send, find, receive, and integrate) routinely or sometimes. From 2018 to 2023, hospitals increased routine engagement in all four interoperable exchange domains (Figure 2).[3] The domains of exchange are:

1. *Find*: Querying external patient health information.
2. *Send*: Electronically sending care summaries to other organizations.
3. *Receive*: Receiving electronic care summaries from external sources.
4. *Integrate*: Integrating external care summaries into the hospital's EHR without manual input.

The analysis reveals that interoperability among acute care hospitals has made substantial progress despite facing persistent challenges in achieving seamless health information exchange. In the five-year span, the percentage of hospitals engaging in all four domains rose between 78% and 92%. By 2023, 43% of hospitals routinely engaged in interoperability, up from 29% in 2021, while those engaging "only sometimes" declined.[3]

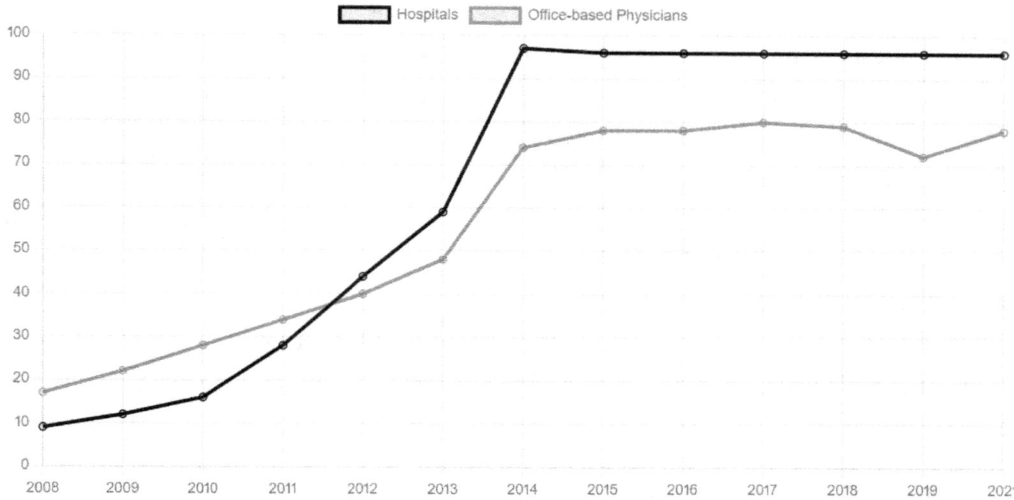

As of 2021, nearly 4 in 5 office-based physicians (78%) and nearly all non-federal acute care hospitals (96%) adopted a certified EHR. This marks substantial 10-year progress since 2011 when 28% of hospitals and 34% of physicians had adopted an EHR.

FIGURE 1. Trends in Hospital and Physician EHR Use

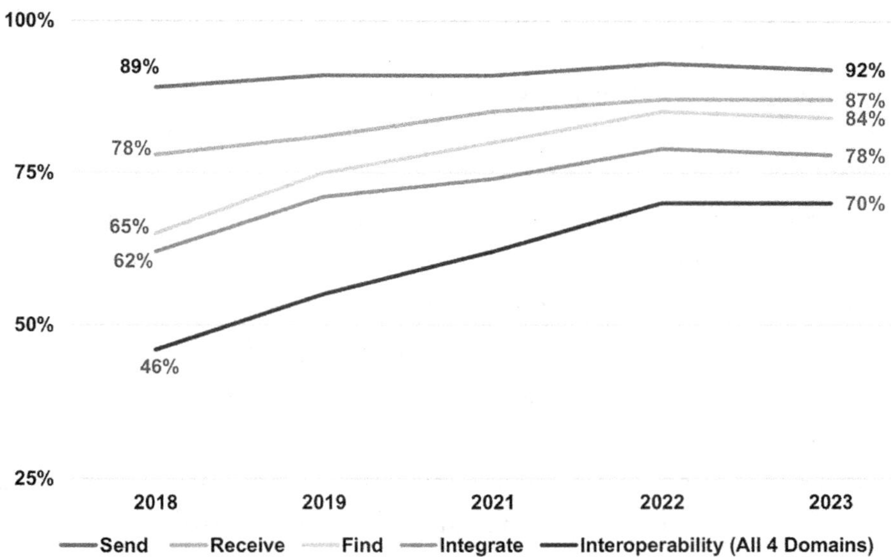

Source: 2018-2023 AHA Annual Survey Information Technology Supplement.
Notes: Study population are non-federal acute care hospitals. Please refer to the Definitions and Methods sections of this brief for more information. Please see full trend graph from 2014 to 2023 available here: https://www.healthit.gov/data/quickstats/electronic-health-information-exchange-hospitals

FIGURE 2. Percent of Non-Federal Acute Care Hospitals Engaging in Electronically Sending, Receiving, and Integrating Summary of Care Records 2014–2023

EHR implementation requires substantial investment, with large systems costing millions of dollars and smaller practices spending $35,000–$70,000 on average. Federal programs like Medicare and Medicaid Promoting Interoperability (formerly the Medicare and Medicaid EHR Incentive Programs) offer incentives of $44,000–$63,750; non-compliance leads to penalties. Evaluating the economic impact of EHR-based clinical decision support (CDS) systems is complex; although they show potential for reducing healthcare waste (estimated at $760 billion–$935 billion annually), development and maintenance costs often overshadow savings.[4]

This points to a need for broader engagement and investment in interoperability across the healthcare continuum to address these gaps and ensure equitable information access.

Clinical Documentation Auditing and Improvement Strategies

Do current EHR systems effectively support continuity of care, patient safety, and seamless integration to enhance physician workflows?

WORKFLOW IS MULTI-DIMENSIONAL IN NATURE

- It spans across *organizations* (e.g., between a clinic and a pharmacy, between a hospital and a clinic, between two clinics or hospitals).
- It occurs *between individuals* (e.g., communication between providers, providers and staff, providers and patients).
- It includes *internal thought processes* often referred to as critical thought processes (e.g., a provider's decision-making about a medication or a procedure).
- It happens *at various stages of patient care*: before, during, or after a patient visit.

Because multiple EMR systems have been implemented by organizations, there are no performance guidelines or mandated requirements for testing the usability and safety of implemented EHRs. Table 1 summarizes the challenges clinicians face with EHR systems and their potential impacts on workflow, efficiency, and patient care.

AI has the potential to transform healthcare through point-of-care learning, clinical documentation, and quality-measurement reporting. By analyzing practice data, search queries, and assessments, AI can deliver personalized updates to physicians, saving them time otherwise spent on irrelevant or redundant content. AI should be viewed as a tool to help physicians in clinical decision-making.

Physician advisors play a crucial role in the design and development of EHR and AI systems that interact with EHRs.[5] Their involvement ensures that these technologies are clinically relevant, user-friendly, and optimized for real-world healthcare settings.

TABLE 1. Challenges with EHR and Its Impact on Workflow

Challenge	Description	Impact
Logging into multiple systems	Clinicians must access several platforms, each requiring separate logins.	Interrupts workflow, consumes time, and increases frustration.
Excessive keyboard usage	Data entry requires extensive keyboard manipulation.	Slows down input and raises the risk of errors.
Medication ordering complexity	Medication orders involve numerous clicks to complete the process.	Makes tasks time-consuming and increases error potential.
Difficulty with non-standard orders	Inputting non-standard orders is challenging due to system constraints.	Reduces flexibility and hinders customization of orders.
Switching between screens	Navigating multiple screens to retrieve and input information.	Causes workflow delays, increases cognitive load, and disrupts efficiency.
Suboptimal data presentation	Critical information like medication profiles is displayed in a non-intuitive manner.	Makes it harder to access vital information quickly.
Cluttered screens	Screens for orders and notes are overcrowded with excessive information.	Obscures key details and slows documentation.
Viewing patient names	Patient names are not clearly displayed in some systems.	Raises the risk of patient identification errors.
Lack of free-text functionality	Limited options for entering free text or using word processing features.	Hinders flexibility and the ability to document accurately and in detail.

For instance, the AMA's Advisory Committee on Physician EHR Usability focus highlighted eight EHR usability priorities for overcoming usability challenges and recommending improvements in processes.[6] The challenges include enhancing physicians' ability to provide high-quality patient care, support team-based care, promote care coordination, offer product modularity and configurability, reduce cognitive workload, promote interoperability and data exchange, facilitate digital patient engagement, and expedite user input into product design and post-implementation feedback.

Here are several key areas where physician advisors' contributions can be vital:

- *Clinical Expertise and Insights*: Physician advisors ensure that AI-based algorithms are aligned with current medical knowledge and practice guidelines, reducing the risk of errors in diagnosis, treatment recommendations, thereby enhancing decision-making and patient care.
- *Collaboration and Workflow Integration:* Physician advisors work with developers to integrate AI features into EHR systems without disrupting existing workflows. They help design user interfaces that are intuitive and align with physicians' routines. For example, at the University of Michigan, a nephrologist chairs the clinical

intelligence committee. The clinician also serves as the health system's associate chief medical information officer for artificial intelligence. This inter-professional committee assesses AI-enabled tools and oversees their deployment across the health system.[5]

- *Ensuring Usability and Acceptance*: Physician advisors provide feedback on the usability of AI features, ensuring that the AI system is easy to navigate, the recommendations are understandable, and the results are actionable. Having human-centric design is the key. Does the technology fit seamlessly into clinical workflows? Is it actually improving the efficiency and quality of care?

Decision Support and Alert Fatigue

The integration of health information technology has brought transformative improvements to healthcare delivery but also introduced several unintended consequences, challenging its overall efficacy. Efficient workflow is critical to supporting effective clinical decision-making. On the other hand, poorly designed workflows, particularly those involving complex or fragmented electronic health records, can disrupt decision-making, increase error rates, and delay critical interventions.

Among the several challenges reported, electronic health record saturation has led to excessive and often redundant data, complicating clinical workflows and detracting from patient care.[7] Practices like "copy and paste" within EHRs create bloated, uninformative, unintelligible notes that obscure critical patient information, potentially leading to unsafe outcomes and impaired clinical decision-making.[8]

Another major consequence is alert fatigue, stemming from the overuse of computerized physician order entry (CPOE) systems. While alerts, particularly hard alerts,[9] can prevent unsafe practices and improve outcomes, such as reducing duplicate lab orders[10] or embedding risk assessment tools to lower preventable venous thromboembolism (VTE) rates,[11] mismanagement of alerts often overwhelms clinicians, leading to work around behaviors and further exacerbating fatigue. Research indicates that effective alert systems require iterative design, long-term studies, and continuous feedback to achieve sustainable success.[12]

Physician burnout, closely linked to EHRs, has become a pressing concern, with key drivers identified as poor usability, excessive documentation requirements, and alert fatigue. Burnout not only affects clinician well-being, it also jeopardizes patient care and system efficiency.[13] To address this, many suggest the potential of AI-driven decision support systems,[14] which utilize vast data sets, spanning patient history, clinical guidelines, and real-time wearable device data, to provide precise, timely clinical insights.

While AI offers promise, its integration into healthcare systems demands careful evaluation, addressing both technical capabilities and human factors, to support clinicians without introducing new burdens.

Many believe that AI-driven decision support systems, which utilize vast data sets, spanning patient history, clinical guidelines, and diagnostic evaluations, can provide precise, timely clinical insights.[14]

AI's role in diagnostic support also has the potential to reduce cognitive load on physicians in the realm of diagnosis and problem solving.[15] In dermatology, AI-based technologies have diagnosed skin pathologies for some conditions at nearly the same level as dermatologists. Early studies in pathology indicate that a synergistic approach with AI-based technologies and human intelligence results in a far more efficient and accurate diagnostics.

Optimizing EHRs and incorporating AI-driven solutions represent pivotal steps in alleviating the cognitive and operational demands on clinicians, helping to foster a more effective and sustainable healthcare environment.

While AI offers promise, its integration into healthcare systems demands careful evaluation that addresses both technical capabilities and human factors in order to support clinicians without introducing new burdens.

Physician and End-User Engagement in IT Strategies

User-centric design models involving clinicians ensures the EHR system meets the practical needs and aligns with workflows, ensuring the maximum benefit. End-user engagement, including co-designing and co-planning with physician leaders and IT professionals, is the key driver for success.

In a recent publication from Memorial Sloan Kettering,[16] authors highlight a user-centered design model to support patient-centered care initiatives by creating a feature in EHR to centrally view information about the patient's values, goals, and preferences. User-centered design methods were applied to create a new "Values Tab" in the EHR system. The design process included using user stories, card sorting, user testing, and an iterative approach with an interdisciplinary project team.

Many projects capture data pertaining to point of care; however, applying design methodology to create an EHR section about patient values for all stages of cancer care was the goal of this six-week project.

Involving healthcare leaders in IT design and decision-making is crucial to ensure that technological solutions are aligned with the organization's broader goals, such as improving patient care, increasing operational efficiency, and achieving long-term sustainability.

Here are several key reasons healthcare leaders are key stakeholders:[17]

- *Strategic Alignment*: Healthcare leaders are well-versed in the organization's strategic objectives. Their involvement in IT design ensures that new technologies and systems are developed with clinical and financial goals in mind, leading to better integration of IT solutions into the organization's workflow and objectives.

- *Resource Allocation*: Healthcare leaders control budgets and resources, so their input is critical in determining the feasibility of IT projects.
- *Workforce Buy-in*: When healthcare leaders are engaged in the design and decision-making process, it fosters a sense of ownership and accountability. This leadership buy-in is vital for ensuring successful implementation and usage of EHRs.
- *Policies and Regulations:* Healthcare leaders can ensure that IT solutions adhere to legal and ethical standards and meet industry-specific requirements.
- *Improving User Adoption:* Healthcare leaders can help ensure that new IT systems meet the needs of end users, such as clinicians, administrators, and support staff. By being involved in the design process, they can advocate for solutions that improve usability, reduce clinician burnout, and enhance patient outcomes.
- *Organizational Change:* Implementing new IT systems often requires significant organizational change. Healthcare leaders play a pivotal role in managing this change, ensuring that the organization is prepared for transitions and staff are adequately trained.
- *Evaluation and Continuous Improvement:* Healthcare leaders are often tasked with overseeing performance metrics and outcomes. Involving them in IT design helps ensure that the system includes mechanisms for ongoing evaluation and adjustment, based on feedback from users and the performance data, to continuously improve the technology's effectiveness.

With the increasing adoption of EHRs and rise of competency-based medical education, educators should address the gaps in the training of future physicians to better prepare them to provide high quality care for their patients and communities.

Developing EHR competencies in areas like information entry and medication management can be enhanced through future curricular focus, including experiential training via extracurricular activities and early clinical exposure. The Association of American Medical College (AAMC), Alliance for Clinical Education, and Liaison Committee on Medical Education,[18] have issued guidance stating that the ability to work in an EHR is a core competency for medical students before beginning residency.

As frequent EHR users, medical students and residents can quickly assess new features or updates, providing rapid feedback to developers.[19] They can participate in usability testing, providing feedback on features before large-scale implementation. The most important role they play is advocating for EHR tools that support education, such as templates for differential diagnoses or integrated clinical decision support tools. In a study of 147 students, there was emphasis on increased experiential training rather than didactic formats.[20] Their unique perspectives as learners, front-line caregivers, and technology adopters can drive meaningful improvements in EHR systems, ultimately enhancing patient care and clinician satisfaction.

Workforce Engagement and Compliance with Institutional Systems

Interoperability issues within EHRs have profound financial and clinical implications, affecting the efficiency of care delivery and escalating costs across healthcare systems.

Table 2 summarizes clinical and financial implications of issues with the interoperability of EHR.

TABLE 2. Clinical and Financial Implications in Workflow and Operations

Clinical Implications	Loss of Clinical Decision Support	Over- or underuse of clinical decision-support tools (e.g., alerts, reminders) within EHRs can lead to missed opportunities for preventive care or treatment interventions.
	Delayed or Inappropriate Treatment	Faulty records can lead to delays in diagnosing or treating patients, compromising care quality.
	Patient Safety Risks	Errors in medication orders, allergies, or diagnoses can lead to adverse patient outcomes, including harm or death.
	Communication Breakdown	Inaccurate or incomplete data can hinder communication among care team members, affecting coordinated care.
	Data Integrity Compromises	Lack of connectivity between EHRs can lead to fragmented or incorrect patient data information, affecting continuity of care.
	Decrease in Physician Work Efficiency and Burnout	Issues related to EHR and workflow efficiency can lead to a decrease in productivity and affect physician well-being.
Financial Implications	Billing and Reimbursement Issues	Inaccurate EHRs can result in incorrect billing codes, leading to denied claims or overpayments that require repayment.
	Increased Cost for Corrections	Correcting errors in EHRs often requires significant resources, including staff time and external consultants.
	Loss of Revenue	Poor EHR functionality can slow down workflows, affect reimbursements, and result in revenue loss.
	Regulatory Fines and Penalties	Non-compliance with regulatory standards due to faulty EHRs can lead to fines.
	Legal Liabilities and Malpractice Claims	EHRs affecting workflow and clinical decision-making can significantly affect patient care outcomes leading to stemming lawsuits, costing millions in settlements or judgments.
	Cost of Systems Overhaul	Optimizing, fixing, or adopting a new EHR could lead to substantial financial investment.

The inability of disparate EHR systems to seamlessly exchange patient data not only leads to redundant testing and delays in treatment but also increases administrative burdens, contributing to higher operational expenses. A human-centric approach and

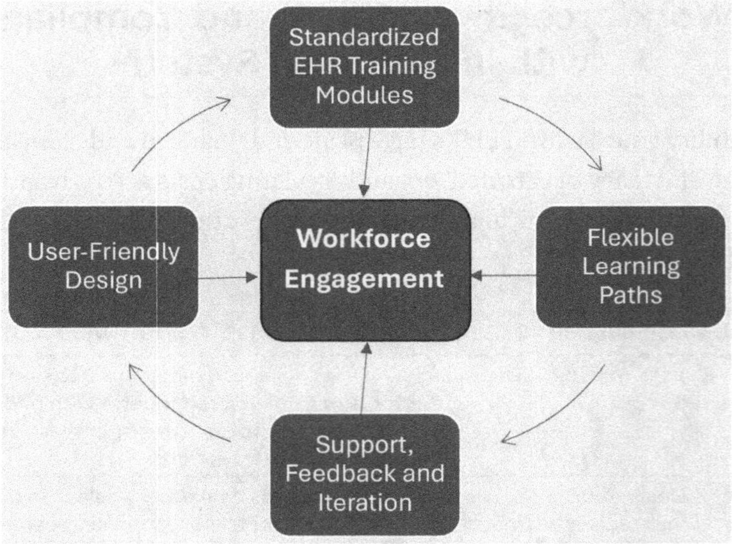

FIGURE 3. Keys to Workforce Engagement

interpersonal interactions may be necessary to drive the effectiveness of interoperability and rip the full benefit of health information technology.[21]

A recent review revealed methodological issues in EHR implementation studies, including vague user-centered design descriptions, limited participatory design, and inconsistencies in user involvement, often restricted to one development stage.[22] There is a need for a more structured, comprehensive approach to user involvement in EHR development, recommending broader participant inclusion.

Effective workforce engagement and compliance with Electronic Health Records (EHR) systems would enhance productivity, reduce errors, and alleviate burnout, thereby fostering a healthy organizational culture. Several key factors would influence workforce engagement (see Figure 3):

1. *Standardized EHR Training Models*
   Standardized training ensures that all employees, regardless of department or role, receive the same foundational knowledge of the EHR system. Training can be divided into clear, manageable structured modules that focus on specific tasks, such as patient charting, order entry, or documentation compliance. This approach allows staff to learn at their own pace and return to specific modules when they need a refresher.
2. *User-Friendly Design*
   Given the complex nature of EHR systems, user-friendly training models often leverage interactive and visual learning elements. Tools such as simulation software, step-by-step guides, and visual aids can help clinicians better understand workflows and system functionality. Having real-world scenarios like "Day in the

life of a physician," or simulate environments such as an ER visit and order entry, helps physicians understand clinical workflows.

3. *Flexible Learning Paths*
   To accommodate diverse learning styles and schedules, EHR training should combine various formats, such as self-paced eLearning, live webinars, and in-person workshops. Microlearning, such as 5- to 10-minute instructional videos or interactive quizzes, helps reinforce key concepts and keeps the workforce engaged. On-demand access also allows healthcare workers to revisit specific sections whenever needed.
4. *Support, Feedback and Iteration*
   As EHR systems often undergo optimization, regular refresher courses and assessments ensure that employees stay up to date with new features or changes in compliance regulations. Gathering feedback from the users about the training content and delivery is an iterative approach leading to improved engagement and systems compliance.

Chapter Summary

EHRs have significantly evolved since their inception, offering opportunities to enhance healthcare delivery and patient outcomes. However, persistent operational challenges, including inefficiencies and cognitive burdens on physicians, limit their potential. Addressing these challenges requires a coordinated, collaborative effort among healthcare providers, administrators, HIT vendors, policymakers, informatics researchers, funding bodies, and external developers.

By working together, these stakeholders can design, implement, and optimize solutions to overcome current barriers and fully harness the capabilities of a digitized health system, ensuring both efficiency and clinician well-being.

REFERENCES

1. Improving Patient Flow Helps This California Hospital Dramatically Improve Metrics. TeamHealth blog. Accessed December 17, 2024. https://www.teamhealth.com/blog/improving-patient-flow-dramatically-improve-metrics/?r=1
2. National Trends in Hospital and Physician Adoption of Electronic Health Records- HealthIT.gov. Accessed December 9, 2024. https://www.healthit.gov/data/quickstats/national-trends-hospital-and-physician-adoption-electronic-health-records
3. Gabriel MH, Richwine C, Strawley C, et al. ONC Data Brief, Interoperable Exchange of Patient Health Information Among U.S. Hospitals: 2023. May 2024. Accessed December 9, 2024. https://www.healthit.gov/sites/default/files/2024-05/Interoperable-Exchange-of-Patient-Health-Information-Among-U.S.-Hospitals-2023.pdf
4. Lewkowicz D, Wohlbrandt A, Boettinger E. Economic Impact of Clinical Decision Support Interventions Based on Electronic Health Records *BMC Health Serv Res.* 2020;20(1):871.
5. Butcher L. Artificial Intelligence and Machine Learning: What Physician Leaders Need to Know.

Physician Leadership Journal. 2023;10(3):31–33. https://doi.org/10.55834/plj.6915833702

6. Practice Management. American Medical Association. Accessed December 17, 2024. https://www.ama-assn.org/practice-management
7. Colicchio TK, Cimino JJ, Del Fiol G. Unintended Consequences of Nationwide Electronic Health Record Adoption: Challenges and Opportunities in the Post-Meaningful Use Era. *J Med Internet Res.* 2019;21(6):e13313. doi: 10.2196/13313
8. Siegler EL, Adelman R. Copy and Paste: A Remediable hazard of Electronic Health Records. *Am J Med.* 2009;122(6):495–496.
9. Powers EM, Shiffman RN, Melnick ER, et al. Efficacy and Unintended Consequences of Hard-Stop Alerts in Electronic Health Record Systems: A Systematic Review. *JAMA.* 2018;25(11):1556–1566.
10. Procop GW, Keating C, Stagno P, et al. Reducing Duplicate Testing: A Comparison of Two Clinical Decision Support Tools. *Am J Clin Pathol.* 2015;143 (5): 623–626.
11. Haut ER, Lau BD, Kraenzlin FS, et al. Improved Prophylaxis and Decreased Rates of Preventable Harm with the Use of a Mandatory Computerized Clinical Decision Support Tool for Prophylaxis for Venous Thromboembolism in Trauma. *Arch Surg.* 2012;147(10):901–907.
12. Borycki E, Dexheimer JW, Hullin Lucay Cossio C, et al. Methods for Addressing Technology-Induced Errors: The Current State. *Yearb Med Inform.* 2016;(1):30-40. doi: 10.15265/IY-2016-029.
13. Li C, Parpia C, Sriharan A, Keefe DT. Electronic Medical Record-Related Burnout in Healthcare Providers: A Scoping Review of Outcomes and Interventions. *BMJ Open.* 2022;12(8):e060865. doi: 10.1136/bmjopen-2022-060865
14. Giordano C, Brennan M, Mohamed B, Rashidi P, Modave F, Tighe P. Accessing Artificial Intelligence for Clinical Decision-Making. *Front Digit Health.* 2021;3:645232. doi: 10.3389/fdgth.2021.645232. eCollection 2021.PMID: 3471311
15. Pavuluri S, Sangal R, Sather J, Taylor RA. Balancing Act: The Complex Role of Artificial Intelligence in Addressing Burnout and Healthcare Workforce Dynamics. *BMJ Health Care Inform.* 2024;31(1):e101120. doi: 10.1136/bmjhci-2024-101120
16. Michael CL, Mittelstaedt H, Chen Y, Desai AV, Kuperman GJ. Applying User-Centered Design in the Electronic Health Record (EHR) to Facilitate Patient-Centered Care in Oncology *AMIA Annu Symp Proc.* 2021;2020:833–839.
17. Solutions for Healthcare Executives and Senior Leaders. Virginia Mason Institute. https://www.virginiamasoninstitute.org/solutions-for-you/healthcare-executives-and-senior-leaders/
18. Allowing Medical Student Documentation in the Electronic Health Record Compliance Advisory. *AAMC.* 2014. Accessed February 21, 2025. https:// www.aamc.org/em/aamc/compliance_advisory.pdf
19. Rajaram A, Hickey Z, Patel N, Newbiggin J, Wolfrom B. Training Medical Students and Residents in the Use of Electronic Health Records: A Systematic Review of the Literature. *JAMIA.* 2020;27(1):175–180. https://doi.org/10.1093/jamia/ocz178
20. Lander L, Baxter SL, Cochran GL, et al. Self-Perceptions of Readiness to Use Electronic Health Records Among Medical Students: Survey Study. *JMIR Med Education.* 2020;6(1):e17585. doi: 10.2196/17585.
21. Amano A, Brown-Johnson CG, Winget M, et al. Perspectives on the Intersection of Electronic Health Records and Healthcare Team Communication, Function, and Well-being. *JAMA Netw Open.* 2023;6(5):e2313178. doi:10.1001/jamanetworkopen.2023.13178
22. Busse TS, Jux C, Laser J, et al. Involving Health Care Professionals in the Development of Electronic Health Records: Scoping Review. *JMIR Hum Factors.* 2023;10:e45598. doi: 10.2196/45598

CHAPTER 16

Information Technology Security, Privacy, and Operations

John Rasmussen, MBA, MA, CISSP

HALM CORE CONTENT:

- 4.7 Information security management (e.g., PHI, HIPAA, FOIA, the release of information)
- 4.8 Management of information security breaches
- 5.3 Compliance (e.g., HIPAA security requirements, HITECH Act meaningful use requirements)
- 5.5 Data management
  - 5.5.1 Security breaches, malware, ransomware, etc.
  - 5.5.2 Ongoing innovation, maintenance
  - 5.5.3 Upgrading and conversions
- 5.10 HIPAA
- 5.11 HITECH Act meaningful use
- 5.12 Information systems continuity and redundancy

CASE SCENARIO:

A healthcare organization's operations are running smoothly at the beginning of the week. Very early on Tuesday morning, access to the electronic health record (EHR) system is lost. Thirty minutes later, clinical workstations display a ransomware message that renders the machines unusable and displays the message "You have 24 hours to pay $3 million in Bitcoin or your patient data will be released on the internet and deleted from all of your machines." What is the potential scope of this incident and the extent of its impact on the provision of care? How does the organization respond to these events? What actions should be taken to protect systems, recover data, and maintain the continuity of care?

THE HEALTHCARE SECTOR INCLUDES a wide variety of businesses, including pharmacies, insurers, medical device manufacturers, software companies, and durable medical equipment providers. Each has its own unique cybersecurity challenges and can have an additional regulatory burden depending on how or where the business operates. This chapter will focus on the provider space, where care is delivered directly to the patients, which includes hospitals, clinics, urgent care, and specialty clinics.

Information technology (IT) systems are an integral part of the delivery of care and day-to-day operations in healthcare. The scope of services provided by IT systems is broad and reaches into every aspect of the organization. Additionally, healthcare organizations, no matter what size, are governed by a variety of regulations meant to protect both the privacy of patient data and the safety of care delivery systems and other IT systems that support healthcare operations.

Given the integration of IT systems in operations, the importance of these systems to operations, and the regulatory requirements that govern the use of data and system security, the maintenance of cybersecurity controls is key to keeping these systems available and not running afoul of legal requirements.

Healthcare Information Technology Operations and Security Controls

Healthcare IT is made up of many kinds of technology, including electronic health records, billing systems, timekeeping, productivity tools such as spreadsheets, documents, and presentations. Industry-specific systems like pharmacy, radiology, and medical devices add another layer of complexity. Additionally, the technology includes items that are not normally considered IT systems, such as heating and air conditioning controllers, temperature tracking for refrigerators, badge access systems, elevators, pneumatic tubes, and camera systems.

Technology has been a central component of healthcare operations for decades. Electronic medical devices have become important parts of diagnostic, monitoring, and treatment tools for patient care. Imaging systems, O_2 monitors, infusion pumps, and proton therapy devices are just a fraction of the available medical devices.

As computers came into healthcare, they reached every aspect of operations, including capturing electronic health information, finance, payment and claims processing, timekeeping for staff, and any number of business use cases. Moreover, healthcare facilities rely on information systems to manage elevators, heating and air conditioning systems, inventory, bed management, food service, and credit card payment processing.

Advancements in programming and computer processing have enabled the development of personal health devices, including health monitoring devices like glucose or

O_2 monitors or implanted medical devices like pacemakers or cardiac monitors. These items can often be described as physician-prescribed and third-party-managed devices.

The scope of information technology as a part of healthcare operations is vast and vital to care delivery — so much so that hospitals and health systems are considered part of the United States' critical infrastructure and must be protected to the same degree as water treatment facilities, power plants, or airports.

IT in healthcare can be managed by different departments within the organization. Many organizations opt to have a central IT leader, a chief information officer (CIO), or a chief technology officer. Smaller organizations may have an IT director. The CIO is typically responsible for the day-to-day maintenance and operations of IT systems, the network, and applications. They may also have additional responsibilities in data management and telephony.

CIOs are strategic business partners and work with senior leadership to develop a technology roadmap that meets the business requirements of the organization. They should be on top of new technology developments and the benefits of implementing these systems. Current innovations include cloud-based applications, commonly known as "software as a service" (SaaS), and artificial intelligence.

Other departments may manage IT platforms specific to their business. Some systems commonly managed by the department include radiology imaging systems, clinical engineering medical devices, the facilities department's environmental control systems, and the public safety department's physical safety systems like cameras and door badging systems.

The complexity of managing a variety of systems and platforms makes ensuring security challenging. Three types of security controls should be applied to all systems: administrative, physical, and technical safeguards.

- Administrative safeguards are policies, standards, security education, and guidelines that govern the use of systems, access to data, and acceptable use of data.[1]
- Physical safeguards are applied to real-world scenarios that could put patient data at risk, such as physical access restrictions to certain areas of a hospital, cameras to monitor areas with restricted data, and physical locks that protect sensitive information.[2]
- Technical safeguards include security tools like firewalls, virtual private networks (VPNs), anti-virus software, software patching systems, and identity and access management tools including multi-factor authentication, and system hardening.[3]

While administrative and physical safeguards can generally be applied to systems and devices, technical safeguards can create complications in the IT landscape. For example, systems can be exploited by hackers who gain access through software or operating system vulnerabilities. Each organization should have a plan to regularly identify and patch vulnerabilities as soon as the patch has been released by the vendor to prevent these intrusions.

For some systems, patching may require downtime as the patch is applied. For critical systems, this patching window is usually determined by the time of least usage for the system. In some cases where the organization has deemed the system to be vital to operations, the patching window must be carefully considered. For other systems, like medical devices, the system has approval to be used on patients through the Food and Drug Administration (FDA).[4] If a patch alters the capabilities of the medical device, the approval process may need to be revisited.

The FDA has ruled that security patches do not typically alter the functionality of a device and can be applied; however, since these devices are often in use, the vendor or clinical engineering must carefully evaluate when to apply patches, thus leaving them open to potential exploit while they remain unpatched.[5] This requires coordination between medical staff and IT to ensure the patch is applied and the system is operating as it should.

Technical safeguards, or compensating controls, are usually applied in layers across the network so the endpoint is not solely reliant on its onboard safeguards. These controls include firewalls, network intrusion detection, virtual local area network segmentation, and other controls applied to access points.[5]

A particular challenge for healthcare is the cost and longevity of certain systems. While a laptop computer may have a usable life of five years, an MRI system or infusion pump may have a 10–15-year lifespan and cost much more than the laptop. When a device or system has a long usable life, the underlying operating system may come to the end of vendor support. Once vendor support for the operating system has expired, there are no additional security patches created to plug vulnerabilities, leaving these systems vulnerable to exploit.

Healthcare Regulatory Environment

Most healthcare businesses are required to comply with the Health Insurance Portability and Accountability Act (HIPAA). In other countries, there are equivalent laws that protect the security and privacy of patient data. When HIPAA was signed into law in 1996, the law was written to ensure continued insurance coverage and care for patients who changed jobs. Regulators later added the Privacy Rule (2003)[6] and Security Rule (2005)[6] to protect patient data from being made available to those who did not have a direct care relationship with patients.

In 2013, the HIPAA Omnibus rules went into effect. These rules were based on the Health Information Technology for Economic and Clinical Health Act (HITECH), which promoted the adoption of electronic health records through incentives and was part of the American Recovery and Reinvestment Act of 2009. The HITECH Act extended regulatory requirements to business associates and their sub-contractors, added additional patient rights, and increased the penalties for violations of HIPAA.

HIPAA applies to covered entities (CEs) and business associates (BAs). A CE is a healthcare provider, insurer, or clearinghouse that conducts specific transactions with insurance carriers.[7] A BA is an organization that utilizes patient information on behalf of the CE for the purpose of managing care or payment.[7] Examples of BAs include EHR system vendors like Athena, Epic, or Cerner. They can also include providers of transcription services, data analytics groups, attorneys, SaaS providers, etc.

Under the Privacy Rule, patients are given certain rights, including the ability to obtain copies of their medical records, request amendments to their records, and request restrictions on uses and disclosures of their information.[8] The Privacy Rule can be confusing and requires a good understanding of the law and healthcare operations to be effectively applied.

The Security Rule in HIPAA requires that CEs implement cybersecurity controls to protect patient data. These controls include administrative, technical, and physical safeguards to protect health data from unauthorized access, use, or disclosure, as mentioned in the section above.[9]

The key goal of HIPAA and other requirements is to protect the confidentiality, integrity, and availability of health information, whether in electronic format, spoken, or in other formats, such as EKG strips, radiology films, etc. Confidentiality refers to the protection of sensitive information related to a patient, including name, address, social security number, credit card numbers, diagnosis, medications, and test results. Some diagnoses or health information are more sensitive than others, such as genetic information, sexually transmitted disease information, or alcohol and drug abuse information and can be protected by additional international, state, or local laws.

Management of Information Security Incidents and Breaches

When a security incident or a breach occurs, the organization needs to be prepared to face it head-on. In the case study at the beginning of the chapter, two different systems are impacted by different incidents. This is not an unusual occurrence; simultaneous incidents can and do occur with some frequency.

Other incidents can occur that can affect the uptime of systems, but these do not usually have the same level of impact on operations that a cybersecurity incident or breach can have to an organization. All providers should be aware that wherever these incidents occur, they could have an impact on patient care, an impact in organizational operations, and long-term repercussions.

One approach to handling security incidents can be boiled down to a five-step process derived from the NIST Special Publication 800-61 Revision 2. NIST is the National Institute for Standards and Technology and provides standards and guidelines based on industry best practices. The five stems to incident handling are:[10]

- Preparation
- Identification
- Containment
- Eradication
- Recovery

Preparation consists of several components that are meant to lower the overall impact of an incident. Major components of preparation include:[10]

- Developing and testing an incident response plan.
- Conducting a business impact analysis based on risk to prioritize systems.
- Implementing redundancies like system backups and eliminating "single point of failure" systems.
- Implementing technical safeguards at different levels within the network from the border to the desktop to harden the environment and make it more difficult for the attacker to gain a foothold.
- Train staff to identify risky cybersecurity behavior like clicking on or responding to phishing messages.

Identification is the point where an organization realizes that something has gone amiss.[9] This can happen when an end user calls the help desk with an error message or the IT team detects anomalous behavior on the network. Identification can come from any point in the organization.

The important aspect of this step is that the organization has the ability to correlate and escalate issues when they arise. Some things, no matter how small, can turn into enterprise-wide events, like a report to the help desk of someone clicking on a suspected phishing email. If the user downloads malicious code, it can spread like wildfire over the network and cripple systems quickly.

In 2017, the NotPetya ransomware quickly overtook the Merck Pharmaceutical network and resulted in an estimated $1.4 billion in losses.[11] If the help desk and IT security team are not in sync, an event could go unnoticed, and correlation will not occur until it is too late.

Containment is the stage of incident response where teams focus on stopping the spread of the issue, whether it is a virus, ransomware, or another kind of intrusion.[10] This typically entails shutting down a network node, unplugging a system from the network, cutting off internet access inbound and outbound, or all the above.

As you can imagine, containment can impact the entire organization. If the electronic medical record is hosted by a vendor, access can be completely cut off. Transfers of data to insurers or clearinghouses for payment may be stopped. Pharmacy systems may not be able to transmit prescriptions to pharmacists, and credit card transactions may not go through. This is just a limited example of the potential operational impact of containment.

The eradication phase removes the threat from the environment.[10] This phase can also cause long disruptions. When a system is infected with malware or there is a persistent intruder located within, the system cannot be trusted and may need to be rebuilt from the ground up. In many cases, conducting a cleanup of a virus can leave remnants behind that can allow the attacker back in and the system cannot be trusted. In some extreme cases, the drives or firmware may be corrupted, and a complete system replacement is needed.

Recovery may be the most prolonged phase of incident response.[10] This phase requires the organization to restore systems to their original state and may result in the permanent loss of data. If data from a local hard drive are not backed up, a ransomware infection may render that information unrecoverable. Systems may need to have data restored from backup. If this is the case, there will be gaps in the data between the incident and recovery.

This is especially important in the provision of care. If the Medication Administration Record (MAR) has gaps in data, this could lead to a patient safety event. If patient notes are recorded on paper during the incident, the organization will need to scan these notes and update the medical record to reflect any care that has occurred. Long term, there may be information that cannot be recovered or is overlooked when updating systems. If this is the case, it could lead to future care issues or potential liability issues for the provider.

It is important to note that these steps are not sequential. Any of these phases can occur at any time during an incident.

Managing and Maintaining Cybersecurity

While maintaining an incident response plan and contingencies for an incident, the best way to prevent an incident is to ensure that IT systems are appropriately managed, patched, and monitored. Since systems can be maintained by separate departments, the main role of the head of cybersecurity, commonly called the chief information security officer (CISO), is to ensure that an organizational strategy for cybersecurity is applied across the entire organization. (HIPAA requires that CEs name a security official in addition to a privacy officer).[11] The CISO works with the CIO and other department heads to understand the technologies in place and what is on the technology roadmap.

Together, the technology managers assess the risk to the organization and identify practices to manage these risks. Key to creating a cybersecurity strategy is having an accurate inventory of systems, devices, and users. These assets all need to have security controls defined.

For systems, which can be standalone or enterprise software systems, the organization should have agreements in place with the vendors to keep the systems secure. These agreements should spell out the minimum cybersecurity controls needed. For example, the vendor should be continually assessing the security of their product and applying updates in a timely manner to address vulnerabilities. Additionally, the organization will need to maintain the security of the platforms that host these systems.

Whether a server, workstation, or portable device, security maintenance is one of the key lines of defense against attack or loss of the device. Mobile device management tools can set up controls on smartphones and tablets used in the environment. These controls can require encryption, passwords, patching, and a minimum level of operating system for them to keep access to organizational information. Servers and desktop/laptop computers can be automatically patched by the IT team and should also include system hardening (blocking unnecessary ports or communication to the device), anti-virus software, access management, and system logging and monitoring.

The most challenging asset to security is the system user. These are usually employees but can include vendors, providers with facility privileges, and volunteers. Each user should be centrally managed and giving the minimum necessary access to systems; for example, a volunteer working in a gift shop should not have access to the EHR. These entitlements are based on the role of the user.

User access should be logged and monitored and promptly revoked when the user leaves the organization. The user should also be trained to maintain the security of the systems. They should never share their password with anyone for any reason. They should be aware of cybersecurity scams and phishing that could introduce ransomware into the environment, and they should be trained on maintaining patient privacy.

Technology and cybersecurity tools in healthcare are costly recurring expenses. Many systems typically have low profit margins, and when IT systems are one of the largest spending categories in healthcare, there is a temptation to cut spending on IT. Much of the technology in the cybersecurity toolkit cannot demonstrate a return on investment and thus becomes a cost center, not a revenue generator. Providers should carefully consider the risk of an IT incident or cybersecurity event when they are creating their annual budgets. When a ransomware attack or an outage occurs, the risks to patient safety, legal compliance, and reputational harm can cost the organization millions of dollars, whereas putting security controls can prevent these issues from happening. As they say, "An ounce of prevention is worth a pound of a cure."

Chapter Summary

A cybersecurity incident in healthcare can have a serious impact on day-to-day operations and the provision of care by affecting vital systems like the electronic health record, medical devices, and vital business systems used to process payments or supplies needed by the provider. Long-term impacts of an incident can financially or reputationally harm the system. Privacy breaches can result in class action lawsuits, scrutiny from regulators, and financial impact through the response process. While insurance coverage may offset some of these costs, insurance premiums will rise and the healthcare entity will be under the microscope of insurers.

Most importantly, any cybersecurity incident could have an impact on patient safety and the continuity of care. If patient monitoring systems or infusion pumps are impacted by a cybersecurity attack, the consequences can be severe by causing delays in care or diverting patients away from the facility. Timely and accurate information is important to the provision of care and anything that alters these systems' ability to operate has a direct impact on healthcare operations.

Leveraging best practices for securing healthcare systems and devices is the best method of lowering the probability of a successful cyberattack. This, however, requires an organization to understand what they have, how it is exposed to attack, and having staff and controls that can react to a cyberattack.

REFERENCES

1. Office for Civil Rights. Summary of the HIPAA Security Rule. Section 8. U.S. Department of Health and Human Services. https://www.hhs.gov/hipaa/for-professionals/security/laws-regulations/index.html. October 19, 2022. Accessed November 2, 2024.
2. Office for Civil Rights. Summary of the HIPAA Security Rule. Section 9. U.S. Department of Health and Human Services. October 19, 2022. Accessed November 2, 2024. https://www.hhs.gov/hipaa/for-professionals/security/laws-regulations/index.html.
3. Office for Civil Rights. Summary of the HIPAA Security Rule. Section 10. U.S. Department of Health and Human Services. October 19, 2022. Accessed November 2, 2024. https://www.hhs.gov/hipaa/for-professionals/security/laws-regulations/index.html.U.S. Food and Drug Administration. Learn About Drug and Device Approvals. February 21, 2020. Accessed November 2, 2024. https://www.fda.gov/patients/learn-about-drug-and-device-approvals.
4. U.S. Food and Drug Administration. Postmarket Management of Cybersecurity in Medical Devices Guidance for Industry and Food and Drug Administration Staff. December 28, 2016. Accessed November 2, 2024. https://www.fda.gov/media/95862/download.
5. Alder S. "HIPAA History." HIPAA Journal, http://www.hipaajournal.com/hipaa-history/. December 31, 2023. Accessed November 2, 2024. (Paragraph 2)
6. U.S. Department of Health and Human Services Office for Civil Rights. HIPAA Administrative Simplification. http://www.hhs.gov/sites/default/files/hipaa-simplification-201303.pdf. March 26, 2013. Accessed November 2, 2024. (Page 12)
7. U.S. Department of Health and Human Services. "Your Rights under HIPAA." HHS.gov, , http://www.hhs.gov/hipaa/for-individuals/guidance-materials-for-consumers/index.html. January 19, 2022. Accessed November 3, 2024. (Section 9)
8. U.S. Department of Health and Human Services. "The Security Rule." HHS.gov. http://www.hhs.gov/hipaa/for-professionals/security/index.html. October 20, 2022. Accessed November 3, 2024. (Section 1)
9. Cichonski P, et al. Computer Security Incident Handling Guide. *Computer Security Incident Handling Guide*. 2(2):21. https://doi.org/10.6028/nist.sp.800-61r2. November 2, 2024. Accessed November 2, 2024.
10. Vanderford R. Insurers Say Cyberattack That Hit Merck Was Warlike Act, Not Covered. *The Wall Street Journal*. February 8, 2023. Accessed November 2, 2024. http://www.wsj.com/articles/insurers-say-cyberattack-that-hit-merck-was-warlike-act-not-covered-11675897657.
11. U.S. Department of Health and Human Services Office for Civil Rights. HIPAA Administrative Simplification. March 26, 2013. Accessed November 2, 2024. http://www.hhs.gov/sites/default/files/hipaa-simplification-201303.pdf.

CHAPTER 17

Data and Analytics

Rubayet Hossain, MD; Nicholas Gavin, MD, MBA, MS; and Robbie Freeman, DNP, RN

HALM CORE CONTENT

- 5.7 Healthcare Analytics
- 5.8 Big Data
- 5.9 Augmented Intelligence

CASE SCENARIO:

An organization is facing enormous penalties for hospital-acquired pressure injuries among inpatients on various clinical services. There is a hypothesis that many community-acquired pressure injuries are not being adequately documented to avoid the penalty of a hospital-acquired condition. How can the organization quantify baseline documentation of Community-Acquired Pressure Injuries (CAPIs)? How can they measure the impact of an education campaign targeting CAPI identification during the admission process? And, how can they identify patients who are at high risk of CAPI so that there can be targeted screening and intervention prior to admission?

Healthcare Analytics

HEALTHCARE ORGANIZATIONS THAT FOCUS on direct patient care often lag behind other industries in the implementation and use of data for strategic insights — what is commonly referred to as business intelligence.[1] There are several reasons for this. For one, healthcare as a field tends to be more conservative than sectors like finance, logistics, or technology. Consider the historical context: despite decades of strong technical development in the 20th century, widespread enthusiasm for electronic health records (EHRs) only emerged in the 21st century after the government introduced financial incentives and subsequent penalties.[2]

Another contributing factor is that leaders in healthcare — physicians, nurses, physician assistants, social workers, respiratory therapists, and others — spend their formative years focused intensely on patient care at the bedside. This educational and professional immersion often leaves little room for developing analytical literacy.

While this chapter cannot resolve these longstanding challenges in one fell swoop, it does aim to provide healthcare leaders with a foundational level of data literacy. By clarifying what healthcare analytics encompasses, illustrating the types of questions a variety of analytical tools can answer, and encouraging creative thinking about potential applications, this chapter seeks to help healthcare leaders appreciate the value of building analytics capabilities. Ultimately, the goal is to inspire them to commit resources toward cultivating analytics expertise within their own organizations — converting data into actionable insights.

There are three types of analytics: descriptive, predictive, and prescriptive. A logical starting point is descriptive analytics, which focuses on understanding what has already occurred within the organization. For example, one might ask, "In the past six months, how many patients have been admitted with particular conditions?" This retrospective view sets the stage for moving toward predictive analytics, which leads to the question, "Based on historical trends, what might happen next month or next year?"

With predictive analytics, one can start making informed guesses about the future. From there, the natural progression leads to prescriptive analytics. If the forecasts are sound, how should they prepare for what's coming? This is where data begin to guide strategic decision-making and resource allocation.

It's important to recognize certain constraints. The types of answerable questions depend on the quality and relevance of the data and on the maturity of the analytic capabilities. For instance, one wouldn't trust current patient data to predict disruptive technologies emerging in healthcare 15 years down the road — that is not what the data are meant to do. Similarly, one wouldn't try to forecast next year's patient volumes without a solid grasp of what's happening right now. Ultimately, a perfect answer to the wrong question is worthless.

The progression from descriptive to predictive to prescriptive analytics should be guided by an appropriate scope of inquiry and a realistic assessment of what the organization can meaningfully address at each stage of data literacy.[3] All three stages depend on a foundation of data integrity and appropriate governance.

INTEGRITY AND GOVERNANCE IN HEALTHCARE ANALYTICS

The accuracy and reliability of any given insight depends on the underlying data's integrity. The integrity of the underlying data has implications for patient safety, clinical effectiveness evaluations of a given intervention, compliance, and research. Examples of data integrity issues in healthcare include missing data, duplicate records, and transcription errors.[4]

To ensure proper data integrity, health systems must have robust data governance structures in place. Governance should oversee all data security, access, management, and quality across the organization. As a best practice, in large academic health systems, there should be shared data governance between the health system and the academic entity.

DESCRIPTIVE ANALYTICS

Descriptive analytics answers a fundamental question: What has happened in a specific situation within the healthcare organization up to this point in time? It does not attempt to predict the future, nor does it guide one in how to respond to upcoming challenges. Instead, descriptive analytics is simply a restatement of past events — a historical account.

For example, one might want to know how many patients arrived in the emergency departments each day over the past week, how many appointments at the clinics were canceled and why, or how many hip and knee replacement surgeries were completed daily last month. Because it deals only with what has already occurred, descriptive analytics tends to be the simplest form of analytics and carries the least amount of risk. After all, if the data are complete and reliable, there is little uncertainty about what happened in the past.

There are both benefits and drawbacks to relying on descriptive analytics. On the positive side, it is the easiest type of analytics to implement and requires minimal data science expertise. It doesn't require formal training in complex forecasting models or optimization procedures. Instead, data sources can be simply queried to summarize the results with basic mathematical transformations.

Descriptive analytics is also straightforward to understand. For example, if last month the inpatient length of stay averaged 6.5 days with a standard deviation of 2.2 days, it is easy to deduct that most hospitalizations fell between roughly 2 and 11 days with no need to revisit advanced statistical concepts.

One can also conduct rudimentary forms of A/B testing. For instance, if the organization has implemented certain quality improvement interventions and has a control population for comparison, perhaps using an interrupted time series design, they can measure whether the intervention clearly outperforms the baseline.[5,6]

On the other hand, descriptive analytics provides the least guidance for future planning. By focusing solely on restating past events, there is often an implicit assumption that the future will mirror the past, which is not always the case. Populations grow, legislation changes, competitors react, and countless other external factors may arise. It is naïve to assume one can plan for the future based only on historical portrayals.

Furthermore, descriptive analytics can be misleading if the type and depth of data displayed are insufficient. For example, if trying to improve asthma management in the patient population and the dashboard shows only readmission rates, emergency department visit frequencies, and inpatient lengths of stay, one might be ignoring critical data, such as the proportion of patients who are prescribed controller medications, have pulmonology referrals, or are under the care of a primary care physician. Without these metrics, there will be a failure to capture the interventions that matter most.

When evaluating descriptive analytics, always ask whether the data are both sufficient and relevant to the needs. If safeguarded against unfounded assumptions and realistic about what descriptive analytics can and cannot provide, it becomes a powerful tool for understanding the past and current health of the organization.

PREDICTIVE ANALYTICS

Predictive analytics seeks to answer the question: Based on what has happened in the past, what can be expected to occur in the future? For instance, in preparation for flu season, when stocking up on testing kits and personal protective equipment, an organization might consider examining the volume of flu patients in past years to identify any upward or downward trends and determine whether there are cyclical patterns (such as a spike during holidays). Similarly, to improve the staffing model, they will need to predict how many patients will be cared for on a given day and anticipate the level of complexity and resource needs.

By progressing from descriptive to predictive analytics, there is a shift of focus to the future which adds the ability to make strategic decisions. Strategy, after all, is about achieving future success, not re-living past accomplishments.

Before diving into predictive analytics, establish strong and reliable descriptive capabilities. If historical data are incomplete or inaccurate, any forecasts generated will be equally unreliable. As the saying goes, "Garbage in, garbage out."

Predictive analytics offers several advantages. Most notably, it goes beyond simply recounting history to provide a mathematically informed glimpse of what lies ahead. This perspective enables leaders to make strategic decisions about resource allocation, staffing, supply management, and more. Additionally, while some predictive models consider complex patterns like trends, seasonality, and heteroscedasticity, many questions can be answered using relatively simple techniques, such as linear regression.[7] This will not need costly outside consultants with black-box models; in many cases, in-house analytical talent and a willingness to experiment are sufficient to get started.

There are drawbacks, however. Predictive models require an understanding of statistical principles and should not be oversimplified. Suppose a forecast predicts 55 patient arrivals at a clinic tomorrow. This must also consider the confidence interval that accompanies this prediction. If the range is 45 to 65 arrivals, receiving 63 does not invalidate the model. Quite the opposite; the model allowed for that outcome.

Another drawback is that a confidence interval inherently includes the possibility of being wrong some percentage of the time. A 95% confidence interval means that the range might be off 5% of the time. Adjusting confidence levels is a trade-off. Increasing the confidence level (from 95% to 99%, for example) produces a wider range and makes it harder to pinpoint an exact number.

Ultimately, the usefulness of certain forecasts depends on how detrimental it would be to make a wrong prediction and how much flexibility there is to respond to a range of potential outcomes. Predictive analytics is thus a balancing act, aiming for enough accuracy and precision to guide strategic decisions without expecting flawless foresight.

PRESCRIPTIVE ANALYTICS

Prescriptive analytics addresses the question: If there are reliable forecasts, what should be done to optimize the objective? Consider the emergency department staffing example. Suppose it can accurately be predicted that between 230 and 260 patients will arrive tomorrow, with about 60% low acuity, 35% high acuity, and 5% critical. With this information, one can determine how many nurses to schedule for each shift, what proportion should be critical care–trained, and how to arrange staffing to minimize cost while adhering to nurse-to-patient ratios, shift length restrictions, and other constraints.

Similarly, if the desire is to maximize profit from the joint replacement program and have reliable forecasts of patient demand, the organization can decide how many surgeons, anesthesiologists, physician assistants, CRNAs, secretaries, and environmental services staff to schedule. The goal might be to optimize the number of surgeries performed during a 10.5-hour day without violating constraints such as room turnover times, the number of operating rooms available, and patient registration and evaluation times.

At its core, prescriptive analytics involves three key elements: objectives (what is hoped to be achieved), decision variables (the adjustable factors to meet the objectives), and constraints (what cannot be altered due to safety, regulatory, or practical reasons). This level of analytics is the pinnacle of business intelligence because it relies on strong descriptive abilities, reliable predictive capabilities, and the expertise to construct and solve optimization models.[8] Although it requires significant mathematical and technical skill, the investment is often worthwhile. By removing guesswork and focusing on data-driven decisions, it reduces waste, eliminates bottlenecks, improves resource utilization, and minimizes variability.

The advantages of prescriptive analytics are clear, but it's important to consider the drawbacks. This approach demands strong in-house expertise, typically found in large health systems or academic medical centers.[9] If such talent isn't readily available, it may need to be developed.

The good news is that if the organization already has robust descriptive and predictive capabilities, the next step may be less costly than expected. For example, investing in training with the current analytics team may be easier since it involves individuals who already understand the data structures and tools. Formal degrees aren't usually necessary, and effective training programs might last only three to six months.

Another challenge involves interpreting the results. Optimization software packages like CPLEX, Gurobi, GAMS, and R can produce outputs that are not immediately intuitive to healthcare leaders accustomed to clinical or traditional research roles. Clear communication from the analytics team is essential, as is a high level of trust in their expertise. Nevertheless, the value of prescriptive analytics is undeniable, and its impact only grows as it harnesses one of the greatest assets the electronic health record system can provide: big data.

Big Data

Big data refers to the vast volume of data generated in the modern digital age from various sources across the internet of things, including transactions, social media, academic research, and the electronic health record. These data are often qualified by their volume, velocity, variety, and veracity, all of which create unique challenges to manage and analyze.[7] Through the power of machine learning and artificial intelligence, big data has the potential to transform healthcare.

Sources of big data in healthcare include traditional data from the EHR but also genomic data, data from wearable devices, medical imaging data, and measurements of social risk. The integration of these diverse data sets offers unprecedented and, to this point, untapped opportunities to improve patient outcomes and reduce the total cost of care. One of the most significant areas where big data is making an impact is genomics, which has the power to enable personalized medicine.[10]

Genomics has grown rapidly due to advances in technology that allow for the sequencing of entire genomes at a low cost. By analyzing the genetic makeup of individuals, populations and cancer tissues, researchers can identify variations that may predispose people to particular conditions or variations that are amenable to particular treatment.[11] This influx of genomic data, when combined with data from other sources including other -omics, is creating a new frontier in personalized medicine.[12]

Personalized medicine is an approach that tailors medical treatment to the individual characteristics of a particular patient, considering their genes and environment.[13] Only through the analysis of big data can the potential of personalized medicine be realized through the identification of genetic markers associated with particular diseases, prediction of patients' responses to therapy, and recognition of markers that may fully prevent disease. One specialty where big data has found applications is in advancing personalized cancer treatment.[14] Numerous other specialties and the conditions they treat stand to benefit from these advancements.

The integration of big data into healthcare presents unique challenges. Interoperability between various information systems, the need to protect individual's privacy, and the potential for data overload can hinder its full potential. Despite these challenges, the future of healthcare is undoubtedly intertwined with the continued advancement and application of big data which holds the promise of transforming healthcare into a more efficient and individualized delivery system.

Augmented Intelligence

Predictive and prescriptive analytics often are derived from artificial or augmented intelligence (AI) technologies that can be embedded into clinical workflows. Adopting such technologies in healthcare settings requires a structured and collaborative approach to maximize potential. Successful implementation hinges on clear planning, continuous evaluation, and seamless integration into clinical workflows.

Best practices for deploying AI tools include defining clear success criteria, co-designing workflows with front-line clinicians, and leveraging iterative improvement methods. Implementing AI systems in healthcare demands careful consideration of infrastructure, stakeholder engagement, and change management. Healthcare leaders must assess institutional readiness by evaluating data quality, integration capacity with electronic medical records (EMRs), and organizational familiarity with AI tools. Early stakeholder engagement is critical, involving multidisciplinary teams such as clinicians, IT, compliance, finance, risk management, and administrators to align goals and expectations.

An effective organizational governance structure is essential for ensuring oversight, adherence to organizational policies, and the safe, responsible use of AI products. Such a structure facilitates comprehensive evaluation of potential risks, addresses ethical considerations, and ensures accountability throughout the AI implementation process. Before any AI product is introduced into the clinical setting, prospective evaluations must be conducted to assess its safety, effectiveness, biases, and alignment with institutional goals.

The governance structure should include a diverse group of stakeholders to ensure multidisciplinary oversight. Clinical leaders play a key role in ensuring AI tools address clinical needs and prioritize patient safety. Ethics experts contribute by addressing ethical considerations and promoting responsible AI use, while data scientists and AI specialists evaluate the technical performance and limitations of these tools. IT and cybersecurity specialists ensure data integrity, system security, and seamless integration with existing infrastructure, while regulatory and compliance officers help maintain adherence to healthcare regulations, standards, and privacy laws.

Executive leadership provides strategic alignment and decision-making authority, and patient representatives ensure the initiatives reflect patient-centered values. Additionally, legal counsel can navigate liability risks and legal challenges, while quality improvement experts monitor outcomes and drive continuous refinement.

Effective governance programs build transparency across an organization, which is essential for building trust, with clear communication about how AI tools work, their benefits, and limitations. Developing training programs equips clinicians and staff with the necessary skills to interpret AI outputs and integrate them into clinical decision-making effectively.

Defining clear success metrics is essential to measure the impact and sustainability of AI tools. These criteria should align with institutional priorities and encompass clinical outcomes such as reducing adverse events, improving patient safety, and enhancing care quality. Operational efficiency metrics might include shorter hospital stays, optimized resource allocation, and improved workflow efficiency. Success also hinges on user adoption and satisfaction, with high rates of clinician engagement and positive feedback on usability.

Integrating AI tools into existing workflows requires a collaborative approach grounded in experience-led, human-centered design practices. Co-designing workflows with end users — clinicians, administrators, and researchers — ensures that the technology seamlessly complements existing practices rather than disrupts them. Human-centered design prioritizes understanding the needs, behaviors, and challenges of users through in-depth research to uncover pain points and workflow bottlenecks. By leveraging these insights, teams can create customized interfaces with intuitive, role-specific workflows and notifications that align with daily routines.

An organizational governance structure can provide oversight and ensure adherence to organizational policies and that AI products are used in a safe and responsible manner. Prospective evaluation should be performed before an AI product is used in the clinical setting.

Building feedback loops is critical for fostering a culture of continuous improvement, providing users with channels to voice concerns, suggest refinements, and share real-world experiences. This iterative process helps address barriers to adoption while ensuring the technology evolves in response to user needs. A focus on user experience not only enhances usability and satisfaction but also drives sustained engagement with the AI system, ensuring its long-term impact and success in improving clinical and operational outcomes.

The Plan-Do-Study-Act (PDSA) cycle is a proven framework for continuous quality improvement, making it ideal for refining AI implementations. Leaders can define specific objectives for deployment, such as reducing response times for clinical deterioration alerts or increasing early detection rates of malnutrition. Piloting the system in a controlled setting helps evaluate performance and identify challenges. Analyzing data and user feedback enables leaders to assess the tool's effectiveness and identify areas for improvement. Subsequent refinements and scaling ensure the AI tool evolves in response to real-world needs, enhancing its utility and impact.

Effective implementation of AI in the healthcare settings requires a structured approach rooted in collaboration, clear goals, and continuous evaluation. By focusing on comprehensive planning, measurable success criteria, user-centered workflow design, and iterative improvement methods, healthcare leaders can maximize the benefits of AI technologies. These strategies drive innovation, improve patient care, and advance institutional missions.

Chapter Summary

The decisions needed to transform healthcare in the United States must be data-driven. Increasingly, predictive analytics will lead to prescriptive guidance. Integration of that guidance into actual clinical workflows and strategic decision-making for health systems requires an interdisciplinary approach that is guided by traditional principles of quality improvement.

REFERENCES

1. Smith M, Saunders R, Stuckhardt L, McGinnis JM, eds. *Best Care at Lower Cost: The Path to Continuously Learning Health Care in America*. Washington, DC: National Academies Press; 2013.
2. Blumenthal D, Tavenner M. The 'Meaningful Use' Regulation for Electronic Health Records. *N Engl J Med.*. 2010;363(6):501–504.
3. Davenport TH, Harris JG. *Competing on Analytics: The New Science of Winning*. Boston, MA: Harvard Business School Press; 2007.
4. Bowie MJ, Green MA. *Essentials of Health Information Management: Principles and Practices, 4th ed*. Cengage Learning; 2018.
5. Ramsay CR, Matowe L, Grilli R, et al. Interrupted Time Series Designs in Health Technology Assessment: Lessons From Two Systematic Reviews of Behavior Change Strategies. *Int J Technol Assess Health Care*. 2003;19(4):613–623.
6. Penfold RB, Zhang F. Use of Interrupted Time Series Analysis in Evaluating Health Policy Interventions. *Acad Pediatr*. 2013;13(6 Suppl):S38-44.
7. Raghupathi W, Raghupathi V. Big Data Analytics in Healthcare: Promise and Potential. *Health Information Science and Systems*. 2019;2(1):1–10. doi:10.1186/2047-2501-2-3.
8. LaVelle S, Lesser E, Shockley R, et al. Big Data, Analytics and the Path From Insights to Value. *MIT Sloan Management Review*. 2011;52(2):21–31.
9. Davenport TH, Patil DJ. Data Scientist: The Sexiest Job of the 21st Century. *Harvard Business Review*. October 2012.
10. Collins FS, Varmus H. A New Initiative on Precision Medicine. *N Eng J Med*. 2015;372(9):793–795.
11. Posey JE, Lupski JR. Genomics in Clinical Practice. *N Engl J Med*. 2023;388(17):1619–1620. doi: 10.1056/NEJMe2302643. Epub 2023 Apr 12. PMID: 37043638.
12. Haendel MA, Chute CG, Robinson PN. Classification, Ontology, and Precision Medicine. *N Engl J Med*. 2018;379(15):1452–1462. doi: 10.1056/NEJMra1615014. PMID: 30304648; PMCID: PMC6503847.
13. Jameson JL, Longo DL. Precision Medicine—Personalized, Problematic, and Promising. *N Engl J Med*. 2015;372(23):2229–2234. doi: 10.1056/NEJMsb1503104. Epub 2015 May 27. PMID: 26014593.
14. Low SK, Zembutsu H, Nakamura Y. Breast Cancer: The Translation of Big Genomic Data to Cancer Precision Medicine. *Cancer Sci*. 2018;109(3):497–506. doi: 10.1111/cas.13463. Epub 2017 Dec 30. PMID: 29215763; PMCID: PMC5834810.

SECTION 6

Human Resource Management and Workforce Development

CHAPTER 18

Workforce Recruitment

Timothy Craig Allen, MD, JD, FCAP, FASCP, and Amyn M. Rojiani, MD, PhD, CPE, DFAAPL

HALM CORE CONTENT:

- 6.1 Compensation and benefits practices
- 6.4 Diversity, inclusion, and equity strategies
- 6.10 Recruitment and retention approaches and techniques

CASE SCENARIO:

Elsewhere Medical Center (EMC) has had challenges recruiting quality physicians to its medical staff. More recently, Dr. Yolanda Ozbenroff approached the chair of medicine to inform him that she is being actively recruited by a private practice group located in West Virginia. The practice is in a more rural location but promises to be satisfying in terms of the case mix and environment - and the compensation offer is significantly higher than her current compensation package.

The chief of medicine met with the EMC president, and they discussed the implications of this news. Factors they considered included the cost of recruiting a replacement, disruption in services at EMC until a replacement is recruited and up to speed, the possibility of providing a retention package that may match the offer, inequity that such a compensation package may create with current faculty, promoting Dr. Ozbenroff to a leadership position as vice chair in recognition of her contributions to the department's quality and outreach initiatives, as well as other possibilities such as attempting to enforce the noncompete clause in her current contract.

Despite being presented with most of these options, she decided to make the career move to West Virginia. EMC did not pursue enforcing the noncompete clause.

Compensation and Benefits Practices

Physician compensation plans have evolved over the last few decades and vary significantly based on a plethora of specific factors. The most obvious factor is specialty, followed by academic or non-academic practice positions and geographic location. Business models have changed from independent, individual, or small-group practices to the large-group practice model or a model in which physicians are employed rather than being owners or partners. Beyond these three elements, there are a whole host of variables that have created a wide variety in compensation plans.

Today's basic compensation plans revolve around productivity and the revenue that each physician brings to the group practice, whether academic or other. The fundamental model is essentially one that guarantees a base salary or net income, supplemented by a non-guaranteed, variable bonus or incentive. While a host of "perks" may be added to sweeten the pot, the defining factor will always be that compensation is most closely aligned with the marketplace.

A caveat to this basic model was described by Andrew Hajde, CMPE, director of consulting at the MGMA, who pointed to two big-picture developments that are starting to take hold in physician compensation structures: value-based care metrics that call for care efficiency, equitability, timeliness, and safety; and risk-based contracts, in which specified quality metrics are tracked and physicians (or their employers) are accountable for providing quality care while avoiding excess hospital readmissions or other suboptimal outcomes. According to Hajde, "These movements, long in transit, are really picking up pace now, so we're just starting to see these value-based components showing up in physician compensation models."[1]

The chronological stage of one's career, acknowledging years of training and years of experience, is clearly a determining factor and will influence aspects of any recruitment package. The recent graduate, completing years of residency and possibly fellowship training, however, is unlikely to have a significant say in the compensation offered.[2] They, with few exceptions, are most likely coming to the table with a substantial education debt, often are just starting families, and are at the first stages of their professional practice. These factors limit the choices new-in-practice physicians make, often leaning them toward positions that will help ease that financial burden. They may have less negotiation prowess and are more likely to take what is offered.

In this situation, it is important that the physician make their choice based on whether this is truly the right opportunity rather than the most financially sound. It is these early formative years that will influence one's perspective on the practice of medicine, often for many years, even decades. One needs to look beyond compensation at some intangible components of the package, such as size of the group/institution, patient population, on-call time, duration of workweek, productivity criteria, geographic location, ability to work from home some days, additional CME time or money, and other factors that will influence lifestyle choices and well-being, physical and mental.

The choice of an academic practice versus a non-academic position, solo practice versus small or large group practice, rural versus suburban or urban practice, is a very individual decision. It is important, therefore, to understand that compensation will vary, sometimes quite significantly, between one and the other. While one may assume that compensation in an urban setting must be higher to cover the cost of living, a small rural practice may have to offer a higher starting salary simply to attract individuals or may present perks that might make it more attractive.[3]

The databases that employers use to determine base salary can be quite different from one institution to another and from one practice type to another. The most frequently used salary tables for academic positions are those generated by the Association of American Medical Colleges (AAMC). The annual AAMC Faculty Salary Report displays total compensation statistics for full-time medical school faculty.

Total compensation is the sum of fixed/contractual salary, medical practice supplement, and bonus/incentive pay. It is important to note that these numbers represent total compensation and not just base salary.

Additionally, the salary report breaks out total compensation by degree, rank, department/specialty, medical school type, region, gender, and race/ethnicity. Tables show the faculty count, mean, median, and the 10th, 25th, 75th, and 90th percentiles for each combination of six faculty ranks (instructor, assistant professor, associate professor, professor, chief, and chair) and two-degree types (MD or equivalent degree and PhD or other doctoral degree) across 100 departments/specialties in basic and clinical sciences.[4]

Additional salary databases include the 2024 MGMA Provider Compensation and Production report *Provider Pay and the Dawn of a New Era of Productivity*, reflecting 2023 data from more than 211,000 physicians and advanced practice providers (APPs).[5]

Sullivan Cotter's Physician Compensation and Productivity Survey continues to be the largest and most comprehensive physician compensation survey published. With data reported on over 215,400 physicians and PhDs, this survey continues to lead the market in all areas – sample sizes, contemporary and emerging pay practices and the number of specialties and position levels surveyed.[6]

A number of other compensation reports are regularly conducted and published, including Doximity and Medscape, as well as those by individual specialty organizations. Each one provides a slightly different set of variables. In the final analysis, however, these are simply guideposts and not absolute numbers, often subject to wide variability and negotiation.

The physician compensation models in general, employ one or more of the following methods:

- Measuring productivity as a function of RVUs or relative value units is the easiest to measure, is transparent, and physicians can control how little or how much they work. On the downside, they can incentivize overutilization of services and may not prioritize preventive medicine.
- Base salary models provide stability with predictable income, allowing for quality patient care without prioritizing revenue. The biggest disadvantage is that this model does not enhance motivation to increase workload or take on new responsibilities. Lack of an incentive component often fails to attract or retain physicians.
- Value-based compensation models place an emphasis on delivering high-quality care but also balancing costs. While easy to understand, these are difficult and complex to measure objectively.

Many models simply incorporate elements of the above with a base salary, an opportunity to earn incentives and some measures of quality care delivery.

Recruitment and Retention Approaches and Techniques

Employee recruitment and retention is critically important for institutional success. Healthcare talent scarcity, predating the pandemic, is generally due to changing demographics and population growth, increased and early retirement by healthcare workers, and insufficient amount or access to quality medical training programs and facilities.[7]

Institutions must continuously attract new talent, and with the growing global shortage of quality workers, especially healthcare workers, which is predicted to last for decades, healthcare institutions will compete not just as traditionally for patients and market share but also for quality employees. To be attractive to these quality candidates, institutions must create and maintain a welcoming and enabling culture.[8]

Scarcity is a vicious circle; having too few quality employees results in overwork, stress, and, ultimately, burnout, which then prompts additional employees to leave, worsening the shortage.[7] One pre-pandemic study found that 43% of just-licensed nurses left their institution within their first three years of employment, generally blaming unmanageable stress as a consequence of having little autonomy, feedback, or mentorship and worsening nurse-patient ratios.[9]

Institutional leaders are challenged in their recruitment efforts by, among other things, intense competition for increasingly scarce qualified healthcare workers, growing budget limitations, balancing hiring quality with speed, increasingly long hiring processes, lengthening time-to-fill positions, high rates of employee turnover, managing multiple openings, difficulty adapting to new technologies, and increasingly burdensome regulatory and compliance rules.[10]

The recruiting landscape has changed, with institutions facing increased competition and employee expectations of competitive salary and benefits, flexible work hours and settings, minimizing administrative burdens, offering effective mentoring and preceptorship, identifying and increasing opportunities for increased responsibility, asking for and delivering frequent feedback, and improving effective administrative communication.[7,8,11]

Despite these variables, certain considerations apply to almost every physician recruitment process. Some of these are described below:

- Have a recruitment strategy that begins before candidates even interview. Various advertising methods may increase an institution's chances of hiring success. While posting advertisements on conventional job boards remains beneficial, more focused positioning on healthcare job boards often provides more successful and quicker hiring results, as those posts extend directly to necessary healthcare candidates.
- Ensure that the compensation package is competitive. A fair market value assessment including the cost of living in that community (particularly real estate costs) is important for any applicant.
- If a higher base salary is not an option, emphasize benefits and market the advantages of the community, such as great schools, low crime, transportation, recreational opportunities, etc. Work–life balance in terms of call schedule, work-from-home options, telemedicine opportunities, and possibly less than full-time positions may also be of particular interest.
- Be as transparent as possible without necessarily compromising negotiation advantages.
- Have in-person, on-site interviews, if possible. While online interviews are a good screening option, an in-person, on-site interview allows the applicant to get a reasonable perspective of their work environment and colleagues while at the same time allowing the recruiter to interact, understand body language, and initiate developing a rapport that may affect the remainder of the recruitment process.
- Create a compelling careers internet page to better distinguish the institution from its often-numerous competitors and immediately communicate the institution's mission, vision, and values to prospective employees.[12]
- Consider obtaining or updating existing recruiting software. These software packages can track candidates throughout the hiring process, provide valuable analytic data; improve the ability of current employees to become involved in the recruiting, hiring, and onboarding process; and better track passive candidates.[12]
- Engage with leadership/decision-makers in the group. Candidates should feel that they are important enough for others to make the time and simultaneously want to meet the individuals who will impact their future.
- Finally, if recruitment has been a challenge, or the team is seeking a different approach, work with a professional, well-established recruiting firm. Although not an essential strategy, nor an inexpensive one, in certain situations, their contribution may be quite valuable.

Recruiting with a strong eye on cultural fit improves the probability of successfully recruiting and retaining by ensuring that the candidate's values align with those of the institution. The candidate should receive clear communication regarding work and professionalism expectations, and time should be taken during the process to ensure that the candidate will relate well with current employees.

It is also important during the interview process to assess a candidate's soft skills, including skills related to communication and professionalism.[12]

THE IMPORTANCE OF EMPLOYEE RETENTION

Successful healthcare employee retention is multifactorial, with many of the same challenges and strategies as with recruitment. According to the American Medical Association (AMA), healthcare organizations can spend anywhere from $250,000 to $1 million replacing an existing physician, or two to three times the annual salary of the departing physician.[13,14] The loss of revenue during the period the position is vacant, the onboarding process, and the time it takes to get up to speed all factor into this expense.

Employee retention, an institution's capability of preserving its current employees, begins with its ability to recruit quality employees at the outset. As such, retention strategy is merely the other side of the coin of recruitment strategy, and the strategies overlap and merge. There are no simple answers, and successful healthcare employee retention is dependent on many factors and these challenges must be addressed strategically. A new hire's degree of integration into the team early on has a great effect of ultimate success at that institution. This is particularly true when the new employee is outside the institution's traditional group.[7]

Employee recognition is a valuable retention tool. Employees can be rewarded in numerous ways, both financially and socially. Recognition should be public recognition, as it is beneficial for other employees to recognize that employee appreciation occurs. Recognition should not only be for successful results but also for efforts, as acknowledgment of disappointing or unsuccessful results supports morale and encourages employees to continue to work for success rather than feel defeated.

People stay in organizations based in part on connections with colleagues.[6] Recognizing and praising employees for their quality work is necessary to maintain and enhance employees' feeling of appreciation. This feeling, when offered genuinely by leadership, can be a powerful retention tool.

It has been proposed that tying that appreciation to monetary rewards undermines its usefulness, and, in fact, may have a negative influence on employees. The concern is that tying quality work directly to a monetary reward makes employees winners and losers, competitive with each other rather than cooperative with each other and working as a strong team. As such, it has been proposed that recognition for quality work be separated from competition.

Healthcare employees crave recognition, not contests. A system of recognition by which notes of praiseworthy work by an employee are provided in suggestion boxes and read by senior leadership, who then follow up with personalized notes of appreciation directly to that employee, preserves the integrity of the employee's intrinsic motivation.[15]

Employees' administrative task burden also prompts them to leave healthcare. Unfortunately, many EHR and other administrative systems do not communicate with each other, which exacerbates the situation. Where possible, consolidation of systems onto a single platform increases interoperability. Further, AI-based natural language speech recognition software can minimize the time employees must spend completing documentation and other paperwork.[7]

Employee burnout, which lowers employee retention, has been shown to be more related to how employees experience their workload than the literal number of hours they work. Factors that lead to employee burnout include a feeling of unfair treatment at work, unmanageable workload, unclear communication from management, lack of manager support, and unreasonable time pressure. Increased employee engagement, clear leadership communication, and consistent management and transparency reduce the risk of employee burnout.[16]

One retention factor is related to the quality of managers. A 2018 study showed that almost half of employees quit because of bad managers. A good manager acts as a coach and a member of a team, providing employees guidance, advice, and support while providing a high degree of employee autonomy. A bad manager, however, tends to act as a boss and is viewed as an unsatisfiable source of demand, micromanaging every aspect of employees' work.

Ultimately, other than noncompetitive salary and benefits, employees typically quit because of feeling overworked, unsupported, or burned out; having no or limited ability to grow or advance; need a better work-life balance; are unhappy with management or corporate culture; or have a better employment opportunity elsewhere. Finally, successful offboarding of those who retire or find more personally suitable employment provides assurance to employees that they will be taken care of whenever they move on themselves.[17]

Recruitment and retention require workforce development. Healthcare leaders must ensure their organizations adopt comprehensive strategies, prioritize continuous professional development, and foster positive workplace environments. Policies alone are insufficient; there must be adequate resources available, the use of new technology must be fostered and encouraged, and employee well-being, including mental health, must be prioritized. Much more needs to be understood about the current recruitment and retention environment, and it would behoove healthcare organizations, policymakers, and academic institutions to collaborate in pursuing innovation and improvement in healthcare recruitment and retention.[16]

Ultimately, motivated candidates and employees frequently want an employment relationship for which leadership provides appreciation. For example, leaders acknowledge employee efforts and successes, provide employees appropriate space and control, and respect and accept employees as who they are.[18]

Institutions in search of highly qualified and talented candidates find that those candidates are in turn looking for a workplace that provides a welcoming environment, creates true opportunities for professional and personal development and professional advancement, treats them with respect and dignity, and enables them to feel valued as contributors to the institution's overall success. They are looking for a place where they can affect the success of the institution and, for some, make a difference in the world.[8]

Healthcare leaders must understand that the workplace landscape has changed, and a uniform employment policy will no longer suffice; increasing burnout among healthcare employees now requires intentional and effective institutional support for family life, and the feeling of being valued members of the healthcare team is essential in retention.[16]

Diversity, Inclusion, and Equity Strategies

As an institution's recruitment goal is to attract top talent, systematically excluding large segments of potential applicants will lead to a less successful search. Further, employees benefit from their associations with colleagues from diverse backgrounds.[19]

The primary goal of diversity, equity, and inclusion (DEI) programs, undertaken to assist people of diverse races, genders, and socioeconomic backgrounds, is to increase these people's access to workplace employment. Nondiscrimination is a compelling governmental interest and is protected by the Equal Protection Clause of the 14th Amendment to the Constitution. DEI originated with the enactment of the Civil Rights Act of 1964, which prohibits, among other things, employment discrimination based on a protected class, such as national origin, gender, race, and religion. One year later, President Lyndon B. Johnson issued Executive Order 11246, barring discrimination in federal employment and requiring federal contractors to implement and maintain affirmative action programs. Since then, public and private employers have developed DEI policies and programs. Title IX of the Education Amendments of 1972 prohibits gender discrimination in federal fund-supported education programs.

Strong case law has arisen from United States Supreme Court holdings, many of which are college admission cases. It is reasonable to assume that these United States Supreme Court holdings also are related to faculty hiring and, by extension, to some extent to other federal employee hiring.

The 1978 *Bakke* case[20] upheld affirmative action, noting that race can be one factor in college admission policy. The 2003 *Grutter* case[21] upheld *Bakke* but held that quotas are not permissible. The 2016 *Fisher* case[22] reaffirmed the key principles of strict scrutiny by courts of affirmative action admission cases, with judicial deference to well-reasoned explanations for pursuing student body diversity but lack of judicial deference in determining if the use of race in admission processes had been as narrowly tailored as possible.

New federal executive administrations bring with them differing DEI philosophies that are exhibited by conflicting federal emphases reflected in agency laws and regulations. The healthcare industry and its individual institutions may be subject to change and additional compliance requirements as governmental administrations change. It behooves institutional leadership to be aware of local, state, and federal laws and regulations regarding DEI, address them with their legal counsel, and act on them accordingly.[23]

Irrespective of the federal executive administrative position, institutional leaders should consider following several good practices. In the promotion of diversity hires, promotion standards should be clearly communicated in writing, and uniformly followed.[24] Inconsistent, scattered, or isolated DEI initiatives typically fail to support an institution's DEI need to show narrowly tailored action as mandated by the United States Supreme Court and may put the institution at risk for allegations of reverse discrimination.

It is also important to avoid any perception that DEI hiring choices are not merit-based; as such, it is prudent to avoid over-involvement in the hiring process by institutional DEI officers, and where a search committee is used, to select a search committee that itself is diverse. Collectively, these efforts can balance the need and opportunity to ensure diversity in recruitment while protecting institutions from facing negative legal actions.

Chapter Summary

This chapter has addressed some of the key models and issues around physician compensation, recruitment challenges and a balanced approach to diversity and inclusion. A review of compensation packages, databases providing benchmarks for both academic and non-academic positions, and the significant costs associated with recruiting a replacement are presented, as well as strategies for enhancing success in recruitment efforts and steps that can be taken to improve retention. Finally, an overview of reasonable efforts at ensuring diversity and inclusion, without generating misperceptions and challenges, is also included.

REFERENCES

1. Darves B. Physician Compensation Models Seeing Modest Shifts. NEJM Career Center. September 20, 2021. Accessed January 20, 2025. https://resources.nejmcareercenter.org/article/physician-compensation-models-seeing-modest-shifts/
2. Darves B. Physician Compensation Models: The Basics, the Pros, and the Cons. NEJM Career Center. October 18, 2021. Accessed January 20, 2025. https://resources.nejmcareercenter.org/article/physician-compensation-models-the-basics-the-pros-and-the-cons/

3. Darves B. Demystifying Urban Versus Rural Physician Compensation. NEJM Career Center. March 4, 2019. Accessed January 20, 2025. https://resources.nejmcareercenter.org/article/demystifying-urban-versus-rural-physician-compensation/
4. AAMC. AAMC Faculty Salary Report. 2025. Accessed online February 13, 2025. https://www.aamc.org/data-reports/workforce/report/aamc-faculty-salary-report
5. MGMA. Provider Pay and the Dawn of a New Era of Productivity. 2024 Provider Compensation and Production Report. 2024. Accessed January 20, 2025. https://www.mgma.com/data-report-provider-comp-2024
6. SullivanCotter. 2024 Physician Compensation and Productivity Survey. 2024. Accessed January 20, 2025. https://sullivancotter.com/surveys/physician-compensation-and-productivity-survey/
7. Preston R. Strategies for Improving Healthcare Workforce Retention. Oracle. March 17, 2023. Accessed January 26, 2025. https://www.oracle.com/human-capital-management/healthcare-workforce-retention/
8. Miller FA, Katz JH. *The Inclusion Breakthrough: Unleashing the Real Power of Diversity.* San Francisco, CA: Berrett-Koehler Publishers, Inc; 2002:15–19.
9. Shaffer FA. Curtain L. Nurse Turnover: Understand It, Reduce It. *American Nurse.* August 10, 2020. Accessed January 26, 2025. https://www.myamericannurse.com/nurse-turnover-understand-it-reduce-it/
10. Jorgovan J. Key Challenges in Healthcare Recruitment and How to Overcome Them. Jake Jorgovan blog. Accessed January 28, 2025. https://jake-jorgovan.com/blog/challenges-in-healthcare-recruitment
11. American Hospital Association. Strengthening the Health Care Workforce: Strategies for Now, Near and Far. American Hospital Association. June 2022. Accessed January 20, 2025. https://www.aha.org/workforce-strategies/recruitment-retention-strategies
12. Marinaki A. How to Hire: 6 Tips to Succeed in Healthcare Recruiting. September 2023. Accessed January 18, 2025. https://resources.workable.com/tutorial/healthcare-recruiting-tips
13. Shanafelt T, Goh J, Sinsky C. The Business Case for Investing in Physician Well-being. *JAMA Intern Med.* 2017;177(12):1826-1832. doi:10.1001/jamainternmed.2017.4340
14. Berg S. How Much Physician Burnout Is Costing Your Organization. American Medical Association. October 11, 2018. Accessed January 20, 2025. https://www.ama-assn.org/practice-management/physician-health/how-much-physician-burnout-costing-your-organization
15. Lee F. Cease Using Competitive Monetary Rewards to Motivate People. In: MT B, ed. *If Disney Ran your Hospital: 9 ½ Things You Would Do Differently.* Bozeman, MT: Second River Healthcare Press; 2004:173-180.
16. Owolabi OR, Olatoye FO, Elufioye OA, Okunade B. Human Resources Management in Healthcare: Recruitment, Retention, and Workforce Development: A Review. *World Journal of Advanced Research and Reviews.* 2024;21:950–957. doi:10.30574/wjarr.2024.21.2.0522
17. Crail C. Effective Employee Retention Strategies. *Forbes.* April 30, 2024. Accessed January 27, 2025. https://www.forbes.com/advisor/business/employee-retention-strategies/
18. Stone D, Heen S. *Thanks for the Feedback: The Science and Art of Receiving Feedback Well.* New York: Penguin; 2014:111.
19. Girod SC. In: Roberts LW, ed. *Roberts Academic Medicine Handbook: A Guide to Achievement and Fulfillment for Academic Faculty.* 2nd ed. Springer Nature; 2020:443:chap How to Be an Effective Team Leader and Committee Member or Chair.
20. *Regents of the University of California v Bakke, 438 U.S. 265 (1978).* https://tile.loc.gov/storage-services/service/ll/usrep/usrep438/usrep438265/usrep438265.pdf
21. *Grutter v. Bollinger et al,* 539 U.S. 306 (2003). https://tile.loc.gov/storage-services/service/ll/usrep/usrep539/usrep539306/usrep539306.pdf
22. *Fisher v University of Texas,* 579 U.S. 365 (2016).https://www.justice.gov/d9/fisher_v._university_of_texas_no._14-981_issued_06-23-16.pdf

23. Janisch K. The State of Diversity, Equity and Inclusion Laws Today. GovDocs blog. April 13, 2022. https://www.govdocs.com/the-state-of-diversity-equity-and-inclusion-laws-today/
24. Allen TC. The Legal Aspects of Diversity in Academic Pathology. *Acad Pathol.* Jan-Dec 2018;5: 2374289518811142. doi:10.1177/2374289518811142

CHAPTER 19

Workforce Operations and Strategies

Nikhil Sood, MD, and Anthony D. Slonim, MD, DrPH, FAAPL

HALM CORE CONTENT:

- 6.2 Conflicts and dualities of interest (e.g., industry relationships)
- 6.3 Conflict resolution and grievance procedures
- 6.5 Employee safety, security, and health issues (e.g., OSHA, workplace violence)
- 6.6 Employee satisfaction assessment, engagement, motivation, and career development tools
- 6.7 Labor relations and laws (e.g., FMLA, FLSA, EEOC, ERISA, worker compensation)
- 6.8 Performance management systems (e.g., performance-based evaluation, rewards systems, disciplinary policies, and procedures)
- 6.11 Staffing models, productivity management, and the impact of changes on the quality of care
- 6.12 Interprofessional care delivery teams
- 6.13 Succession planning models
- 6.14 Workforce cultural competency strategies
- 6.15 Utilization and impact of external staffing agencies

CASE SCENARIO:

A large, urban healthcare organization serving a culturally diverse population has several significant strategic challenges. There are conflicts among inter-professional teams leading to high employee turnover, and nurses, physicians, and administrative staff report conflicts over workload, communication, inadequate staffing, and supplies that compromise patient safety.

The organization struggles with employee retention because a lack of clear career paths leaves employees disengaged and prone to burnout. Although feedback surveys and staff forums are held to encourage communication, employees rarely receive feedback regarding how their suggestions were implemented.

To address these issues, the leadership begins to closely monitor key performance indicators (KPIs) related to workload, patient outcomes, and employee satisfaction to detect signs of strain or dissatisfaction. Additionally, they hold periodic review meetings with managers and team leaders to discuss challenges and to foster a proactive approach to addressing workforce and operational concerns.

Structured conflict resolution procedures, including regular team-building sessions, are implemented to improve inter-professional relationships. The performance management system is revised to include equitable rewards and career growth opportunities. Workforce cultural competency strategies and training are introduced, improving the team's ability to deliver patient-centered care in this diverse setting. Enhanced safety policies and compliance with labor laws reinforce a supportive environment for all employees that encourages open communication and is blame-free.

HEALTHCARE ORGANIZATIONS TAKE GREAT PRIDE in their buildings, technology, and the physical environment where caregivers provide services. However, with their knowledge, skills, expertise, and compassion, the people working in healthcare help differentiate great healthcare organizations from good ones. In large healthcare organizations, managing workforce operations is complex due to the numerous legal and regulatory requirements, a diverse workforce and teams, and high patient volumes.

The physician leader's most important strategic activity is to align organizational goals with employee well-being. An approach that includes operations to support employee health and safety, manage team dynamics, and address conflict, boosts employee engagement. Engaged, valued, and supported employees will perform efficiently and provide better patient care.[1,2] In contrast, unregulated and undefined organizational expectations lead to stress, reduced productivity, and a long-term impact on the organization's performance.

Laws, Regulations, and Best Practices that Guide Healthcare Organizations

Healthcare organizations are subjected to a hierarchy of "rules" to ensure safe and efficient operations patients and employees (Figure 1).[3] This hierarchy is composed of laws, regulations, and best practices. Compliance with local, state, and federal laws that govern healthcare operations, such as labor laws, patient privacy laws (HIPAA), and workplace safety (OSHA), help create a solid base.

Regulations are mandated by accrediting bodies like The Joint Commission and governmental agencies like the Centers for Medicare & Medicaid Services. They ensure healthcare organizations meet quality and safety benchmarks.

Best practices represent evidence-based strategies that guide clinical and operational excellence, improving patient outcomes and workforce efficiency. Research, industry standards, and continuous quality improvement initiatives often influence these practices. This structure ensures that healthcare organizations operate within a legal framework while striving for high-quality, compliant, patient-centered care.

FIGURE 1. A Hierarchy of Rules that Govern a Healthcare Organization's Strategy and Operations

Culture versus Climate

The rules hierarchy provides guardrails for an organization's culture and climate. Culture and climate support how people in the organization relate to one another (Figure 2). The culture represents shared values, beliefs, and norms that define the organization's identity and guide employee behavior.[4] Culture is steeped in history and tradition and influences how employees think, feel, and behave.[5] When the culture is strong, employees feel loyalty and belonging, which promotes collaboration and alignment with organizational goals, drives motivation and engagement, and strengthens retention.[4,5]

The organizational climate reflects employees' collective perceptions and attitudes about their immediate work environment. Climate is measured through employee surveys focusing on job satisfaction and the relationships between employees and

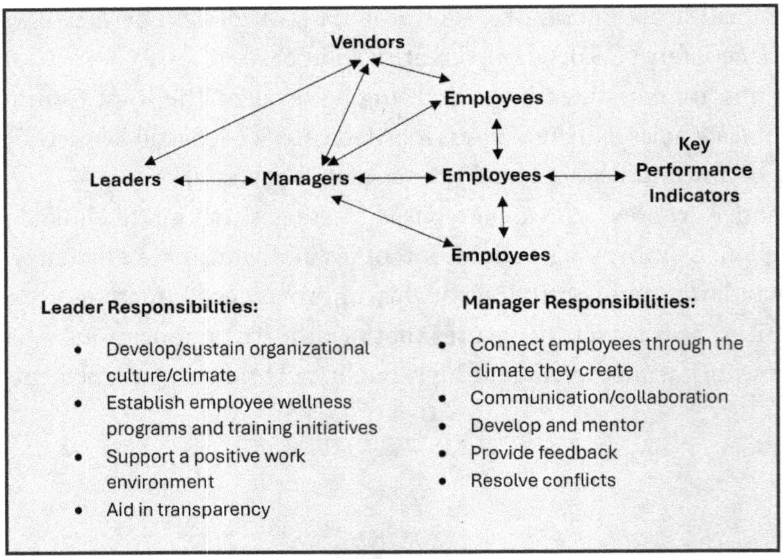

FIGURE 2. Interactions between Key Players of Healthcare Organizations

managers. Culture develops over time through history, purpose, and values. Climate is more operational and, hence, more dynamic, often shifting based on leadership style, policies, or external events.[6]

Both culture and climate are interrelated and play a pivotal role in shaping workforce operations. Effective leadership is essential for cultivating a positive culture and climate. Physician leaders who model organizational values and respond proactively to employee feedback can create an environment where staff feel valued, respected, and empowered to contribute to the organization's success.

How Individuals Relate to the Whole

An organization's human capital allows it to achieve its strategic and operational goals. Employees relate to each other through workplace processes established by leadership and accountable through management. Figure 2 illustrates the interpersonal relationships that operate within organizations to achieve their KPIs. The figure emphasizes the importance of open communication, collaboration, mentorship, conflict resolution, and transparency. Note that physician leaders may find themselves in the role of employee, manager, leader, or vendor.

Employees are connected to their manager, other employees, and vendors. These connections are strengthened by bidirectional communication and collaboration. Managers are important "connectors" of leadership to front-line employees, and their major role includes a focus on development and mentorship, providing feedback, both positive and negative, and conflict resolution when necessary.

Other relationships, like vendors, may be employed outside the organization but can still meaningfully affect the quality of the care being delivered. Vendors may interact directly with leadership, management, and the organization's employees. These relationships are subject to potential conflicts of interest; collaboration and transparency are essential in providing appropriate oversight and controls.

Finally, leadership oversees all groups and is responsible for developing and sustaining the organization's climate and culture. Leaders may promote wellness programs and training initiatives that support a positive work environment.

Conflicts and Dualities of Interest

Conflicts and dualities of interest arise from organizational relationships between healthcare organizations and industry partners or other vendors when distinct interests from the parties coexist in a decision-making setting.[7] Conflicts also relate to personal relationships between physicians and staff within an organization or across organizations.

These relationships can provide access to new technologies and business processes and often lead to clinical and financial benefits. However, these relationships are often subject to policies, procedures, and guidelines that establish ethical practices to preserve clinical independence and patient care quality.[8] Further, relationships that extend beyond a professional domain to one that is personal can raise concerns about perceived inequities, undue influence of a supervisory role, sexual harassment, or favoritism.[9] To establish and maintain a cooperative work environment, the physician leader must know how to understand, avoid, and address potential and real conflicts.

Organizations have codes of conduct to provide guidance, policies, and procedures to address real or potential dualities of interest. An annual disclosure process that requires physicians and executives to disclose potential conflicts arising from business practices, including their families' business practices, is also an important step. These conflicts should be reported as they arise.

Triangulated relationships or dualities of interest often require oversight to ensure compliance and may arise through competing businesses between the physician and employer or the physician's relationships with vendors that also do business with the organization. Audits are essential to monitor these relationships and ensure their integrity. By fostering transparency, reinforcing ethical boundaries, and engaging directly with staff, leadership upholds an environment where patient-centered care remains uncompromised.

Conflict Resolution and Grievance Procedures

Conflict resolution and grievance procedures are essential to a healthy workplace.[9] Leadership styles that emphasize a collaborative, multifaceted, dynamic, and transparent process are more effective at resolving conflict. Grievance procedures provide a formal process for employees to raise concerns, without fear of retaliation from management, when the response to their complaint is unsatisfactory. The topics range from workload and scheduling issues to harassment or pay disparities.

Structured tools, such as mediation or arbitration, may be used to manage conflicts that cannot be addressed internally. Effective conflict management enhances the organizational climate by improving job satisfaction, reducing turnover, promoting teamwork, and upholding high patient care standards.[9,10] Effective conflict resolution supports a positive work culture, facilitating open dialogue and preventing misunderstandings. Table 1 highlights interventions for physicians to address conflict resolution and grievances.

Prevention also matters. For example, meetings with smaller groups of employees to listen to their concerns can identify major issues before conflicts arise.

TABLE 1. Conflict and Grievance Interventions that Aim to Improve Workplace Climate and Culture

Intervention	Climate	Culture
A Policy on Reporting	Creates a safe and open environment for staff to report issues without fear of retribution.	Reinforces organizational values of transparency and accountability.
Conflict Resolution Training for Managers	Provides managers with the skills to address conflicts swiftly and constructively, enhancing day-to-day work relations.	Fosters a long-term cultural norm of respectful and effective communication.
Feedback Loops and Surveys	Measures employee perceptions regularly to identify and address emerging concerns.	Encourages a culture of continuous improvement and openness to feedback.
Team-Building Workshops	Improves team cohesion and collaboration in the short term.	Builds a culture of trust and mutual respect over time.
Regular Safety Drills and Training	Ensures immediate awareness and response to safety concerns, affecting perceived safety climate.	Establishes a culture of prioritizing safety and preparedness.

Employee Safety, Security, and Health Issues

Ensuring the physical and mental safety of employees and team members is an important responsibility for physician leaders. To be effective, the physician leader must understand the major laws and regulations governing the healthcare environment. Table 2 outlines key safety standards and practices, highlighting the measures needed to ensure a safe and compliant healthcare environment.[11] Complying with these safety regulations is crucial for maintaining a safe and resilient workforce.

TABLE 2. A Summary of the Major Aspects of Employee Safety, Security, and Health Relevant to Healthcare Organizations

Safety/Health Issue	Description	Relation to Our Case Study
Workplace Violence Prevention	OSHA and The Joint Commission require measures to prevent workplace violence, ensuring a secure environment for staff and patients.	Critical to prevent incidents and ensure staff feel safe and protected at work.
Infection Control	The Joint Commission mandates rigorous infection control protocols, and OSHA emphasizes protection from biohazards.	Ensures staff are safeguarded from communicable diseases, supporting a healthy workplace.
Hazardous Materials Management	OSHA and The Joint Commission outline the safe handling and disposal of hazardous materials to protect staff and patients.	Relevant for maintaining safety, especially in high-risk areas like emergency and operating rooms.
Emergency Preparedness	The Joint Commission requires comprehensive emergency plans, while OSHA focuses on readiness to handle workplace emergencies.	Essential for preparing staff to respond effectively, minimizing chaos and ensuring safety during crises.
Ergonomics and Injury Prevention	OSHA provides guidelines for ergonomic practices to prevent injuries, supported by The Joint Commission's emphasis on staff well-being.	Helps prevent injuries among employees, particularly those performing repetitive tasks or heavy lifting.
Mental Health Support Program	The Joint Commission recommends mental health support, while OSHA emphasizes the need for stress management resources.	Supports staff well-being, reduces burnout, and improves overall job satisfaction.
Substance Abuse Policies	OSHA and The Joint Commission require strict substance abuse policies to ensure a safe and effective working environment.	Helps maintain a safe workplace and ensures employees are fit to perform their duties.
Incident Reporting Systems	The Joint Commission mandates robust incident reporting systems, with OSHA emphasizing prompt and thorough documentation.	Enables swift action to prevent recurrence and fosters a culture of transparency and safety.
Safety Training and Drills	OSHA and The Joint Commission require regular safety training and drills to prepare staff for emergencies.	Keeps employees well-prepared and ensures quick, effective responses to potential threats or emergencies.

Employee Satisfaction Assessment, Engagement, Motivation, and Career Development

Employee engagement and motivation are closely tied to job satisfaction and career growth with high levels of job satisfaction being linked to better patient outcomes, reduced turnover, and a positive workplace culture.[12]

EMPLOYEE SATISFACTION ASSESSMENT

Regularly assessing employee satisfaction through surveys can identify areas where the organization can improve work conditions, processes, or policies that enhance staff well-being. Tools like anonymous surveys, focus groups, and suggestion boxes provide insights into staff concerns, and exit interviews can reveal issues that contribute to staff turnover. These assessments can help organizations create a more responsive and supportive work environment, increasing staff loyalty and commitment.[13]

ENGAGEMENT AND MOTIVATION

Employee engagement and motivation are essential for maintaining high productivity and quality of care. Engagement initiatives, like recognition programs, team-building events, and feedback mechanisms, enable employees to feel valued and respected.[14] Financial incentives, such as performance-based bonuses, are also effective in motivating staff. Still, non-financial incentives like extra paid time off, flexible schedules, and personal development opportunities are equally impactful.

Managers can drive engagement through regular meetings with employees to understand their goals, concerns, and motivations.[15] They provide personalized support and encouragement to keep them committed to their work.

CAREER DEVELOPMENT TOOLS

Career development is vital to retaining skilled healthcare professionals and reducing turnover.[16,17] Organizations that invest in career development demonstrate a commitment to their employees' professional growth, which enhances loyalty and reduces burnout. Mentorship programs, where experienced staff guide newer employees, can help in skill-building and orienting employees.[17] Continuing education opportunities, such as workshops, certifications, and online courses, provide employees with new skills and organizational growth.

Labor Relations and Laws

Labor relations and laws, such as the Family Medical Leave Act (FMLA), Fair Labor Standards Act (FLSA), and Equal Employment Commission (EEOC) regulations,

TABLE 3. Organizational Labor Laws

Law	Description	Impact
Family and Medical Leave Act (FMLA)	Provides eligible employees up to 12 weeks of unpaid, job-protected leave for family or medical reasons.	Helps employees balance health/personal issues without job risk; fosters a supportive environment.
Fair Labor Standards Act (FLSA)	Establishes minimum wage, overtime pay eligibility, and child labor standards.	Ensures fair compensation for overtime, supporting workforce morale and preventing burnout.
Equal Employment Opportunity Commission (EEOC)	Prohibits discrimination based on race, color, religion, sex, or national origin.	Promotes a diverse, inclusive workplace essential in large, multicultural healthcare settings.
Occupational Safety and Health Act (OSHA)	Ensures safe and healthy working conditions by enforcing standards and providing training.	Enhances safety through training on workplace hazards, which is crucial for reducing stress and promoting security.
Employee Retirement Income Security Act (ERISA)	Protects employee benefits, like pensions and health insurance.	Supports long-term employee satisfaction and loyalty, which are key in a competitive healthcare job market.
Worker Adjustment and Retraining Notification (WARN) Act	Requires employers to provide advance notice of significant layoffs.	Helps manage large workforce adjustments, creating transparency and reducing job insecurity.
Americans with Disabilities Act (ADA)	Prohibits discrimination and requires accommodations for employees with disabilities.	Ensures accessibility and inclusivity, which strengthens employee morale and reinforces equitable treatment.
National Labor Relations Act (NLRA)	Protects employees' rights to unionize and engage in collective bargaining.	Supports fair employee representation and advocacy, which is important in resolving systemic issues in large groups.

(table continues)

ensure that healthcare organizations remain compliant while protecting employees' rights (Table 3). Adhering to these laws fosters a fair and equitable work environment, promoting job satisfaction and reducing the risk of legal disputes (Table 3).

Performance Management Systems

Performance management systems ensure employees perform their roles effectively and contribute to the organization's goals. These systems encompass performance-based evaluations, rewards programs, and disciplinary policies. Performance-based evaluations involve assessing employees against clearly defined metrics that align with patient care and operational efficiency.[18] This process should be objective, transparent, and frequent, allowing employees to understand their performance and where improvement is needed.

TABLE 3. Organizational Labor Laws *(continued)*

Law	Description	Impact
Health Insurance Portability and Accountability Act (HIPAA)	Protects patient and employee health information privacy.	Maintains confidentiality, fostering trust among healthcare staff, and managing sensitive patient information.
Civil Rights Act, Title VII	Prohibits workplace discrimination and promotes equal opportunity in hiring and employment practices.	Reinforces a commitment to a diverse, non-discriminatory work culture.
Consolidated Omnibus Budget Reconciliation Act (COBRA)	Provides continuing healthcare coverage after job loss or other qualifying events.	Offers staff continuity of benefits, supporting them through transitions and reducing potential stressors.
Genetic Information Nondiscrimination Act (GINA)	Prohibits discrimination based on genetic information in employment and health insurance.	Protects employees' privacy and personal information, contributing to an environment of trust and security.

Managers play a crucial role in providing constructive feedback and setting performance goals that are achievable yet challenging. A well-structured evaluation system fosters a culture of accountability and continuous improvement. Rewards can include financial incentives, such as bonuses for exceptional performance, and non-financial rewards, such as public recognition, additional training opportunities, or paid time off. These rewards motivate employees and increase job satisfaction, improving patient outcomes.

Disciplinary policies are another component of performance management systems. These policies should be communicated to all staff and outline the consequences of failing to meet performance standards or violating organizational policies and procedures. Effective disciplinary measures should be fair and consistently applied and aim to correct behavior rather than punish employees. By implementing a balanced performance management system, healthcare organizations can ensure that employees are motivated, supported, and aligned with organizational goals.

Staffing Models, Productivity Management, and the Impact on Quality of Care

Leadership and staffing are fundamental factors for quality.[19] Staffing directly influences productivity and quality. Traditional staffing models often involve fixed schedules and rigid staff-to-patient ratios, leading to inefficiencies during fluctuating patient volumes and acuity. More flexible models, such as per-dem staffing, cross-training for multiple roles, or using part-time employees, can optimize resources while maintaining high standards of care. Productivity management involves measuring and improving how

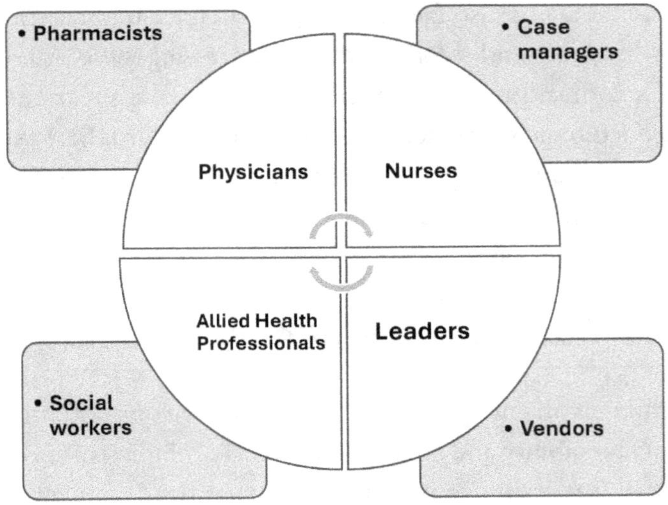

FIGURE 3. Interactions among Inter-Professional Care Delivery Team Members

efficiently staff perform without compromising patient safety.[20] It is also important to avoid overburdening staff, which can lead to burnout and reduced quality.

Changes in staffing models, such as moving to more flexible scheduling or using technology to automate administrative tasks, can significantly impact care delivery. For example, implementing predictive analytics to anticipate patient volumes can help allocate staff more efficiently, reducing wait times and improving patient satisfaction. Effective staffing and productivity management strategies are essential for delivering high-quality in an evolving healthcare landscape. Balancing productivity with employee well-being ensures that patients receive the highest level of service.

Inter-Professional Care Delivery Teams

Inter-professional care delivery teams are integral to modern healthcare, as they bring together professionals from various disciplines to manage patient care collaboratively. These teams often include physicians, nurses, pharmacists, social workers, and allied health professionals who work together to develop and implement comprehensive care plans (Figure 3).

The team's leadership often relies upon a "dyad model" that includes a physician leader paired with an operational leader to ensure oversight of a business unit's strategic, operational, and workforce goals. The goal is to leverage each team member's unique skills and perspectives to improve patient outcomes and ensure that care is holistic, efficient, and patient-centered. Effective inter-professional collaboration relies on clear communication, mutual respect, and understanding each member's role.[21] Communication tools, such as shared electronic health records (EHRs) and regular inter-professional meetings, can facilitate collaboration and reduce the risk of errors.

Inter-professional teams also face challenges, such as hierarchical structures and role confusion, which can hinder collaboration. Addressing these issues requires strong leadership and a commitment to fostering a culture of respect and inclusiveness. Leaders should encourage team members to speak up, share their expertise, and feel valued, regardless of their position. Inter-professional teams improve patient care by promoting collaboration, reducing redundancies, and ensuring that all aspects of a patient's needs are addressed.

Succession Planning Models

Succession planning is an enterprise approach that develops potential candidates for organizational sustainability and business continuity.[22] Effective succession planning reduces the risk of leadership gaps and ensures that the organization can maintain stability and deliver high-quality care.

The process begins with talent identification, where leaders assess the skills and potential of employees across various departments. Tools like performance evaluations, leadership assessments, and career aspiration interviews can help identify future leaders. Once high-potential individuals are identified, organizations should provide targeted development opportunities, such as mentorship programs, leadership training, and job rotations.

These experiences help prepare candidates to take on greater responsibilities and understand the complexities of healthcare management preparing high-potential employees to assume critical roles when vacancies occur due to retirements, promotions, or unexpected departures.

Succession planning includes a formalized mentorship program where experienced leaders guide and coach emerging talent. This mentorship accelerates future leaders' development and fosters a sense of belonging and engagement. Additionally, cross-training staff to handle various roles ensures that the organization remains agile and can adapt to changes quickly.

Transparency is vital in succession planning. Communicating the organization's commitment to developing future leaders helps build trust and encourages employees to invest in their professional growth. By having a robust succession plan, healthcare organizations can ensure they are well-positioned to navigate future challenges and maintain a high standard of care.

Workforce Cultural Competency Strategies

Cultural competency strategies are important for delivering patient-centered care in diverse communities. It involves understanding and respecting patients' and colleagues' cultural backgrounds, beliefs, and needs. This means creating an environment where staff are trained to recognize cultural differences and provide culturally sensitive and inclusive care.

Training programs that educate employees on cultural awareness, implicit biases, and effective communication across cultural barriers are key components of these programs.[23] Workshops, role-playing exercises, and case studies can help staff practice cultural sensitivity in real-world scenarios. Organizations should also encourage using interpreters and culturally appropriate educational materials to improve communication with non-English-speaking patients.[24]

A focus on recruiting and retaining a diverse workforce that reflects the community's complexion can create a team with unique perspectives and insights to enhance patient care and promote innovation. Employee resource groups (ERGs) and diversity committees can provide opportunities for staff to discuss cultural challenges and recommend improvements.

Leadership plays a crucial role in fostering a culturally competent environment. By modeling inclusive behavior and supporting cultural initiatives, leaders set the organization's tone. Regular assessments, such as patient satisfaction surveys and staff feedback, help to measure the effectiveness of these strategies and identify areas for improvement. Ultimately, a culturally competent workforce improves patient trust, reduces disparities in care, and fosters a more inclusive workplace.

Utilization and Impact of External Staffing Agencies

Staffing agencies provide flexibility for staffing shortages or unexpected patient volume by adjusting workforce to meet patient demands, reducing staff burden and burnout. Temporary nurses, physicians, allied health professionals, and leaders can fill critical gaps and ensure continuity of care. Agencies often have access to a large pool of qualified professionals who can be deployed on short notice, which is crucial during emergencies or peak times, such as flu season.

However, staffing agencies can also present challenges that must be managed effectively to minimize disruptions. Reliance on external staffing can impact team dynamics and patient care quality.[25] Temporary staff may be less familiar with the organization's protocols, technology, or culture, leading to communication errors and inefficiencies. Organizations should implement comprehensive onboarding programs for temporary staff to mitigate these risks and ensure they understand essential procedures and are integrated into the care team.

Cost is another consideration. External staffing is expensive, and over-reliance may strain the organization's budget. To balance financial efficiency with patient care needs, healthcare leaders should strategically plan staffing levels, using predictive analytics to anticipate demand and minimize the need for temporary staff. Building relationships with reliable staffing agencies and negotiating favorable contracts to help control costs.

Chapter Summary

Effective workforce strategies are vital for healthcare organizations. This chapter explored essential knowledge for physician leaders to manage their workforce and enhance patient care. By grasping areas like conflict resolution, labor relations, and performance management, leaders can cultivate an engaging and satisfying work environment. The importance of balancing interests, such as industry relationships, was discussed to ensure transparency and ethical conduct. Strategies for employee safety, compliance with OSHA, and handling workplace violence were also addressed.

Key labor laws, including FMLA, FLSA, and EEOC regulations, serve as foundational knowledge for managing a diverse workforce. The chapter examined how staffing models influence productivity and care quality, providing insights for optimizing staffing levels. The integration of inter-professional care teams was emphasized as essential for effective patient-centered care. Succession planning and cultural competency strategies ensure healthcare providers meet diverse patient needs. The use of external staffing agencies was discussed as a solution for staffing shortages. Overall, the chapter equips physician leaders with tools to build and maintain an engaged workforce, enhancing patient care quality.

REFERENCES

1. Reich MR, Javadi D, Ghaffar A. Introduction to the Special Issue on "Effective Leadership for Health Systems." *Health Syst Reform*. 2016;2(3):171–175.
2. Bhati D, Deogade MS, Kanyal D. Improving Patient Outcomes Through Effective Hospital Administration: A Comprehensive Review. *Cureus*. 2023;15(10):e47731. doi: 10.7759/cureus.47731. PMID: 38021686; PMCID: PMC10676194.
3. Essex R, Kennedy J, Miller D, Jameson J. A Scoping Review Exploring the Impact and Negotiation of Hierarchy in Healthcare Organisations. *Nursing Inquiry*. 2023;30: e12571. https://doi.org/10.1111/nin.12571
4. Tsai Y. Relationship Between Organizational Culture, Leadership Behavior and Job Satisfaction. *BMC Health Serv Res*. 2011;11:98. doi: 10.1186/1472-6963-11-98. PMID: 21569537; PMCID: PMC3123547.
5. Tran SK. GOOGLE: A Reflection of Culture, Leader, and Management. *Int J Corporate Soc Responsibility*. 2017;2(1). https://doi.org/10.1186/s40991-017-0021-0
6. Parker CP, Baltes BB, Young SA, et al. Relationships Between Psychological Climate Perceptions and Work Outcomes: A Meta-Analytic Review. *J Organiz Behav*. 2003;24:389–416. https://doi.org/10.1002/job.198
7. Figueroa CA, Harrison R, Chauhan A, et al. Priorities and Challenges for Health Leadership and Workforce Management Globally: A Rapid Review. *BMC Health Serv Res*. 2019;19:239. https://doi.org/10.1186/s12913-019-4080-7
8. Institute of Medicine (US) Committee on Conflict of Interest in Medical Research, Education, and Practice; Lo B, Field MJ, editors. 6, Conflicts of Interest and Medical Practice. *Conflict of Interest in Medical Research, Education, and Practice*. Washington, DC: National Academies Press; 2009. https://www.ncbi.nlm.nih.gov/books/NBK22944/
9. Cullati S, Bochatay N, Maître F, et al. When Team Conflicts Threaten Quality of Care: A Study of Health Care Professionals' Experiences and Perceptions. *Mayo Clin Proc Innov Qual Outcomes*.

2019;3(1):43–51. doi: 10.1016/j.mayocpiqo.2018.11.003. PMID: 30899908; PMCID: PMC6408685.

10. Ronquillo Y, Ellis VL, Toney-Butler TJ. Conflict Management. [Updated 2023 Jul 3]. In: *StatPearls [Internet]*. Treasure Island, FL: StatPearls Publishing; 2024 Jan-. https://www.ncbi.nlm.nih.gov/books/NBK470432/
11. Committee on Department of Homeland Security Occupational Health and Operational Medicine Infrastructure; Board on Health Sciences Policy; Institute of Medicine. 3, A Comprehensive Framework for Ensuring the Health of an Operational Workforce. *Advancing Workforce Health at the Department of Homeland Security: Protecting Those Who Protect Us*. Washington, DC: National Academies Press; 2014 Jul 3. https://www.ncbi.nlm.nih.gov/books/NBK231901/
12. Gustavsson K, van Diepen C, Fors A, Axelsson M, Bertilsson M, Hensing G. Healthcare Professionals' Experiences of Job Satisfaction When Providing Person-Centred Care: A Systematic Review of Qualitative Studies. *BMJ Open*. 2023;13(6):e071178. doi: 10.1136/bmjopen-2022-071178. PMID: 37295826; PMCID: PMC10277035.
13. Huebner LA, Zacher H. Following Up on Employee Surveys: A Conceptual Framework and Systematic Review. *Front Psychol*. 2021;12:801073. doi: 10.3389/fpsyg.2021.801073. PMID: 34956026; PMCID: PMC8696015.
14. Frampton A, Fox F, Hollowood A, et al. Using Real-Time, Anonymous Staff Feedback to Improve Staff Experience and Engagement. *BMJ Qual Improv Rep*. 2017;28;6(1):u220946.w7041. doi: 10.1136/bmjquality.u220946.w7041. PMID: 28469897; PMCID: PMC5411713.
15. Mazzetti G, Schaufeli WB. The Impact of Engaging Leadership on Employee Engagement and Team Effectiveness: A Longitudinal, Multi-Level Study on the Mediating Role of Personal- and Team Resources. *PLoS One*. 2022;17(6):e0269433. doi: 10.1371/journal.pone.0269433. PMID: 35767536; PMCID: PMC9242457.
16. Shiri R, El-Metwally A, Sallinen M, et al. The Role of Continuing Professional Training or Development in Maintaining Current Employment: A Systematic Review. *Healthcare (Basel)*. 2023;11(21):2900. doi: 10.3390/healthcare11212900. PMID: 37958044; PMCID: PMC10647344.
17. Sood N, Hoque F, Slonim AD. Mentorship for Non-academic, Mid-Career Hospitalist Physicians: The Journey Taken Less Often. *J Gen Intern Med*. 2024. doi: 10.1007/s11606-024-09174-y. Epub ahead of print. PMID: 39482472.
18. U.S. Department of Health and Human Services. Performance Management Appraisal Program (PMAP) Handbook. Accessed November 18, 2024. https://www.hhs.gov/sites/default/files/asa/ohr/manual/files/430-2.pdf.
19. Havig AK, Skogstad A, Kjekshus LE, et al. Leadership, Staffing and Quality of Care in Nursing Homes. *BMC Health Serv Res*. 2011;11:327. https://doi.org/10.1186/1472-6963-11-327
20. Cain C, Haque S. Chapter 31- Organizational Workflow and Its Impact on Work Quality. In: Hughes RG, ed. *Patient Safety and Quality: An Evidence-Based Handbook for Nurses*. Rockville, MD: Agency for Healthcare Research and Quality US; 2008. https://www.ncbi.nlm.nih.gov/books/NBK2638/
21. Bosch B, Mansell H. Interprofessional Collaboration in Health Care: Lessons To Be Learned from Competitive Sports. *Can Pharm J (Ott)*. 2015;148(4):176-9. doi: 10.1177/1715163515588106. PMID: 26448769; PMCID: PMC4530359.
22. Bano Y, Omar SS, Ismail F. (2022). Succession Planning Best Practices for Organizations: A Systematic Literature Review Approach. *International Journal of Global Optimization and Its Application*. 2022;1(1):39–48. https://doi.org/10.56225/ijgoia.v1i1.12
23. Mouboua PD, Atobatele F, Akintayo O. Cross-cultural Competence in Global HRD: Strategies for Developing an Inclusive and Diverse Workforce. *International Journal of Science and Research Archive*. 2024;12:103-113. 10.30574/ijsra.2024.12.1.0765.
24. Andrulis DP, Brach C. Integrating Literacy, Culture, and Language to Improve Health Care Quality for Diverse Populations. *Am J Health Behav*. 2007;31 Suppl 1(Suppl 1):S122-33. doi: 10.5555/ajhb.2007.31.supp.S122. PMID: 17931131; PMCID: PMC5091931.

25. Aiken LH, Clarke SP, Sloane DM. Hospital Staffing, Organization, and Quality of Care: Cross-National Findings. *International Journal for Quality in Health Care*. 2002;14(1):5–14. https://doi.org/10.1093/intqhc/14.1.5

CHAPTER 20

Workforce Retention

Reka Danko, MD

HALM CORE CONTENT

- 6.9 Physician satisfaction assessment and engagement tools and techniques
- 6.15 Workforce wellness
- 6.16 Burnout mitigation
- 6.17 Impaired individuals

CASE SCENARIO:

Crises surround healthcare. The COVID-19 pandemic was an example of physicians bringing the best of their skill set to save and protect others, triage crashing patients, give out vaccinations on demand, safely repurpose supplies and equipment on shortage, answer questions about developing science, all while facing numerous fears and trying not to get sick. How do physicians care for themselves? How do they care for each other to ensure they can safely practice what they teach and advise to patients?

HEALTH IS NOT DEFINED by the absence of disease; defining wellness is quite complex. The World Health Organization defines health as "a state of complete physical, mental, and social well-being and not merely the absence of disease or infirmity."[1] Medical schools go into depth about how the body systems work in physiology and how they break down in pathology.

While treatments have evolved over time, the only constant in medicine and science is that they continue to change regarding prevention, diagnostic modalities, and treatments of acute and chronic conditions. Additional complexity arises in how the body systems interact, how illnesses may prevent or interfere with the treatment of other illnesses, and how thought patterns, coping strategies, and emotional health contribute to the overall physical and mental health states. Social determinants of health and how those social, physical, and environmental factors have a major impact on well-being must also be considered.

The Triple Aim has been widely accepted as a model for optimizing healthcare performance and comprises the quality care of the individual while delivering population health in a cost-effective model of care.[2] With widespread focus on burnout in the healthcare workforce, it has become clear that the Quadruple Aim, which adds the goal of improving the work life of healthcare providers, including clinicians and staff, should be the model for delivery of healthcare.[3]

It is an honor and privilege to practice medicine. It is a privilege to learn confidential information from patients about all areas of their lives — physical, emotional, spiritual, environmental, and behavioral — and to be entrusted to put the data together to diagnose and develop a treatment plan. This privilege is not to be taken lightly. It comes with a heavy burden of responsibility, duty, and continuous assessment by rigorous testing, commitments to licensing and credentialing requirements, and oversight standards by numerous governing agencies at state and federal levels.

Along with the honor and responsibility comes the human component. Doctors and healthcare clinicians are human. Humans face physical, mental, and emotional struggles both external to the jobs and within the jobs themselves. It is challenging to hear sad stories, witness difficult outcomes, and process tragedy and loss. They may face their own mortality at times when treating patients. They also take an oath to practice medicine: to treat the ill to the best of their ability, to preserve each patient's privacy, and to teach the practice of medicine to the next generation.

The practice of medicine integrates science, the individual patients, and their pathologies, and meets them where they are in their treatment plans. This task is challenging, and they do this best when they care for themselves and each other. If they are not in a state of wellness, it may compromise their ability to keep the oath and treat the ill to the best of their abilities.

Physician Satisfaction Assessment and Engagement Tools and Techniques

A phrase heard frequently in hospitals and other healthcare settings in 2020 was, "I cannot wait until this COVID-19 pandemic is over." Most medical conditions don't resolve without effort or treatment and neither did the COVID-19 pandemic. It did, however, teach adaptability, as it required finding and balancing the combination of factors to provide benefits and reduce risk for patients and the workforce. Just as it would not be wise to advise patients to ignore symptoms and seek treatment only on the brink of cardiovascular collapse, we should not ignore physician wellness due to a perceived risk of collapsing the ability to provide safe and effective healthcare.

Medicine's founding oath is "First, Do No Harm."[4] It weighs the risks and benefits of all testing, treatments, procedures, surgeries, and interventions and, after discussing the options with patients, must only proceed if the benefits outweigh the risks and do no harm. It should also be the founding promise to physicians and practitioners of medicine to first do no harm to themselves.

The Green Cross Academy of Traumatology established the standards of care for practice in any field to provide standards of self-care.[5] The focus of the published guidelines is to (1) do no harm to oneself in the line of duty when helping and treating others and (2) to attend to physical, social, emotional, and spiritual needs as a way of ensuring high-quality services to those who look to physicians for support as human beings.[5]

As previously mentioned, providing care to others has innate responsibility, honor, and privilege; it is unethical to provide care that may be compromised. The Green Cross Academy of Traumatology guidelines provide a straightforward framework for prioritizing self-care and potential steps for preventing imbalance between work and life.

It is important to note that self-care must be individualized. Just as medications work with a range of efficacies and must be tailored to each individual, so must burnout prevention and self-care routines.

According to the guidelines, the principles of self-care include respect for dignity and self-worth, responsibility of self-care, and the requirement of self-care in the duty to perfom.[5] The guidelines further define the standards for the practice of self-care to include the right to wellness, physical and emotional rest and nourishment, and sustenance modulation, knowing that certain foods, drinks, substances, or behaviors may compromise competency.[5]

Standards are also set for expecting appreciation and compensation, including seeking appreciation from supervisors and clients to increase worker satisfaction, making it standard to be recognized for service that increases worker satisfaction, and selecting one or more advocates who monitor the efforts of ongoing self-care.[5]

In focus on establishing and maintaining wellness, the sections are broken into commitment of self-care and strategies for letting go of work. Both of these components are based on making a formal, tangible commitment; setting deadlines and goals; and generating strategies that work and can be followed.[5]

The third section, strategies for gaining a sense of self-care achievement, relies on finding strategies for acquiring adequate rest and relaxation and practicing effective daily stress reduction methods.[5]

Keeping an inventory of ongoing self-care practices is also vital. This includes personal and professional inventories. The personal inventories may include the physical aspects of monitoring parts of the body for tension and finding techniques to reduce tension, effective sleep induction and maintenance strategies, and effective methods for assuring proper nutrition.

The psychological inventory may include:

- Effective behaviors and practices to sustain a balance between work and play.
- Effective relaxation time and methods.

- Frequent contact with nature or other calming stimuli.
- Effective methods of creative expression and skills for ongoing self-care, such as time management, cognitive restructuring, interpersonal communication, stress reduction, and assertiveness.
- Effective skill and competence in meditation or spiritual practice that is calming.
- Effective methods of self-assessment and awareness.

In the social and interpersonal inventory, the assessments of the social support network, getting help, and social activism may result in a better work environment and sense of satisfaction.

The professional inventory may include:

- Balance between work and home.
- Boundaries and limit settings, such as time boundaries, professional boundaries, personal boundaries, dealing with multiple roles, and balancing between change and acceptance.
- Getting support and help at work through peer support, supervision, consultation, and role models.
- Generating work satisfaction by remembering the joys and achievements of the work.[5]

Prevention plan development may include reviewing current self-care and functioning, selecting goals, analyzing resources for achieving the goals and implementing the plans, and evaluating the plan with the support person(s).[5]

To be stewards of the practice of medicine and delivery of healthcare, physician leaders are tasked with creating cultures of wellness. Yet, healthcare workers often are afraid to seek help due to stigma, shame, lack of time, fear of confidentiality conflicts, or fear of losing the ability to practice and care for patients. We must normalize getting help and set standards that it is not acceptable or ethical to practice medicine unless physicians and healthcare professionals are in a state of wellness.

Leaders must take the time to ask each other and their teams how they are doing and find tangible ways to improve satisfaction. Though they cannot change the entirety of how healthcare systems operate in the United States, physician leaders can find ways to optimize the safety and efficiency of working in the current system.

Workforce Wellness

Public health depends on delivering the correct level of high-quality care to individuals. That requires a coordinated and healthy workforce — teams whose members maintain wellness, communicate effectively, and work well together.

Burnout is defined as a long-term stress reaction characterized by depersonalization, including cynical or negative attitudes toward patients, emotional exhaustion, a feeling of decreased personal achievement and a lack of empathy for patients.[6] The rate of physician burnout ranges from 30–65% across medical specialties, with the highest rates among physicians in the front-line of care.[6]

The American Medical Association (AMA) provides multiple resources, assessments, and tools for physician burnout. The seven steps to prevent burnout recommended by the AMA are:[7]

1. Establish wellness as a quality indicator for the practice.
2. Start a wellness committee and/or choose a wellness champion.
3. Distribute an annual wellness survey.
4. Meet regularly with leaders and/or staff to discuss data and interventions to promote wellness.
5. Initiate selected interventions.
6. Repeat the survey within the year to re-evaluate wellness.
7. Seek answers within the data, refine the interventions and continue to make improvements.

Building wellness into the workforce may also be aided by encouraging discussions about purpose and passion. Understanding the reasons for the goals and practice promotes transparent communication. Transparency builds trust in the reasons for the policies, procedures, and processes and may decrease frustration simply by increasing understanding.

Burnout Mitigation

Burnout is a work-related stress syndrome stemming from chronic exposure to job stress.[8] The word burnout was introduced in the 1970s by Freudenberger and later defined by Maslach and colleagues to encompass three dimensions: emotional exhaustion, cynicism and depersonalization, reduced professional efficacy, and personal accomplishment.[8] The consequences of burnout may include personal and professional fallout and may lead to lower patient satisfaction, impaired quality of care, medical errors, a potential increase in malpractice lawsuits, and increased costs for caregivers and hospitals.[8] According to the Centers for Disease Control and Prevention (CDC), 46% of healthcare workers reported feeling burned out in 2022, up from 32% in 2018.[9]

Providing care has multiple components in addition to knowing and understanding the standards of medicine: documenting using appropriate electronic records, following state and federal laws of prescribing and care guidelines, working with care partners, balancing workforce shortage and rising costs of labor and supplies, and communicating and working with payer partnerships in claims authorization and payments.

The United States spends more on healthcare than any other developed country, yet people continue to struggle to access affordable insurance. Though there is not a quick fix to the healthcare system, learning about the current system and working with care partners in the community or nationally to implement positive changes to help optimize the care provided to patients across the care spectrum may help mitigate burnout.

Any stress response creates a known cascade of interactions in the body. Activation of the sympathetic nervous system prepares for a fight, flight, or freeze response. Increased emotionality from the amygdala increases communication to the hypothalamic pituitary axis, which releases cortisol and adrenaline. Overactive release of the stress response overflows the system with cortisol (a steroid) and adrenaline. This consistent perceived threat creates floods of stress hormones, which inflame the physiologic system and risk creating physical, emotional, mental, and social problems.

Positivity, on the other hand, may combat this stress. Positivity releases dopamine and floods the pleasure center with reward. These rewards decrease inflammation and provide natural healing to the system and may lead to an increase in mindfulness and present-focused attention, broaden problem-solving, increase the ability to give and receive emotional support, increase resilience from stressors, build resistance from illness and decrease risks of health complications.

A positive orientation helps to perceive events as predictable and generally in the best interest, and process events in life and work as less threatening, see life- and work-related goals as more attainable, and be more resilient to the impact of the challenges and stressors resulting from daily experiences and social interactions.[10] Also, a positive orientation may contribute to work-life balance by fostering high tolerance to stress, resiliency, and commitment to valued goals such as self-care.[10]

There are many ways to increase positivity and creative change in the workforce. Examples may include practicing thankfulness and gratitude (such as building thankfulness lists, laughing at jokes or funny things, or writing thank you cards), mindfulness and calming programs, online courses or apps, stress reduction techniques, peer support and reaching out to others, therapy and counseling, exercise, yoga, acupuncture, positive affirmations, positive thinking practices, or anything promoting positivity to help ourselves and others.

To address burnout, physicians can focus on (1) building relationships with family, friends, and colleagues; (2) including religious or spiritual practices; (3) finding fulfillment in work as well as choosing and limiting the type of medicine being practiced; (4) cultivating self-care practices; and (5) adapting a specific life philosophy based on a positive outlook.[8]

Impaired Individuals

Physicians are under close societal scrutiny concerning their physical and mental competence.[11] Physician *impairment* refers to situations in which physicians are unable to perform their professional responsibilities safely or adequately because of a variety of health problems, including medical disease, psychiatric problems, or substance use.[11] The American Medical Association states that "it is the physician's ethical responsibility to take cognizance of a colleague's inability to practice medicine adequately because of physical or mental illness including alcoholism and drug dependence."[12]

It is important to separate impairment from addiction. An impaired state may be related to stress, untreated medical or behavioral health conditions, intoxication or withdrawal from substances, or life changes or adjustments. Addiction is defined as a chronic relapsing brain disease characterized by ongoing use of substances or behaviors despite negative consequences.

If impairment is suspected, regardless of its etiology, it should be reported and investigated immediately for the safety of the physician and the patient. Licensing boards and governing bodies have protocols and pathways for the evaluation and management of substance-use-related impairments and pathways to safe work reintegration.

Data regarding the prevalence and patterns of substance-use disorders in physicians is lacking. However, studies show the most frequent, problematic substance for use by physicians is alcohol, consistent with the general population.[13] Also consistent with the general population, the strongest predictor of substance-use disorders in physicians is a family history of substance-use disorder.[13]

The Federation of State Medical Boards defines impairment as the inability to practice with reasonable skill and safety due to illness. By this definition, not all physicians with substance use disorders meet the definition of impairment.[13] If any impairment is confirmed or suspected, or substance use that may lead to impairment is suspected, it is prudent for the physician to stop medical practice until an assessment of fitness to practice is completed.[14]

Physician health programs (PHPs) are vital in promoting and supporting early intervention, appropriate treatment, and rigorous monitoring of the response to treatment. The treatment outcomes for participants in PHPs are among the best in addiction treatment,[13] which is why referral and reporting to the programs through licensing and specialty boards and regulatory entities remains vital. Helping physicians receive treatment for impairment and addiction ensures physician wellness and safe patient care.

Chapter Summary

The 2022 U.S. Surgeon General's Advisory on Building a Thriving Health Workforce titled *Addressing Health Worker Burnout* states, "During the pandemic, each shift and overtime hour for a health worker often meant putting their own health and their family's health at risk in order to heal, comfort, and protect others. Fear, loneliness, and uncertainty were pervasive. The threat of targeted harassment and violence underscored many interactions. Some health workers were forced to wall themselves off from their loved ones. In addition, too many served as the final comfort for patients walled off from theirs. COVID-19 has been a fully and uniquely traumatic experience for the health workforce, and for their families."[14]

This advisory addresses steps that healthcare organizations; federal, state, local, and tribal governments; health insurers and payers; healthcare technology companies; academic institutions, clinical training programs and accreditation bodies; family members, friends and communities; and health workers can take to address health worker burnout.[14] Though many of the recommendations require structural change and diligent follow-up planning, it is vital to protect and nurture our healthcare workforce to continue to provide the vital care to patients and our communities.

A simple solution to eradicate burnout from healthcare does not exist; however, awareness and adaptation to wellness models, prevention strategies, and normalizing the conversation around this important topic are key to promoting wellness for physicians and healthcare workforce.

All healthcare settings should consider providing training in coping strategies, interpersonal skills, management of negative emotions, communication skills, and relaxation techniques.[15]

Physician leaders will need to be agile to adapt to changes in medicine, healthcare, and healthcare delivery and become stewards of high-quality care, foster health in communities, and care for each other with compassion, kindness, and openness. In this approach, they may lead health and wellness by example. Only then will they achieve the goals of healthy and optimized healthcare delivery and work through crises with ease, supporting each other along the way.

REFERENCES

1. World Health Organization. Constitution. Accessed November 15, 2024. https://www.who.int/about/governance/constitution
2. Berwick DM, Nolan TW, Whittington J. The Triple Aim: Care, Health, and Cost. *Health Aff* (Millwood). 2008;27(3):759–769.
3. Bodenheimer T, Sinsky C. From Triple to Quadruple Aim: Care of the Patient Requires Care of the Provider. *Ann Fam Med.* 2014;12(6):573–576.
4. First, Do No Harm. Centers for Medicare and Medicaid Services. March 16, 2023. Accessed November 15, 2024. https://www.cms.gov/blog/first-do-no-harm
5. Standards of Care. Green Cross Academy of Traumatology. Accessed November 15, 2024. https://greencross.org/about-gc/standards-of-care-guidelines/ and https://greencross.org/wp-content/uploads/2017/11/Standards-of-Self-Care-Guidelines.pdf
6. Corder JC. We Need to Reflame the Fire Before It Burns Out. *Mo Med.* 2018 Mar-Apr;115(2):108-111. PMID: 30228694; PMCID: PMC6139869.
7. Linzer M, Guzman-Corrales L, Poplau S. Preventing Physician Burnout. American Medical Association. Accessed November 15, 2024. https://amaalliance.org/wp-content/uploads/2019/01/preventing_physician_burnout-stepsforward-ama.pdf
8. De Hert S. Burnout in Healthcare Workers: Prevalence, Impact and Preventative Strategies. *Local*

Reg Anesth. 2020 Oct 28;13:171–183.

9. Centers for Disease Control and Prevention. Health Workers Face a Mental Health Crisis. Accessed November 15, 2024. https://www.cdc.gov/vitalsigns/health-worker-mental-health/index.html
10. Orkibi H, Brandt YI. How Positivity Links With Job Satisfaction: Preliminary Findings on the Mediating Role of Work-Life Balance. *Eur J Psychol*. 2015;11(3):406-418. doi: 10.5964/ejop.v11i3.869. PMID: 27247666; PMCID: PMC4873052.
11. O'Connor PG, Spickard A. Physician Impairment by Substance Abuse. Med Clin North Am. 1997;81(4):1037–1052. doi: 10.1016/s0025-7125(05)70562-9.
12. American Medical Association Council on Mental Health. The Sick Physician: Impairment By Psychiatric Disorders, Including Alcoholism and Drug Dependence. JAMA. 1973;223(6): 684–687.
13. Selzer J. Chapter 41: Physician Health Programs and Addiction Among Physicians. In: Ries R, Ries RK, Fiellin DA eds. *The ASAM Essentials of Addiction Medicine. 5th ed*. LWW:245–251.
14. Addressing Health Worker Burnout. The U.S. Surgeon General's Advisory on Building a Thriving Health Workforce. U.S. Department of Health and Human Services. Accessed November 15, 2024. https://www.hhs.gov/sites/default/files/health-worker-wellbeing-advisory.pdf and https://www.hhs.gov/surgeongeneral/priorities/health-worker-burnout/index.html
15. Wiederhold BK, Cipresso P, Pizzioli D, Wiederhold M, Riva G. Intervention for Physician Burnout: A Systematic Review. *Open Med* (Wars). 2018;13:253–263.

SECTION 7

Leadership In Patient Safety and Quality Improvement

CHAPTER 21

High-Reliability Organization, Structure, and Performance Monitoring

Edgar G. Chedrawy, MD, MSc, FRCSC, FACS, MHA, CPE, FAAPL, MCPDC

HALM CORE CONTENT:

- 7.1 Benchmarking standards to define, monitor, and assure evidence-based, efficient, timely, appropriate, cost-effective, equitable, patient-centered care
- 7.2 High-reliability care organizational (HRO) principles, tools, and monitoring processes (e.g., error reduction, serious safety event and near-miss reporting, just culture, root cause analysis, regulatory safety event reporting requirements, corrective action plans, and error disclosure)
- 7.3 Performance standard-setting, documentation, measurement, and monitoring (e.g., evidence-based clinical pathways, value-based care, population health, pay-for performance, patient satisfaction)

CASE SCENARIO:

An organization is focused on reducing the average length of stay after cardiac surgical procedures. Multiple factors, including the nature of the surgical procedure, patient age and comorbidities, postoperative complications, discharge planning, and patients' (as well as caregivers') preferences for transition of care influence the length of stay.

To provide patient-centric care in a fiscally responsible manner, physician leaders must meet well established standards with a high-reliability organization collective mindset, commitment and adherence to well-balanced healthcare performance metrics. This chapter explores benchmarking standards for patient-centred care, reviews the principles of high-reliability organizations, and discuss performance standards for value in healthcare.

The Institute of Medicine listed patient centered care (PCC) as one the six aims for improvement in its 2001 report, "Crossing the Quality Chasm." The institute defines patient-centered care as care that respects and responds to the individual patient's preferences, needs, and values, and ensures that clinical decision incorporates the patient's values.[1]

Since the Institute of Medicine report, the United States health system has been under increased scrutiny for adverse events, quality, and patient safety issues. Advancement in the realm of patient safety is due mostly to the aviation industry. The drive toward process improvement in high-reliability organizations, however, is thanks to process improvement in engineering and other industries. This chapter explores the ultimate goal of the health system: to deliver PCC in a fiscally responsible and sustainable manner through process improvement and performance management.

Benchmarking Standards to Define, Monitor, and Assure Evidence-Based, Efficient, Timely, Appropriate, Cost-effective, Equitable, Patient-Centered Care

Patient- centered care (PCC) is a model for delivering healthcare services that focuses not only on the patient's clinical signs and symptoms but also on emotional, social, and financial factors that affect their life and their personal value system. PCC emphasizes respect for patients' (and their significant others/families) values in individual care decisions and in improving care practices delivered by health systems. PCC is a true partnership between the patient, their healthcare provider and health system.[1-4]

The concept of PCC emerged in the late 1970s. The British Picker-Commonwealth Program for Patient Centered Care, which was initiated in 1987, stated that *"respecting patients' individuality is the foundation of humane medical care."* The book *Through the Patient's Eyes*, edited by Margaret Gerteis *et al*,[2] presented the material gathered for the Picker-Commonwealth Program for Patient Centered Care and addressed three important themes: (1) the association between patients' interactions with healthcare providers and health systems and the patients' subjective experience of illness and wellbeing; (2) the extent to which the health systems work to meet patients' needs; and (3) the incorporation of patients' perspectives on healthcare quality by healthcare providers and managers.[2-5]

Patient centered care is a process of shared decision-making by patient and physician where the patient: (1) understands the risk of the disease or condition; (2) understands the healthcare service being offered, including the risks, benefits, and alternatives; (3) has weighed his or her values regarding the potential benefits and harms associated with treatment; and (4) has engaged in a shared decision-making process at a level that he or she desires and feels comfortable.

Patients differ across age, gender, and ethnicity, in the extent to which they wish to be involved in decision-making for their medical care and treatment. Cultural competence and understanding are at the core of equitable PCC. The healthcare team must tailor the medical care per the preferences of patients and their significant others/families.[6-8]

The core principles at the center of patient-centered care are:[3-8]

- *Timely* access to healthcare services by *patient-trusted* professionals.
- *Transparent communication* and *respect* for patient preferences in decision-making.
- *Care continuity* and *effective transitions* with *family* and *caretaker* involvement and support.
- *Empathy* and emotional support with consideration of *environmental* and *physical* needs.

BENCHMARK STANDARDS OF PCC

Benchmarking standards ensure that care is patient-centered, evidence-based, efficient, timely, appropriate, cost-effective, and equitable. Some benchmarking approaches include the following.[9-11]

Internal benchmarking involves comparing performance metrics within different departments or locations within the same organization. It helps identify best practices and areas for improvement within the organization.

For example, a physician leader may want to know whether the surgery clinic or pediatric clinic scores higher for overall patient satisfaction. Monitoring this measure across the organization may shed light on issues that need to be addressed and help specific units improve their processes or practices. Individual clinics may learn best practices from other clinics in the same organization. Other internal benchmarks or key performance indicators (KPIs) include readmission rates, average length of hospital stays, patient drug costs per stay, and hospital-acquired complication rates.

Peer benchmarking compares an organization's performance metrics to those of its competitors or peers in the same or different markets. It helps organizations understand their relative position in the local/regional market and identify areas where they can improve to stay competitive.

For example, comparing metrics (such as average length of stay) against competitor hospitals in the same geographic area will help determine the standing against those in the market. Also, physician leaders may look at similar hospitals and clinics (peers) that serve a different market (because they are not competing against these entities). They can use the data to learn from one another and further improve their processes.

Functional benchmarking compares an organization's performance metrics to those of organizations in other industries that have similar processes or metrics. Physician leaders can learn from other industries and apply best practices to their own operations. For example, in the aviation industry, safety is not just a priority, it's part of the culture. From the aviation industry, physician leaders learned how to reduce medical errors to almost never events with tools such as time-outs and OR checklists.

Regulatory benchmarking compares an organization's performance to regulatory standards set by government agencies or professional bodies such as The Joint Commission and the Food and Drug Administration. It ensures that the organization meets the required standards for quality, safety, and patient care. An example is the R3 Report (Requirement, Rationale, Reference) from The Joint Commission: Patient-Centered Communication Standards. [12]

Once the health system has determined which benchmarking approach to follow, certain KPIs for patient-centered care may be identified and monitored to ensure that healthcare services are tailored to the needs and preferences of patients in an evidence-based, efficient, timely, appropriate, cost-effective, and equitable manner. Some KPIs that help healthcare organizations monitor and improve the quality of patient-centered care they provide include:[13-15]

1. *Respect for Patients' Values and Preferences.* Healthcare providers must listen to and honor patient values and preferences. The physician leader can measure patient satisfaction through surveys and feedback forms.
2. *Information, Communication, Education, Coordination, and Integration of Care.* To provide patients with clear, comprehensive information about their conditions and treatments with care well-coordinated across different healthcare settings and providers, the physician leader may evaluate the clarity and comprehensiveness of information provided to patients and track patient care transitions and integration through feedback surveys, audits, and case studies.
3. *Physical Comfort and Emotional Support.* Patient comfort, pain management, and emotional support are critical. The physician leader may assess patient comfort levels, pain management effectiveness, and the availability and effectiveness of emotional support services through surveys, pain checklists, and patient (and caregiver) feedback.
4. *Involvement of Family and Friends.* Family and friends should be encouraged to participate in patient care. The physician leader may track and evaluate family involvement in the care process through caregiver feedback and case studies.
5. *Access to Care with Seamless Continuity and Transition.* To ensure timely access to care and smooth transitions between different healthcare settings, the physician leader will measure wait times, appointment availability, and patient satisfaction

with access to care, and will monitor the effectiveness of transition processes through patient feedback and audits.

6. *Overall Patient Experience.* To continually assess and improve the overall patient experience, the physician leader will use comprehensive patient satisfaction surveys and feedback mechanisms.

High-Reliability Care Organizational Principles, Tools, and Monitoring Processes

Two decades after the publication of the Institute of Medicine's "To Err is Human," medical errors continue to be a leading cause of death in the United States.[1,16-18] As a result, many healthcare systems have turned to other industries, including nuclear power and aviation, that have experience in transforming to "high-reliability organizations" or HROs.

High-reliability organizations are defined as organizations that "*operate in complex and high-hazard domains, for extended periods, without serious accidents or catastrophic failures.*" The theory underlying HRO is that creating a culture of "collective mindfulness" — in which workers look for and report small problems — can help systems address issues before they pose a risk to the overall organization or harm individuals.

The following HRO principles have been successfully adapted to healthcare settings:[16-18]

- *Sensitivity to Operations (StO):* To have heightened awareness of the state of relevant systems and processes and to observe management operations and their effects on delivery of services. HROs in healthcare maintain situational awareness and realize that unexpected events can begin during routine operations from a hidden condition or system interaction that is normally dormant and quickly cascade into a larger problem if not recognized and thwarted early in their development.

  Physician leaders recognize there is a difference between *work-as-designed* and *work-as-performed* and remain alert to this drift in implementation that can lead to an unwanted result. An example of this would be crisis drills during the pandemic and in emergency departments.
- *Reluctance to Simplify (RtS):* To accept that work is complex with potential to fail in new and unexpected ways, and to resist the urge to simplify assumptions about the world. HROs understand their operating systems and the interconnectedness of their processes and do not accept simple interpretations of what might be an indicator of a systemic problem. Physician leaders analyze incident reports as well as process changes to look for unwanted system interactions so they can be addressed before causing or exacerbating a problem, such as continuity of care issues.

- *Preoccupation with Failure (PwF):* To view near misses as opportunities to improve rather than proof of success or failure; to examine failure as a window on the health of the actual system. HROs are aware that process or system lapses are symptoms of problems that must be investigated. Physician leaders encourage the reporting of near misses and unexpected events to learn from them and do not become complacent due to past success, such as root cause analysis.
- *Deference to Expertise (DtE):* To value insights from staff with the most pertinent safety knowledge over those with greater seniority and to create a climate of deference to the experts. HROs recognize that the expert in the room may not be the one with the most experience or the highest rank.

  Physician leaders follow normal communication hierarchy for routine operations but make decisions close to the front-lines during distress and defer to the person with the most knowledge of the condition and situation. Creating a zone of psychological safety is of outmost importance — for example, cardiac arrest codes.
- *Commitment to Resilience (CtR):* To prioritize and sustain emergency training for many unlikely but possible system failures and to develop resilience to manage these unexpected events.[16-18] HROs can detect, contain, and bounce back from small perturbations that occur unexpectedly in all operations and are able to contain them at the lowest level of disruption. Physician leaders do not pretend to be error-free, but their errors do not disable the operation; rather, they are contained at the lowest level possible (e.g., simulation training in the OR and ER).

The first three principles or mindfulness practices address "anticipation" of unexpected problems *(StO, RtS, and PwF),* whereas the final two principles *(DtE and CtR)* address the ability to "contain" unexpected problems. Evidence suggests that implementation of HRO principles into health systems may contribute to improved staff ratings of safety culture and improved patient safety outcomes.[16-18]

HOW TO BECOME A HIGH-RELIABILITY ORGANIZATION

There are five levels of maturity to becoming a high-reliability organization: Level 1 is "Silent," Level 2 is "Starter," Level 3 is "Stable," Level 4 is "Sustain," and Level 5 is "Summit." The progression through the five stages is documented in Table 1.[17]

Learning tools identified to help with HRO maturation include debriefing, simulation, crew resource management, and reporting systems to disseminate safety messages.[17-22]

Debriefing involves deconstructing incidents using reflective questions, while simulation training utilizes asking staff to relive the event by performing the task(s) in a role-play scenario. Crew resource management is a set of training procedures that focus on communication, leadership, and decision-making.

Sophisticated incident-reporting systems provide valuable information on hazards and are widely recommended as a way of disseminating key safety messages following

TABLE 1. Patient Safety Healthcare Maturity Grid

HRO Principle:	Level 1 (Silent)	Level 2 (Starter)	Level 3 (Stable/ Standardize)	Level 4 (Stable/ Sustain)	Level 5 (Summit)
StO: Flexibility in making small adjustments can prevent errors from accumulating.	Meetings rare, without quality, no focus on long- or short-term organization aims.	Occasional meetings with no defined purpose, outcome, or terms of reference.	Regular meetings with defined terms of reference, purpose, and outcomes.	Regular meetings with outcomes allocated to individual roles.	Regular meetings with outcomes allocated to individual roles and monitored for completion.
RtS: Organization pays close attention to weak signals of failure and views near misses as symptoms of larger problems within the system rather than proof of effective safeguards in the system.	Sceptics may be victimized and punished. Culture of distrust among employees/ departments.	Sceptics are not always victimized or punished but may be viewed negatively. Pockets of distrust among employees/ departments.	A process for challenging exists. Culture permits challenge to normal or new processes, but challenges are often ignored, paid lip service to, or implementation delayed by excessive bureaucracy.	Sceptics and out-of-the-box thinkers are respected and often implemented by management. Evidence of frank and open cooperation between employees/departments.	Management actively creates forums to challenge the norm or new processes. Out-of-the-box thinkers are rewarded. Teams work together synergistically and have each other's backs.
PwF: Incidents/ near misses and culture of learning.	Not reported, no peer review. Secretive, defensive culture prevalent.	Sometimes reported. Focus on narrative and not root causes. Secretive, defensive culture prevalent. Focus on individual's blame and competency. Punitive actions may follow.	Generally reported and investigated by skilled peers. Root causes are identified but not always shared. Staff often blamed directly or indirectly. Training and supervision used as punitive tools. Culture remains defensive and insular.	Always reported and investigated by skilled peers. Root causes are identified, widely shared. Staff not singled out or blamed. Environmental, operational, and human factors considered in root causes and learning. Open culture of learning together.	Always reported, triaged, appropriately investigated, outcomes monitored. Patients participate in framing and investigating incidents. No-blame culture, open, transparent collaborative culture prevalent. Reporting of incidents / near misses is actively rewarded.

(table continues)

TABLE 1. Patient Safety Healthcare Maturity Grid *(continued)*

HRO Principle:	Level 1 (Silent)	Level 2 (Starter)	Level 3 (Stable/ Standardize)	Level 4 (Stable/ Sustain)	Level 5 (Summit)
DtE: During a problem or crisis, decision-making migrates to the person or staff with the most expertise with the problem at hand, regardless of authority or rank.	In an emergency, the most senior person takes responsibility irrespective of experience. It is difficult to know who has the most expertise for each emergency.	Hierarchical rank takes precedent during an emergency. The most senior person feels insulted if not in charge during emergencies. Staff know who has the most expertise in an emergency.	There is a formal process to determine who takes responsibility in an emergency. Views from experienced staff may be solicited. Lack of clarity and confidence may ensue.	The most senior person yields responsibility to the person with the most expertise during the emergency. The expert accepts responsibility professionally and yields back after the emergency. Expertise for all emergencies is readily available.	There is mutual respect for one another's jobs. No job is considered more important than the other. Staff are encouraged to take expert decisions irrespective of hierarchy during emergencies. Staff feel responsible until problems are resolved.
CtR: Developing capabilities through sustained training to cope with, contain, and bounce back from mishaps that have already occurred before they worsen and cause more serious harm.	Organization does not organize / sponsor training. Competencies and skills are not routinely assessed. There is no emergency response or contingency plan.	Training exists but is only used to reward favored front-line staff. Individual leaders assess competencies and skills in their own way. There are emergency response and contingency plans, but staff are not aware of them. Drills are regarded as a nuisance.	There is a formalized, well-funded training program, equitable and open to all staff. Skills and competencies are routinely assessed in a standard manner across all departments. Emergency drills are done routinely, staff are mandated to participate, understand the emergency response and contingency plans.	Leaders and staff work together to identify training and development gaps and close them. Competency assessment is an on-going process and feedback is constructive and supportive. Staff actively seek to understand and review the emergency response and contingency plans. Staff regard drills as valuable and a potential way to save lives.	Staff are skilled and competent to do their job and act during emergencies. Competence and skills assessment is a proactive process. Emergency response and contingency plans are robust and grounded and the responsibility for implementation is shared among all staff. Everyone trusts one another and relies on another during emergencies.

– Adapted from Mitchell *et al.*, 2023[17]

safety incidents. These learning tools were found to have a positive impact on learning if conducted soon after the incident with efficient facilitation and administration/ senior physician leadership support.

To build a high-reliability organization (Level 5, Summit) the "collective mindfulness" must adopt an "informed culture" or else a single person committed to HRO mindfulness will be silenced by the dominant "organizational culture" (Level 1, Silent).

The informed culture has four components:[17-22]

1. *Reporting culture* – People share their accounts of what went wrong.
2. *Just culture* – The organization treats people fairly and clearly defines "acceptable and unacceptable" action and does not punish failures that arise from acceptable behavior. When something goes wrong, seek reasons, not scapegoats.
3. *Flexible culture* – If your work is variable, don't depend on a rigid, slow hierarchy. Foster individual discretion and variation instead of uniformity.
4. *Learning culture* – Increase everyone's capacity to share information.

Performance Standard-Setting, Documentation, Measurement, and Monitoring

After the COVID-19 pandemic, healthcare systems were pushed to evolve into high-reliability organizations delivering patient-centered care in financially sustainable macro-environments.[23-27] To measure the performance of an HRO system delivering PCC in a fiscally responsible and sustainable manner, a well-rounded clinical, financial, and organizational performance measurement tool must be used.

Outside of healthcare, the balanced scorecard (BSC) is the standard. Kaplan and Norton[27] introduced the concept of a balanced scorecard as *a performance measurement framework that added strategic non-financial performance measures to traditional financial metrics to give managers and executives a more "balanced" view of organizational performance.*

The BSC approach is a strategic planning and management system that is used extensively in business, government, and nonprofit organizations worldwide to align business activities to the vision and strategy of the organization, improve internal and external communications, and monitor organizational performance against strategic goals.

The BSC combines four distinct perspectives:[26,27]

1. *Financial* perspective (economic value-added, revenue growth, costs, profit margins, cash flow, net operating income, etc.).
2. *Customer (or patient)* perspective (the value proposition that an organization adopts to satisfy its customers).
3. *Internal business* perspective (the internal business processes that create and deliver the customer value proposition).

4. *Learning and growth* perspective (internal skills and capabilities necessary to support the value-creating internal processes). Figure 1 shows a typical BSC in healthcare:

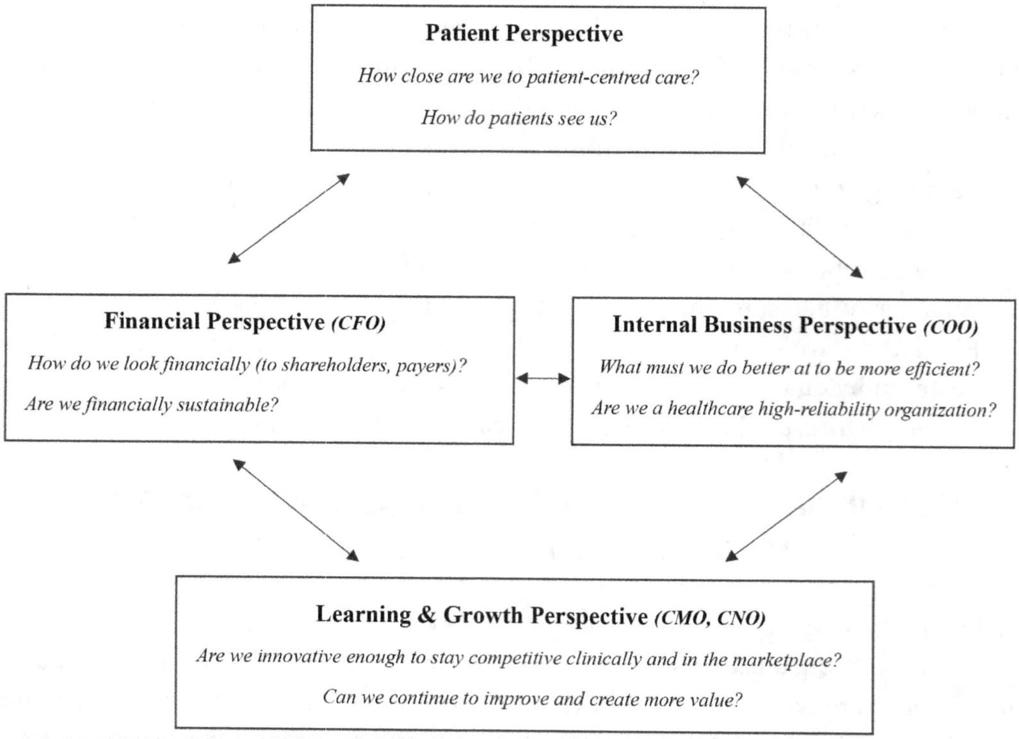

CFO: chief financial officer, COO: chief operating officer, CMO: chief medical officer, CNO: chief nursing officer

FIGURE 1. Healthcare Balanced Score Card Links Performance Measures

VALUE AND PAY FOR PERFORMANCE IN HEALTHCARE

The definition of *value* in healthcare (unlike other industries) remains elusive. In healthcare, *value* may be defined as the health outcomes achieved per dollar spent. To achieve a high-value healthcare delivery system, safety, equity, and efficiency must be achieved and patient-centric care, with all its attributes, must be delivered in a cost-effective and sustainable system.

Porter described the three principles of value-based healthcare delivery.[24] The first principle in creating a high-value delivery system is for each participant to define value as the goal, not reducing cost, maximizing revenue, or providing every service. Improving value requires improving outcomes per unit of cost.

The second principle of value-based delivery is that care should be organized around the way value is created in the total care of a patient's medical condition over the full cycle of care (patient-centered). Value is not created in a system organized around specialties and departments (professional-centered). For example, diabetes care does not only revolve around blood glucose control and endocrinology issues but also eye issues, vascular issues, and kidney issues (end-organ) among others. Integrated care is at the core of value in healthcare.

The third principle of value-based delivery is the need to accurately measure value (patient-centered outcomes and cost). Without measuring outcomes and costs, it is difficult to improve. Monitoring efforts focused on measuring processes, and not outcomes, do not add value to PCC. The attention to compliance (with guidelines and processes) rather than measuring how well patients do is misleading.

Pay for performance in healthcare (P4P),[25] also known as value-based payment, comprises payment models that attach financial incentives/disincentives to provider performance.

P4P is part of the overall U.S. national strategy to transition healthcare to value-based medicine.[23-27] While it still utilizes the fee-for-service (FFS) system, it pushes providers toward value-based care because it ties reimbursement to metric-driven outcomes, proven best practices, and patient satisfaction, thus aligning payment with value and quality.

There are two basic types of pay for performance designs being deployed for hospitals. With the first, payers lower global FFS payments and use the funds to reward hospitals based on how well they perform across process, quality, and efficiency measures. In the second, hospitals are penalized financially for sub-par performance, and the penalties are either translated into direct cost savings for payers or are used to generate an incentive pool.

Chapter Summary

Physician leaders are asked to deliver patient-centered care in a fiscally responsible and sustainable manner. We are ideally positioned to transform healthcare institutions into high-reliability organizations by cultivating the collective mindfulness of an HRO, identifying the benchmark standards of patient-centered care and appropriately measuring, and acting upon, our performance metrics.

REFERENCES

1. Institute of Medicine. *Crossing the Quality Chasm: A New Health System for the 21st Century.* Washington, DC: National Academy Press; 2001.
2. Gerteis M, Edgman-Levitan S, Daley J, et al. *Through The Patient's Eyes: Understanding and Promoting Patient-Centered Care.* San Francisco, CA: Jossey-Bass; 1993.
3. Hobbs JL. A Dimensional Analysis of Patient-Centered Care. *Nurs Res.* 2009;58(1):52–62. doi: 10.1097/NNR.0b013e31818c3e79
4. Mead N, Bower P. Patient-Centeredness: A Conceptual Framework and Review of the Empirical

Literature. *Soc Sci Med.* 2000;51:1087–1110. https://doi.org/10.1016/S0277-9536(00)00098-8

5. Saha S, Beach MC, Cooper LA. Patient Centeredness, Cultural Competence and Healthcare Quality. *J Natl Med Assoc.* 2008;100(11):1275–1285. https://doi.org/10.1016/S0027-9684(15)31505-4
6. Jayadevappa R, Chhatre S. Patient Centered Care — A Conceptual Model and Review of the State of the Art. *Open Health Serv Policy J.* 2011;4:15-25. http://dx.doi.org/10.2174/1874924001104010015
7. Leino A. Planning Patient-Centered Care. *Am J Nurs.* 1952;52(3):324–325.
8. Levenstein JH, McCracken EC, McWhinney IR, et al. The Patient Centered Clinical Method-A Model for the Doctor-Patient Interaction in Family Medicine. *Fam Pract.* 1986;3:24–30. https://doi.org/10.1093/fampra/3.1.24
9. Oh A. 4 Types of Healthcare Benchmarking (& The Benefits of Each). ClearPoint Strategy. August 19, 2024. Accessed November 1, 2024. https://www.clearpointstrategy.com/blog/4-types-of-benchmarking-in-healthcare-benefits-of-each#4-types-of-healthcare-benchmarking-and-the-benefits-of-each.
10. What Is Benchmarking in Healthcare? (Plus Types and Guide). Indeed. August 15, 2024. Accessed November 13, 2024. https://www.indeed.com/career-advice/career-development/benchmarking-in-health-care
11. Young M, Smith MA. Standards and Evaluation of Healthcare Quality, Safety, and Person-Centered Care. [Updated 2022 Dec 13]. In: *StatPearls [Internet]*. Treasure Island, FL: StatPearls Publishing; January 2024. https://www.ncbi.nlm.nih.gov/books/NBK576432/
12. The Joint Commission. *R3 Report — Requirement, Rationale,* Reference. Issue 1, February 9, 2011. Patient-centered Communication Standards for Hospitals. https://www.jointcommission.org/standards/r3-report/r3-report-issue-1---patient-centered-communication//
13. Gangannagaripalli J, Albagli A, Myers SN, et al. A Standard Set of Value-Based Patient-Centered Outcomes and Measures of Overall Health in Adults. *Patient.* 2022;15:(3):341–351. https://doi.org/10.1007/s40271-021-00554-8
14. Cano SJ, Pendrill LR, Melin J, et al. Towards Consensus Measurement Standards for Patient-Centered Outcomes. *Measurement.* 2019;141: 62–69. https://doi.org/10.1016/j.measurement.2019.03.056
15. Reeve BB, Wyrwich KW, Wu AW, et al. ISOQOL Recommends Minimum Standards for Patient-Reported Outcome Measures Used in Patient-Centered Outcomes and Comparative Effectiveness Research. *Quality of Life Research.* 2013;22(8):1889–1905.
16. Veazie S, Peterson K, Bourne D, et al. Implementing High-Reliability Organization Principles into Practice: A Rapid Evidence Review. *J Patient Saf.* 2022;18(1):e320–e328.
17. Mitchell C, Van Laar D, Strevens C, Labib A. No Harm in Learning–A Balanced High Reliability Organisation (HRO) Approach in Healthcare. *J Soc Econ Stat.* 2023;12(2):1-19. https://doi.org/10.2478/jses-2023-0006
18. Weick KE, Sutcliffe KM. *Managing the Unexpected (Vol. 9). Resilient Performance in an Age of Uncertainty.* San Francisco: Jossey-Bass; 2001.
19. Cantu J, Gharehyakheh A, Fritts S, et al. Assessing the HRO: Tools and Techniques to Determine the High-Reliability State of an Organization. *Safety Science.* 2021;134:105082. https://doi.org/10.1016/j.ssci.2020.105082
20. Cantu J, Tolk J, Fritts S, et al. High Reliability Organization (HRO) Systematic Literature Review: Discovery of Culture as a Foundational Hallmark. *J Contingencies Crisis Manage.* 2020;28(4):399–410. https://doi.org/10.1111/1468-5973.12293
21. Hales DN, Chakravorty SS. Creating High Reliability Organizations Using Mindfulness. *J Bus Res.* 2016;69(8):2873–2881. https://doi.org/10.1016/j.jbusres.2015.12.056
22. Serou N, Sahota LM, Husband AK, et al. Learning from Safety Incidents in High-Reliability Organizations: A Systematic Review of Learning Tools That Could Be Adapted and Used in Healthcare. *Int J Qual Health Care.* 2021;33(1): mzab046. https://doi.org/10.1093/intqhc/mzab046
23. Vincent C, Burnett S, Carthey J. Safety Measurement and Monitoring in Healthcare: A Framework to Guide Clinical Teams and Healthcare Organisations in Maintaining Safety. *BMJ Qual Saf.*

2014;23(8):670–677. https://doi.org/10.1136/bmjqs-2013-002757

24. Porter ME. Value-based Health Care Delivery. *Ann Surg.* 2008;248(4):503–509.
25. What Is Pay for Performance in Healthcare? *NEJM Catalyst.* March 1, 2018. https://catalyst.nejm.org/doi/full/10.1056/CAT.18.0245
26. Betto F, Sardi A, Garengo P, et al. The Evolution of Balanced Scorecard in Healthcare: A Systematic Review of Its Design, Implementation, Use, and Review. *Int J Environ Res Public Health.* 2022;19(16):10291. https://doi.org/10.3390/ijerph191610291
27. Kaplan R, Norton D. The Balanced Scorecard-Measures That Drive Performance. *Harv. Bus. Rev.* 1992;70:71–79.

CHAPTER 22

Case Management and System-Based Engagement

Julie T. Joseph, MD, MBA, MPH, CPE

HALM CORE CONTENT:

- 7.8 Utilization review and leadership of case management teams
- 7.9 Education in identifiable gaps in system-based practice
- 7.10 Longitudinal understanding of the system-wide organizational structure
- 7.11 Community initiatives (e.g., violence prevention)
- 7.12 External agency engagement (e.g., NAHQ, AHRQ, NAM, etc.)

CASE SCENARIO:

A physician's patient has had multiple admissions at hospitals throughout various boroughs in New York City for asthma exacerbation. Effective case management is hindered because case managers at each hospital are unable to communicate and share information on this patient with other hospitals in the city.

What resources can be utilized to improve patient outcomes? Can case management at the health maintenance organization be of assistance? How can utilization management data from the health maintenance organization be used to assist case management at the payer?

THE INFORMATION COLLECTED through utilization management at the health maintenance organization can be provided to the case manager at the health insurance company to connect, assess, provide, and monitor patient care. Case management can facilitate communication about the patient to hospitals on each admission, in addition to assisting with the coordination of care, especially with discharge planning and transition of care. Case managers not only connect patients to resources and services, but they also connect patients to healthcare providers. Case managers are liaisons to healthcare providers and the healthcare facilities.

Utilization management is dynamic and evolving with changes in medical advancements and regulations from regulatory bodies such as the Centers for Medicare and Medicaid Services (CMS). In addition, data analysis done in utilization management can identify trends and allow case managers to streamline processes and adjust the provision of medical services needed. Collaboration and communication between utilization management and case management is critical in ensuring optimal delivery of care before, during, and after hospitalization.

Utilization Review and Leadership of Case Management Teams

Utilization management and case management are key processes in the healthcare delivery system that ensure patients get the right care at the right time in the right place while maintaining a high quality of care. Utilization management ensures that patients receive necessary and appropriate care, while case management coordinates the utilization of resources to provide care in an effective and timely manner.

Utilization management and case management involve several stakeholders. The key stakeholders are patients, healthcare providers, case managers, hospitals, and health maintenance organizations. The health maintenance organization's utilization management department reviews a patient's medical records to determine if a request from a healthcare provider for services or procedures is medically necessary. The utilization management team at the health maintenance organization uses evidence-based clinical guidelines, such as InterQual or Millman Care Guidelines (MCG), to assist in determining medical necessity.[1]

With the assistance of the utilization management team, the case management team at the health maintenance organization identifies patients who have complex medical and social barriers to care and enrolls them to receive case management services.

Health insurance companies perform three types of utilization review (Figure 1):[2]

1. Prospective review (Pre-authorization Review)
2. Concurrent review
3. Retrospective review

A prospective review, or precertification, is an authorization review of a medical service or procedure before it is done. A medical service or procedure must be approved before it is provided. These types of reviews are typically done for elective surgeries or procedure.[3] The main purpose of a prospective review is to eliminate unnecessary and ineffective medical care or treatment.

A concurrent review, or a continued stay review, is an authorization review of a patient's ongoing care during their hospital stay to evaluate for medical necessity. This is typically done when a patient is being moved to a unit or facility for a different

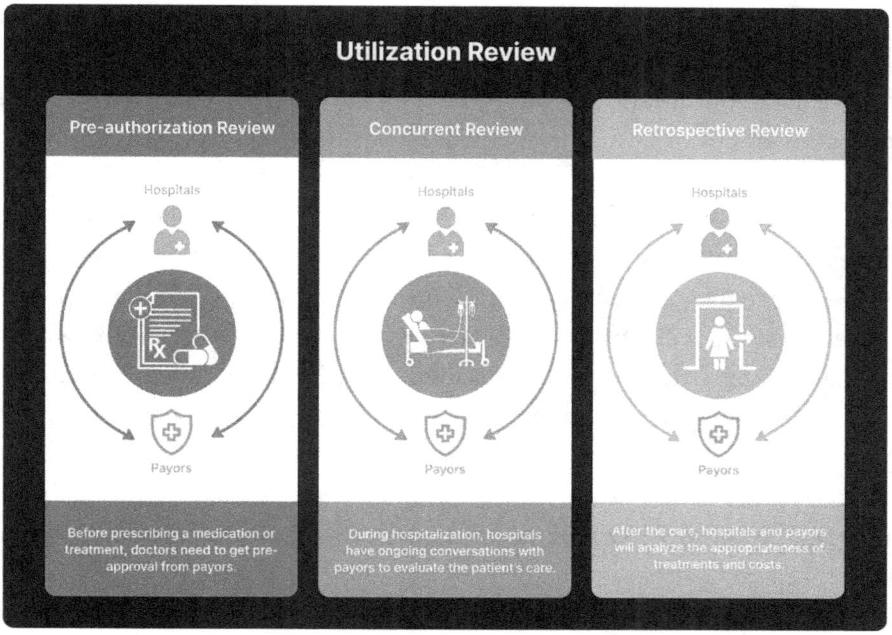

FIGURE 1. Three Types of Utilization Reviews

level of care.[4] The patient's progress during the hospitalization is monitored, allowing case management to track utilization of resources and to coordinate care upon discharge. Discharge planning ensures a patient receives the appropriate level of care and resources upon discharge from the hospital.

A retrospective review is an authorization of a medical service or procedure after it has been completed. This typically involves reviewing medical records and claims data submitted after care was delivered to determine medical necessity.[5]

The cross-disciplinary collaboration between utilization management and case management is vital in maintaining and providing quality care to patients while improving patient outcomes.

Education in Identifiable Gaps in System-Based Practice

Gaps are areas of vulnerability where a patient receives care that falls short of the recommended standard of care. Identifiable gaps in healthcare system-based practice are seen with care coordination, care transition, and interoperability. Gaps with care coordination revolve around poor communication between providers and specialists, missed follow-up appointments, and referrals.[6] These gaps in care coordination can lead to fragmented care, delayed or missed treatment, medication errors, duplicate tests, and increased hospital readmission rates that ultimately lead to poor patient outcomes.

The gaps in care coordination can also lead to inefficient transition of care between different care settings, leading to poor patient outcomes.[7] The underlying impediment to effective care coordination and transition of care is poor data sharing, or lack of interoperability.[8]

Interoperability is the ability of health information systems in various healthcare entities such as hospitals, providers, and health insurance companies, to seamlessly exchange patient data across organizations to advance the effective delivery of healthcare.[9] Healthcare data are largely held by providers, hospitals, and health insurance companies in different electronic formats. Each stakeholder collects and owns specific types of patient data that the other stakeholder needs and is not easily shared.

Medical decisions on treatment and diagnoses depend on access to timely and complete patient information. Incomplete health data contributes to an increased likelihood of redundant testing, transcription errors, and adverse events.[10] The lack of transparency and poor collaboration among stakeholders creates an obstacle in providing optimal healthcare.

Historically, there have been several impediments to achieving interoperability across the U.S. healthcare system, however, recently there have been advances toward achieving this goal.

The lack of universal adoption of a standardized electronic health record (EHR) system, the complex privacy and security challenges, and the impact on health providers' workflow and weak or misaligned incentives are some historical impediments to achieving interoperability in the U.S. healthcare system.[11]

Fragmentation of the EHR system along with competing standardized formats among EHRs have resulted in incompatible information exchange and lack of interoperability. Privacy and security laws vary from state to state, making cross-state health information exchange and interoperability difficult. The workflow processes providers follow to care for patients are not standardized, and when these workflows are redesigned to allow for interoperability, it causes significant negative impact on a provider's day-to-day workflow.

In addition, historically there were no incentives provided by the government to promote interoperability or widespread information exchange with external organizations outside a provider's health system.

According to the National Academy of Medicine's Procuring Interoperability: Achieving High-Quality, Connected, and Person-Centered Care report, "health care organizations are therefore not just seeking the ability to transmit records electronically from point A to point B; they are looking for *clinically meaningful* interoperability that improves patient safety and workflow, enhances value, and enables person-centered care."[12]

Current advances toward achieving interoperability have been through incentives the government has provided for value-based reimbursement. Unlike traditional fee-for-service reimbursement, value-based reimbursement has a positive effect on interoperability and health information exchange.[13]

Interoperability is vital in achieving value-based reimbursement and thus contributes to increased health information exchange. The shift from a fee-for-service model to a value-based model has positively influenced providers in adopting interoperability tools.

Longitudinal Understanding of the System-Wide Organizational Structure

Nurses play a central role in utilization management. Once a healthcare provider or a healthcare facility sends an authorization request to the payer, the utilization management nurse at the health maintenance organization conducts the initial review of the prior authorization request. The nurse collects the medical records, interprets the clinical information in the patient's medical records, and reviews it for appropriateness.[14]

If the request does not meet InterQual or MCG criteria, the request is escalated to a medical director at the payer for review. A decision is made and sent to the requesting physician or healthcare facility. If the request is denied, the physician or healthcare facility can proceed through the appeals process with the health insurance company.

Social workers and nurses play a central role in case management. Case managers assess, plan, implement, and coordinate resources and services for patients. Case managers assess the patient's needs and discusses potential services and resources to meet these needs. They can also assist with making follow-up appointments, obtaining referrals as well as prior authorizations.[15]

In addition, case managers work with patients and their providers to develop and implement a plan of care. Case managers monitor progress and update providers. It is crucial that there is effective communication and interdisciplinary collaboration between case managers and utilization management nurses to improve patient care and safety.

Community Initiatives: Violence Prevention

The Centers for Disease Control and Prevention (CDC) considers violence an urgent public health matter with a goal to stop violence before it begins. According to the World Health Organization, "almost 500 people die every day as a result of interpersonal violence in the Americas."[16] The CDC National Violent Death Reporting System, a U.S. database that tracks violent death including homicides and suicides, reports homicide as one of the top five causes of death between the ages of one and 44 years of age.[17]

The CDC proposes a four-level social-ecological model to understand the multiple factors that increase one's risk for violence. The four levels include: individual, relationship, community, and societal (Figure 2).[18]

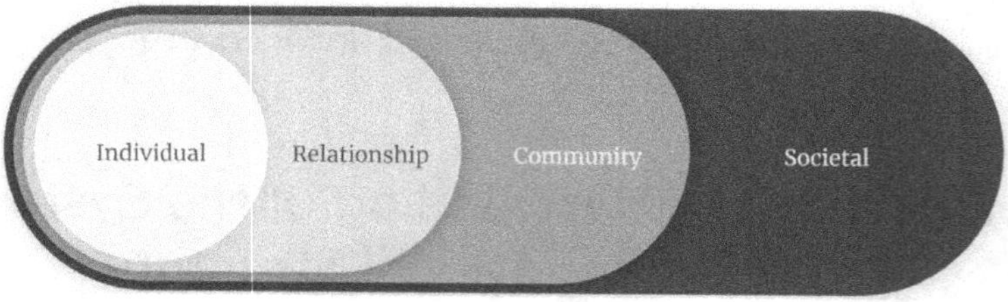

FIGURE 2. CDC's Four-Level Social-Ecological Model Related to Risk of Violence

Individual. The first level explores biological and personal history factors that increases one's risk of experiencing or engaging in violence. Biological and personal history risk factors include history of abuse, age, education, income, delinquent peers, low IQ, mental/behavioral condition, male sex, unstructured free time and substance use. Prevention strategies should address an individual's feelings, beliefs and behaviors regarding violence.

Relationship. The second level evaluates close relationships with the patient that may increase their risk of exposure to violence. Close relationships include individuals such as friends, partners, or family members. Risk factors are low socioeconomic status, poor parent-child relations, separation from parents, family history of suicide, and substance misuse. Prevention strategies may involve prevention programs or sessions that involve the individual in the close relationship.

Community. The third level examines community settings such as school, workplace, and neighborhoods, which may increase one's risk to violence. Risk factors include status of school and housing, size and geographic location of school, involvement with gangs witnessing or experiencing violence, media portrayals, access to gun, alcohol, or drugs. Prevention strategies include developing safe places to live, learn, work, and play.

Societal. The fourth level identifies broad social factors such as health, economic, and cultural norms that support violence. Risk factors involve oppression, family dynamics, mental illness, and weak social ties. Prevention strategies involve educating on social norms that protect against violence and strengthen educational and employment opportunities.

The CDC's public health approach to violence prevention involves a four-step process (Figure 3).[19]

The first step in preventing violence is understanding the basics of the problem, such as "who," "what," "when," "where," and "how." This can be accomplished through data analysis of various sources such as death certificates, hospital charts, law enforcement reports, and medical examiner reports.

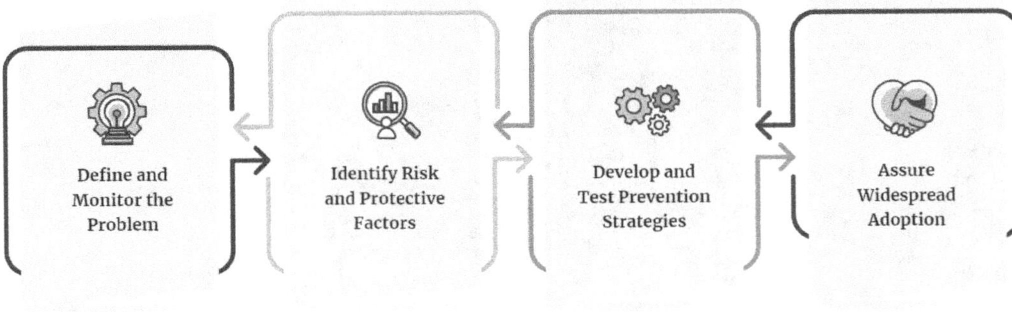

FIGURE 3. CDC's Public Health Approach to Violence Prevention

The second step identifies factors that put individuals at risk of violence as well as factors that protect them from violence. Risk factors increase the likelihood of encountering violence; protective factors decrease the likelihood of experiencing violence.

The third step designs and tests prevention strategies. Evidence-based data is used to develop prevention strategies that undergo extensive testing and evaluation. The goal is to generate and establish the most effective violence prevention strategies.

The fourth step is to promote widespread adoption of the most effective prevention strategies through training, networking, and evaluation. Continuous assessment is needed to make sure the prevention strategies are appropriate and useful.

Healthcare providers must receive appropriate training and education in identifying risk factors for violence and addressing violence prevention, as well as recognizing and reporting violence when identified. Healthy People 2030 identify public health priorities to improve health and well-being in the U.S. over the next decade. Healthy People 2030 emphasize the use of interventions to reduce violence to keep people safe in all settings from their home, school, workplace, and community.[20]

External Agency Engagement

Quality management is fundamental to utilization management and case management. The goal of utilization management and case management is to improve patient care by providing high-quality care in an effective manner. CMS national quality strategy goals include advancing health equity, increasing individual and community engagement, improving patient safety, enabling a resilient healthcare system to improve quality, aligning across patient care settings, improving interoperability, encouraging scientific advancement, and improving patient outcomes (Figure 4).[21]

The four main healthcare quality agencies are: NAHQ, AHRQ, NAM, and NCQA.

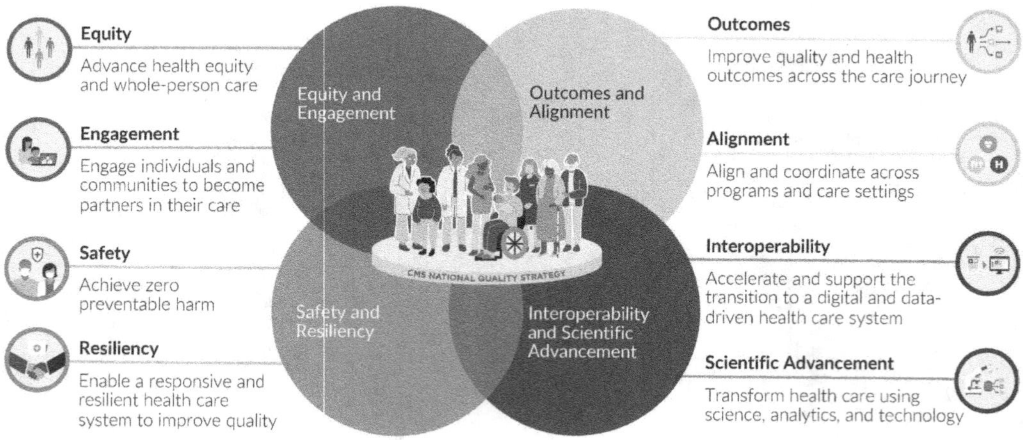

FIGURE 4. CMS National Quality Strategy Goals

The **National Association for Healthcare Quality (NAHQ)** was established in 1976 to educate and empower healthcare professionals to reduce variability in care delivery and to drive value through improved quality and safety outcomes. NAHQ looks to set the industry standard for healthcare quality and safety and offers the Certified Professional in Healthcare Quality (CPHQ) certification, a certification endorsed by The Joint Commission — the only accredited healthcare quality certification.[22]

NAHQ created the Healthcare Quality Competency Framework to recognize a high-functioning quality program and it established the industry standard for workforce competencies in quality. The Healthcare Quality Competency Framework includes eight domains:[23]

1. Professional Engagement
2. Quality Leadership and Integration
3. Performance and Process Improvement
4. Population Health and Care Transitions
5. Health Data Analytics
6. Patient Safety
7. Regulatory and Accreditation
8. Quality Review and Accountability

The **Agency for Healthcare Research (AHRQ)** is one of 12 agencies in the United States Department of Health and Human Services. It was established in 1989 to enhance the quality, appropriateness, effectiveness, and equitability of healthcare services through research.

AHRQ is known for its Consumer Assessment of Healthcare Providers and Systems (CAHPS) program, which is a multi-year initiative to better understand the patient experience with a range of healthcare services in various healthcare settings. The CAHPS program supports investigator-led research to assess the patient experience, report survey results, and provide organizations with the results to improve the quality of care.

The CAHPS survey uses standardized questions to assess the patient experience with the healthcare system from their communication with their provider to understanding their medication instruction.[24]

The National Academy of Medicine (NAM), formerly known as the Institute of Medicine, is a nonprofit organization founded in 1970 that publishes reports on the future of quality.[25] In fact, the AHRQ collaborates with NAM to develop reports on improving the quality of healthcare.

The **National Committee for Quality Assurance (NCQA)** is a nonprofit organization that seeks to improve healthcare quality. NCQA is a leader in health plan accreditation, and they are the only program that sources their results on consumer experience (CAHPS) and clinical experience (HEDIS). HEDIS stands for Healthcare Effectiveness Data and Information Set and it is a standardized set of performance measures used to evaluate and compare the quality of healthcare services provided by health plans.

Some HEDIS measures revolve around immunization status, cancer screening, blood pressure control, and medication adherence. HEDIS includes more than 90 measures across six domains of care:[26]

1. Effectiveness of Care
2. Access /Availability of Care
3. Experience of Care
4. Utilization and Risk Adjusted Utilization
5. Health Plan Descriptive Information
6. Measures Reported Using Electronic Clinical Data Systems

Healthcare quality agencies have developed certifications and tools to monitor quality that have become industry standard to ensure patients receive high-quality care and safety.

Chapter Summary

Effective utilization management and case management lead to better patient outcomes and efficient use of healthcare resources. Nurses lead utilization management teams, while social workers lead case management teams. The cross-disciplinary collaboration between utilization management and case management is vital in maintaining and providing quality care to patients while improving patient outcomes.

Identifiable gaps in healthcare system-based practice are present in care coordination, care transition and interoperability, which lead to poor patient outcomes. The underlying impediment to the effective care coordination and transition of care is the lack of interoperability. Historically, there have been several impediments to achieving interoperability across the U.S. healthcare system, however, recently there have been advances toward achieving this goal.

The Centers for Disease Control and Prevention (CDC) considers violence an urgent public health matter with a goal to stop violence before it begins. The CDC proposes a four-level social-ecological model to understand the multiple factors that increase one's risk for violence. It is critical that healthcare providers receive appropriate training and education on identifying risk factors for violence and addressing violence prevention, as well as recognizing and reporting violence when identified.

The establishment of healthcare quality agencies and quality measurement tools have set the industry standard for healthcare quality and safety monitoring.

REFERENCES

1. Allam S. Advancing Patient-Centered Care: A Nationwide Analysis of Hospital Efficiency and Morbidity Using Innovative Propensity Score Techniques. *Cureus*. 2024;16(12):e76370.
2. Hartman V. What Is Utilization Review. Abstractive Health. December 7, 2022. Accessed February 6, 2025. https://www.abstractivehealth.com/article/what-is-utilization-review
3. Giardino AP, Wadhwa R. Utilization Management. 2023 Jul 10. In: *StatPearls* [Internet]. Treasure Island, FL: StatPearls Publishing; 2025 Jan–. PMID: 32809641.
4. Bailit HL, Sennett C. Utilization Management as a Cost-Containment Strategy. *Health Care Financ Rev*. 1992 Mar;1991(Suppl):87–93. PMID: 25372048; PMCID: PMC4195135.
5. Institute of Medicine (US) Committee on Utilization Management by Third Parties. Controlling Costs and Changing Patient Care? The Role of Utilization Management. Gray BH, Field MJ, ed. Washington, DC: National Academies Press; 1989. PMID: 25144100.
6. Timmins L, Kern LM, O'Malley AS, et al. Communication Gaps Persist Between Primary Care and Specialist Physicians. *Ann Fam Med*. 2022;20(4):343–347. doi: 10.1370/afm.2781. PMID: 35879085; PMCID: PMC9328695.
7. Mansukhani RP, Bridgeman MB, Candelario D, Eckert LJ. Exploring Transitional Care: Evidence-Based Strategies for Improving Provider Communication and Reducing Readmissions. *P T*. 2015 Oct;40(10):690-694. PMID: 26535025; PMCID: PMC4606859.
8. Samal L, Dykes PC, Greenberg JO, et al. Care Coordination Gaps Due To Lack of Interoperability in the United States: A Qualitative Study and Literature Review. BMC *Health Serv Res*. 2016;16:143.
9. Interoperability in Healthcare. HIMSS. Accessed February 6, 2025. https://gkc.himss.org/resources/interoperability-healthcare
10. Stewart BA, Fernandes S, Rodriguez-Huertas E, Landzberg M. A Preliminary Look at Duplicate Testing Associated with Lack of Electronic Health Record Interoperability for Transferred Patients. *J Am Med Inform Assoc*. 2010;17(3):341–344. doi: 10.1136/jamia.2009.001750. PMID: 20442154; PMCID: PMC2995707.
11. Health Information Technology Policy Committee. Report to Congress Challenges and Barriers to Interoperability. December 2015. Accessed February 6, 2025. https://www.healthit.gov/sites/default/files/facas/HITPC_Final_ITF_Report_2015-12-16%20v3.pdf
12. Wang YC, Zenooz A, Sriram RD, Samitt C, Karney M, Johnson W, Goldman J, Gettinger A, Fridsma DB, Bono RC, Palmer S, Johns MME, Pronovost P (eds). National Academy of Medicine; The Learning Health System Series. Procuring Interoperability: Achieving High-Quality, Connected, and Person-Centered Care. Washington, DC: National Academies Press; 2018. PMID: 37733889.
13. Maximizing Data Interoperability and Integration to Support Value-Based Care. March 2020. US DHHS Office of Assistant Secretary for Planning and Evaluation. Accessed February 7, 2025. https://

aspe.hhs.gov/sites/default/files/private/pdf/264456/Data-Integration-Brief.pdf

14. Flarey D. Nursing Case Management and the Utilization Review Role. American Institute of Health Care Professionals. October 14, 2022. Accessed February 7, 2025. https://aihcp.net/2012/05/31/nursing-case-management-and-the-utilization-review-role/
15. Flarey D. Case Management and Utilization Review. American Institute of Health Care Professionals. December 18, 2024. Accessed February 7, 2025. https://aihcp.net/2024/04/05/case-management-and-utilization-review/
16. Violence Prevention: Why Violence Matters to Public Health? Pan American Health Organization. Accessed February 7, 2025. https://www.paho.org/en/topics/violence-prevention
17. Centers for Disease Control and Prevention. Injuries and Violence Are Leading Causes of Death. CDC WISQARS. Accessed February 7, 2025. https://wisqars.cdc.gov/animated-leading-causes/
18. Violence Prevention. CDC. Accessed February 7, 2025. https://www.cdc.gov/violence-prevention/about/index.html
19. About The Public Health Approach to Violence Prevention. CDC. Accessed February 7, 2025. https://www.cdc.gov/violence-prevention/about/about-the-public-health-approach-to-violence-prevention.html
20. Violence Prevention. Healthy People 2030. Accessed February 7, 2025. https://odphp.health.gov/healthypeople/objectives-and-data/browse-objectives/violence-prevention
21. CMS National Quality Strategy. CMS.gov. Accessed February 7, 2025. https://www.cms.gov/medicare/quality/meaningful-measures-initiative/cms-quality-strategy
22. CPHQ: The Certified Professional in Healthcare Quality certification. *NAHQ*. Accessed February 7, 2025. https://nahq.org/credentials/cphq-certified-professional-in-healthcare-quality/
23. The Healthcare Quality Competency Framework. *NAHQ*. Accessed February 7, 2025. https://nahq.org/why-nahq/healthcare-quality-competency-framework/
24. The CAHPS Program. AHRQ. Accessed February 7, 2025. https://www.ahrq.gov/cahps/about-cahps/cahps-program/index.html
25. National Academy of Medicine (NAM) Reports. *AHRQ*. Accessed February 7, 2025. https://www.ahrq.gov/patient-safety/reports/national-academy-medicine.html
26. HEDIS and Performance Measurement. *NCQA*. Accessed February 7, 2025. https://www.ncqa.org/hedis/

CHAPTER 23

Patient Safety, Risk Management, and Peer Review

Brijen J. Shah, MD, AGAF, and Anne Roberts, Esq., CPMSM, CPCS

HALM CORE CONTENT:

- 7.4 Principles of patient safety, methods, and legal aspects of medical staff credentialing and peer review, including Focused Professional Practice Evaluations (FPPE) and Ongoing Professional Practice Evaluations (OPPE)
- 7.7 Risk management principles and programs (e.g., insurance, education, workplace safety, injury management, patient complaints, patient and staff safety, and security)

CASE SCENARIO:

Oceanside Hospital is a mid-size suburban hospital with a growing cancer program. A large gastroenterology group in the area has been providing inpatient consultation and on-call coverage for several years. The group recently hired a new physician who has finished their gastroenterology and advanced endoscopy training. The hospital and cancer program have welcomed this addition, as many cancer patients need advanced GI procedures as part of their cancer care.

During the first six months of the physician being on the medical staff, there have been a series of safety events that have resulted in investigations. In the first event, a patient was scheduled to have two procedures: an ultrasound of the head of the pancreas with a possible biopsy and an exam of the biliary tract with a brushing. The ultrasound and biopsy were performed; however, the exam of the biliary tract was not completed. Once the patient was in the recovery area, the GI physician realized that the patient required a biliary tract exam. The patient was brought back the next day. This event was reviewed by the hospital safety team.

The second event involved a patient with early gastric cancer who was referred for evaluation and possible endoscopic resection. During this procedure, the patient developed a perforation and required emergency surgery to address the issue.

The third case, a week later, occurred during an endoscopic retrograde cholangiopancreatography (ERCP). The sphincter of Oddi required an incision to remove the stone during a gallstone removal. The patient developed a post-procedure bleed 24 hours later. The nurse in the room noted during the debrief that the physician required multiple attempts to insert the catheter into the bile duct.

HEALTHCARE LEADERS MUST TAKE a broad view of patient safety and risk management in their leadership roles. Enterprise risk management encompasses patient safety and extends beyond this to the workforce and the environment of care. This chapter uses Reason's Swiss Cheese Model of Defense as a foundation for all safety and risk mitigation work and shares tools to examine a safety breach. Specific domains of risk management are then explored, including clinical performance management, malpractice, employee safety, and patient grievances.

Risk identification, analysis, and continuous monitoring are crucial to mitigating risks. An important part of risk mitigation includes ensuring the organization has developed a culture and structure for staff to feel comfortable reporting safety concerns, which is another essential duty of physician leaders. In this chapter, the principles of patient safety and risk management are discussed, and the importance of linking these principles to credentialing and peer review is explored. A crucial component of a solid peer review program is proactively developing comprehensive risk assessment processes that monitor not only individual provider performance or specialty-specific metrics, but also identify risks to the organization.

Principles of Patient Safety

Patient safety is the reduction of the risk of unnecessary harm associated with the process of healthcare to an acceptable minimum per the World Health Organization (WHO report).[1] These events include "errors," "deviations," and "accidents."[2] Patient safety events occur due to human interactions and multiple systems interacting to deliver healthcare. The field of patient safety encompasses reporting events, analyzing patient safety events, developing a culture of safety, and creating safety solutions.[3]

James Reason's Theory of Active and Latent Failures describes how systems and humans interact, leading to safety events.[4] Care is delivered through the coordination of many systems. Each system has safety barriers such as engineering controls (alarms), procedures (double checks), or administrative controls (policies) to safeguard from an event. Humans interact with these systems, and ideally, these safety barriers will prevent an adverse event.

Even with the best design, each system has a vulnerability or a hole in its design, like a slice of Swiss cheese. These vulnerabilities set up a condition for a potential safety event or a latent condition. These conditions are often hidden and do not reveal themselves until they are combined with human action or other latent conditions. Reason described two types of latent conditions: one condition that can set up for an error (time pressure, fatigue, high volume) and the permanent destruction of a safeguard (inaccurate measurement devices, low sensitivity alarms).

Active failures are the actions of humans who come in contact with the system.[5] These actions can be blatant violations of a safety process, a "workaround" or "shortcut," slip, lapse, or mistake. The majority of safety events are a combination of active failures and one or more latent conditions (Figure 1).

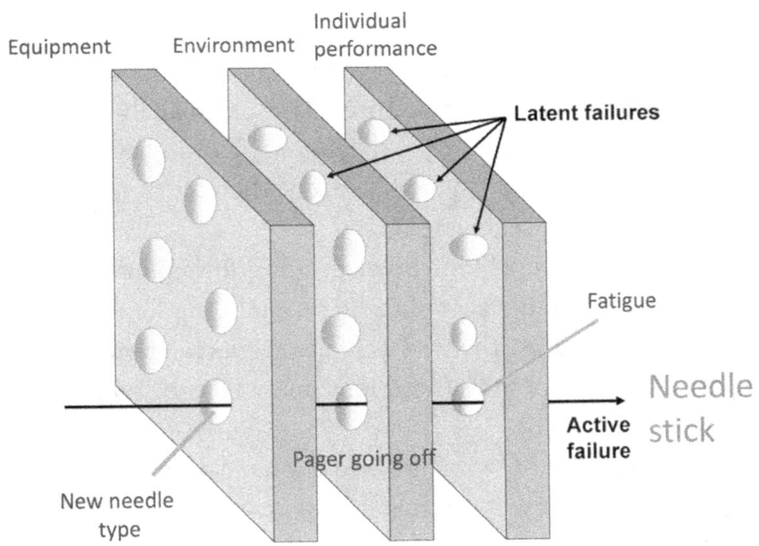

FIGURE 1. Swiss Cheese Model of Defense.[4]

A safety culture is a core component of developing structure and processes, and ultimately, defining outcomes for patient and staff to mitigate risk. The ability of patients, families, and staff to speak up if there is a possible or actual safety condition is a foundation of safety culture.

Organizations need mechanisms for front-line staff and consumers to be able to report if there is a safety, ethical, or compliance concern. These systems, often electronic, should be secure and easy to use. They should collect key information and route it to relevant stakeholders for information and investigation. Most systems have an anonymous and confidential mechanism of reporting. Organizations should safeguard privacy risks when designing and implementing these systems and safeguard reporters from retaliation.[6] A patient safety organization is one structure that facilitates this effort.

TOOLS FOR PATIENT SAFETY ANALYSIS

Several tools are available to help analyze patient safety. Two tools that The Joint Commission references for patient safety are the failure modes effect analysis (FMEA) and root cause analysis (RCA).

FMEA uses a multidisciplinary team discussion to look for potential risks and the likelihood of detecting the risks.[7] Once the team identifies the greatest risk points in a process, the team develops solutions to decrease the risk. This tool is useful when redesigning a complex process or when creating a new process.

The process begins with a process map. At each step, participants consider what could go wrong (failure mode), why it could go wrong, and what the consequence would be. For each failure, participants rate the likelihood of occurrence, detection, and severity. A risk profile number (RPN) is then calculated as a product of each of the likelihoods. The processes with the largest RPNs should be the focus of the redesign.

A root cause analysis (RCA) is a structured, fact-based analysis that identifies the causal linkages from the consequence to the underlying root causes(s) and identifies the corrective actions that, if taken, will prevent the recurrence of this particular consequence and related consequences.[7]

This tool is used retrospectively and involves a multidisciplinary team. The process has three phases: collecting the facts of the case, analyzing the facts for root causes, and developing safety solutions. The case facts and events can be depicted in a timeline or a process map. A variety of tools (described below) can be created to capture and depict causes (Figures 2 and 3).

The 5 Whys: The question of "why" is asked to elucidate the cause of an event and then asked again for each cause — up to five times —to get to granular causes.[8]

Fishbone/Ishikawa Diagram: This line diagram (Figure 2) categorizes contributors to the safety event. The event is placed in the "head" of the fish. Teams brainstorm to create a list of factors that caused the event and then categorize them into larger groups such as materials, people, processes, technology, and equipment. The 5 Whys strategy can be used for each item on the fishbone to get to more detail.

Causal Tree: This tool is a logic diagram (Figure 3) that lists the event at the top and then asks a series of whys for two or three levels to hone in on the key specific reasons for an event. These causes can then be classified into broader categories such as human resource, process, policy, education, etc.

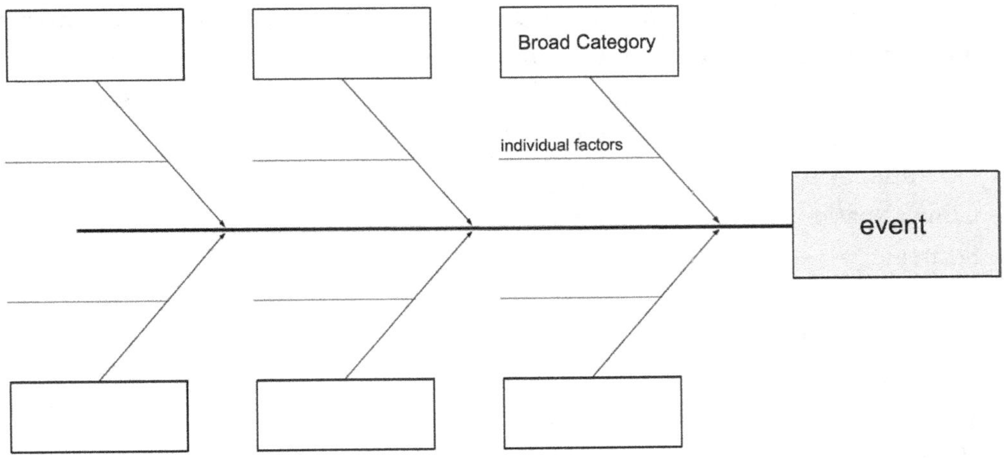

FIGURE 2. Fishbone Diagram

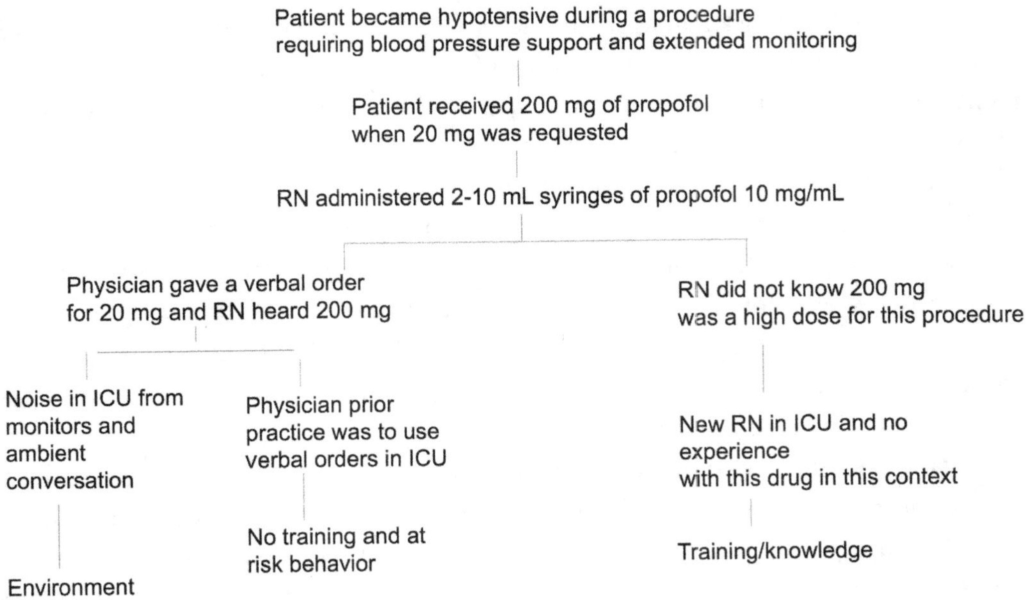

FIGURE 3. Causal Tree Example

Risk Management: Principles and Programs

While healthcare's primary focus on risk management has been on the safe delivery of care, healthcare organizations have had to develop programs for the entire enterprise. The purpose of an enterprise risk management program is to detect, monitor, assess, mitigate, and prevent risks in the clinical and administrative arenas.[9] Pandemics, cyber-attacks, and threats to supply chains are some of the forces that have required healthcare organizations to shift from a reactive to a proactive approach. The Joint Commission requires an emergency planning structure and process for each organization.[10]

The American Society of Healthcare Risk Management defines enterprise risk management according to the following domains:[11]

- Operational
- Clinical/patient safety
- Strategic
- Financial
- Human capital
- Legal/Regulatory
- Technology
- Hazard

Technology can assist healthcare organizations in mitigating risks. Data analytics help clarify risk, prioritize vulnerabilities, and make decisions and investments.

An organizational risk management plan should include education and training of all staff during initial orientation and annually thereafter at minimum. Risk management and risk mitigation are an important part of the daily responsibilities of executive physician leaders and administrative executives, including how to aggregate data that identifies risks and develop solutions for risk mitigation.

The U.S. Congress passed the Patient Safety and Quality Improvement Act (PSQIA) to develop effective strategies for reducing medical errors and increasing patient safety.[12] The Agency for Healthcare Research and Quality, a significant part of PSQIA, created patient safety organizations (PSOs), federally listed third-party agencies that work with providers to improve quality and safety through the collection and analysis of aggregated, confidential data on patient safety events.

Organizations use patient safety evaluation systems (PSES) to collect incident reports, near-miss reports, and other patient safety events to help them identify potential risks and opportunities for improvement. The metrics collected in the PSES are then reported confidentially to the PSO contracted by the organization. The PSO provides feedback aimed at promoting learning and preventing future patient safety events.

Another key component of PSQIA is the identification of patient safety work product (PSWP). PSWP includes but is not limited to data, reports, analysis data (such as root cause analysis), written and oral statements, and other data collected in an effort to improve patient safety, healthcare quality, or outcomes.

The data, which must include information related to the organization's deliberations and analysis of the data, is assembled for reporting to a PSO analysis. Information that is PSWP is considered legally privileged, meaning it is not subject to subpoena in civil, criminal, or administrative proceedings and not subject to legal discovery or the Freedom of Information Act. Organizations can disclose PSWP to a PSO without needing patient authorization; however, the safe handling of identifiable patient information is still mandatory under the provisions of the Healthcare Insurance Portability and Accountability Act (HIPAA).[13]

The Centers for Medicare and Medicaid Services (CMS) sets forth specified requirements for participating hospitals, including a formal process for addressing patient complaints and grievances and the duties and responsibilities of the medical staff to oversee the quality of care provided to patients.[14]

Timely response to patient and family grievances is another key component that is coordinated across clinical and administrative departments. The Joint Commission requires hospitals to respond to patient complaints and grievances in seven days and to share aggregate trends and metrics with the governing body. The review of complaints should include a clinical review of care and a review of standards of service. Leaders need to be vigilant about complaints, concerns, and safety risks being shared online and should have a monitoring plan for this medium.

The hospital needs an internal and external communication plan for risks and threats. The regulatory function of a hospital will need to submit reports to external agencies such as county, state, and federal agencies, when there is a sentinel event or breech.

Occupational and employee health are key components of a risk management plan. All healthcare workers face an increasing number of occupational risks and may suffer physical and mental harm as a result. They should undergo annual health assessments and any identified risk should result in a mitigation plan for the employee. Staff should be offered personal protective equipment and vaccinations commensurate with risk in their role.

The security service helps to ensure staff and patient safety. This service, often contracted to a third party, will help with patient flow, and visitor management, and ensure that only credentialed employees and vendors are permitted into the building. Security services include identifying and handling any materials that may be hazardous to the environment, such as firearms, and will partner with local services and emergency management in planning for and responding to emergencies.

With an increase in workplace-based healthcare violence, security team members may be called to assist in helping to manage the violent or aggressive patient, family member, or staff member. Leaders should include security has part of their risk mitigation plans.[15]

Credentialing and Peer Review

Preliminary screening and credentialing are the first steps in identifying potential risks to patients and to the organization. The Joint Commission (TJC), the primary accrediting body for most hospitals across the nation, mandates that the organized medical staff oversee the quality of patient care, treatment, and services provided by physicians and other licensed practitioners privileged through the medical staff process.[10]

GUIDANCE FOR PRE-SCREENING

Prior to issuing a credentialing application, the hospital should conduct a preliminary analysis to evaluate the education, training, and qualifications for each practitioner. Conducting thorough interviews can help physician leaders confirm that the practitioners' training and experience align with the expectations of the clinical setting in which they will be working and will be able to meet the needs of the patient population.

Asking probing questions during an interview, such as whether they have ever been investigated or disciplined by a state medical board or any healthcare organization, what their malpractice history includes, and discussing their prior clinical experience can help them make an informed decision *prior to* extending a credentialing application.

Ask the provider to submit a copy of a self-query of the National Practitioner Data Bank (NPDB). The U.S. Department of Health and Human Services (HHS) mandates that state medical boards, malpractice companies, and hospitals report specific disciplinary actions or malpractice settlements to the NPDB. All hospitals are required to also query the NPDB as a part of the credentialing and re-credentialing process.[16] It is important to note, however, that despite it being a national law, many organizations fail to appropriately report peer review actions to the NPDB, which is one of many reasons a thorough credentialing process is essential.

ENSURING THOROUGH CREDENTIALING PRACTICES

Once a credentialing application is received, the credentialing process includes a comprehensive gathering of information through primary source verifications as it relates to education, work history, criminal background checks (and a review of any civil cases that may involve crimes of moral turpitude), and verification of all current and prior licenses, certifications, etc.

When granting clinical privileges, an organization should obtain clinical evaluations from program directors or recent department chairs to assess the applicant's *current* clinical competence for the privileges requested (not just peer references). In addition to clinical evaluations, case logs are typically requested to demonstrate recent clinical experience, to confirm they've had sufficient clinical activity over the last 12-24 months, and to presume they've maintained their current clinical skills at a level expected to exercise the privileges that they have requested.

Any issues or concerns that are identified during the credentialing process are called "red flags." It is the duty and the responsibility of the medical staff (department chair or physician designee and the credentials committee) to thoroughly evaluate the totality of information, with a high focus on any red flags, to identify potential future risks to patient safety or to the organization, and to make a determination on their current clinical competence before granting clinical privileges. Failing to identify or take red flags into consideration, and/or failure to confirm current clinical competence prior to granting clinical privileges can lead to allegations of negligent credentialing.

Initial Focused Professional Practice Evaluation

Subsequently, upon initial grant of clinical privileges, all practitioners must undergo an initial focused professional practice evaluation (FPPE), a comprehensive process of closely monitoring the overall performance of new practitioners during their initial review period (typically set by organizations as four to six months). An initial FPPE is also required when a practitioner requests new/additional privileges.

An initial FPPE should include reviewing a specified number of clinical cases that span the scope of the clinical privileges granted and a full assessment that follows the six-general competencies set by the ACGME.[17]

Ongoing Professional Practice Evaluations

A comprehensive ongoing professional practice evaluation (OPPE) process is essential and includes monitoring clinical performance metrics and complications, as well as all practitioner performance data (e.g., patient satisfaction scores, patient complaints and grievances, compliance with the bylaws, policies, and procedures, etc.).

The gathering of OPPE data begins immediately upon the granting of clinical privileges and The Joint Commission requires organizations to evaluate the data at least annually. When issues arise through the OPPE process, the medical staff should determine the appropriate action based on the practitioner's prior performance history and the significance of the issue at hand, and identify if there are any hospital/system issues that need to be addressed.

Often, significant concerns related to a practitioner's clinical competence may lead to a "for cause" FPPE, often viewed as a remediation plan, which may or may not include a formal restriction of clinical privileges. Medical staff leaders can use the OPPE process to evaluate at that time whether clinical privileges should continue to be granted to the practitioner. For example, do they have sufficient volume to measure quality outcomes and thus justify the continued grant of privileges, are there concerns that require the initiation of an investigation, etc.?

ADDRESSING PERFORMANCE CONCERNS

Many factors that are taken into consideration include the significance of the issue/ patient harm that occurred, an immediate risk to patient safety, or a pattern or trend

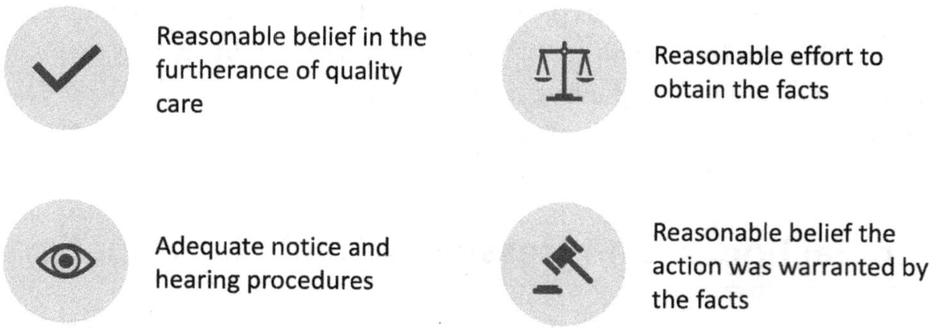

FIGURE 4. Healthcare Quality Improvement Act Standards

of behaviors or performance concerns with this practitioner. Organizations also must balance ensuring that the practitioner's rights are protected and organizational policies and the medical staff bylaws are followed consistently across the hospital for all practitioners, ensuring a fair peer review process using Just Culture principles.

Organizational performance enhancement policies may set forth a suggested progressive action plan for addressing these matters, such as starting with a peer-to-peer conversation for minor issues or concerns (when no prior issues are noted), then stepping up to formal collegial intervention/coaching conversation with the physician's direct supervisor and then considering a formal remediation plan (for cause FPPE).

In the case of egregious concerns or a discernable pattern or trend that's concerning, a progressive approach may not be an option and immediate action may be warranted. Certain actions taken such as mandating proctoring via direct observation, requiring the plan of care be approved in advance are considered a limitation or restriction of clinical privileges. Depending on the circumstances, these actions may be reportable to the state medical board or to the NPDB. However, it is important that the medical staff evaluate the issue, determine the appropriate course of action to protect patients, the wellness of the practitioner, and the organization, and *then* evaluate if the action is then reportable.

PEER REVIEW LEGAL PROTECTIONS

The FPPE and OPPE processes are components to an organization's overall performance enhancement (peer review) program. In evaluating legal protections, the peer review statutes in each state may vary so it is important to consult with legal counsel when considering corrective or disciplinary action.

At the federal level, the Healthcare Quality Improvement Act (HCQIA)[18] offers immunity against civil litigation damages to physicians and hospitals that participate in peer review if the peer review process meets a four-way test (Figure 4).

Chapter Summary

In sum, linking risk management principles to credentialing, privileging, and peer review is an essential duty for all organizations to ensure safe, quality patient care. Risk analysis is done at the time of recruitment/onboarding and credentialing; risk identification and mitigation are ongoing processes that have many components, including assessment of provider-specific concerns, system errors that may contribute to patient safety events, and evaluating the overall risk to the organization.

REFERENCES

1. World Health Organization. The Conceptual Framework for the International Classification for Patient Safety. January 15, 2009. Accessed February 5, 2025. https://www.who.int/publications/i/item/WHO-IER-PSP-2010.2 on.
2. Cooper JB, Gaba DM, Liang B, et al. The National Patient Safety Foundation Agenda for Research and Development in Patient Safety. *MedGenMed*. 2000;2(3):E38.
3. Hershey K. Culture of Safety. *Nurs Clin North Am*. 2015;50(1):139–152. doi: 10.1016/j.cnur.2014.10.011. Epub 2014 Dec 2. PMID: 25680493.
4. Reason J. Human Error: Models and Management. *BMJ*. 2000;320(7237):768–770. doi: 10.1136/bmj.320.7237.768. PMID: 10720363; PMCID: PMC1117770.
5. Reason J. *Human Error*. New York: Cambridge University Press; 1990.
6. Health Quality Ontario. Patient Safety Learning Systems: A Systematic Review and Qualitative Synthesis. *Ont Health Technol Assess Ser*. 2017 Mar 1;17(3):1–23. PMID: 28326148; PMCID: PMC5357133.
7. Root Cause Analysis. *PSNet* [internet]. Rockville, MD: Agency for Healthcare Research and Quality, US Department of Health and Human Services. 2019.
8. Card AJ. The Problem with "5 Whys." *BMJ Quality & Safety*. 2017;26:671–677.
9. What is Risk Management in Healthcare? *NEJM Catalyst*. April 25, 2018. https://catalyst.nejm.org/doi/full/10.1056/CAT.18.0197
10. Joint Commission on Accreditation of Healthcare Organizations. *Comprehensive Accreditation Manual for Hospitals: The Official Handbook*, 2025 ed. Oak Brook, IL: Joint Commission Resources; 2024.
11. Enterprise Risk Management. American Society for Health Care Risk Management. Accessed February 6, 2025. https://www.ashrm.org/system/files?file=media/file/2019/06/ERM-Tool_final.pdf
12. Agency for Healthcare Research and Quality. (2021, November). Strategies to Improve Patient Safety: Draft Report to Congress. November 2021. Accessed January 31, 2025. https://pso.ahrq.gov/sites/default/files/wysiwyg/strategies-to-improve-patient-safety_draft-report.pdf
13. Understanding Patient Safety Confidentiality. U.S. Department of Health & Human Services. Accessed January 31, 2025. https://www.hhs.gov/hipaa/for-professionals/patient-safety/index.html#:~:text=Enforces%20confidentiality%20protections%20for%20%E2%80%9Cpatient,of%20the%20Delegation%20of%20Authority.
14. Title 42, Chapter IV, Subchapter G, Part 482. (n.d.). In *Code of Federal Regulations*. essay. Retrieved from https://www.ecfr.gov/current/title-42/chapter-IV/subchapter-G/part-482.
15. White KR, Griffith JR. *The Well-Managed Healthcare Organization*. Chicago, IL: American College of Healthcare Executives; 2019: 381-382.
16. U.S. Department of Health and Human Services. National Practitioner Data Bank. Accessed January 12, 2025. https://www.npdb.hrsa.gov/
17. Correa R, Curran M, Eno C, Graese P, et al. Milestones Guidebook for Residents and Fellows.

American College of Graduate Medical Education. Accessed January 12, 2025. https://www.acgme.org/globalassets/pdfs/milestones/milestonesguidebookforresidentsfellows.pdf

18. H.R.5540 - 99th Congress (1985-1986): Health Care Quality Improvement Act of 1986 | congress.gov | library of Congress. (n.d.-a). Accessed January 12, 2025. https://www.congress.gov/bill/99th-congress/house-bill/5540.

CHAPTER 24

Quality and Quality Improvement

Daniel A. Handel, MD, MBA, MPH, CPE

HALM CORE CONTENT:

- 7.5 Process and quality improvement principles, measurement tools, and techniques (e.g., plan-do-study-act, lean daily management, Six Sigma)
- 7.6 Quality program leadership, strategic planning, operations, and financing

CASE SCENARIO:

An organization is focused on reducing central line-associated bloodstream infections (CLABSIs). Because the data aren't available until almost a month after the fact, it is challenging to use such a lagging metric alone to drive change. What leading daily or weekly metrics can the organization use? It turns out the measurements of insertion and maintenance line bundle compliance are leading process metrics and have a high correlation with CLABSI rates. How do the units with central lines track these on a continuous basis to drive improvement? What daily standard work and huddles create visibility and accountability around these leading indicators?

QUALITY IMPROVEMENT WORK is a core part of physician leaders' responsibility, whether they are front-line practicing clinicians, medical directors, or working at the level of a chief quality officer or chief medical officer. While the focus on quality improvement may primarily be on the efforts of other physicians within the healthcare organization, it is important for physician leaders to work closely with nursing and other dyad/triad leaders to ensure efforts are aligned toward a larger set of common objectives and goals. For example, quality improvement and patient satisfaction are frequently the primary focus of dyad work with nursing leaders.[1]

The history of healthcare quality improvement dates back to the time of Hippocrates, advancing to Florence Nightingale's infection control practices during the Crimean War, likely influenced by the work of Ignaz Semmelweis a couple of decades prior, and Jonathan Letterman's battlefield triaging model during the American Civil War.[2,3] In 1910, Abraham Flexner, under the aegis of the Carnegie Foundation, issued his seminal report with recommendations that transformed the medical education system and, in the process, closed half of the existing medical schools that did not meet the new quality standards.[4]

Almost a century later, the Institute of Medicine (IOM) released two reports that quantified the extent of errors and harm to patients in the U.S. healthcare system. In the first, *To Err is Human: Building a Safer Health System*, published in 1999, the IOM estimated that as many as 98,000 people died annually in hospitals due to medical errors that could have been prevented.[5]

In 2001, the IOM released a more detailed report that further fleshed out the foundational problems within the U.S. healthcare system. *Crossing the Quality Chasm: A New Health System for the 21st Century* emphasized how underuse, overuse, and misuse of treatments and resources drove the poor-quality outcomes. To combat this, the IOM recommended improvement in six dimensions: patient safety, care effectiveness, patient-centeredness, timeliness, efficiency, and equity.[6]

These dimensions, which have come to be known as the six domains of quality healthcare, have evolved into an analytical framework upon which quality improvement efforts have been structured since the start of the 21st century.[7]

In this chapter, guiding principles and processes will be defined, along with tools and measurement techniques to drive sustained improvements in a complex setting such as healthcare.

Process and Quality Improvement Principles

The study and history of quality improvement extends well beyond healthcare, with many lessons to be learned from other high-reliability industries such as aviation and manufacturing.[8] W. Edwards Deming is considered the father of modern quality improvement work through the manufacturing techniques he developed in the 1940s that subsequently spread to other industries, including healthcare.

The World Health Organization (WHO) defines quality of care as "the degree to which health services for individuals and populations increase the likelihood of desired health outcomes."[9] As a healthcare organization and its leaders engage in quality improvement work, four principles frame the process:[10]

- The healthcare system is complex.
- The focus is on the patient.

- Data drive improvement.
- Healthcare must be delivered by teams, not individuals.

In 1993, in what would be the last year of Deming's life, he stated at a seminar in Phoenix, "A bad system will beat a good person every time."[11] Therefore, it is incumbent upon physician leaders to develop systems and processes where the path of least resistance for work drives optimal quality outcomes for every patient every time. In other words, relying on individual efforts of teams and providers will not lead to sustained and consistent outcomes. Failures will happen, so it is important that the physician leader focuses on the processes that need to be reviewed and revised and resists the urge to assign personal blame for failures.

Quality improvement is hard work. Managing large, highly educated teams of people who have been trained to lead as individuals requires an intentional approach over a long period of time. To be effective, the team should create specific, measurable, attainable, relevant, and timely (SMART) goals and hold themselves accountable for achieving them. As Peter Drucker famously said, "You can't improve what you don't measure."

Quality Measurement Tools

Kaoru Ishikawa, an engineering professor at Tokyo University, emphasized seven quality improvement tools:[12]

- Cause-and-effect diagram (also known as fishbone): Used to identify possible causes and sort them into categories (see Figure 1).

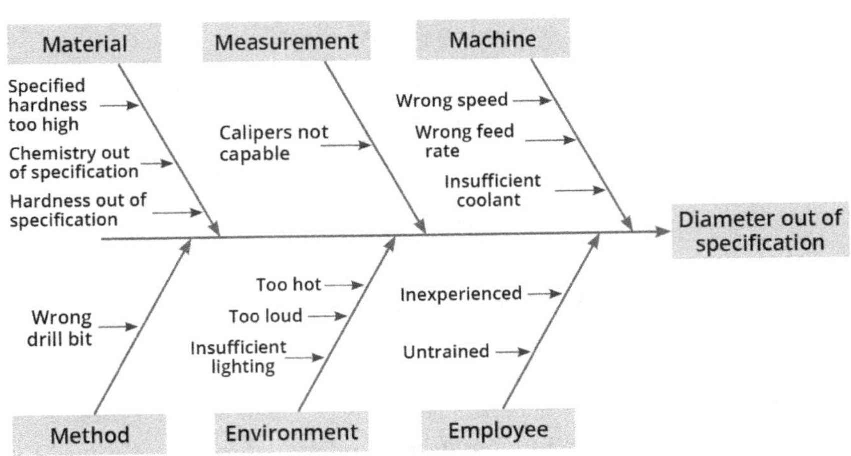

FIGURE 1. Fishbone Diagram Example

- Check sheet: A structured way to collect and analyze data used for a wide range of purposes.

- Control chart: Used to look over time process changes; delineate whether or not the variation is caused by common or special causes (see Figure 2).

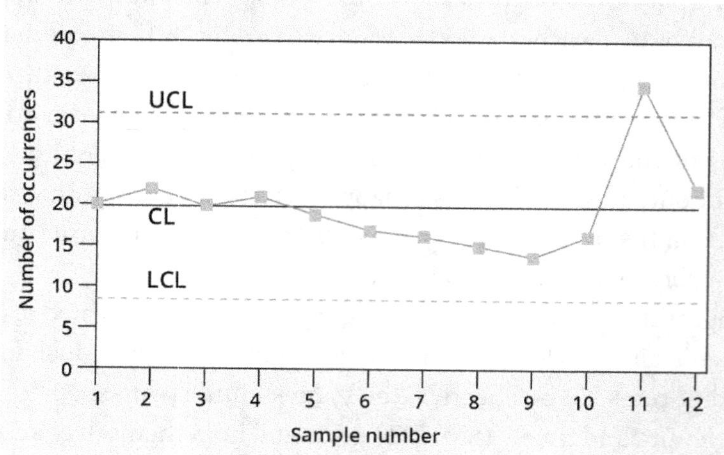

FIGURE 2. Control Chart Example

- Histogram: Used to present frequency distributions (see Figure 3).

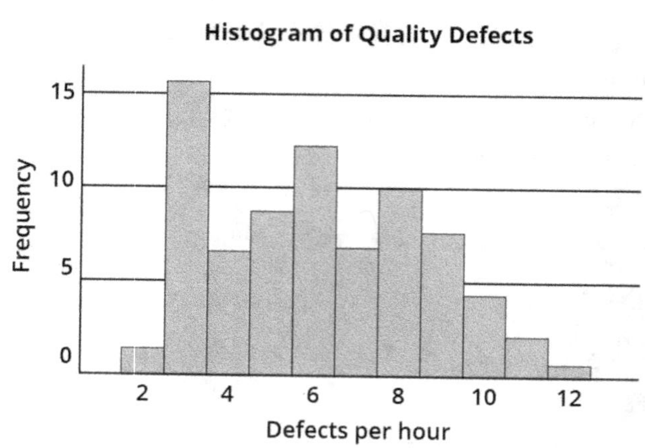

FIGURE 3. Histogram Example

- Pareto chart: Prioritizes the most significant factors (see Figure 4). The Pareto Principle states that 20% of the errors typically cause 80% of the problems.
- Scatter diagram: Pairs data when looking for relationships (see Figure 5).
- Stratification: Separates data to better visualize patterns (see Figure 6).

The greatest challenge in quality improvement work is that measurement results for most key performance indicators (KPIs) are lagging in nature, which means that corrective efforts are reactive, occurring long after the patient has been affected. To

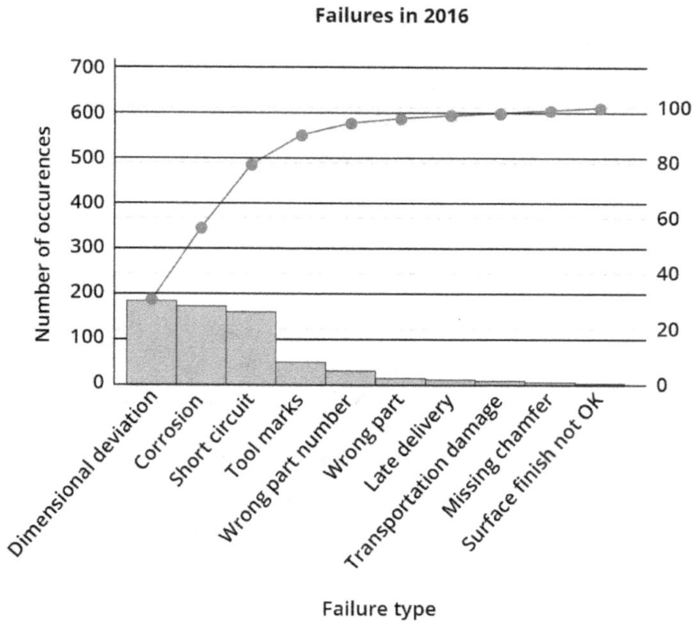

FIGURE 4. Pareto Chart Template Example

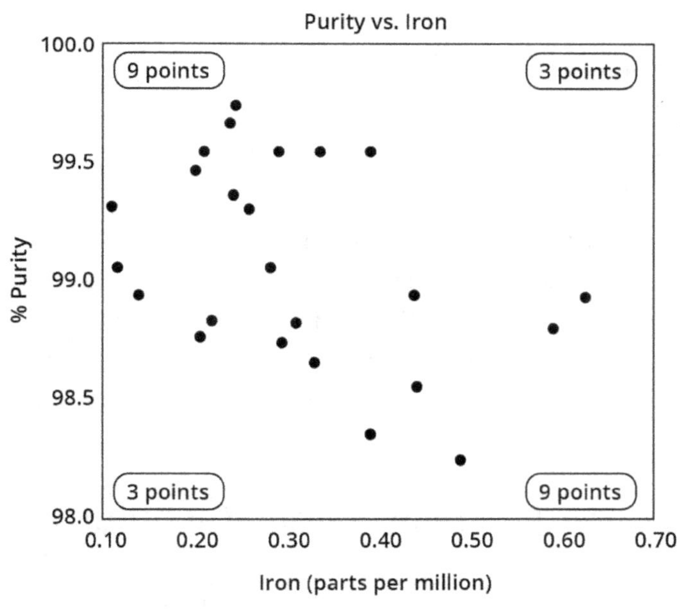

FIGURE 5. Scatter Diagram Example

drive quality improvement, it is important to identify leading metrics that can be measured and tracked daily or weekly and that, if performed well, will improve the KPIs.

Using tools such as the four disciplines of execution outlined below, quality improvement teams can create standard daily work with transparent metrics and clear lines of accountability. The four disciplines of execution are:[13]

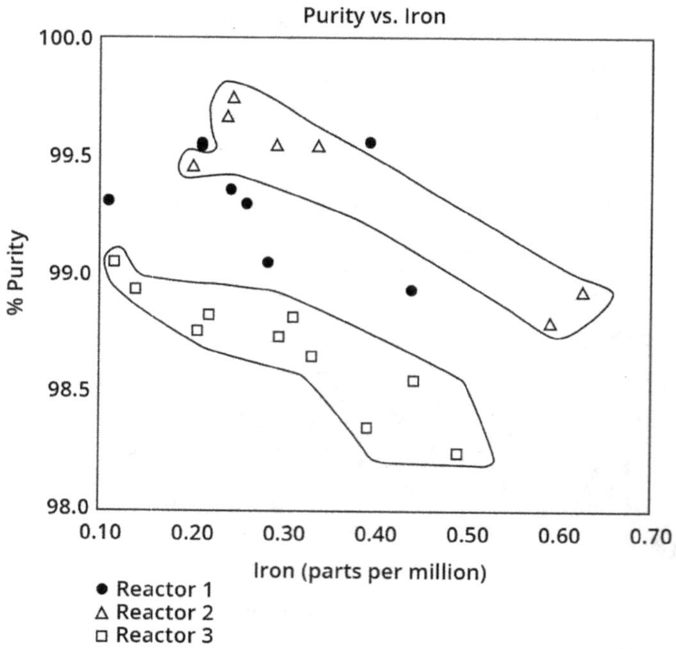

FIGURE 6. Stratification Diagram

- Focus on the wildly important goals (WIGs).
- Act on the lead measures.
- Keep a compelling scoreboard.
- Create a cadence of accountability.

A related strategy is the use of objective and key results (OKRs). Created by Andy Grove during his tenure at Intel and based on the work of Peter Drucker,[14] OKRs force quality improvement efforts to quantify what the objective is (the lagging metric) and how it will be accomplished by achieving one or more measurable key results (leading metrics). To drive a cadence of progress, it is ideal to set deadlines for every key result to ensure the timely completion of the work.

Quality Measurement Techniques

Plan-Do-Study-Act (PDSA) cycles are frequently used to create a cadence of continual improvement. Also known as the Deming Wheel or Deming Cycle, this tool was first used at Bell Laboratories in New York in 1939.[15]

In the planning step, teams identify what needs to be accomplished, define what success looks like from a metrics perspective, and then put the plan into action. During the "do" stage, teams collect data as the plan is implemented.

During the study phase, the team reflects on what outcomes were achieved and validates what succeeded and failed in the plan while identifying possible areas for improvement. Finally, the cycle loop is closed in the act phase, where the lessons learned are analyzed and integrated into the process for the next cycle of planning, which starts the cycle all over again. With this continuously iterative process, the hope and intent are that the quality process and metric performance will perpetually improve over time.

As a corollary to the four disciplines of execution, creating a *lean daily management* system in the healthcare setting is a highly effective tool to connect the standard daily work of front-line caregivers to the organization's larger KPIs. Lean daily management must be directed to look at all work being done throughout the day and classify it as value-added, non-valued added but necessary, and waste.[16] Waste must be eliminated to the extent possible.

Lean daily management systems have four main tools:[17]

- Daily Accountability Process: A tiered huddle structure starting at the local unit level identifies and then escalates issues so that they can be resolved in real time before they negatively affect patient care. This holds front-line team members and leaders accountable for fixing problems.
- Leader Standard Work: What are the actions a leader must perform on a daily, weekly, or monthly basis to keep the organization on track toward improvement? Creating a standard cadence for this work ensures that a leader does not always get pulled into the whirlwind of constant crises that arise in a busy healthcare setting and instead remains focused on the larger strategic direction of the organization.
- Gemba Walks: Gemba is the Japanese term for "actual place" and emphasizes the importance of healthcare leaders physically going to where the work is being done. If a physician leader continues to work clinically, this is one source of feedback, but the perspective should not be limited to one specialty if the scope of the leader's oversight is broad.

  A physician leader who is no longer doing clinical work should intentionally block out time to regularly round in the clinical areas under their purview and create a system to gather input to close the loop on issues identified in the process.
- Process Confirmation: A system must be established to ensure critical processes are being followed consistently. This can be accomplished through observation and data tools to measure as close to real-time as possible.

Six Sigma methodology is a quality improvement tool that uses statistics, financial analysis, and project management to identify and reduce errors, thereby improving quality and efficiency.

This methodology was first used in the manufacturing industry at Motorola in the 1980s. It then spread to finance and eventually to healthcare. While Six Sigma focuses on optimizing process control and reducing process variation, adding lean methodology, adopted from the Toyota Production System (Lean Six Sigma), focuses more on defect prevention rather than simply defect detection.

Several Six Sigma tools can drive process improvements:[18]

- DMAIC: This methodology uses data to improve processes. The phases are (1) Define the problem, goals, etc.; (2) Measure the process's performance; (3) Analyze the process to identify causes of poor performance; (4) Improve process performance by addressing and eliminating the identified causes; and (5) Control the improved process and future performance.
- 5S: When used in Lean Six Sigma, the 5Ss refer to the five Japanese words to create a clean, uncluttered work environment that reduces waste and improves safety and productivity. The words are (1) Seiri (separate needed tools from unneeded ones); (2) Seiton (neatly arrange parts and tools to ease use); (3) Seiso (clean up the work area); (4) Seiketsu (conduct the first 3Ss daily to maintain the work area); and (5) Shitsuke (form the habit of following the first 4Ss).
- Seven Wastes (Muda): In Lean Six Sigma, the seven wastes to eliminate are: (1) overproduction, (2) waiting, (3) unnecessary materials transport, (4) over-processing due to poor design, (5) high inventory, (6) unnecessary movement of people, and (7) defective part production.
- Value Stream Mapping: By mapping out the current process, one can identify what waste exists. Based on this information, a future state map can be created to improve process efficiencies.
- Flow: This is an analysis of how tasks move along in the value stream, looking for ways to improve along the way.
- Visual Workplace: By creating an environment where information can be better shared, better precision and reliability lead to quality and safety improvements.
- Voice of the Customer: All processes should be designed with the needs of the customer (patient) in mind.

Quality Program Leadership

As organizations transition from a volume-based to a value-based model, the leaders of the organization's quality management program need to be intentional in its design and organizational structure. According to the Institute for Healthcare Improvement, there are five high-impact leadership behaviors:[19]

- Person-centeredness
- Front-line engagement
- Relentless focus
- Transparency
- Boundarilessness

From a top-down perspective, the senior-most leaders need to align organization-level goals and incentives to drive quality improvement. Given the current CMS value-based programs,[20] there is a strong financial reason to focus on quality in addition to the long-standing moral imperative.

The organization's leadership must also devote a sufficient amount of personnel and infrastructure resources to ensure that the designated quality-improvement team has sufficient time and support to focus on the long and endless journey of quality improvement. Leaders must also be present on the front lines on a regular basis through Gemba walks to see firsthand how the work is executed.

From a bottom-up viewpoint, how do front-line leaders connect the standard daily work they do to quality improvement efforts? Investing in dashboards that connect leading process metrics to larger KPIs on a daily basis and maintaining transparency and clear accountability will drive ongoing improvement. The focus needs to be on the data and what systemic barriers exist, not on who is responsible for the failures.

Leaning on dyad/triad leadership teams at all levels is essential to ensure a collaborative approach is taken by defining what roles and respective metrics need to be accomplished to improve quality outcomes. Only through a unified multidisciplinary front can boundaries be removed and the focus be squarely on improving processes rather than on assigning blame.

Quality Strategic Planning

As with any strategic plan, it is important for healthcare organizations to think about and plan for not only what their quality goals are for the upcoming year but also where they want to be three to five years in the future. Several factors play into this long-term target, most importantly the population health needs of the communities they serve. This can be determined in part through a community health needs assessment, which is required at least every three years to maintain tax-exempt status in nonprofit organizations.

In terms of outcome metrics, life expectancy rates are at the highest level. How do those of the community compare to the state, region, and nation? If levels are lower, what can the organization do to drive improvement?

Breaking down where the greatest opportunities for improvement lie is the first step for action planning, which can then focus the work moving forward. Are there particular social drivers of health, including patient populations from particular racial, gender, or ethnic backgrounds, that have worse outcomes? What are their barriers to receiving high-quality care?

Next, what are the chronic comorbidities that burden the community? What is driving an increase in emergency department and hospitalization rates, and what can be done to shift the curve to keep patients at home and in more preventive health settings?

While much of health continues to be reimbursed on a volume basis, the future is in value-based care, so it is not a question of if, but when healthcare payer reimbursements will pass the tipping point in that direction. Healthcare organizations that plan for that inevitable reality will not only be ahead of their competitors but more proactive at addressing the community's needs earlier.

A hierarchal model that can be adopted starts with the individual patient in mind, looking at how access and personal accountability intersect to drive improved outcomes. Built on top of that is institutional management, which then rolls up to regional and national work (see Figure 7).[21]

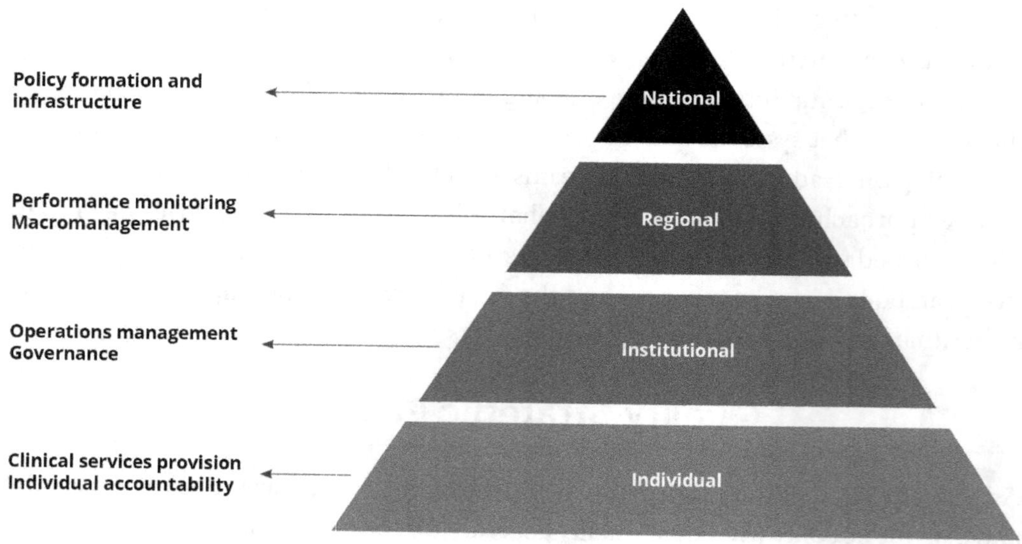

FIGURE 7. Hierarchical Model of Patient Care

Quality Operations

Quality improvement must be incorporated into daily and long-term operations and not be seen as separate from it. A quality improvement effort not only improves patient outcomes but represents a sound business strategy perspective as it reduces waste and improves financial outcomes. Quality improvement is a part of the holistic model to deliver high-value care by decreasing variation, inappropriate care, preventable injury and death, and waste.[22]

The foundation of quality operations is creating and sustaining a data infrastructure that drives improvement. As discussed earlier in this chapter, the opportunity for improvement must be defined with SMART goals set to be accomplished by a certain date (OKRs). Organizations must have the discipline to define these goals early and stick to them.

Goals should not be created in a leadership vacuum; they must involve front-line staff, who will not only help define the appropriate goals but will engage them in the work. Every organization should have project champions at multiple levels who believe in the importance of the work and who can spread enthusiasm across the organization.

With interventions designed to target the root causes, PDSA cycles need to be created to measure results, adjust, and continuously learn and iterate. If improvement stalls, then the processes are not designed correctly; the right process makes doing the right thing easy.

Physician leaders should celebrate wins with their teams and continuously connect the work occurring at the front lines to the positive impact it is having, not only on the patients directly under their care, but the larger communities they serve. Creating this sense of purpose will empower and sustain organizations over time, as quality improvement operations is a journey with no finish line.

Quality Improvement Financing

In the healthcare setting, diminishing operating margins have placed increased scrutiny on indirect services. Consequently, quality improvement programs and resources deemed "non-essential" are among the first areas to be cut during hard financial times. However, there is a risk of a self-fulfilling prophecy, as hospital financial performance is associated with better patient outcomes, quality and safety processes, and an increased focus on patient-centered care.[23]

The return on investment (ROI) in building and sustaining quality improvement programs is clear in light of this evidence, and it is important for physicians and other clinical leaders to advocate for ongoing investment to not only support continued work in this area to improve patient care, but to support the long-term financial health of the organization.

Chapter Summary

With an intentional structuring of quality team leadership, backed by a sufficient quantity of resources to support it, quality improvement programs must use the appropriate measurement techniques to detect the effectiveness, or lack thereof, of processes to drive positive change. Physician leaders must be well-versed in these techniques and incorporate them into their standard practice.

REFERENCES

1. Sanford K, Moore S. *Dyad Leadership in Healthcare: When One Plus One is Greater than Two.* Philadelphia: Wolters Kluwer; 2015.
2. Hines, K, Mouchtouris N, Knightly JJ, Harrop J. A Brief History of Quality Improvement in Health Care and Spinal Surgery. *Global Spine J.* 2020;10(1 Suppl):5S-9S.
3. Sheingold BH, Hahn JA. The History of Healthcare Quality: The First 100 Years 1860-1960. *International Journal of Africa Nursing Sciences.* 2014;1:18–22.

4. Flexner A. *Medical Education in the United States and Canada: A Report to the Carnegie Foundation for Advancement of Teaching.* New York: Merrymount Press; 1910.
5. Institute of Medicine, Committee on Quality of Health Care in America. *To Err is Human: Building a Safer Health System.* Washington DC: National Academies Press; 2000.
6. Institute of Medicine, Committee on Quality of Health Care in America. *Crossing the Quality Chasm: A New Health System for the 21st Century.* Washington DC: National Academies Press; 2001.
7. Six Domains of Healthcare Quality. Agency for Healthcare Research and Quality, Rockville, MD. Content reviewed December 2022. Accessed April 30, 2024. https://www.ahrq.gov/talkingquality/measures/six-domains.html.
8. Evans JR, Lindsay WM. *The Management and Control of Quality: 6th ed.* Mason, OH: Thomson South-Western; 2005.
9. World Health Organization. Quality of Care. 2024. Accessed May 1, 2024. https://www.who.int/health-topics/quality-of-care#tab=tab_1.
10. Neutze D, Wiggs B. Quality Improvement. In: Daaleman TP, Helton MR, eds. *Chronic Illness Care: Principles and Practice.* Springer International Publishing; 2023. https://doi.org/10.1007/978-3-031-29171-5_38
11. Hunter J. A Bad System Will Beat a Good Person Every Time. The Deming Institute. February 26, 2015. Accessed May 1, 2024. https://deming.org/a-bad-system-will-beat-a-good-person-every-time/.
12. American Society for Quality. The 7 Basic Quality Tools for Process Improvement. Accessed May 2, 2024. https://asq.org/quality-resources/seven-basic-quality-tools.
13. McChesney C, Covey S, Huling J. *The 4 Disciplines of Execution, 2nd ed.* New York: Simon & Schuster; 2021.
14. Doerr J. *Measure What Matters.* New York: Portfolio/Penguin; 2018.
15. The Deming Institute. Explore PDSA. Accessed May 3, 2024. https://deming.org/explore/pdsa/.
16. Lean Enterprise Institute. 7 Wastes. Accessed May 4, 2024. https://www.lean.org/lexicon-terms/seven-wastes/.
17. Pereira R. What Is a Lean Daily Management System? Gemba Academy. Updated March 4, 2024. Accessed July 25, 2024. https://blog.gembaacademy.com/2020/08/07/what-is-a-lean-daily-management-system/.
18. American Society for Quality. What is Six Sigma? Accessed May 5, 2024. https://asq.org/quality-resources/six-sigma
19. Swensen S, Pugh M, McMullan C, Kabcenell A. *High-Impact Leadership: Improve Care, Improve the Health of Populations, and Reduce Costs.* IHI White Paper. Cambridge MA: Institute for Healthcare Improvement; 2013.
20. Centers for Medicare & Medicaid Services. What Are the Value-based Programs? Modified September 6, 2023. Accessed May 6, 2024. https://www.cms.gov/medicare/quality/value-based-programs.
21. Leatherman S, Gardner T, Molloy A, Martin S, Dixon J. Strategy to Improve the Quality of Care in England. *Future Hosp J.* 2016 Oct;3(3):182–187. doi: 10.7861/futurehosp.3-3-182.
22. The Top Five Insights into Healthcare Operational Outcomes Improvement. Health Catalyst. May 13, 2020. Accessed July 25, 2024. https://www.healthcatalyst.com/insights/healthcare-operations-top-5-improvement-insights.
23. Akinleye DD, McNutt LA, Lazariu V, McLaughlin CC. Correlation between Hospital Finances and Quality and Safety of Patient Care. *PLoS One.* 2019 Aug 16;14(8):e0219124. doi: 10.1371/journal.pone.0219124.

SECTION 8

Organizational Leadership and Communication Skills

CHAPTER 25

Leadership Structure and Support

Steven D. Brass, MD, MPH, MBA, FACHE, and Vijay Khatri, MBChB, MBA, FACS, FSSO, FASGO

HALM CORE CONTENT:

- 8.1 Clinical operational leadership for interprofessional teams across the continuum (e.g., planning, direction, execution, evaluation) for:
  - 8.1.1 Ancillary services (e.g., lab, radiology, pharmacy)
  - 8.1.2 Providers (e.g., nonprofit, for-profit, federal, public health)
  - 8.1.3 Support services (e.g., the environment of care, plant operations, materials management, supply chain management, hospitality services)
- 8.7 Team Leadership
  - 8.7.1 Change management
  - 8.7.2 Conflict resolution
  - 8.7.3 Diversity, equity, and inclusion
  - 8.7.5 Group dynamics
  - 8.7.7 Organizational culture development and resources
  - 8.7.9 Risk communication
  - 8.7.10 Situational leadership skills
  - 8.7.11 Team building
    - 8.7.11.1 Assembly
    - 8.7.11.2 Development

CASE SCENARIO:

The department of surgery at an academic health system participates in the American College of Surgeons National Surgical Quality Improvement Project (NSQIP) as a means to track internal metrics and compare them to national standards. The clinical data sets submitted are collected and audited rigorously for accuracy.

The department chair receives the quarterly report, which reveals that the surgical site infection (SSI) for colorectal surgery for the institution has slowly increased from 1.5 times the national rate to now 2.2 times the national rate. For this metric, the institution is now in the lower 10th decile.

The chair shares the results with the lead colorectal surgeon to address this quality deficiency, as SSIs are associated with higher morbidity, increased length of stay, lower patient satisfaction rate, and increased cost to the institution.

The surgeon recognizes that a team approach will be necessary to effect change as the care continuum involves the outpatient clinic, preoperative unit, operating room, post-anesthesia care unit, and the surgical floor. The interdisciplinary team will include surgeons, anesthesiologists, nursing staff, pharmacists, infectious disease specialists, dieticians, surgical educators, surgical quality nurses, and discharge planners.

In addition to the "rank and file" caregivers, engagement of the ambulatory, operative surgical suite, peri-operative care unit, and surgical floor will be needed. While the lead surgeon performed the majority of the colorectal resections, it was notable that such surgeries were performed by 15 other members of the surgical faculty, each with their own approach.

Clinical Operational Leadership

A SUCCESSFUL HEALTHCARE SYSTEM is based on leadership that creates an environment where inter-professional teams work collaboratively across the system for the ultimate customer: the patient. When thinking about what drives operations at a system level, one can think about different categories of teams that affect the patient, including providers, ancillary services, and support services (Figure 1).

Providers: A "healthcare provider" is a licensed healthcare professional who provides direct patient care. Examples include a doctor of medicine or osteopathy, a podiatrist, a dentist, a chiropractor, a clinical psychologist, an optometrist, a nurse practitioner, a nurse-midwife, or a clinical social worker. They are authorized by the state to practice within the scope of their practice as defined by state law.

Ancillary Services: Ancillary services support providers with regards to patient care by assisting with diagnosis or therapy. Examples of ancillary services include radiology, laboratory, pharmacy, hospice care, and physical therapy.

Support Services: Support services include departments that ensure the coordination of care, which may or may not directly touch a patient. Support services include environmental care services, health information technology, and patient transportation.

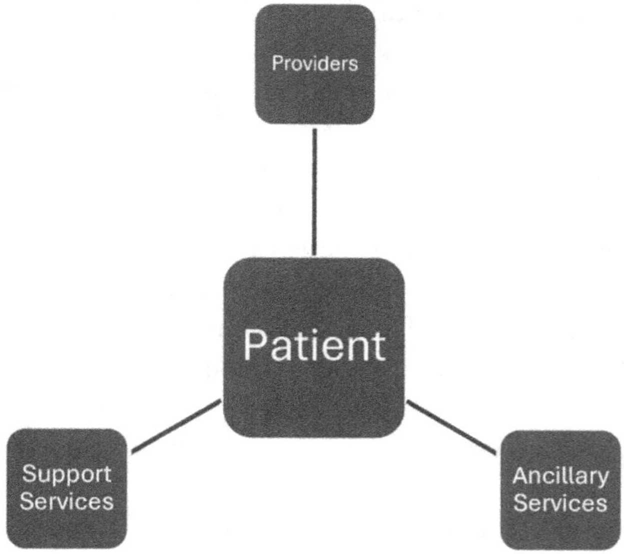

FIGURE 1. Inter-professional Teams in Healthcare

To achieve institutional goals, these three categories of services need to work collaboratively while acknowledging that, at times, there will be conflicts. These conflicts are to be anticipated, and awareness of them is necessary to manage them effectively. Management requires situational leadership, experience in conflict resolution, and awareness of the prevailing culture.

While it is natural for departments to operate in silos with an internally oriented view, members from the providers, ancillary services, and support services groups must assemble as a team. Knowledge about team building and group dynamics is critical to effecting change and being successful.

Change Management

Successful leaders understand the concept of change management in healthcare, which is undergoing intense transformation from technology (artificial intelligence), policy and regulatory changes (Centers for Medicare & Medicaid Services regulations), or even from clinical issues as discoveries and new diseases evolve (vaccines). A successful leader not only understands change management but leads it.[1-4]

In order to best understand change management, one of the best-known models of leading complex change is the Kotter Eight-Step Change Model (Figure 2).[5] Kotter described a change in the system based on the following:

1. *Create urgency.* Leaders must create a compelling case by explaining why the *status quo* is no longer acceptable. One must explain the current status and why it's a danger to quality and patient safety and have a sense of urgency.

2. *Form a powerful coalition.* Identify key stakeholders who can act as change champions and can serve as partners in the change process.
3. *Create a vision for change.* The vision for change must be patient-centered, clear, and direct.
4. *Communicate the vision.* Communication of the vision for the future is crucial and cannot be done by email alone. Face-to-face meetings, intense discussions, and listening to the stakeholders' concerns and feedback are vital to be successful.
5. *Empower action.* Any barriers, real or perceived, must be removed. They may be operational, financial, emotional, or a combination. Feedback on whatever the barriers are to change is important and must be addressed.
6. *Create quick wins.* It is crucial to track and identify any short-term wins and milestones for the project. This will help further the project by celebrating the early successes.
7. *Build on the change.* It is important to monitor and communicate progress with the front-line staff to ensure reliability in the process.
8. *Make it stick.* In order to best anchor the new change in the culture, metrics and targets need to be implemented and integrated into the organization's standard work surrounding the change.

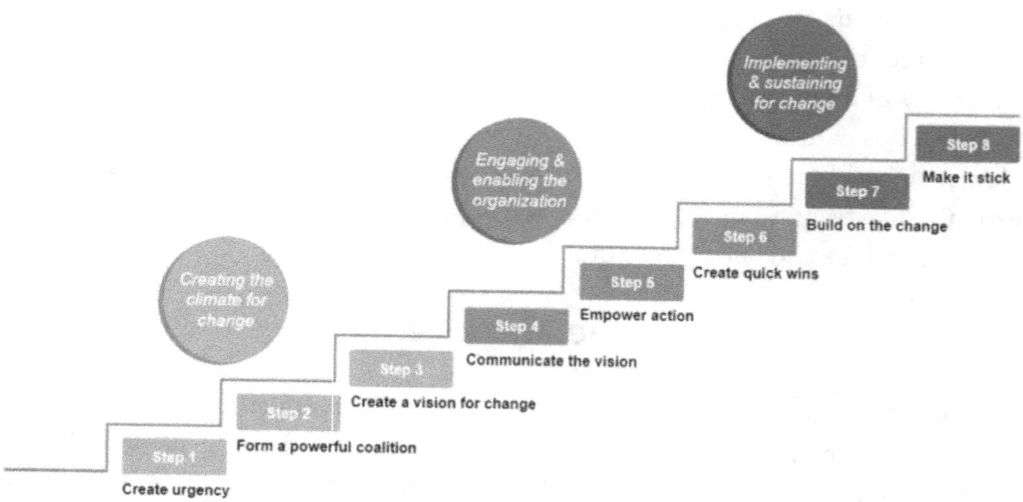

FIGURE 2. Kotter's Eight-Step Change Model

Resistance to change is common, and healthcare leaders must acknowledge resistance as part of a change management process. Kubler-Ross described a model of how people go through different stages of mourning as they adapt to the death of a loved one. The same model has been used analogously for individuals when dealing with change.[6]

The emotional reaction has five stages: denial, anger, bargaining, depression, and acceptance (Figure 3). By understanding where a healthcare employee or the organization is on the change curve, the physician leader can ensure appropriate support is provided.[6]

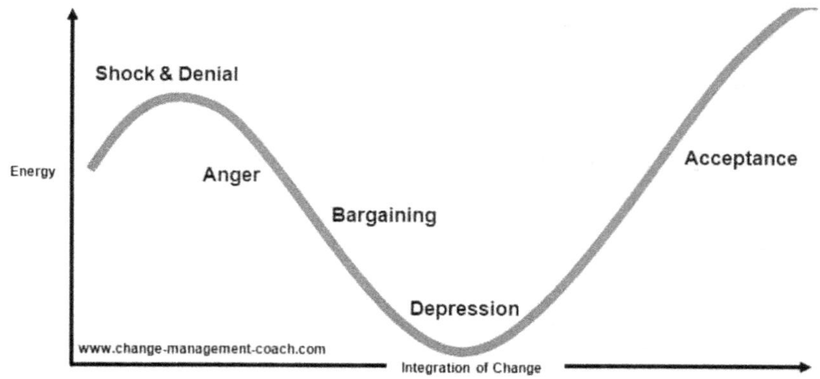

FIGURE 3. The Kubler-Ross Change Curve

The best way healthcare leaders can deal with some of the resistance is to educate early on why that change is needed and what is in it for them. It is important to involve key stakeholders early on instead of at the end and emphasize how leadership is interested in hearing their input to address barriers to change.

Empathizing with the teams regarding their feelings surrounding the change is important, along with over-communicating these changes in several forums at multiple levels in the organization. In addition, there will need to be an appropriate time for the change to sink in to allow acceptance. After implementation, verify and validate the change has occurred and is sustained by ensuring that there are clear metrics of accountability.[6]

Organizational Culture Development and Resources

Research shows even the best plans can go off track if leaders don't understand how company culture works. Culture is the unspoken rules and secret sauce of the organization. It can be loosely defined as "how we do things around here." It is the "tactical social order, attitudes, behaviors, and norms that define what is encouraged, discouraged, accepted, or rejected within a group."[7]

Researchers point out two main aspects of organizational culture: (1) how people interact and (2) how they deal with change.

Eight cultural styles have been reported across organizations.[7]

1. *Caring culture*: friendly and collaborative.
2. *Purpose-oriented culture*: focus on helping others.

3. *Learning culture*: all about creativity and exploration.
4. *Enjoyment culture*: prioritize fun and engagement.
5. *Results-driven culture*: aim for achievement and winning.
6. *Authority culture*: competitive and bold.
7. *Safety culture*: value predictability and careful planning.
8. *Order culture*: focus on structure and rules.

Cultures can change based on outside pressures; for example, a purpose-oriented culture is key in healthcare but not so much in the consumer goods industry. Once leaders know where their company's culture stands, they can see if change is needed. Making sense of the culture is crucial for effective leadership and guiding change in the organization.[7]

Group Dynamics

Group dynamics refers to how employees interact and collaborate. This has an overall impact on team performance, patient outcomes, and overall job satisfaction. Several characteristics are necessary to ensure group dynamics are optimized. Clearly defined roles and responsibilities prevent confusion and enhance accountability. Structured communication through methods like SBAR (Situation, Background, Assessment, Recommendation) decreases communication errors, especially during care transitions.

Effective leadership via formal and informal approaches is necessary to drive change and manage conflicts. Conflicts must be addressed constructively to prevent harm to teamwork, as unresolved issues can hinder collaboration.

Inclusive decision-making encourages input from all members, promoting a sense of investment and engagement in the process, with structured approaches like consensus-building aiding in effective decisions. Finally, cultural competence training equips teams to navigate varying communication styles and patient care approaches more effectively.[8]

Team Building

Research has shown that several features can drive the team toward success in the organization. Orientation and training that focus on teamwork and leadership skills can improve everyone's ability to communicate better and handle conflicts. Regular team meetings are necessary to keep everyone in the loop about goals and progress and build stronger relationships among team members.

An inclusive leadership style goes a long way, too. When everyone feels encouraged to share their ideas, it creates a richer conversation and leads to more creative solutions. Psychological safety is crucial. Team members must feel safe to take risks and voice their ideas without worrying about being judged.

Organizations must also have resources in place for managing conflicts constructively, as this can turn disagreements into chances for the team to grow together. When team members feel supported in managing their time and stress, everyone benefits from improved morale and productivity.

Finding the right mix of people is crucial, as choosing individuals with varied skills and backgrounds helps create a well-rounded team. Good leaders empower team members, encourage open communication, and hold everyone accountable, making sure each person feels their contributions matter.[8]

By prioritizing both assembly and development, health systems can develop teams that are able to drive outstanding patient care while also balancing the challenges posed by modern healthcare systems. The assembly of teams within a health system is critical for delivering high-quality, patient-centered care. Team assembly begins with identifying the roles and skills needed to address the goals of the health system, such as improving patient outcomes and streamlining operations.

When assembling the team, it is crucial to consider diverse experiences and backgrounds, as this encourages innovative solutions to complex challenges. Role clarity is crucial when assembling a team; all key stakeholders must have a clear understanding of their responsibilities and the organization's overarching mission.

The development of a team is based on a triad of effective communication, trust-building, and ongoing training. Communication, whether through formal or informal processes, is foundational for the team to develop. Leaders are important to ensure there is feedback and team-building exercises, which can ensure positive team dynamics and, ultimately, engagement and alignment of team players. Leaders also need to address any perceived barriers, resolve conflicts promptly, and advocate for resources that empower the team.

Amy Edmondson, professor of leadership and management at Harvard Business School, reported on four tools leaders use to establish successful teams. The first tool is "emphasizing purpose." This is necessary to motivate the team toward change. "Psychological safety" allows others to raise questions, acknowledge errors, and raise issues without fear of retribution. "Allowing teams to embrace failure" provides essential information and a learning platform that can guide the next steps. Finally, "putting conflict to work" is necessary. While at times it can feel challenging, learning from conflict allows the team to have different perspectives and ultimately grow and improve.[8,9]

Situational Leadership

There are a plethora of books and courses on leadership, each with its own definition and nomenclature to describe the various leadership styles. In essence, leadership reflects a set of observable behaviors employed by individuals to influence, motivate, and guide their employees and colleagues. The six common leadership styles are transformational, delegative, authoritative, transactional, participative, and servant leadership.[10]

There are various theories about leadership traits; some think that it is innate, though this is often confused with charisma. Many assert that it is a learned ability. In reality, an individual's leadership style is cultivated through a combination of innate personality (especially self-awareness, empathy, and adaptability), lived experiences, personal values, and communication abilities.

To be effective, leaders should be aware of their leadership style and know whether a situation requires a leader who can make an executive decision or a consultant who might suggest the best path forward. Furthermore, a leader needs to know the most effective leadership style for an organization or situation to succeed. Understanding one's leadership style allows a leader to take ownership, control, and responsibility for the size and scope of the tasks ahead.

No one leadership style fits all organizations or all situations, and there may be a need to strategically switch between different leadership styles. Situational theories of leadership assume the most effective style of leadership changes from situation to situation. To be most effective and successful, leaders should have the ability to adapt their style and approach to diverse circumstances.

It is important for individuals to be aware of the various leadership styles and their advantages and disadvantages. The right approach is often determined by assessing the environment and the people. The variables include:

1. The type of organization and its culture.
2. The nature of work to be accomplished.
3. Team competency such as level of experience and skill set.
4. The personality of the leader.

When such a multifactorial assessment is developed with the use of the above factors, one can determine the appropriate leadership style to adopt. Flexibility is critical. Understanding one's leadership style and the ability to be flexible based on changing circumstances has the potential advantage of improving communication and collaboration and increasing employee engagement, thereby leading to the strengthening of team effectiveness.[11,12]

Conflict Resolution

Conflict is an essential part of being human, and therefore, as leaders, awareness of the skills and strategies to address such situations is critical. Conflict resolution can be defined as the informal or formal process that two or more parties use to find a peaceful solution to their dispute. Effective conflict resolution is not designed to avoid disagreements; rather, conflict resolution skills facilitate discussions, increase mutual understanding, and control the associated emotional responses that can derail the process.[13-16]

In addition to the adverse effects of emotional responses, it is important to be aware of unconscious cognitive errors that lead to unproductive or unresolved conflict.[15,16] These effects include:

- *Conflict avoidance*: To prevent personal discomfort, it is often easier for humans to circumvent an adverse situation with hopes of self-resolution. Unfortunately, this approach allows the conflict to fester.
- *Overconfidence*: Such a stance may lead an individual to overestimate their chance of success and thereby fail to see others' perspectives, possibly preventing an opportunity for early resolution.
- *Escalation of commitment*: This is similar to the financial concept of "sunk cost," where prior investment losses should not influence decisions about the future. An individual either continues to raise the stakes of an existing argument or puts forward additional issues, thus delaying resolution.
- *Self-serving fairness*: Rather than approach from a neutral stance, there is a singular focus on one's own benefit and thus deciding what is "fair" from a biased point of view.
- *Blame game, emotional volatility, and insults*: These tactics are always counterproductive and lead to an explosive situation that renders resolution virtually impossible.

Conflicts at corporate and institutional levels are usually resolved with the use of broad strategies such as negotiation, mediation, arbitration, and litigation. Regarding the clinical vignette described here, the common approach is that of negotiation. Negotiation to achieve conflict resolution between two or more parties is most successful with active listening, open communication, patience, emotional intelligence, solution orientation, and collaboration. Pre-negotiation preparation includes exploring the interests of the underlying parties' positions, developing options and possible acceptable tradeoffs, and always having a BATNA (best alternative to a negotiated agreement) ready. Negotiating is a humbling process, so be prepared to make mistakes, apologize if necessary, and don't hesitate to reach out to someone in the organization for advice and guidance.

Resolving conflicts through successful negotiation will foster relationship building and secure commitment (buy-in), and may open the door to new ideas and innovative problem-solving. It is also an opportunity to promote self-development and ongoing learning.[13-16]

Risk Communication

Risk is defined as the probability that a hazard will give rise to harm. Risk communication is defined as a "process of exchanging information among interested parties about the nature, magnitude, significance, or control of a risk."[17] Risk communication can be described as a combination of conflict resolution, public participation, and two-way messaging.

Physicians, especially surgeons and proceduralists, routinely discuss risks associated with medical treatment. It is an integral part of the consent process, which promotes shared decision-making, addresses asymmetric knowledge, allays fears, and, above all, establishes "buy-in" so that the patient becomes an integral and important part of the treatment team.

This approach enhances patient satisfaction and, thereby, risk reduction, not only for the surgeon, but for the institution, due to improvement in quality outcomes. Accuracy and scientific strength of the information are necessary so that the recipient can make an informed decision based on the best available information. In the case scenario, such a tactic was used to introduce enhanced recovery after surgery (ERAS), which is a patient-centered, evidence-based program.[18-21]

When this concept of risk communication is extended to group activity, delivery of timely and accurate information in an open style dialogue is essential to building the trust among the team members.

In their 1989 report titled "Improving Risk Communication," the National Academy of Sciences panel defined risk communication as an interactive process that includes an exchange of information, including opinion (categorized as level V evidence in medicine) among individuals, groups, and institutions.[22] The critical components of the communication process include the risk communicator (source of information), the message, the message channel, and the message recipient.

While such an analytic process suggests a linear series of events, communication is usually a complex interactive process that includes feedback loops from participating members. As a result, misinterpretations can occur at various levels due to the impact of cultural differences, biases, and other mental shortcuts such as preconceived assumptions that help people navigate daily life.

Remember, that with risk communication, understanding is considered the most important goal. If risk communication does not lead to a change in behavior, it is not a failure in communication; rather, it is the result of decisions made by the information recipient who may take into consideration a variety of other factors, such as offsetting benefits. While physicians may have learned the basics of communication through their clinical training, additional competencies in this area involve understanding team and institutional dynamics.

Advantages of risk communication include improved decision-making, effective team coordination, streamlined operations, efficient resource management, and compliance with regulations. Finally, don't forget to deliver information with empathy, as team members feel more valued and better understood, thereby creating a stronger workplace culture that drives productivity while building a sense of compassion. After all, humans are social animals, and the communication process centers around nurturing relationships to achieve mutually beneficial goals using emotional intelligence to navigate complex situations with calmness and compassion. A related concept is the possession of situational leadership skills as previously mentioned.[18-21]

Diversity, Equity, and Inclusion

Having a workforce diverse in race, gender, age, religion, disability, and socioeconomic background creates a better organizational understanding of the unique needs of various patient populations. This allows the patient to better identify with the health team and has been shown to improve communication between the patient and the healthcare team, which leads to more accurate diagnoses and better treatment plans. Considering various perspectives on a healthcare topic leads to an overall better outcome.[23]

There is a difference between equity and equality. Equity means distributing resources based on specific needs; equality means providing the same resources to everyone. Ensuring equitable access to healthcare is crucial in addressing disparities that lead to poorer health outcomes among certain groups. These disparities can result in broader public health crises.

Achieving equity in healthcare is vital for overall population health and is supported by research emphasizing its importance in meeting global health goals. It is well known that the social determinants of health, 80% of which are unrelated to clinical care, have an impact on the health outcomes of the population. Some of the social determinants of health include access to food, housing, legal services, and employment.[24]

Inclusion means creating an environment where everyone feels as if they have a voice at the table and has equal opportunities to contribute. This is important for healthcare workers, as creating a culture of inclusivity leads to higher job satisfaction, reduced turnover, and better patient care experiences.[25]

Over the past few years, organizations have adopted DEI policies, but often with "one size fits all" interventions such as unconscious bias, racial sensitivity, and cultural competency training. Instead, leadership should initially perform employee surveys, focus groups, and DEI data analysis, and then use this information to identify the unique internal challenges. Interventions should be designed with desired outcomes (primary and secondary endpoints, short- and long-term results).[26] DEI efforts should employ a scientific approach to implement evidence-based interventions.

Chapter Summary

Physicians are trained to employ critical thinking, evidence-based decisions, and good problem-solving skills in patient care. Physician leaders should apply these same approaches when serving in healthcare management roles. This chapter introduced several concepts that allows physician leaders to broaden their armamentarium of skills to steer meaningful health system change.

Effective healthcare leadership requires fostering collaboration across teams, including providers, ancillary services, and support services, to deliver high-quality, patient-centered care. Leaders must understand the concepts of change management, conflict resolution and creating psychological safety among the team. Situational leadership allows leaders to adapt their approach based on team needs and the organizational environment. Physicians who ensure clear communication, address conflict, and develop their team will become successful healthcare leaders that will ultimately improve outcomes.

REFERENCES

1. Kotter JP. Leading Change: Why Transformation Efforts Fail. *Harvard Business Review*. May–June 1995. Accessed December 1, 2024. https://hbr.org/1995/05/leading-change-why-transformation-efforts-fail-2
2. Beer M, Nohria N. Cracking the Code of Change. *Harvard Business Review*. May–June 2000. Accessed December 1, 2024. https://hbr.org/2000/05/cracking-the-code-of-change
3. Goleman D, Boyatzis R, McKee A. The Emotional Reality of Teams. *Journal of Organizational Excellence.* February 2000. Accessed December 1, 2024. https://doi.org/10.1002/npr.10020.
4. Garvin DA, Roberto MA. Change Through Persuasion. *Harvard Business Review*. February 2005. Accessed December 1, 2024. https://hbr.org/2005/02/change-through-persuasion.
5. Kotter JP. *Leading Change*. Boston, MA: Harvard Business School Press; 1996.
6. Kübler-Ross E. *On Death and Dying*. New York, NY: Macmillan; 1969.
7. Groysberg B, Lee J, Price J, Cheng JY. A Leader's Guide to Corporate Culture. *Harvard Business Review*. January-February 2018. Accessed December 1, 2024. https://hbr.org/2018/01/a-leaders-guide-to-corporate-culture.
8. Edmondson AC. Psychological safety and learning behavior in work teams. *Adm Sci Q*. 1999;44(2):350-383. Doi:10.2307/2666999.
9. Edmondson AC. Teamwork on the Fly. How to Master the New Art of Teaming. *Harvard Business Review*. April 2012. https://hbr.crg/2012/04/teamwork-on-the-fly-2.
10. Goleman D. Leadership That Gets Results. *Harvard Business Review*. March-April 2000. https://hbr.org/2000/03/leadership-that-gets-results
11. Hersey P, Blanchard KH. *Management of Organizational Behavior: Utilizing Human Resources. 5th ed.* Englewood Cliffs, NJ: Prentice Hall: 1988.
12. Graeff CL. Evolution of Situational Leadership Theory: A Critical Review. *The Leadership Quarterly*. 1997;8(2):153-170.
13. Sudhakar G. A Review of Conflict Management Techniques in Projects. *Brazilian Journal of Operations & Production Management*. 2015;12(2):214-232.
14. Adham TK. Conflict Resolution in Team: Analyzing the Conflicts and Best Skills for Resolution. *Sch J Eng Tech*. 2023;8:152-162.
15. Aydoğan R, Baarslag T, Gerding E. Artificial Intelligence Techniques for Conflict Resolution. *Group Decision and Negotiation*. 2021;30(4):879-883.
16. Madalina O. Conflict Management, a New Challenge. *Procedia Economics and Finance*. 2016;39:807-814.
17. Covello VT. Risk Communication: An Emerging Area of Health Communication Research. *Annals of the International Communication Association*. 1992;15(1):359-373. doi:10.1080/23808985.1992.11678816

18. Balog-Way D, McComas K, Besley J. The Evolving Field of Risk Communication. *Risk Analysis*. 2020;40(S1):2240-2262.
19. Rohrmann B. Risk Perception, Risk Attitude, Risk Communication, Risk Management: A Conceptual Appraisal. Presented at: 15th International Emergency Management Society (TIEMS) Annual Conference; 2008.
20. Calman KC. Communication of Risk: Choice, Consent, and Trust. *The Lancet*. 2002;360(9327):166-168.
21. Trevena LJ, Zikmund-Fisher BJ, Edwards A, et al. Presenting Quantitative Information About Decision Outcomes: A Risk Communication Primer for Patient Decision Aid Developers. *BMC Medical Informatics and Decision Making*. 2013;13:1-15.
22. National Research Council. *Improving Risk Communication.* Washington, DC: National Academy Press; 1989.
23. Esparza CJ, Simon M, London MR, Bath E, Ko M. Experiences of Leaders in Diversity, Equity, and Inclusion in US Academic Health Centers. *JAMA Network Open*. 2024;7(6):e2415401. doi:10.1001/jamanetworkopen.2024.15401.
24. Kelly R. Effect and Outcome of Equity, Diversity, and Inclusion Programs in Healthcare Institutions: A Systematic Review Protocol. *BMJ Open*. 2024;14(2):1-8. doi:10.1136/bmjopen-2024-085007.
25. Cozier Y, Mellman L, Galea S. The Evolving Role of Diversity, Equity, and Inclusion Programs in Academic Health Institutions. *JAMA Health Forum*. 2022;332(7):531-532. doi: 10.1001/jama.2024.9951.
26. Sitzmann T, Schwartz S. Why Is Progress Toward Diverse Representation So Slow? Contrasting Management Practices' Prevalence Versus Effectiveness for Achieving Diverse Representation. *Business Horizons*. 2024. https://doi.org/10.1016/j.bushor.2024.02.012.

CHAPTER 26

Leadership Techniques and Skills

Rex Hoffman, MD, MBA, FACHE, CPE; Rajesh Ranadive, MD; and Amy Herold, MD, MBA, MPH

HALM CORE CONTENT:

- 8.2 Collaborative techniques for engaging and working with physicians
- 8.3 Contingency planning (e.g., emergency preparedness, disaster management, National Incident Management System)
- 8.4 Organizational systems (e.g., span of control, chain of command, interrelationships of organizational units)
- 8.6 Resource allocation methods and related conflict management

CASE SCENARIO:

The administrator on call of a hospital is awakened at midnight with reports of rapidly spreading wildfires in the area due to multiple lightning strikes on a hot, windy night. First responders are mobilizing, and a helicopter has started dropping off people rescued from engulfed hilltops on the hospital's helipad, as it is the closest one available. Hundreds of people are being evacuated from the surrounding areas, and thick smoke is rapidly filling the air. The only other hospital in the area is preparing to evacuate due to the rapidly approaching fire. How does the hospital leadership respond to this potential crisis? Who should be part of the collaborative response?

PHYSICIAN ENGAGEMENT, PARTNERSHIP, AND COLLABORATION are the bases for the success of any healthcare organization, including group practices, hospital organizations, and insurance companies, including accountable care organizations (ACOs). Studies have shown that a collaborative environment benefits the patients and the community at large through better clinical outcomes, patient and staff satisfaction, reduction in error rates, decreased length of stay, physician recruitment, growth, and retention.

Collaborative Techniques For Engaging And Working With Physicians

Three categories of factors influence inter-physician collaboration: personal factors, professional factors, and organizational factors.[1]

Personal factors include language, gender, age, culture, autonomy, personal goals and challenges, and reluctance to change. Being part of an organization with appropriate support, coaching/mentoring, onboarding, and monitoring are some ways to tackle these factors if they become an obstacle to collaboration.

Professional factors that affect inter-physician collaboration include medical specialty, hierarchy, responsibilities, workload, stress, and stereotypes. Organizational factors include leadership, culture, communication, and shared goals.

Effective leadership centers around having quality champions who are inclusive, transparent, and open-minded; who can address challenges to collaboration, building a culture of inclusion and transparency; and who are invested in and committed to employee growth.

ENHANCING INTER-PHYSICIAN COLLABORATION

The pathway to success for inter-physician collaboration requires addressing the categorical challenges listed above. Understanding the importance of collaboration to organizational success and dedicating the necessary resources to enhancing collaboration ultimately benefits everyone. Leaders can promote collaboration through positive communication; inclusive collaborative goal setting; and teamwork.

A culture of collaboration requires open and frequent communication to build trust and rapport. Increased emphasis should be placed on listening to and acknowledging physician concerns and being empathetic. Rather than making an issue personal, the leader should listen and understand the root cause, provide honest and direct communication, be prepared to offer solutions, be supportive and encouraging, and be fair and consistent. Providing feedback with positive reinforcement and physician recognition is a good strategy, and gratitude and appreciation go a long way.

Involving physicians and physician leadership in the early discernment process for setting goals, protocols, and changes in policies and procedures promotes engagement and fosters collaboration.

In general, physicians are trained to be individual thinkers and often take charge of a situation and find solutions. Having strong organizational leadership who can not only communicate well with physicians and physician leadership but who are also willing to get them involved is important.

Contingency Planning

Emergency preparedness and disaster management are areas many new leaders don't know what they need to know about until they need to know it. An emergency and a disaster can be brought on by the same event; the difference in outcome is related to preparedness and relative resources.

Disasters can be natural or technological.[2] Natural disasters include weather and climate events with acute onsets such as hurricanes, floods, extreme heat, tornados, tsunamis, volcanic eruptions, blizzards or extreme cold, droughts, earthquakes, and wildfires. Technological or man-made disasters can include nuclear accidents, explosions, bioterrorism, cyberthreats, and epidemics.

The two categories can overlap. Recall the 2011 earthquake in Japan that triggered a tsunami that caused a nuclear accident at the Fukushima Power Plant.[2] As technology advances, so does the risk of concurrent or sequential emergencies between natural and man-made disasters.

A critical element of emergency preparedness is the hazard risk assessment (HRA) tool, which determines what events are most likely to occur in the area where a facility is located. For example, hurricanes are more likely on the east coast and earthquakes are a threat on the west coast. Internal disasters include utility failures or fires; external threats of ransomware attacks are becoming more prevalent, especially in the healthcare setting.

An effective HRA examines the stability of the organization and the most likely threats to a community. This analysis includes using historical data to review past incidents and their severity and scientific data to look ahead at predictive threats. The assessment is critical to creating plans to mitigate and manage these hazards.

Emergency management plans should include provisions for the specific facility, contain policies for different scenarios, and consider partnerships with other responding agencies. The critical elements are structure (resources, equipment, and staff), process (response and communication), and outcomes (restoration of operations and maintenance of health status).[3]

Similar to the ABCs of CPR, immediate response to an emergency in a facility is centered on three main questions:

1. Is the building structurally intact and safe?
2. Are the utilities working to allow function and is the air safe to breathe? Does additional equipment need to be set up?
3. Do evacuation or shelter-in-place measures need to be taken immediately and can appropriate resources, including staff, be adequately mobilized and moved throughout the facility?

Healthcare workers' response to emergencies is critical to response capacity.[4] Workers are less likely to respond if they fear for their personal safety or that of their families, if they feel they don't have adequate training, or if they believe they are not important to the outcomes.[5] Clerical and support staff tend to feel less important than clinical staff. Drills and training can improve these outcomes. Self-efficacy is a psychological attribute that empowers people to be confident in high-stress situations.[6] Workers are nearly 10 times more likely to respond to an emergency if they feel important to the response. The sense of efficacy outweighs the perception of risk of the threat in a worker's willingness to respond. When training in responding to specific hazards includes a discussion on willingness, not just readiness, response rates drastically improve.[4]

The elements of the response process involve the successful operational performance of the plan and depend on preparation, training, and drills to ensure teams know their roles in an emergency and can activate the plan quickly and efficiently.

Communication is a critical component of the process, as it is necessary to mitigate panic during an emergency. Communication needs to be bidirectional with communications coming in and being transmitted. Because many disasters can cause disruption of phone lines, the ability to go "analog" is important. Use of pagers, Wi-Fi calling, and radio stations to broadcast locally can mitigate digital and cellular downtime.

Perception of risk decreases when people feel some sense of control and familiarity. Information going out should be simple and easily digested. Use the "rule of threes" in effective message mapping:

1. Identify the audience and their questions/concerns.
2. Develop risk messages.
3. Deliver your messages.

Communicate three key facts in descending priority to keep information organized and concise.[7]

The outcomes of an emergency response plan are based on the preparation work. The ultimate goal is the restoration of normal operations and the subsequent health and safety of the community and the response team, including mental health. For every person physically affected by disasters, 4 to 50 times that may suffer psychological effects, and the distress is greater in man-made disasters than natural ones.[4]

Mitigating psychological effects early in a disaster can help prevent overloading available resources with the "worried well." Effective risk communication and mobilization of support resources into the community can reduce long-term psychological effects for victims and responders. These effects can range from mild symptoms of fear, worry and transient sleep disturbance, to moderate symptoms of insomnia and anxiety and increased alcohol or tobacco use, to severe symptoms of PTSD and major depressive disorder. Children can become regressive or aggressive in response to disasters.[2] Disaster plans should always make a provision for behavioral health resources and reunification plans for children.

The National Incident Management System (NIMS), provided by FEMA for all responders to a disaster, offers training in structure, resource availability, response frameworks, and mutual aid.[8] A sub-training program called the Hospital Incident Command System (HICS) covers setting up an incident command center, the roles necessary to manage the incident, and the forms mandatory to submit to local and federal authorities, especially if FEMA reimbursement will be sought for expenses.[9]

This training is important not only to better understand how to manage emergencies locally and in collaboration with all other agencies who speak the same "language" but is mandated by the Centers for Medicare and Medicaid Services (CMS).[10]

CMS created an Emergency Preparedness Rule with the following four requirements:

1. Risk assessment.
2. A communication plan: internal, external, and interagency.
3. Policies and procedures.
4. Training and testing.

Returning to the case study, now that the wildfire emergency has been identified, the critical first steps are:

1. The hospital incident command center is opened.
2. Communication regarding the opening of the command center and its location is sent to all necessary personnel and staff are called in.
3. Roles in the command center are assigned.
4. The facility is inspected for structural integrity and safety and to ensure that utilities or the backup systems are functioning. Rooms with ventilators must be adequately powered to ensure patient safety.
5. Windows and doors are secured to prevent contaminated smoky air from entering the facility. Air scrubbers are deployed to high-risk areas (ICU, OR, NICU) with vulnerable patients.
6. Communication is initiated with internal unit leaders at a scheduled cadence to ensure continued operational integrity and identify needs for resource deployment.
7. Communication channels with external agencies — county, state, and fire — are established with a schedule for check-in times.
8. All units follow their internal emergency management policies.
9. Triage areas are set up for the potential influx of patients: the injured and the evacuated.

Organizational Systems

A high-functioning organization adopts a structure to bring clarity, efficiency, and optimization to its operations. This structure helps employees and leadership understand job responsibilities, decision-making, communication, and intra-departmental and inter-departmental interactions. Recruitment and retention are also salient features of a well-structured organization.

A variety of structural models are available; their success depends on the organization's culture, size, needs, market environment, and other factors. It is common for an organization to implement a conglomerate of various models.

PREREQUISITES FOR DEVELOPING AN ORGANIZATIONAL STRUCTURE

A leader or leadership team needs to address the question "What is the purpose of the organizational chart and is it clear?" The fundamental principles for an organizational chart are as follows.

- *Alignment of Goals and Culture.* The model must represent goals and cultural values.
- *Chain of Command.* A detailed chain of command helps develop protocols and brings clarity and accountability.
- *Roles and Responsibilities.* In addition to bringing clarity to a job description, descriptions of roles and responsibilities helps with recruitment and accountability, which leads to higher retention and better job satisfaction.
- *Decision-making and Scope of Control Authority.* Defining parameters fosters efficiency and optimization, which helps an individual employee, team, or department appropriately escalate concerns or address their concerns through the proper channels.
- *Intra- and Inter-Departmental Operations.* A model should reflect how the structure addresses the needs of an employee, team, and department. Furthermore, it should foster a culture of collaboration for the success of the organization.

ORGANIZATIONAL STRUCTURES

Organizational structures vary by organization.[11]

1. *Centralized versus Decentralized.*The centralized model is traditional and more commonly used. Senior leadership are responsible for making major decisions and guiding the organization. Well-defined responsibilities are cascaded down to individual teams and employees. Clear communication, transparency, and chain of command are well established and are essential for its success.

   The decentralized model, in contrast, provides more autonomy to individual divisions, departments, and teams. This structure is commonly seen in organizations or conglomerates that are geographically dispersed.
2. *Hierarchical versus Circular.* The hierarchical model is a pyramid-based organizational chart with a well-established chain of command. Moving down the pyramid, authority and responsibilities become more granular, limited, and focused on the specific department.

In a circular model, the core leadership is at its center and information flows out in all directions.

3. *Vertical versus Flat.* In the vertical model, core leadership is at the top/center of the organization chart and has a clear chain of command and escalation path.

   In the flat model, an employee can have responsibilities in multiple departments and can report to more than one manager across departments.

SPAN OF CONTROL

The span of control is defined as the number of employees who report directly to a manager or leader. The span of control is calculated by dividing the total number of employees the supervisor manages by the number of supervisors. Independent of the organizational structure or model, a span of control plays a vital role in productivity, efficiency, motivation, and culture building. Strong, experienced leadership with good communication skills is essential for success in engaging employees and inter-departmental collaboration.

There are two types of spans of control.[12]

1. *Wide Span of Control.* In this model, fewer managers oversee many employees. This is generally seen in organizations with flat structures. Some benefits are more direct communication, low overhead costs (lower manager salaries), a feeling of employee empowerment due to less oversight, more accountability and decision-making authority, and increased engagement and innovation.
2. *Narrow Span of Control.* In this setup, a manager is responsible for a smaller team. This is generally seen in departments requiring closer supervision, especially those handling complex jobs. A manager can provide closer attention with direct oversight, which helps with employee development, team guidance, and communication. Multiple layers of leadership, high cost (more managers), more bureaucracy and a slower decision-making process are some of the potential challenges. This type of span of control is generally seen in organizations with centralized, hierarchical types of structure.

CHAIN OF COMMAND

A chain of command is a ladder of authority such that those in charge of an organization or company direct and control employees below them. In the business world, it is the hierarchy that delineates the reporting structure and the roles an individual plays within the organization. Generally, there are three types of roles in the chain of command: senior management, middle management, and regular employees.

Pros of a chain of command structure include:[13]

- Clear structure of authority.
- Quick decision-making.
- Specialization of skills and function.

- Accountability.
- Increases stability.

Cons of a chain of command structure are:[13]

- Lack of flexibility and delayed reactions.
- Decreased employee morale.
- Communication breakdown.
- Micromanagement.
- Misuse of power.

When developing, reviewing, and implementing a well-defined chain of command policy, the following factors should be taken into consideration. [14]

- Eliminating/limiting the barriers
- Structured communication
- Employee education
- SBAR reporting (**S**ituation, **B**ackground, **A**ssessment, **R**ecommendation)
- CUS Statement (I'm **C**oncerned; I'm **U**ncomfortable; **S**top the line)
- Evaluate effectiveness

INTER-DEPARTMENTAL COLLABORATION

Inter-department collaboration is fundamental to the success of any organization.[15] It can bring efficiency, optimization of resources, a positive culture, employee satisfaction, and retention. Experienced leadership with strong communication skills play an important role in fostering collaboration. When recruiting for leadership roles, it is important to keep this in mind. Challenges to inter-departmental collaboration include:

- Communication barriers
- Conflicting priorities
- Lack of accountability
- Resistance to change
- Potential power struggles
- Conflict

Inter-departmental collaboration is essential for a successful, financially stable, and growing organization. Strategies that bring efficiency, optimization of resources, employee growth, and satisfaction to the organization and promote inter-departmental collaboration include transparency, trust and rapport, celebration of wins, and collaborative decision-making.[16]

Conflict Management

Being well-versed in conflict management (or resolution) is an important component of effective leadership. A strong leader sees conflict not as a barrier to overcome, but as an opportunity for growth and deeper understanding. A leader who manages conflict effectively prioritizes the growth and well-being of individuals. This leader actively listens, empathizes, and empowers team members, fostering a culture of collaboration and trust. By looking out for their team's needs, leaders cultivate an environment where individuals feel valued and motivated to contribute their best efforts. When team members see their leader exemplifying these qualities, they are more likely to adopt similar approaches in their interactions, contributing to a better work environment.

Conflict resolution involves navigating disagreements to find a mutually acceptable solution. Doing so helps maintain team cohesion, enhances performance, and promotes a culture of respect. Leaders who excel in conflict resolution can transform potential negative situations into opportunities for growth. They recognize that conflict, if managed well, can lead to innovative solutions, strengthen relationships, and improve overall team dynamics.[17]

Conflict resolution:

1. Fosters a positive work environment.
2. Improves team performance.
3. Encourages open communication.
4. Develops problem-solving skills.

Essential strategies for conflict resolution include:

1. Practicing active listening.
2. Remaining neutral.
3. Encouraging collaboration.
4. Addressing issues early.
5. Establishing clear processes.
6. Empowering team members.

Best Practices for Leaders

The following strategies can help leaders develop their conflict resolution skills:

1. Develop emotional intelligence (EI). EI is the ability to recognize and manage one's own emotions and the emotions of others.
2. Lead by example. Leading by example focuses on maintaining composure, showing respect, and focusing on solutions rather than blame.
3. Receive conflict resolution training. Such training introduces leaders to important communication skills, negotiation techniques, and conflict resolution strategies.
4. Seek feedback and reflect. Feedback from team members, mentors, and colleagues provides insights into what worked well and what could be improved.
5. Promote a culture of respect. A culture of respect helps prevent and resolve conflicts.

Resource Allocation Methods

A scarce good is a good that has more quantity demanded than quantity supplied at \$0.[18] Scarcity falls into three distinctive categories: demand-induced, supply-induced, and structural. Demand-induced scarcity happens when the demand for the resource increases and the supply stays the same. Supply-induced scarcity occurs when the supply of a resource is very low compared to the demand. Lastly, structural scarcity occurs when part of a population does not have equal access to resources due to political conflicts or location.[19] Throughout history, the need has arisen to decipher how best to allocate scarce resources, whether it was food during World War II, water in the African desert, or oil to different parts of the world; however, the COVID-19 pandemic, more than any other occasion, highlighted the glaring need to have a transparent, ethical, and evidence-based process in place.

The COVID-19 pandemic highlighted the importance of conflict management in the context of scarce resources. Strategies such as open communication, collaborative decision-making, and equitable distribution were used to resolve disputes that arose when individuals or groups competed for limited resources, such as vaccines and therapeutics like Remdesivir. These techniques helped mitigate tensions and found solutions that benefited all parties involved.

When resources are limited, individuals or groups may perceive a need to compete for access, leading to conflict due to differing priorities or perceptions of fairness in distribution.

Such scenarios tend to result in competition where individuals or teams feel pressure to prioritize their own needs over the collective, miscommunication because of a lack of transparency, and perceived inequity if resource allocation is seen as unfair, which can lead to resentment and conflict.

Strategies used to manage these conflicts during COVID-19 included:

1. Open communication where transparent discussion was encouraged about resource constraints and individual needs. An important component of this was incorporating active listening to understand different perspectives.
2. Collaborative decision-making by involving stakeholders in the decision-making process to identify potential solutions and compromises. The stakeholders involved often brainstormed to generate creative options for resource allocation.
3. To ensure fair distribution, clear criteria for resource allocation based on objective factors and organizational goals were established. Needs based on urgency or impact were considered.

In addition, mediation provided a neutral space for parties to discuss issues and reach a mutually agreeable solution, and negotiation strategies helped parties find a middle ground that satisfied everyone.

The experience at Providence Holy Cross during the COVID-19 pandemic illustrates how several of these strategies and techniques were implemented successfully.[20]

Chapter Summary

In summary, this chapter has provided a review of several important leadership techniques and skills. Successfully responding to real life scenarios, such as the one highlighted in the beginning of this chapter, often requires a leader to have mastered the art of collaborating and engaging with physicians and being well-versed in contingency planning. In addition, leaders should understand the concepts of chain of command and span of control and be cognizant of resource allocation methods and how to manage conflict. A leader who has a good command of each of these concepts, will more often than not be set up for success.

REFERENCES

1. Braam A, Buljac-Samardzic M, Hilders CGIM, van Wijngaarden JDH. Collaboration Between Physicians from Different Medical Specialties in Hospital Settings: A Systematic Review. *J Multidiscip Healthc.* 2022;15:2277–2300. https://www.dovepress.com/collaboration-between-physicians-from-different-medical-specialties-in-peer-reviewed-fulltext-article-JMDH
2. Landesman LY. *Landesman's Public Health Management of Disasters: The Practice Guide, 4th edition.* Washington, D.C.: APHA Press; 2017.
3. Nelson C, Lurie N, Wasserman J. Assessing Public Health Emergency Preparedness: Concepts, Tools, and Challenges. *Annu Rev Public Health.* 2007;28:1–18. doi: 10.1146/annurev.publhealth.28.021406.144054.
4. Barnett DJ, Thompson CB, Errett NA, et al. Determinants of Emergency Response Willingness in the Local Public Health Workforce by Jurisdictional and Scenario Patterns: A Cross-Sectional Survey. *BMC Public Health.* 2012;12(1):164. https://doi.org/10.1186/1471-2458-12-164.
5. Santinha G, Forte T, Gomes A. Willingness to Work During Public Health Emergencies: A Systematic Literature Review. *Healthcare (Basel).* 2022;10(8):1500. doi: 10.3390/healthcare10081500.
6. Bandura A. Self-efficacy: Toward a Unifying Theory of Behavioral Change. *Psychological Review.* 1977;84(2):191–215. doi: 10.1037/0033-295X.84.2.191.
7. Environmental Protection Agency. Risk Communication. https://semspub.epa.gov/work/11/174720.pdf.
8. Emergency Management Institute. National Incident Management System. FEMA. https://training.fema.gov/nims/
9. California Emergency Medical Services Authority. Hospital Incident Command System. https://emsa.ca.gov/disaster-medical-services-division-hospital-incident-command-system-resources/
10. Emergency Preparedness Rule. Centers for Medicare and Medicaid Services. Accessed November 28, 2024. = https://www.cms.gov/medicare/health-safety-standards/quality-safety-oversight-emergency-preparedness/emergency-preparedness-rule.
11. Organ C. 7 Organizational Structure Types (with Examples). Forbes Advisor blog. May 29, 2004. https://www.forbes.com/advisor/business/organizational-structure
12. What Is Span of Control In Business and Management? Organimi. May 1, 2024. https://www.organimi.com/span-of-control-in-business/
13. Bennett G. Understanding the Chain of Command in Business. The OneDirectory blog. December 2022. https://www.onedirectory.com/blog/the-chain-of-command-in-business/

14. Icenhower M. The Chain of Command: A Powerful Patient Safety Tool. *Coverys*. August 10, 2023. https://www.coverys.com/expert-insights/chain-of-command-a-powerful-patient-safety-tool
15. How to Improve Interdepartmental Collaboration. Adobe. Accessed December 6, 2024. https://www.adobe.com/acrobat/business/hub/tips-for-interdepartmental-collaboration.html?msockid=05ca32130928620c0dbe275e082f6396
16. 11 Ways to Improve Interdepartmental Collaboration and Communication. *eResource Scheduler* https://www.eresourcescheduler.com/blog/11-ways-to-improve-interdepartmentalcollaboration
17. Dallago D. Unlocking Success: Why Conflict Resolution is the Key to Effective Leadership. Interaction Management Associates Blog. August 12, 2024. Accessed December 4, 2024. https://imamediation.com/blog/unlocking-success-why-conflict-resolution-is-the-key-to-effective-leadership
18. Scarcity. Wikipedia. Accessed December 6, 2024. https://en.wikipedia.org/wiki/Scarcity
19. Kennedy B. Environmental Scarcity and the Outbreak of Conflict. Population Reference Bureau. January 1, 2001. Accessed November 30, 2024. https://www.prb.org/resources/environmental-scarcity-and-the-outbreak-of-conflict/
20. Donovan DW, Hoffman R. Providence Holy Cross Outlines Steps for Ethical Distribution for a COVID Medication. Health Progress. 2020; Fall;57–60.

CHAPTER 27
Communication

Michael D. Patrick, Jr, MD, FAAP

HALM CORE CONTENT:

- 8.5 Principles of media relations, advertising, social media, and community relations
- 8.7.4 Emotional intelligence
- 8.7.6 Interpersonal communication
- 8.7.8 Public relations and media

CASE SCENARIO

Dr. Cheryl Fletcher, a well-respected physician leader, finds herself in the middle of a public health crisis. An outbreak of a preventable infectious disease is affecting her community, and misinformation is circulating online and spilling over into conversations within homes, schools, and workplaces.

Dr. Fletcher faces a lack of public trust in the healthcare system as she begins the daunting task of addressing the community's concerns, engaging traditional and social media, and promoting vaccination in a way that resonates with diverse audiences. She must leverage her communication skills to restore trust, educate the public, and advocate for public health measures to contain the outbreak.

Emotional Intelligence and Interpersonal Communication

Emotional intelligence (EQ) refers to the ability to recognize, understand, and manage one's emotions and behaviors and to recognize, understand, and influence the emotions and behaviors of others.[1] Unlike the intelligence quotient (IQ), EQ is not fixed and can be developed and strengthened over time. From exam rooms and hospital wards to podcast appearances and television interviews, EQ is essential for every conversation in healthcare.

EQ encompasses four key pillars: self-awareness, self-management, social awareness, and relationship management. Each of these pillars can be taught, practiced, and strengthened. The ability to develop EQ is important because elevated EQ in healthcare providers is associated with improved patient satisfaction, better health outcomes, enhanced physician wellness, and reduced burnout.[2,3] In a public health crisis, EQ is essential for managing emotions, building trust, and fostering stakeholder collaboration. Because of its importance, EQ should be introduced early in medical training and reinforced throughout one's career.

The first pillar of EQ, self-awareness, is recognizing and understanding one's emotions, strengths, weaknesses, and goals. Emotions are a set of physiologic reactions to a particular situation. The emotions we feel during a challenging encounter are a complex product of the problem at hand, past experiences, values, beliefs, and our interpretation of the situation.

Self-awareness is the foundation of EQ and is essential for effective communication. It influences the second pillar of EQ, self-management, allowing us to control impulsive behaviors, take a step back, assess the situation, and respond with thought and care. Strong self-awareness and self-management skills enable one to act upon emotions in healthy ways. When experiencing strong emotions, they allow an understanding of what is being felt and how to respond appropriately.

Social awareness is the ability to recognize and understand the emotions and behaviors of others. This awareness leads to empathy, which is the ability to understand a person from their frame of reference and to experience their feelings vicariously. Empathy is crucial to communication as one strives to understand the concerns, fears, and motivations of others. This understanding allows the communicator to tailor a message that resonates with a particular audience.

Responding with empathy also supports the final pillar of EQ: relationship management. Empathy enables people to inspire, influence, and positively affect the emotions and behaviors of others. It lifts people up and supports them through challenging times.

Emotional intelligence is the foundation of interpersonal communication. Combining self-awareness, self-management, social awareness, and relationship management with active listening, nonverbal communication, feedback, context, and an understanding of other situational factors, physician leaders can successfully navigate complex and nuanced conversations.

Community Relations

Community relations has always been an important activity for physicians. Counseling patients and families in the exam room, serving on hospital committees, and speaking to school boards, legislators, and the media are important ways medical professionals engage their community with education and advocacy.

In the internet age, community has greatly expanded, giving medical professionals an easy-to-reach sphere of influence at state, national, and international levels. This expanded reach is possible through websites, blog posts, infographics, podcasts, videos, and other forms of digital content.

Whether engaging a single family, hospital staff, or millions of social media followers, the framework for successful communication remains the same: identify the target audience, assess the audience's needs, determine the communication goal, and employ storytelling techniques to share information, influence behavior, and shape health-related outcomes.

IDENTIFY THE TARGET AUDIENCE

Identifying the target audience is the first step in effective community relations.[4] The target audience determines the words and tone used, the channels leveraged, and the strategies employed. Crafting a one-size-fits-all communications strategy would be easy, but this will not resonate with all audiences.

An effective communication strategy requires words and communication channels to be different when addressing colleagues, community officials, schools, and the general public. For example, the language used to share scientific data with colleagues will differ from the language used to educate the general public about vaccinations.

Each audience will be best reached through different communication channels.[5] Updating colleagues on an outbreak can be conducted through public health bulletins and online dashboards, while communicating with local officials and schools may take place during town halls and board meetings. The general public can be informed through television interviews and engagement on social media platforms.

ASSESS THE AUDIENCE'S NEEDS

The needs of each target audience are also different.[6] Colleagues require detailed information about the outbreak, including the number of cases, the affected populations, and the recommended public health interventions. Community officials may seek guidance on protecting residents, and schools will need advice on educating students about the illness in an age-appropriate manner, creating attendance policies for infected children, and handling isolation procedures when exposures occur. The general public will have basic questions about the disease, its symptoms, treatment, prevention, and the benefits and risks of vaccination.

As communication strategies are crafted, each target audience's needs, concerns, and communication preferences should be addressed. One must also consider the cultural, social, and economic factors influencing each audience's health beliefs and behaviors.

Beginning with a blank page for each audience will allow the communicator to identify each stakeholder, their unique needs, barriers, challenges, and the best channels for communicating with them. This focus is essential for building trust, fostering collaboration, and promoting public health interventions in a way that resonates with diverse audiences.

DETERMINE THE COMMUNICATION GOALS

Goals should be set for each group of stakeholders. What knowledge does one want to share and why? What is the desired response from each audience? What decisions and behaviors need to be shaped? Identification of these goals will inform the communication strategy, message development, and evaluation plans.[7] Each goal should be SMART: specific, measurable, attainable, relevant, and time-bound.[8] This will allow an evaluation of the success of the communication efforts and the ability to adjust strategy as needed.

An example of a SMART goal is to ensure that a specific percentage of the population is vaccinated by a particular date. This goal is specific as it identifies the target population, the desired behavior, and the desired outcome. In the case scenario, it is measurable because the percentage of vaccinated individuals can be tracked over time.

The goal is attainable by working with local health departments, pharmacies, community physicians, and schools to provide vaccinations. It is also relevant because vaccination is a critical public health intervention to prevent disease spread.

Finally, the goal is time-bound as it details when a specific percentage of the population should be vaccinated. If the goal is not met, an adjustment in the communication strategy will be needed to reach the audience in question in a manner and place that influences behavior in a way that meets the goal.[9]

USE STORYTELLING

Storytelling is an effective way to meet audience needs while achieving health-related goals. Stories are memorable, engaging, and persuasive. They can simplify complex information, evoke emotion, and inspire action. Stories can be used to share personal experiences, explain scientific concepts, and advocate for public health interventions. Stories are a powerful tool for building trust, fostering collaboration, and promoting behavior change.[10] Stories can be shared through traditional and social media, public presentations, and written materials.

When crafting a story to share with an audience, the reporter's questions can effectively build a framework for the story. Building this framework involves answering the questions of who, what, when, where, why, and how. This framework ensures the story is complete, engaging, and relevant to the audience.[11]

In the example of promoting vaccinations, who should be vaccinated? When and where should vaccination occur? Why is vaccination necessary? How does the vaccine work? What side effects will it cause, and what risks will it present?

Answering the reporter's questions ensures the public has the information to make informed decisions, which can be strengthened by sharing experiences of infected patients and recounting vaccine success stories from other communities.[12] Physician leaders can also advocate for public health funds and private and public insurance to cover the costs of the shots. This advocacy will help ensure everyone has access to the vaccine and increase the likelihood of containing the outbreak.

CURATE CONTENT

After choosing a target audience, defining the goal, and crafting a story, it's time to communicate that story with the audience. There are many ways to communicate a story, and it's not always to start from scratch; trustworthy, evidence-based sources already exist. Content curation involves identifying, selecting, and sharing existing content with the audience.[13]

There are many sources from which to curate content. For example, the U.S. Centers for Disease Control and Prevention and the World Health Organization are reliable sources of health information. Other valuable sources include the National Institutes of Health, the American Academy of Pediatrics, and the American Medical Association. Local and state health departments and regional hospital websites also provide reliable information. These sites offer content tailored for many target audiences, including medical professionals, public health officials, and the general public. They also provide various easy-to-share artifacts, such as scientific articles, public health bulletins, fact sheets, blog posts, infographics, videos, and podcasts.

Adding a personal touch to curated content can refine the message and increase its impact. In a community health crisis, the physician leader could share a peer-reviewed article or public health bulletin and create an adjacent message highlighting key points, emphasizing recommendations, and explaining how they apply to the local community. Infographics, videos, and podcasts may only tell a portion of the story, but they can be shared and supplemented with comments, personal experience, and practical advice.

Curated content can be shared through many platforms, including websites, social media, traditional media, public presentations, and written materials. Content can also be shared through email, text messages, and phone calls. The key is to reach the audience where they are and in a manner that resonates with them based on each target audience's communication preferences and the most effective channels for each group. Reaching diverse audiences with a resonating message builds trust, fosters broad collaboration, and promotes public health interventions.[14]

Respecting copyright and intellectual property rights is essential when curating and sharing content. Online content-sharing should include a link to the original source; this gives the author credit for their work, increases traffic to their site, and provides a trustworthy source for the audience to obtain additional information. Content for public presentations and written materials should include a citation of the source. If the content will be used in a manner that generates profit, it is essential to secure the appropriate permissions. When in doubt, one should contact the content creator and ask permission to use their work.[15]

CREATE CONTENT

While curating and sharing content is an effective way to communicate a story, there are times when this method is not sufficient. Perhaps there is a particular lens through which the story should be told, or existing content may not be ideal for meeting communication goals. The presenter may have a unique style of storytelling that already resonates with audiences or a creative side to produce engaging, memorable, and persuasive messages. In these cases, content creation may be a better approach.[16]

Created content can take many forms. Some examples include blog posts, public service announcements, infographics, videos, podcasts, and written materials. Each form has its strengths and weaknesses. Blog posts are engaging and can be shared easily. Public service announcements are memorable and can be broadcast through traditional media. Infographics are visually appealing and can simplify complex information. Videos are entertaining and easily shared on many social media platforms, and podcasts are convenient when listeners are driving, exercising, or working. Written materials can be physically distributed and consumed at the reader's convenience.

Multiple forms of content can tell the same story. This variety will engage diverse audiences and increase the message's impact on a community.[17] One might tell the story with a blog post on the health department's website, public service announcements broadcast on local television and radio, an infographic shared on Facebook, or a short video posted on YouTube or TikTok. Written material detailing symptoms, management, and prevention strategies can be shared with local hospitals and clinics. Each form of content can be tailored to meet a particular audience's unique needs, concerns, and communication preferences.

Content creation is an opportunity to share a story, build trust, foster collaboration, and promote behavior change.[18] The content can be leveraged to share the experiences of infected patients, explain the benefits of vaccination, and advocate for community support during the outbreak.

Social Media

Social media platforms are ideal for engaging audiences and sharing curated and created content.[19] Some platforms, such as Facebook, Twitter (X), and Instagram, are well known for their broad reach. Others, like LinkedIn, Pinterest, Snapchat, and TikTok, are popular with specific demographics. Each platform has its place in a communication campaign, and the most effective platforms will depend on the target audiences.

Creating a professional presence and regularly engaging on multiple social media platforms should be done long before crisis communication is needed.[20] This will build a following and establish familiarity and trust with the audience. It will also increase the visibility of future posts and the likelihood they will be shared with others.

Social media platforms use complex algorithms to prioritize content for users.[21] The visibility of content can be increased by posting at peak times, sharing content that resonates with the audience, and encouraging followers to like, comment, and share posts.

Hashtags can also be used to increase reach. These are keywords or phrases preceded by the pound (#) symbol. They categorize content, delivering the message to more users and encouraging discovery by larger audiences. Hashtags can be applied to threads of conversation, shared items, and created content.

By creating content, sharing the content on social media platforms, and including relevant hashtags, the story can be delivered more widely and with the greatest impact.

An important consideration when using social media is comments made by those who wish to contradict the communicator's goals by challenging the message or presenting conflicting information. Rather than reacting to these challenges directly, it is permissible to delete comments and block or ban users who habitually attempt to derail health-related content.

Although it's rare, there are times when the physician may feel threatened, directly or indirectly, by comments made by others. In this case, the physician should contact law enforcement, just as they would with in-person threats.

Because social media is a form of interpersonal communication, leaders must employ emotional intelligence and empathy when engaging on these platforms. Comments that seem to challenge the message may be legitimate concerns, given the user's frame of reference. For example, a mother whose child has autism may be vaccine-hesitant because she believes immunizations harmed her child. Responding with care can go a long way to providing appropriate reassurance and alleviating the fears of others watching the conversation from the sidelines.

Media Relations

Television, radio, newspapers, and magazines are essential sources of information for many people. These trusted outlets reach large audiences and are ideal for sharing public health messages, promoting behavior change, and advocating for community support.[22] Traditional media should be leveraged to reach diverse audiences, including those who do not regularly use social media or the internet. Similar to having an established social media presence before a communications campaign is needed, it is also essential for healthcare leaders to develop relationships with traditional media outlets and local reporters before a crisis occurs.

Regularly pitching ideas to traditional media outlets, providing expert commentary on health-related stories, and submitting letters to the editor are effective ways to build relationships with reporters. These relationships can be leveraged during a public health crisis to share accurate information, dispel myths, and advocate for public health interventions. Regular ongoing collaboration with local media builds rapport with reporters and audiences. Then, when a crisis occurs, journalists and community members are more likely to hear, accept, disseminate, and follow the advice of healthcare leaders.[23]

Another way of strengthening relationships with traditional media outlets is to employ a dedicated media liaison through a healthcare organization's marketing and public relations department. This individual can pitch stories, respond to media inquiries, and coordinate interviews. The media liaison can monitor traditional and social media for misinformation and respond with accurate data and recommendations. They should be well-versed in public health, possess excellent communication skills, have established relationships with local media outlets, and be able to work under pressure. The media liaison can assist several leaders within an organization, choosing the best leaders for a given topic and coaching them to share accurate information while remaining on message and presenting themselves professionally.

Public Relations and Advertising

Public relations (PR) is a strategic communications process that builds and maintains mutually beneficial relationships between two or more parties. In the case of healthcare organizations, PR is most often accomplished by providing services, support, education, and advocacy within a community.

Physician leaders can strengthen the positive image of their healthcare organization by behaving professionally and seeking to include all members of a community, regardless of background or beliefs, when providing care, sharing educational messages, and embarking on advocacy work. The community will likely respond to this positive image by seeking services from the organization and encouraging others to do the same.

Advertising is a paid form of communication that reaches a community. Its principles are similar to other communication strategies: identify the target audience, establish goals, craft a story, and share the message through appropriate channels. Advertising is a terrific way to spread awareness for a particular service or a new facility. However, in the case of a public health crisis, advertising is seldom necessary because media outlets are tasked with sharing accurate information with the public, and local healthcare leaders are a convenient and trustworthy source of information. Media outlets are particularly interested in leaders who can share concise messages that resonate with diverse audiences, build trust, and foster collaboration.[24]

An exception to this is paying for sponsored posts on social media platforms. Many platforms allow organizations to pay for increased visibility of their posts. This can be an effective way to share a public health message, promote behavior change, and advocate for community support.[25] Sponsored posts can be targeted to specific demographics, increasing the likelihood that a particular target audience will see them.

Chapter Summary

Effective interpersonal communication is essential for healthcare leaders, and emotional intelligence (EQ) is the foundation for communication success. EQ consists of self-awareness, self-management, social awareness, and relationship management. Working through one's feelings and the emotions of others is crucial for building empathy, which helps the leader understand concerns, fears, and motivations. With this insight, leaders are better equipped to inspire, influence, and positively impact the emotions and behaviors of others.

Choosing a target audience is the first step in effective communication. The audience determines the words and tone used, the channels leveraged, and the strategies employed. Identifying the target audience's unique needs, concerns, and communication preferences is essential for connecting, building trust, changing behavior, and fostering collaboration. SMART communication goals should be tailored for each target audience. A story is then crafted. This considers the leader's goals and the audience's needs while answering the questions of who, what, when, where, why, and how. The story is communicated through curated and created content, which can be shared on social and traditional media.

Media liaisons are valuable members of the healthcare team. They can maintain relationships with the media, pitch stories, respond to inquiries, coordinate interviews, monitor traditional and social media for misinformation, and respond with accurate data and recommendations. Advertising also plays a role in effective communication. Paying for sponsored posts on social media platforms and paid communication with traditional media outlets can increase the visibility and impact of a leader's communication strategy.

The ultimate goal of communication efforts is to engage diverse audiences, build awareness and trust, enhance the public image, and support the relationship between the healthcare organization and the many communities it serves.

REFERENCES

1. O'Connor PJ, Hill A, Kaya M, Martin B. The Measurement Of Emotional Intelligence: A Critical Review of the Literature And Recommendations For Researchers And Practitioners. *Frontiers in Psychology*. 2019;10:1116.
2. Kadadi S, Bharamanaikar SR. Role of Emotional Intelligence in Healthcare Industry. *Drishtikon: A Management Journal*. 2020;11(1):1-37.
3. Vlachou EM, Damigos D, Lyrakos G, et al. The Relationship Between Burnout Syndrome and Emotional Intelligence in Healthcare Professionals. *Health Science Journal*. 2016;10(5):1.
4. Lancaster G, Massingham L. Communications Strategy. *Essentials of Marketing Management* London: Routledge; 2017;199-232.
5. Noar SM. An Audience–Channel–Message–Evaluation (ACME) Framework for Health Communication Campaigns. *Health promotion practice.* 2012;13(4):481-488.
6. McCormack L, Sheridan S, Lewis M, et al. Communication and Dissemination Strategies to Facilitate

the Use of Health-Related Evidence. *Evid Rep Technol Assess*. 2013;213:1-520.

7. Foster D, Jonker J. Stakeholder Relationships: The Dialogue of Engagement. *Corporate Governance: The International Journal of Business in Society*. 2005;5(5):51-57.
8. Bjerke MB, Renger R. Being Smart About Writing SMART Objectives. *Eval Program Plann*. 2017;61:125-127.
9. Haumer F, Schlicker L, Murschetz PC, Kolo C. Tailor the Message and Change Will Happen? An Experimental Study of Message Tailoring as an Effective Communication Strategy for Organizational Change. *Journal of Strategy and Management*. 2021;14(4):426-443.
10. Brooks SP, Zimmermann GL, Lang M, et al. A Framework To Guide Storytelling as a Knowledge Translation Intervention for Health-Promoting Behaviour Change. *Implementation Science Communications*. 2022;3(1):35.
11. McKinnon M, Kudo M, Ouchi S. Chapter 7: Understanding and Using Media in Health Promotion. In: McKinnon M Ed. *Health Promotion: A Practical Guide to Effective Communication*. Cambridge UK: Cambridge University Press; 2021:147.
12. Shelby A, Ernst K. Story and Science: How Providers and Parents Can Utilize Storytelling to Combat Anti-Vaccine Misinformation. *Human Vaccines & Immunotherapeutics*. 2013;9(8):1795-1801.
13. Mihailidis P, Cohen J. Exploring Curation as a Core Competency in Digital and Media Literacy Education. *J Interactive Media in Education*. 2013;(1). https://doi.org/10.5334/2013-02
14. Nuss KE. Content Curation. *Social Media for Medical Professionals: Strategies for Successfully Engaging in an Online World*. Switzerland: Springer; 2019;121-144.
15. Mapua J. *Respecting Digital Content: Using and Sharing Intellectual Property Online*. New York: The Rosen Publishing Group, Inc.; 2018.
16. Dahlstrom MF. Using Narratives and Storytelling to Communicate Science with Nonexpert Audiences. *Proceedings of the National Academy of Sciences*. 2014;111(supplement_4):13614-13620.
17. Scolari CA. Transmedia Storytelling: New Ways of Communicating in the Digital Age. In: *AC/E Digital Culture Annual Report 2014; 69-79.* https://www.accioncultural.es/media/Default%20Files/activ/2014/Adj/Anuario_ACE_2014/EN/6Storytelling_CScolari.pdf.
18. Lopes AR, Casais B. Digital Content Marketing: Conceptual Review and Recommendations for Practitioners. *Academy of Strategic Management Journal*. 2022;21(2):1-17.
19. Luttrell R. *Social Media: How to Engage, Share, and Connect*. Lanham, MD: Rowman & Littlefield; 2018.
20. Capozzi L, Rucci SR. *Crisis Management in the Age of Social Media*. New York: Business Expert Press; 2013.
21. Poleac G, Ghergut-Babii AN. How Social Media Algorithms Influence the Way Users Decide-Perspectives of Social Media Users and Practitioners. *Technium Soc Sci J*. 2024;57:69-81.
22. Anwar A, Malik M, Raees V, Anwar A. Role of Mass Media and Public Health Communications in the COVID-19 Pandemic. *Cureus*. 2020;12(9):e10453.
23. Cairns G, De Andrade M, MacDonald L. Reputation, Relationships, Risk Communication, and the Role of Trust in the Prevention and Control of Communicable Disease: A Review. *J Health Comm*. 2013;8(12):1550-1565. doi: 10.1080/10810730.2013.840696
24. Majid U, Wasim A, Truong J, Bakshi S. Public Trust in Governments, Health Care Providers, and the Media During Pandemics: A Systematic Review. *J Trust Research*. 2021;11(2):119-141. https://doi.org/10.1080/21515581.2022.2029742
25. Freeman B, Potente S, Rock V, McIver J. Social Media Campaigns That Make a Difference: What Can Public Health Learn From the Corporate Sector and Other Social Change Marketers. *Public Health Res Pract*. 2015;25(2):e2521517.

SECTION 9

Professionalism and Ethics

CHAPTER 28

Professionalism

Amy Harrington, MD, CPE, FAPA, and Andrew S. Karson, MD

HALM CORE CONTENT:

- 9.3 Cultural and spiritual diversity of patients and staff as relates to healthcare needs
- 9.4 Patient-centered care and shared decision making
- 9.8 Professional standards, licensure, board certification, code of conduct
- 9.9 Educational program integration and continuing education
  - 9.9.1 Staff
  - 9.9.2 Medical Professionals
- 9.10 Role modeling professionalism in the learning environment
- 9.11 Strategies for management of the disruptive physician

CASE SCENARIO:

The Credentials Committee is reviewing the credentialling application for a newly hired sub-specialist. It took longer to successfully recruit a physician for this position than initially anticipated, and there is a clinical need for this physician to start providing patient care. The application materials include a peer reference that states that despite proficient care, this physician had several patient complaints related to communication and providing culturally sensitive care. How can basic competence in practicing medicine be determined? Why are providing culturally sensitive care and working well with other team members important skills for a physician? Why is it important for senior physicians to model these skills to more junior members of the profession? What are some ways to manage physicians who are technically competent but who receive patient complaints or who are difficult to work with due to personality issues or poor communication skills?

MEDICINE IS CHARACTERIZED in our society as a *profession*, a term that carries specific sociological implications. Members of a profession portray themselves to the public and are, in turn, accepted by the public as people who have specialized skills or knowledge. In addition to a shared educational and training pathway, members of a profession often have common values and hold their peers accountable for maintaining those ideals. As professionals, physicians must understand the role that society expects of them, which in turn comes with certain privileges that must be carefully maintained.

A physician's identity is often shaped by a sense of responsibility, knowledge, and authority within patient care.[1] Physicians agree to adhere to certain ethical standards, and the public recognizes their specific role in society. Licensure and board certification ensure they have demonstrated adequate training to be admitted to the profession, and there is an expectation that they will maintain knowledge of current standards of practice. They will use this to train more junior members of the profession, either through direct teaching or through modeling the professional standards to those still in training.

Licensure, Board Certification

Licensure and board certification are elements that uphold the integrity of the medical profession and ensure that physicians are both competent and accountable. Each U.S. state or jurisdiction has its own medical licensing board and its own licensing process. Although licensing boards are trending toward uniform requirements, reciprocity between states has mostly been eliminated. Physicians must be licensed in each state where they practice medicine, including telemedicine. Physicians practicing telemedicine must adhere to the requirements of the state where the patient, not the physician, is physically located.

During the licensure process, a state board of registration will require verification of education and graduate training. Other information required includes a review of past and current licenses from other jurisdictions, prior hospital privileges, and professional references. Physicians must pass either the United States Medical Licensing Examination (USMLE) or the Comprehensive Osteopathic Medical Licensing Examination (COMLEX) for osteopathic physicians.[2]

While licensure is a basic requirement, board certification has become, at times, an essential next step for physicians, indicating competence within a specific field. After completing a residency, a physician will be eligible to take a board examination in that field. These exams are administered by specialty boards, such as the American Board of Medical Specialties (ABMS) or the American Osteopathic Association (AOA).

Although board certification is voluntary, many payers require a physician to be board-certified to participate in their network. Most specialty boards require participation in maintenance of certification (MOC) programs that ensure physicians stay up to date in their clinical skills and their knowledge of the subject matter. Although criticized at times for the financial and administrative burden it can place on physicians, MOC ensures familiarity with the most up-to-date developments within the field. Many healthcare organizations require board certification to be credentialed and receive clinical privileges.

Healthcare organizations and insurance companies typically require a physician to undergo a credentialing process. The credentialing body will verify an applicant's medical school education and post-graduate training, as well as licensure and board certification. A history of malpractice claims or disciplinary actions is obtained from the National Practitioner Data Bank.

Physicians typically need to provide references from colleagues who can verify their clinical competency, communication skills, and adherence to professional standards. Once all the necessary information is collected and verified, a credentialing committee will review the application and determine if privileges to practice will be granted.

Educational Program Integration and Continuing Education

The ongoing development of physicians is an important consideration. Many physicians have not been formally trained in some key areas related to professionalism, including concepts related to diversity, equity, inclusion, and belonging (DEIB); cultural competency; and optimal physician-patient communication strategies.[3] Internal education and development programs should ideally be aimed at advancing these competencies in the physician workforce.

Formal educational requirements around professionalism are put forth by state medical boards as well as federal regulatory and/or other certifying organizations such as the Centers for Medicare & Medicaid Services and The Joint Commission. It is advised that healthcare organizations include physician representatives in the development and execution of any educational requirements such that there is better physician acceptance of the content and the time that physicians will need to devote to this training.

Providing continuing medical education credits and, when possible, specialty board maintenance of certification credits for trainings enhances physician acceptance and compliance with the training. Some organizations also incorporate monetary bonus incentives to ensure participation. Increasingly, asynchronous electronic trainings are employed for physicians, but some curriculum elements are better done live, such as some communication trainings, especially those related to best practices in having crucial conversations.

While some physicians question the benefits of ongoing maintenance of specialty board certifications, public perception, institutional board of trustee comfort, and often payer mandates require physicians to continue to obtain and maintain their certifications. Some exceptions are reasonable to this requirement — for example, when a provider who is in good standing at their organization and who has long-standing board certification plans to retire within the upcoming two years.

For institutions that support residency and fellowship programs, it is often beneficial to have the organization's focus on professionalism be the same for all of the faculty, residents, and fellows. Enrichment programs should be designed so that they can accommodate all levels of physicians at whatever point they are in in their careers.

Cultural and Spiritual Diversity of Patients and Staff in Relation to Healthcare Needs

Teams that include diverse members have been shown to provide better outcomes than teams with less diversity.[4] This is true in healthcare, where diverse clinical teams have been shown to provide better chronic condition management and improved patient adherence to care plans.[5] The diversity of the physician staff should ideally represent the diversity of the community that it serves.

Leaders must make special efforts to ensure that diverse candidates are sourced and ultimately hired into their organizations. Successful recruitment techniques include having a selection committee with members who represent diverse perspectives and candidate searches that reach out to individuals, organizations, and schools that include physicians who are from groups that are underrepresented in medicine.

Given recent court rulings that may restrict the use of race-based criteria, more "holistic review" methods are increasingly being incorporated into healthcare hiring practices such that a person's broader background is considered such as their economic background, personal paths taken, resilience, and experiences working with historically underserved communities.

In addition to creating a diverse healthcare team, it is important to also educate current workforce members to enhance their cultural competencies and to develop proficiency with concepts related to DEIB.[6] Many healthcare leaders have been advancing DEIB programs at their organizations by creating central offices of experts to drive the programs and by increasingly embedding DEIB liaisons within departments.

Patients have a right to access their healthcare in the language of their choice;[7] communication with patients and their families in their preferred language is a foundational step toward improving the overall care provided. It is recommended that healthcare personnel use dedicated and qualified interpreters when working with patients with limited English proficiency whenever possible. Physicians should be discouraged from doing their own interpretation unless they become certified to do so at their institutions.

Patient-Centered Care and Shared Decision-Making

In recent years, healthcare has increasingly shifted away from the physician-dominated model of medical practice and has embraced the concept of patient-centered care, which emphasizes that patients should actively participate in decisions affecting their own care. This is true at both the individual patient level and more broadly as organizations include the patient and family voice in organizational strategy and decision-making.

Shared decision-making (SDM) is a patient-centered model for involving patients in the determination of a treatment plan. Key aspects of this process include providing the patient with the risks and benefits of the different options while soliciting the patient's values, goals, and preferences so the ultimate decision is aligned with the patient's unique needs.

The SDM process can take place over one visit with a patient or it can be stretched over several visits to allow time for the necessary steps. There are evidence-based models as well as decision-making tools that can guide a physician in this process.

Commonly used models include the Three-Talk Model for SDM, which breaks the conversations down into three phases that each have different goals: team talk, option talk, and decision talk.[8] Other models include the SHARE Approach, which condenses the process into the five words made up by the mnemonic (Seek, Help, Assess, Reach, Evaluate), and Purposeful SDM, which focuses on understanding the problem first before presenting and discussing potential interventions.[9]

It is increasingly common for payers to require documentation of use of a patient decision-aid for reimbursement. The National Quality Forum maintains a National Standards for the Certification of Patient Decision Aids to ensure the tools being used have the ability to adequately walk the patient and provider through the process of SDM.[10]

The incorporation of patient and family wishes on a broader scale is often achieved by the formation of patient and family advisory councils (PFACs). While the research behind the creation of PFACs is just developing,[11] these councils are increasingly seen as important strategic enablers to incorporate patient and family perspectives into organizational planning.

Many institutions have PFACs that advise at an organization-wide level, while also having area-specific PFACs, such as one for their pediatrics department and one for their cancer program. In addition, individual PFAC members increasingly serve individually or in small groups as members of other institutional committees, such as the organization's board of trustees, patient safety council, and patient experience committee, among others.

Best practices in the creation of PFACs include:[12]

1. Select representative patients/families with respect to diversity and to variation in clinical experiences and conditions, including patients/families who have had good experiences and those who have had negative ones.
2. Aim for a council size of 12–18 members such that the group is small enough to facilitate interpersonal dynamics and dialog, but large enough to allow for broad-based idea sharing.
3. Limit healthcare entity staff to at most three or four standing members so that the patient/family input is primary.
4. Membership term limits should be two to three years and term durations should be staggered.
5. Patients/families should be compensated for the expenses they incur while executing their committee activities, for example for travel and parking, and/or for childcare services.
6. Guidelines and bylaws should be created by the council to govern meeting frequency, agenda planning, voting procedures, and other operational processes.

Code of Conduct and Role-Modeling Professionalism in the Learning Environment

Physicians are expected to uphold lifelong learning and be familiar with the latest trends in the delivery of patient care so they can provide the highest standard of patient care in every professional interaction. In addition, they are expected to prioritize patient well-being and maintain professional integrity.

There are many ways in which this Code of Conduct is communicated in medicine, the first being the Hippocratic Oath that all medical school students take at graduation. The American Medical Association (AMA) provides a comprehensive Code of Medical Ethics that outlines behaviors of professional conduct for physicians. In its most recent version from 2016, the code emphasizes the following:[13]

1. Patient welfare and well-being.
2. Patient autonomy.
3. Confidentiality.
4. Honesty and integrity.
5. Respect for others, both patients and colleagues.
6. Competence and maintenance of skills.
7. Justice.

Physicians play a vital role in modeling this code of conduct for residents, students, and other learners, particularly as the perception of what is acceptable physician behavior evolves and as the concept of inter-professionalism plays a greater role in healthcare. As team-based approaches to healthcare become the norm, it will be more important for physicians to work well alongside other healthcare professionals, fostering a respectful and inclusive environment in a patient-centered approach to care.

Inter-professional education plays a greater role in the training of all disciplines of healthcare professionals. The Interprofessional Education Collaborative (IPEC), a coalition of 22 health professions education associations, established core competencies that learners should master in order to provide healthcare that is both patient-centered as well as beneficial from a population health standpoint. The collaborative's 33 sub-competencies fall under four competency areas of values and ethics, roles and responsibilities, communication, and teams and teamwork.[14]

Although no medical education associations are members of the IPEC, many medical schools incorporate inter-professional education into their curricula. This provides medical students with the opportunity to understand the unique skills and knowledge that the physician brings to the collaborative healthcare team.

In 2012, the Accreditation Council for Graduate Medical Education (ACGME) established the CLER Pathways to Excellence, which has been updated twice, most recently in March 2024.[15] The Clinical Learning Environment (CLER) Program emphasizes topics such as teaming, or making certain the clinical learning environment supports high-performance teams, as well as supervision, including ensuring that all members of the care team can raise concerns when the supervision is having a negative impact on the learning environment. Teaming and supervision are two of six focus areas for CLER, the others being patient safety, healthcare quality, well-being, and professionalism. Many institutions with Graduate Medical Education programs have applied these principles internally, creating workflows for how trainees can raise concerns about the professionalism of an attending.

A healthcare institution can expect a CLER assessment by the ACGME every 18–24 months. An institution can take several steps to ensure this evaluation of the quality of the learning environment goes well.[16]

The designated official for each sponsoring institution should meet with C-suite representatives regularly to maintain readiness for the CLER visit. An interview with the CEO as well as the designated official is a part of each assessment visit. Standardized trainings for quality and patient safety will ensure consistent communication with the evaluator about the institution's approach to these topics. Trainers should point out to residents and fellows how their training is related to CLER objectives so trainees are prepared when they are interviewed by the assessors.

As healthcare evolves to be more team-based, physicians can role-model shared decision-making by soliciting input from other providers on the team. They can demonstrate ethical conduct and respectful communication. If a fellow, resident, or medical student observes a supervising attending reading an article when they do not know an answer or self-reporting a near-miss or error, this will set an expectation for the learner that they should be committed to life-long learning and self-improvement. By embracing this role as a mentor in a team-based model of care, physicians will help prepare future healthcare leaders to uphold the standards of professionalism in a changing healthcare environment.

Strategies for Management of Disruptive Physicians

The Joint Commission on Accreditation of Healthcare Organizations (JCAHO) defines disruptive behavior as "personal conduct, whether verbal or physical, that negatively affects....patient care."[17] Disruptive behavior is common among physicians, with 77% of respondents in one survey of healthcare workers having reported observing such behavior by physicians.[18]

The negative impact of such behavior on patient safety is so concerning that The Joint Commission published Sentinel Event 40, which are behaviors that undermine a culture of safety.[19] Since 2009, they have required that hospitals maintain a code of conduct that defines disruptive behaviors and that leaders create and implement a process for managing such inappropriate behaviors.

Healthcare leaders can use several strategies when dealing with a physician displaying disruptive behavior. The first is often coaching.[20] This intervention is evidence-based and can help identify the underlying causes of the behavior and offer strategies for improvement. Professional coaches can help physicians develop emotional intelligence, improve their communication skills, and better manage workplace conflict.

Regular performance evaluations can help identify patterns of concerning behavior so they can be addressed early. When annual performance reviews are done, they should cover not just clinical competence but also communication and teamwork. It is important to provide clear feedback if a physician's behavior is affecting team dynamics and provide specific expectations for anticipated changes in behavior.

If the issues persist or become more serious, a performance improvement plan (PIP) may be required. A PIP is a structured document that outlines specifical behavioral goals, timelines, and consequences for failure to meet these expectations. Again, clear and consistent feedback about both the behavior and about adherence with the PIP is necessary from the supervisor so additional support can be provided if the physician is not meeting goals.

Chapter Summary

Physicians must maintain standards of professionalism to preserve the integrity of the field of medicine and to preserve public trust. Basic requirements include licensure, board certification and credentialing. In recent years, the practice of medicine has placed a greater importance on culturally sensitive and patient-centered care. It is important for physicians to maintain knowledge in their specialized field of medicine as well as to stay current as new concepts take on greater importance so they can serve as mentors and role models for younger members of the profession.

REFERENCES

1. Hall P. Interprofessional Teamwork: Professional Cultures as Barriers. *Journal of Interprofessional Care*. 2004;S1:188–196.
2. Federation of State Medical Boards. About Physician Licensure. Accessed 12/19/24. https://www.fsmb.org/u.s.-medical-regulatory-trends-and-actions/guide-to-medical-regulation-in-the-united-states/about-physician-licensure
3. Smith TK, Hudson Z. Enhancing Curricula About Diversity, Equity, Inclusion and Justice in Undergraduate Medical Education. *Pediatric Annals*. 2023;52(7):e249-e255. doi:10.3928/19382359-20230516-02,
4. McKinsey & Company. Diversity Matters Even Move: The Case for Holistic Impact. December 5, 2023..
5. Perez-Stable EJ, El-Toukhy S. Communicating with Diverse Patients: How Patient and Clinician Factors Affect Disparities. *Patient Education and Counseling*. 2018;101(12):2186–2194
6. Saha S, Komaromy M, Koepsell TD, Bindman AB. Patient-Physician Racial Concordance and the Perceived Quality and Use of Health Care. *Arch Intern Med*. 1999;159(9);997–1004. doi: 10.1001/archinte.159.9.997.
7. Basu G, Phillips Costa V, Jain P. Clinicians' Obligations To Use Qualified Medical Interpreters When Caring for Patients with Limited English Proficiency. *AMA J Ethics*. 2017;19(3):245–252. doi: 10.1001/journalofethics.2017.19.3.ecas2-1703.
8. Elwyn G, Durand MA, Song J, et al. A Three-Talk Model for Shared Decision Making: Multistage Consultation Process. *BMJ*. 2017:359;j4891. doi:10.1136/bmj,j4891
9. Agency for Healthcare Research and Quality. Research in Shared Decision Making. March 2023. Accessed December 4, 2024. www.AHRQ.gov/sdm/research/index.html
10. National Quality Forum. National Standards for the Certification of Patient Decision Aids. December 15, 2016. https://www.qualityforum.org/Publications/2016/12/National_Standards_for_the_Certification_of_Patient_Decision_Aids.aspx.
11. Sharma A, Knox M, Mleczko V, Olayiwola J. The Impact of Patient Advisors on Healthcare Outcomes: A Systematic Review. *BMC Health Services Research*. 2017;17(693). doi: 10.1186/s12913-017-2630-4.
12. Institute for Patient- and Family-Centered Care. Creating Patient and Family Advisory Councils. August 2022. Accessed December 8, 2024. https://www.ipfcc.org/resources/Advisory_Councils.pdf.
13. American Medical Association. AMA Code of Medical Ethics. 2016. Accessed December 20, 2024. https://www.ama-assn.org/topics/ama-code-medical-ethics.
14. Interprofessional Education Collaborative. Core Competencies for Interprofessional Collaborative Practice: Version 3. . November 20, 2023. https://interprofessional-education.uamsdev.com/wp-content/uploads/sites/61/2024/06/IPEC_Core_Competencies_Version_3_2023.pdf.
15. Accreditation Council for Graduate Medical Education. CLER Pathways to Excellence: Expectations for an Optimal Clinical Learning Environment to Achieve Safe and High-Quality Patient Care, Version 3.0. 2024. doi:10.35425/ACGME.0010
16. Kim DI, Garrison RC, Duong C, et al. Field Report: Getting Prepared for Your Next CLER Visit. *American Association for Physician Leadership*. May 15, 2018. Accessed December 7, 2024. https://www.physicianleaders.org/articles/field-report-getting-prepared-your-next-cler-visit.
17. Gautham, KS. Addressing Disruptive and Unprofessional Physician Behavior. *Jt Comm J Qual Patient Saf*. 2020; 42(22):61–63. doi: 10.1016/j.jcjq.2019.12.002
18. Rosenstein, AH, O'Daniel M. A Survey of the Impact of Disruptive Behaviors and Communication

Defects on Patient Safety. *Jt Comm J Qual Patient Saf.* 2008;34(8):464–471 doi: 10.1016/s1553-7250(08)34058-6.

19. The Joint Commission. Sentinel Event Alert 40: Behaviors that Undermine a Culture of Safety. Updated June 2021. Accessed December 12, 2024. https://www.jointcommission.org/resources/sentinel-event/sentinel-event-alert-newsletters/sentinel-event-alert-issue-40-behaviors-that-undermine-a-culture-of-safety/.
20. Palamara K, Shanafelt TD. Physician Coaching: Establishing Standards and Core Competencies. *Mayo Clin Proc.* 2024;99(5):693–696. doi:10.1016/j.mayocp.2024.03.002

CHAPTER 29

Ethics

Mark D. Olszyk, MD, MBA, CPE, FAAPL

HALM CORE CONTENT:

- 9.1 Conflict of interest issues and solutions as defined by organizational bylaws, policies, and procedures (futile care)
- 9.2 Consequences of unethical actions
- 9.5 Ethical implications of human- or animal-subject research
  - 9.5.1 Research enterprise initiatives
- 9.6 Ethics committees' roles, structure, and functions
- 9.7 Patients' rights and responsibilities (e.g., informed consent, withdrawal of care, advance directives)
- 9.12 Organizational policies on misinformation
- 9.13 Medical marijuana

CASE SCENARIO:

You are a physician executive at a large hospital. Your organization has been operating in the red for the past two years and now budget constraints are forcing your team to prioritize cost-saving measures. You are faced with an ethical dilemma. A proposed policy would limit access to an expensive but life-saving treatment for critically ill patients. You must balance fiscal responsibility with the moral obligation to provide equitable and compassionate patient care.

HEALTHCARE ETHICS IS THE CORNERSTONE of responsible clinical care and leadership. It touches on everything we do, especially on such challenging issues as euthanasia, patient confidentiality, informed consent, and resource allocation. Physician leaders must recognize and navigate these concerns while being mindful of their duties to their patients and organizational goals. Limited resources often force difficult decisions; ethical leadership is essential to maintain trust and integrity.

To apply ethics in practice, a physician leader can use four key norms or models:

1. Virtue Ethics: Concerns the leader's personality, such as integrity, benevolence, and humility. This model is oriented around the character and motives of the decision-maker.
2. Deontology: Emphasizes duty, responsibility, and rule-keeping, like confidentiality of patient data and informed consent. This model judges the rightness of an act according to a list of principles, not the consequences of the act.
3. Utilitarianism: Promotes the greatest good for the greatest number, maximizing positive outcomes or minimizing harm. The consequences of an action determine whether it was right or wrong. In healthcare, it focuses on resource allocation, prioritizing patients based on need, and potential benefit, especially in crisis situations.
4. Principlism: Developed in the 20th century as a pragmatic approach with four pillars: autonomy (patient rights), beneficence (well-being), nonmaleficence (no harm) and justice (fairness). Principlism helps leaders balance ethical considerations, both clinically and organizationally.

If one or more of these frameworks are used, physician leaders can make morally appropriate choices for the benefit of patients, operational efficiency, and organizational integrity.

Conflict of Interest (COI) Issues and Solutions as Defined by Organizational Bylaws, Policies, and Procedures

Physician executives in medical organizations confront difficult ethical situations when conflicts of interest (COIs) relate to patient care. COIs can come in a variety of forms — money, family, or outside professional obligations — and they can put a physician's objectivity at risk. Effective management of COIs is crucial to maintaining trust, transparency, and equity in healthcare delivery. These conflicts need to be detected, disclosed, and addressed in bylaws, policies, and procedures of organizations especially when decisions involve high-stakes care issues like futile care.

FUTILE CARE AND ETHICAL DILEMMAS

Futile care refers to medical interventions that are unlikely to benefit the patient or are disproportionate to the potential benefits. Ethical challenges arise when healthcare providers and families have conflicting views on treatment. For instance, physicians might be pressured by family members to continue aggressive interventions despite clinical evidence indicating no benefit. When financial incentives or personal relationships are involved, conflicts of interest can exacerbate ethical dilemmas, leading to decisions that may not align with the best interests of the patient.

Healthcare institutions should deal with this issue by adopting bylaws that demand that physicians identify financial interests or connections that could sway their clinical judgment. Additionally, policies and procedures should establish guidelines for decision-making on futile care that are based on both ethics and clinical practice. Ethics panels can help when there is conflict between the family's wishes and the medical opinion.

EXAMPLE 1: THE CASE OF BABY CHARLIE GARD (2017)

A famous example of a terminally ill baby in the United Kingdom named Charlie Gard serves as an important example of when futile care was unconscionable.[1] His parents had tried experimental treatment overseas and the hospital's medical staff insisted that he would never recover because his disease was irreversible. The ethical issue was about whether it was in Charlie's interest to go on with treatment, with no chance of success.

This case raised questions about physicians' duty to render clinically sound decisions, as well as the influence of family expectations on care. The involvement of courts and ethics committees emphasized the importance of clear institutional policies for managing such situations.

EXAMPLE 2: PHARMA

Another COI ethical issue involves physicians who are connected to pharmaceutical companies. Physicians who prescribe certain drugs receive financial favors or research grants from the manufacturer. Even small gifts, meals, and sponsored events can create a sense of obligation, subtly encouraging doctors to favor certain products. In those cases, the physicians' treatment advice may be biased. This can lead to questions about whether patient care is undermined for commercial gain.

An example published in the *Journal of Law, Medicine & Ethics*[2] illustrated how institutions struggled to resolve these conflicts of interest. When a question was raised about the physicians' prescribing habits, the hospital's ethics committee was instructed to investigate. The case illustrated the need for open policies requiring disclosure of any financial connections and the necessity of institutional measures to maintain patient trust and impartial clinical judgment. This example highlights the larger consequences of conflicts of interest in medicine and how ethics committees can serve to ensure that healthcare remains ethical.

SOLUTIONS

To control COIs and reduce their influence on care decisions, physician leaders need to establish strict conflict-of-interest disclosure policies and make futile care decisions in accordance with clinical protocols and ethical requirements. Regular ethics training, independent review by ethics committees and clear communications with patients and families can reduce the risk that COIs unduly influence medical decisions.[3]

Consequences of Unethical Actions in Healthcare

Unethical medical behavior can have long-lasting and profound effects, not just on those individuals directly involved, but on public confidence, legislation, and the ethics codes that will inform medical practice for generations to come. In the past century, we have seen countless examples where moral delusion has had devastating results, and this reinforces the need for physician executives to remain vigilant with regard to ethics.

1. *The Tuskegee Syphilis Study (1932-1972)*[4,5]

   The Tuskegee Syphilis Study is frequently cited as a shameful case of medical research without informed consent. Studies carried out by the U.S. Public Health Service followed African American men with syphilis. The patients were not treated effectively even after penicillin was developed. This unethical act had several ramifications.

   In the short term, many participants experienced avoidable complications and death. Later, the study's publication undermined the relationship between African Americans and the medical profession – a legacy that still influences healthcare inequities and clinical research to this day. This case led to substantial regulatory reform, including the creation of institutional review boards (IRBs) to regulate research using human subjects ethically.

2. *Thalidomide Tragedy (1957-1961)*[6]

   Thalidomide, which was originally used as a sleep aid and to alleviate morning sickness in pregnant women, led to an international medical disaster when thousands of babies were born with deformed limbs. The drug had not been tested for safety, a scandal of poor oversight of pharmaceutical regulation and marketing.

   The results were devastating to the patients and affected families and led to a shift in the regulatory landscape for drugs, especially in the United States. The U.S. Food and Drug Administration (FDA) mandated more rigorous clinical trials and more adequate safety precautions before drugs are licensed. It was a case that showed the critical importance of ethical accountability in drug development and in communicating risks to patients.

3. *The Case of Henrietta Lacks' (1951)*[7]

   Henrietta Lacks' cells were harvested without her permission while she was receiving treatment for cervical cancer at Johns Hopkins Hospital. Her cells – called HeLa cells – went on to fuel medical innovation and led to a variety of medical breakthroughs, from the polio vaccine to cancer treatments. The ethical transgression was that no informed consent was obtained, and no benefit or recognition was offered to Lacks' family.

Decades later, the case came to light and resulted in demands for an emphasis on patients' rights and informed consent. Likewise, it spurred regulations and policy changes that ensure that material from patients is ethically used and the patients are compensated or recognized appropriately.

The impact of these cases goes beyond the immediate impact on individuals and families. They led to a general distrust of medicine, added pressure for legislation and policy reforms, and highlighted how vital it is for the medical profession to have ethical leadership. It is important for physician leaders to become familiar with these historical lessons so they can promote a culture of practice that values candor, dignity, and autonomy.

Ethical Implications of Human- or Animal-Subject Research

Human and animal research have been vital in improving medicine, but they also raise important ethical questions around obtaining informed consent, minimizing harm, and ensuring that research is worth the risk. Research enterprise initiatives are policies and programs that seek to implement these ethical values into larger-scale research and to ensure that the studies are as transparent and safe as possible.

INFORMED CONSENT AND HUMAN-SUBJECT RESEARCH

Informed consent is essential in any study of humans.[8,9] Participants must be completely informed of the study's purpose, procedures, risks, and rewards, and willingly accept to take part without pressure. Failure to seek adequate consent has caused devastating breaches (Tuskegee Syphilis Study) and led to rigorous policies in the Declaration of Helsinki and the Belmont Report. These models require investigators to place an emphasis on participant autonomy and rights. The National Institutes of Health (NIH) research enterprise programs, for example, enact these guidelines into funding and review, so that ethical work forms part of federally funded research.

ETHICAL USE OF ANIMAL SUBJECTS

Animal studies, which are essential to the mechanisms of disease and treatments, raise ethical issues around animal welfare.[10] Ethical animal studies follow the principle of the "3 Rs": replacement, reduction, and refinement. Replacement advocates the use of non-animal substitutes, when possible, reduction aspires to keep as few animals as possible, and refinement concentrates on the minimization of suffering and enhancement of animal welfare.

Campaigns such as the National Centre for the Replacement, Refinement and Reduction of Animals in Research (NC3Rs) champion them around the world. This center provides grants and works with scientists to create alternative animal models, and it teaches research businesses how to incorporate animal ethics into their planning.

EXAMPLES OF RESEARCH ENTERPRISE INITIATIVES

Several initiatives have been launched to embed ethics deeply into the research landscape:

- *The NIH Clinical and Translational Science Awards (CTSA) Program.*[11] Aims to streamline the process of translating lab findings into clinical applications while upholding rigorous ethical standards for participant safety and data integrity.
- *The All of Us Research Program.*[12] Focuses on building a diverse biomedical database with comprehensive informed consent and participant engagement practices to ensure respect for participants' rights.
- *The European Commission's Horizon Europe.*[13] Prioritizes ethics in research funding, mandating ethical compliance as a prerequisite for grants to protect human and animal welfare.

Such efforts bring ethics to the forefront of research activities. With ethics built into the research business, organizations can create a culture that will not only advance science but also preserve the dignity and well-being of research participants. The ethical concerns about human and animal research go beyond isolated investigations; they shape public opinion, policy and medical science's future. Research enterprise programs help institutionalize these values and ensure that research is done ethically and transparently. Physician executives and scientists must continue to stick to these standards, and support efforts to maintain participant safety and science.

Ethics Committees: Roles, Structures, and Functions

Ethics committees play an important role in healthcare, providing oversight on the way medical practice and research is conducted, ensuring adherence to ethical standards. The primary task is to protect patient rights and aid clinicians in making difficult decisions. These committees should be multidisciplinary to best address the spectrum of ethical problems, from clinical care issues to research oversight.

ROLES OF ETHICS COMMITTEES

The main purpose of an ethics committee is to advise on ethical issues that emerge in clinical and research practice. For example, if a physician is unsure whether to continue or discontinue life-support treatment, the ethics committee can help interpret the matter in an ethically appropriate way, considering patient autonomy, goodwill, non-harm, and justice.[14]

Committees can be educational as well, organizing workshops and trainings to introduce staff to the ethics, regulations, and policies of the institution. They also assist in formulating and updating hospital policies to incorporate current ethical guidelines and legislation. When conducting research, ethics committees (called institutional review boards or IRBs) examine and monitor studies to ensure the rights and welfare of participants. Such boards oversee research designs to ensure informed consent, risk minimization and compliance with ethical standards (for example, the Belmont Report and the Declaration of Helsinki).

STRUCTURE OF ETHICS COMMITTEES

Ethics committees are optimally composed of a broad variety of membership: physicians, nurses, social workers, lawyers, ethicists, and members of the public. This diversity enables the committee to examine ethical questions from multiple angles and to make balanced, broad decisions. For instance, an end-of-life care question benefits from the input of palliative care experts, ethicists, and family activists, so that all the aspects of patient care and ethics are involved.

Apart from permanent members, ad hoc consultants or subject matter experts may be appointed when a particular issue demands specialist expertise. Committees may look different at each institution, but the key principle is to ensure an independent and balanced oversight body.

EXAMPLE FROM CURRENT HEALTHCARE SYSTEMS

Cleveland Clinic's Ethics Committee is a good example of a strong ethics committee that delivers clinical advice, policy guidance, and training to the entire organization.[15] Its members include doctors, ethicists, and legal counsel, and its discussions include patient autonomy, consent issues, and complicated treatment decisions.

Likewise, the Mayo Clinic's Ethics Consultation Service is an inter-professional organization that supports patients, families, and clinicians dealing with ethical dilemmas by providing solutions that integrate ethical theory with clinical medicine.[16]

Such ethics committees not only oversee clinical and research affairs in real time but also determine longer-term policy. For example, they create guidelines to solve new problems such as the ethics of genetic testing and data security. They do so through a formalized process that always puts the interests of the patient at the center of practice, ensuring compliance with ethics and laws.

FUNCTIONS BEYOND CONSULTATION

More than simply solving individual issues, ethics committees can also provide strategic guidance and policymaking. They can even help institutions develop standards for end-of-life, organ transplantation, and equitable allocation of resources. This consultative role also helps maintain the confidence of community and healthcare staff by establishing an ethic of excellence.

Ethics committees, being formal and multidisciplinary, are critical in maintaining the culture of ethical conduct within healthcare systems. From individual patient care to general institutional policy, they ensure that ethical principles are still embedded in medical practice and research.

Patients' Rights and Responsibilities

As they discuss patient rights and duties, physician leaders need to acknowledge patients' desire to preserve morals and autonomy.

Informed Consent: The core of medical ethics, informed consent ensures that patients understand what plan of care they are being offered, and what are the risks, benefits, and alternatives of a procedure or treatment.

The shift toward telemedicine that was propelled by the COVID-19 pandemic undermined older models of consent and highlighted the necessity of ensuring transparency and patient understanding at a distance. New patient safety standards highlight the importance of robust patient engagement to protect these rights.[17,18]

Withdrawal of Care: The decision to withhold care is difficult, especially in intensive care units (ICUs). The death of Alfie Evans, a toddler whose parents tried to keep him on life support despite medical advice, instigated international discussions about patient rights and the boundaries between parental and medical judgment. This case illustrates the importance of clear guidelines and communication in high-stakes care decisions.[19,20]

Advance Directives: Advance Directives allow patients to define their wishes for care if they are unable to make decisions on their own, thereby increasing independence and understanding. Advance directives were a focus of pandemic public awareness, prompting more and more people to codify their medical wishes in the event of a sudden illness. Advance directives allow care providers to treat the patient in accordance with their wishes and thus avoid conflicts.

Overall, ensuring patients have informed consent, documented wishes regarding care withdrawal, and advance directives requires constant compliance with laws and changing patient care standards. Physician leaders must continually train themselves and their staff to maintain patient engagement while providing a high standard of care.

Organizational Policies on Misinformation

Hospitals and health systems need comprehensive organizational policies that promote good communication and respect for public trust to address misinformation. The plans should include employee training and community outreach.

1. *Implementing Policies Internally*. Hospitals should establish clear policies for staff to follow when offering medical information to internal and external audiences. That includes setting up procedures to ensure the accuracy of all health-related information posted in clinical environments and on social media. The American Medical Association (AMA) has stressed that health professionals have an obligation to provide the truth and recommended that hospitals implement policies to counter misinformation.[21]
2. *Education and Training*. Continuing education for healthcare workers can help ensure that they know the importance of accurate communication. Medical practitioners, nurses, and administrative staff can be trained to spot false information and act. Training should include best practices in public outreach, answering patients' questions, rumor control, and myth-busting. Healthcare systems with an informed workforce help to counter false information.
3. *Monitoring and Response Systems*. Hospitals can use monitoring systems to identify false information spreading through their community in order to take appropriate action. The Johns Hopkins Center for Health Security, for instance, has advocated for an early-warning system in which hospitals coordinate with public health departments and online platforms to monitor and correct false data before it gets out to the masses. This includes having teams that can respond quickly to the public in a direct, evidence-based way.[22]
4. *External Organizations Collaboration*. Developing partnerships with the media and tech companies will promote reliable medical data. Health systems can collaborate with social media platforms to identify and remove harmful health content. Hospitals also can join with public health groups in coordinated initiatives to disseminate credible health information to strengthen public confidence.
5. *Hospital Community Outreach*. Hospitals should conduct community outreach activities to promote health literacy and empower the public to make their own decisions about who can be trusted with medical information. These activities include holding workshops, producing local community educational materials, and connecting with trusted community leaders who can share truthful health information. This kind of work creates a well-informed public that is less prone to misinformation.

Medical Marijuana

The medical cannabis market has its own ethical issues, particularly for physician executives dealing with legal, clinical, and social complexities. Cannabis has increasingly become accepted as a treatment for chronic pain, chemotherapy-induced nausea, and even neurological conditions. However, its controversial nature — stemming from its classification as a controlled substance and its varying legality across states and countries — leads to serious ethical issues that doctors must grapple with in practice and in policy.

The fundamental ethical issue in the medical marijuana industry is how to make a choice between patient autonomy and informed consent, and the dangers of marijuana use. Although patients may want marijuana as a supplement or replacement for traditional treatments, physicians need to make sure the treatment is safe, effective, and long-lasting. In addition, physicians are subject to laws and institutions that may prohibit or control its application. This creates tension between respecting patient choices and adhering to professional and legal standards.

Health executives are responsible for crafting regulations on how medical marijuana will be used at their own facilities, ensuring that standards are evidence-based, ethical, and adhere to local regulations. With medical marijuana becoming more accepted, physician executives must remain aware of its use in clinical practice.

EXAMPLE 1: THE CASE OF THE VETERANS HEALTH ADMINISTRATION

In 2020, the Veterans Health Administration (VHA) said it would no longer deny VHA benefits to veterans who legally smoked medical marijuana in their states.[23-25] This was a policy decision that followed decades of controversy surrounding the use of marijuana among veterans with post-traumatic stress disorder (PTSD) and chronic pain.

Ethical concerns arose regarding the safety and clinical efficacy of marijuana, especially as the VHA's policy was not uniformly supported by all healthcare providers. Physician executives at the VHA had to navigate patient advocacy with clinical standards and scientific research, as well as an evolving regulatory environment.

EXAMPLE 2: MEDICAL MARIJUANA USE IN PEDIATRIC POPULATIONS

The use of medical marijuana in children is an especially thorny topic.[26,27] The American Academy of Pediatrics (AAP) warns against the use of medical marijuana among children, citing the lack of definitive evidence regarding its safety and long-term effects.

In pediatrics, the ethical question is whether young people should be offered pain treatment while at the same time reducing the chances of children being exposed early to drugs that have unclear developmental impact. These issues should be addressed by physician executives familiar with pediatric care and who are mindful to protect parental rights and are based on clear standards for children's treatment.

EXAMPLE 3: THE LEGALIZATION DEBATE IN CANADA

Throughout Canada, where medical marijuana has been legal since 2001, a study showed that, despite its popularity, physicians were hesitant to prescribe it because they still had questions about its safety and efficacy.[28,29] The ethical issue here centers on physician discretion and the professional duty to provide evidence-based care. As patients demand medical marijuana, physician leaders must create institutional standards consistent with evolving law and encourage appropriate clinical decision-making.

The ethical issues surrounding medical marijuana must be carefully considered in terms of patient rights, clinical proof, regulations, and laws. Physician executives must ensure that medical marijuana is appropriately integrated into practice in accordance with patient safety, informed consent, and evidence-based care. By developing clear, evidence-driven policies and continuously engaging in conversation about research, physician executives can guide their organizations through this complex problem.

Chapter Summary

A physician executive must become familiar with the variety of ethical dilemmas that will inevitably present themselves: conflicts of interest, concerns surrounding research and experimentation, advanced directives, withdrawal of care, balancing resources and duties to treat, and others. As medical technology progresses and healthcare remains at the intersection of law, politics, economics, and personal choice, a physician executive would do well to understand the frameworks of ethical decision-making (virtue ethics, deontology, utilitarianism, and principlism), the history of medical ethics and the notorious cases that affected not only patients, but society (the Tuskegee experiments, Thalidomide, Henrietta Lacks), as well as current controversies. Collaboration with peers, colleagues, and member of the public is essential to combat misinformation, conflicts of interest, and to set up ethics committees.

REFERENCES

1. Wilkinson D, Savulescu, J. Chapter 1, The Charlie Gard Case. *Ethics, Conflict and Medical Treatment for Children: From Disagreement to Dissensus* [Internet]. London: Elsevier; 2018 Sep 4. https://www.ncbi.nlm.nih.gov/books/NBK537990/
2. Rodwin MA. Conflicts of Interest, Institutional Corruption, and Pharma: An Agenda for Reform. *The Journal of Law Medicine & Ethics*. 2012;40(3):511–522. https://doi.org/10.1111/j.1748-720x.2012.00683.x
3. Gillon R. Medical Ethics: Four Principles Plus Attention to Scope. *BMJ*. 1994:309(6948):184. https://doi.org/10.1136/bmj.309.6948.184
4. Centers for Disease Control and Prevention. About The Untreated Syphilis Study at Tuskegee. September 4, 2024. Accessed November 23, 2024. https://www.cdc.gov/tuskegee/about/index.html#:~:text=The%20U.S.%20Public%20Health%20Service%20(USPHS)%20Untreated%20Syphilis%20Study%20at,after%20it%20was%20widely%20available.
5. Brieger GH. Bad Blood: The Tuskegee Syphilis Experiment. James H. Jones. *Isis*. 1983;74(3):433–434. https://doi.org/10.1086/353329
6. Vargesson N. Thalidomide-induced Teratogenesis: History and Mechanisms. *Birth Defects Research*. 2015;105(2):140–156. https://doi.org/10.1002/bdrc.21096
7. Skloot R. *The Immortal Life of Henrietta Lacks*. New York: Random House; 2010.

8. The Belmont Report. Ethical Principles and Guidelines for the Protection of Human Subjects of Research. *J Am Coll Dent.* 2014;81(3):4–13. https://pubmed.ncbi.nlm.nih.gov/25951677/
9. World Medical Association. WMA Declaration of Helsinki – Ethical Principles for Medical Research Involving Human Participants. Updated December 13, 2024. Accessed November 23, 2024. https://www.wma.net/policies-post/wma-declaration-of-helsinki/
10. Graham JC, Wong L, Adedeji AO, et al. Fostering Animal Welfare and Advancing 3Rs Principles through the Establishment of a 3Rs Advisory Group. *Animals.* 2023;13(24):3863. https://doi.org/10.3390/ani13243863
11. National Center for Advancing Translational Sciences. Clinical and Translational Science Awards (CTSA) Program. Accessed November 23, 2024. https://ncats.nih.gov/research/research-activities/ctsa
12. National Institutes of Health. All of Us Research Program. Accessed November 23, 2024. https://allofus.nih.gov/
13. European Research Council. Ethics Guidance. Accessed November 23, 2024. https://erc.europa.eu/manage-your-project/ethics-guidance
14. Childress JF. *Principles of Biomedical Ethics.* Oxford, UK: Oxford University Press; 1983.
15. Cleveland Clinic Center for Bioethics. About Us. Accessed November 23, 2024. https://my.clevelandclinic.org/departments/bioethics/about
16. Gazelka H, Hellyer JH, Lamer T. P-125 Ethics and Palliative Care Consultation: Mayo Clinic Ethics Consult Service Experience. *BMJ Supportive & Palliative Care.* 2015;5:A82.3–A82. https://doi.org/10.1136/bmjspcare-2015-000978.254
17. Alder S. Patient Rights Under HIPAA. *The HIPPA Journal.* August 28, 2024. Accessed November 23, 2024. https://www.hipaajournal.com/hipaa-rights/.
18. American Medical Association. Ethical Practice in Telemedicine. AMA Code of Medical Ethics. https://code-medical-ethics.ama-assn.org/ethics-opinions/ethical-practice-telemedicine
19. Strand L, Sandman L, Tinghög G, Nedlund A. Withdrawing or Withholding Treatments in Health Care Rationing: An Interview Study on Ethical Views and Implications. *BMC Medical Ethics.* 2022;23(1). https://doi.org/10.1186/s12910-022-00805-9
20. BBC. Who Was Alfie Evans and What Was the Row Over His Treatment? *BBC News.* April 28, 2018. Accessed November 23, 2024. https://www.bbc.com/news/uk-england-merseyside-43754949
21. American Medical Association. AMA Adopts New Policy Aimed At Addressing Public Health Disinformation. American Medical Association Press Release. June 13, 2022. Accessed November 23, 2024. https://www.ama-assn.org/press-center/press-releases/ama-adopts-new-policy-aimed-addressing-public-health-disinformation
22. Johns Hopkins Center for Health Security. Addressing Health-Related Misinformation and Disinformation. Accessed November 23, 2024. https://centerforhealthsecurity.org/our-work/research-projects/addressing-health-related-misinformation-and-disinformation\
23. Kansagara D, Morasco BJ, Iacocca MO, et al. Clinician Knowledge, Attitudes, and Practice Regarding Cannabis: Results from a National Veterans Health Administration Survey. *Pain Medicine.* 2020;21(11):3180–3186. https://doi.org/10.1093/pm/pnz322
24. U.S. Department of Veterans Affairs, Veterans Health Administration. VA and Marijuana—What Veterans Need to Know. Accessed November 23, 2024. https://www.publichealth.va.gov/marijuana.asp.
25. Sarris J, Sinclair J, Karamacoska D, Davidson M, Firth J. Medicinal Cannabis for Psychiatric Disorders: A Clinically-Focused Systematic Review. *BMC Psychiatry.* 2020;20(1). https://doi.org/10.1186/s12888-019-2409-8
26. Stoner MJ, Dietrich A, Lam SH, et al. Marijuana Use in Children: An Update Focusing on Pediatric Tetrahydrocannabinol and Cannabidiol Use. *ProQuest.* 2022;3(4):e12770. https://doi.org/10.1002/emp2.12770
27. Wilson S, Rhee SH. Causal Effects of Cannabis Legalization on Parents, Parenting, and Children:

A Systematic Review. *Preventive Medicine*. 2022;156:106956. https://doi.org/10.1016/j.ypmed.2022.106956

28. Ng JY, Gilotra K, Usman S, Chang Y, Busse JW. Attitudes Toward Medical Cannabis Among Family Physicians Practising in Ontario, Canada: A Qualitative Research Study. *CMAJ Open*, 2021;9(2):E342–E348. https://doi.org/10.9778/cmajo.20200187
29. Bean S, Smith MJ. Medical Cannabis: Identifying Ethical and Policy Implications for Healthcare Organizations in Canada. *J Pain Manag*. 2016;9(4):473–479. https://search.ebscohost.com/login.aspx?direct=true&db=cul&AN=121009955&site=ehost-live

2023 HALM Core Content

www.ingramcontent.com/pod-product-compliance
Lightning Source LLC
LaVergne TN
LVHW080014210926
848481LV00011B/3017